For Jan

Colleague and friend,

with thanks

'Heaver and heartener of the work'

Martin

October 2010

'A Life Lived Quickly'

'A Life Lived Quickly'

Tennyson's Friend
ARTHUR HALLAM
and His Legend

MARTIN BLOCKSIDGE

sussex
ACADEMIC
PRESS
Brighton • Portland • Toronto

2 4 6 8 10 9 7 5 3

First published in 2011 by
SUSSEX ACADEMIC PRESS
PO Box 139
Eastbourne BN24 9BP

and in the United States of America by
SUSSEX ACADEMIC PRESS
920 NE 58th Ave   Suite 300
Portland, Oregon 97213-3786

and in Canada by
SUSSEX ACADEMIC PRESS (CANADA)
90 Arnold Avenue, Thornhill, Ontario L4J 1B5

British Library Cataloguing in Publication Data
A CIP catalogue record for this book is available from the British Library.

Library of Congress Cataloging-in-Publication Data
Blocksidge, Martin.
'A life lived quickly' : Tennyson's friend Arthur Hallam and his legend /
   Martin Blocksidge.
   p. cm.
Includes bibliographical references and index.
ISBN 978-1-84519-418-5 (h/c : alk. paper)
   1. Hallam, Arthur Henry, 1811–1833. 2. Authors, English—19th
century—Biography. 3. Tennyson family. I. Title.
   PR4735.H4Z59 2011
   824'.7—dc22
   [B]
                                                        2010022925

Typeset and designed by Sussex Academic Press, Brighton & Eastbourne.
Printed by TJ International, Padstow, Cornwall.
This book is printed on acid-free paper.

Contents

List of Illustrations

Preface and Acknowledgements

The death of Arthur Hallam at the age of twenty-two prompted the writing of what is perhaps the greatest of all nineteenth-century English poems. Tennyson's *In Memoriam* not only explored the emotion of bereavement in a way which resonated strongly throughout Victorian England (and indeed continues to do so), but also made particularly palpable the elegiac myth that those whom the Gods love die young.

A major purpose of this book is, in a sense, to rescue Arthur Hallam from *In Memoriam*. All Hallam's friends (and they were many) were both shocked and disturbed by his premature death and were fulsome in their praise of his character and abilities. This book seeks to capture Arthur Hallam as he was in life rather than in death, to weigh the man against the reputation, and to set him in his literary and cultural moment. It is the first biographical treatment of Hallam since his father published his Preface to his son's *Remains in Verse and Prose* which first appeared in 1834, the year after his death.

Apart from the *Remains*, any student of Hallam must be indebted to two other works. T.H. Vail Motter's *The Writings of Arthur Hallam* (1943) gathered together for the first time all his known work, including significant material which had been excluded from the *Remains*. Motter exposed all Hallam's writing to rigorous scholarly examination, though with time his edition has been partially superseded, as additions to the canon have appeared and more information about the chronology of Hallam's life has become available. This is mainly due to the work of Jack Kolb whose *The Letters of Arthur Henry Hallam* appeared in 1981. Although some new letters (mainly juvenilia) have come to light since, this edition must inevitably remain the most revealing *vade mecum* to Hallam's life and mind and makes the evolution of a chronological narrative of that life a much more straightforward task than it might otherwise have been.

One of the great pleasures of research is the incurring of debts of gratitude and I have a number of people and institutions to thank. In Clevedon, Jane Lilly and Julia Elton were of invaluable assistance with my research into Hallam's Elton forebears, and Mary Walters kindly showed me round St. Andrew's Church which contains the Hallam family vaults. At Eton, Penny Hatfield and Lynn Sanders provided useful material with great efficiency. I am also grateful to Michael Atkinson, Joseph Francis and Roland Martin.

At Trinity College Cambridge, I would like to thank Jonathan Smith and the staff of the Wren Library for making available to me the extremely large and miscellaneous Hallam archive there, as well as other relevant material. Janet McMullin and the staff of the Library at Christ Church, Oxford bore with cheerful equanimity my several visits to inspect the Hallam family papers. I should also like to thank Grace Timmins of the Tennyson Research Centre in Lincoln and Richard Bowden, Archivist of the de Warenne Estate in London. Thanks are also due to the staffs of the Bodleian Library and, especially, the Rare Books and Music Reading Room of the British Library where, literally, every word of the book was written.

I should particularly like to thank a number of friends and colleagues whose tolerance of my enthusiasm for Hallam has made considerable inroads into their time and effort. Sir Eric Anderson read my chapter on Hallam's life at Eton and, apart from his helpful comments on it, offered encouragement at a time when there still seemed a very long way to go. Ian Littlewood brought his unrivalled knowledge of literary travel and travellers to bear on my treatment of Hallam's visit to Italy in 1827–8. Jonathan Smith and Christopher Stray kindly read my chapter on Hallam's life at Cambridge and saved me from a number of *betises*. Roger Evans directed me to the Hallam and Elton papers in the British Library and kindly loaned me papers and manuscripts of his own. Kelvin Everest helped me with the textual history of Shelley's *Adonais* (in which Hallam had a hand) and Dr. Edward Littleton provided an expert and lengthy diagnosis of Hallam's medical condition at the time of his death. My greatest debt of all is to Jan Piggott who read the entire typescript with a characteristic mixture of rigour and enthusiasm, causing me to benefit immensely from his considerable knowledge of early nineteenth century aesthetics and personalia. He is not responsible for any errors and infelicities which remain.

Some parts of CHAPTER SEVEN appeared in *The Use of English* (Volume 6, No. 2 Summer 2009) and I should like to thank its editor, Ian Brinton, for his permission to reproduce them. I am also grateful to the Ohio State University Press for allowing me to quote from Jack Kolb's edition of Hallam's letters. Permissions to reproduce illustrative material are acknowledged where the illustrations occur.

London, April, 2010

'A Life Lived Quickly'

Tennyson's Friend
ARTHUR HALLAM
and His Legend

CHAPTER ONE

Naturally Disputatious
Father and Son, 1811–1822

The parish church of St. Andrew in the Somerset town of Clevedon is
known locally as The Old Church and was built, possibly in Saxon times,
on a headland overlooking the Bristol Channel. Although in the early
nineteenth century it was the town's only church, it stood at some distance
from the community which it served, being more visible to the shipping
in the Channel than it was in the town itself. Modern-day Clevedon has
straggled out to meet it, and housing estates cluster at the bottom of the
hill on which the church and its graveyard still stand.

Inside the church a visitor is struck by one unexpectedly poignant
feature. On the wall of the south transept is a collection of five memorial
tablets, all commemorating members of one family: father and mother,
and four children. The father is identified (in death as he invariably was
in life) as 'Henry Hallam, The Historian'. His wife Julia Maria, commemorated on the same tablet was: 'daughter of Sir Abraham Elton, Bart., of
Clevedon Court . . . affectionate and cheerful companion of thirty three
years'. Then there are two daughters, Eleanor, and Julia, and a younger
son, Henry Fitzmaurice. But by far the largest and most elaborate of the
tablets is the one that was placed there first, dedicated to the memory of
Arthur Henry Hallam, the family's eldest child. Arthur's father had the
melancholy experience of seeing not only his wife, but three of his four
children predecease him.

Not only is Arthur Hallam's memorial the largest one. Its central position on the wall leads to the other tablets being arranged around it, rather
like satellites around a planet, as if drawing attention to their own inferior status. This is further borne out by the fact that Arthur is referred to,
directly or indirectly, on all the other tablets too. Eleanor's 'remains are
deposited in the same vault with those of her beloved brother'; Henry
Fitzmaurice was 'an image of his elder brother'; Julia Hallam in death 'was
permitted to rejoin the blessed spirits of two dear children'. Clearly Henry
Hallam could not mourn for other members of his family without
mourning afresh for Arthur each time. Arthur in his death was a standard
against whom everyone else had to be measured. Not only was he a
paragon: he had become a legend.

I

The celebration of Arthur Hallam's legendary status went far beyond the confines of Clevedon Church. As is well known, his death in 1833 was the prompting of Alfred Tennyson's poem *In Memoriam* (1850) and this fact, too, is commemorated in Clevedon. Behind the parish church, at the edge of the cliff on which it stands, runs a pathway known as Poets' Walk, which, local tradition asserts, Tennyson and Hallam trod in their youth. Moving back towards the town, there is a Tennyson Road, and also Tennyson House, where, once more, local tradition tells us, Tennyson stayed when he visited the area. Arthur Hallam, Alfred Tennyson, and the relationship immortalised by *In Memoriam,* have thus been carefully cherished in a quiet corner of England. Literary pilgrims, taking their bearings from Tennyson's poem, have been known to search Clevedon churchyard for Hallam's grave, though they have always done so in vain, for Arthur Hallam's life has been (to quote Philip Larkin's words) 'transfigured . . . into untruth.'

Arthur Hallam's personal connection with Clevedon was an indirect one. Strictly speaking the Hallam family itself had no association with Clevedon at all: Clevedon was the home of Arthur's mother's family, the Eltons, and there is only one recorded reference in his letters to the adult Arthur having visited his relatives there (though there had been regular visits in childhood). Alfred Tennyson never visited the town at all during Hallam's lifetime, going there for the first time only after *In Memoriam* had been published. This explains, among other things, the poem's confusion about the precise place of Hallam's interment. He is buried inside the church, not in the 'English earth' of the graveyard, which the poem suggests.[1] There is also an unwittingly erroneous reference in the poem to Hallam's body being brought back by boat, after his death in Vienna, to the nearby shore of the Bristol Channel. But the body actually landed at Dover, a fact of which Tennyson was made aware only late in his life.

There are few figures in English literary history about whom so much has been imagined and so little actually known. Arthur Hallam's life is a largely unexamined one.

That this life has been surrounded, even submerged, by fiction and fable is convenient. It enables Tennyson's *In Memoriam*, not to mention a substantial body of his other poems, to be easily understood by reference to the single event of Hallam's death. Hallam himself emerges, both from Tennyson's poetry and from the reminiscences of his friends and family, in certain very distinct ways: as supremely gifted, well set to become the pre-eminent intellect of his age; a moral example, 'The man' Tennyson 'held as half divine'.[2] Dying as he did at the age of 22, he symbolised perfectly the figure of the golden youth of great promise, whose life was brutally cut short before his abilities were given the opportunity to flourish. So far has legend overtaken reality that even the circumstances of his death have sometimes been confused in the popular imagination. Although Hallam died of natural causes, it has often been

2

assumed that he met his death by drowning, thus enrolling him into the elegiac literary tradition of Shelley and of Milton's *Lycidas*.

The year after Arthur Hallam's death his father compiled a volume of *Remains in Verse and Prose*, containing a liberal selection of Arthur's writings and preceded by a biographical preface written largely by Henry Hallam himself. It is by this preface that the outline and trajectory of Arthur's life has generally come to be known. Henry Hallam writes of his son's early years that he:

> 'was born in Bedford Place, London, on the 1st February, 1811. Very few years had elapsed before his parents observed strong indications of his future character, in a peculiar clearness of perception, a facility of acquiring knowledge, and, above all, in an undeviating sweetness of disposition, and adherence to his sense of what was right and becoming. As he advanced to another stage of childhood, it was rendered still more manifest that he would be distinguished from ordinary persons, by an increasing thoughtfulness, and a fondness for a class of books, which in general are so little intelligible to boys of his age.'

Arthur was proficient in French and Latin by the age of seven and shortly afterwards began composing tragedies 'if we may so call them, either in prose or verse, with a more precocious display of talents, than the Editor [i.e. Henry Hallam] remembers to have met with in any other individual.' Henry adds that his parents were keen to handle this precocity carefully and so 'avoided every thing like a boastful display of blossoms which, in many cases, have withered away in barren luxuriance'.[3]

As will be discussed later (in CHAPTER SEVEN), Henry Hallam's tribute to his son is in many ways surprisingly objective. It is not mere hagiography, a fact, which, given the circumstances of its composition, is surprising. Nevertheless, in speaking of Arthur as 'precocious' (which he undoubtedly was) Henry is guilty, as much out of modesty as anything else, of an important misrepresentation: he suggests that Arthur's precocity sprang, so to speak, fully formed upon the world. In fact it was to a large degree a matter of genetic inheritance. The Hallam family was an extremely gifted one and of Henry's four surviving children three were exceptionally intelligent. Arthur's younger sister, Eleanor (known in the family as Ellen, or Nell), was, like him, a good linguist and an avid reader but also an excellent pianist and singer. The journal which she kept when the family visited Italy in 1827–8 and she was aged eleven is not only stylistically very assured but is remarkably authoritative in its discussion of paintings and architecture, about which Ellen is clearly very well informed. The youngest member of the family, Henry Fitzmaurice (always known as Harry), was also very able. Although thirteen years younger than Arthur, he followed in his footsteps to Eton and Trinity College, Cambridge, where his career was, in formal terms, at least as distinguished as his brother's: he gained a better degree than Arthur and was encouraged to sit for a Trinity Fellowship.

Henry Hallam himself had also shown comparable precocity. At the time of Arthur's birth he was in the process of acquiring a reputation as a man of letters. In due course was to become early nineteenth-century England's most celebrated historian, hence his soubriquet 'Hallam the historian'. This was in an age before professional academic historians existed, as the subject (in England at least) was not studied in universities. Henry Hallam's career as a historian thus owed a great deal to his individual talent and effort, and in his own lifetime his name was far better known than Arthur's. It is Henry who is celebrated on the blue plaque which can still be seen on the front of 67 Wimpole Street, the family's London home for many years.

The name of Hallam can be found in parish records from as far back as the thirteenth century, and one ancestor could well have been Robert Hallam, an early fifteenth-century Bishop of Salisbury and member of the Council of Coustance. The name is toponymic in origin, relating to the village of Hallam, in South Yorkshire. Indeed the area now largely covered by the city of Sheffield was once known as Hallamshire. The village name itself is derived from the old English word for 'hall' or 'manor house'. There were Hallams in Yorkshire and Nottinghamshire, but Henry Hallam's forebears were from Boston in Lincolnshire. The earliest reference to the family is in the Boston Parish Records for 1685 when 'Cheyney, son of Isaac & Sarah Hallam [was] baptised 23 September'. The persistence throughout this and subsequent generations of the names of Nathaniel, Daniel and Isaac, seems to suggest Puritan stock, a fact which may well have contributed indirectly to the Whig rather than Tory bias of Henry Hallam's historical writings. (He remained throughout his life suspicious of High Churchmen). In the eighteenth century the family appears to have grown in prosperity and eminence. Isaac Hallam (1702–68), Henry's grandfather, described usually as an apothecary (though sometimes as a surgeon) and twice Mayor of Boston, sent his only son, John, Henry's father, after a brief spell at Boston Grammar School, to be educated at Eton.

This departure from the normal expectations of a provincial family must have owed something to John Hallam's unusual ability, and his entry to Eton College was the first stage in what would eventually be a distinguished career in the church. Entering Eton in 1742 at the age of thirteen, he was two years later elected a King's Scholar. He became a Scholar of King's College, Cambridge in 1748 and was subsequently a Fellow for twelve years. He became Canon of Windsor in 1775 (the year of his marriage at the age of 47) and proceeded to the degree of Doctor of Divinity at Cambridge in 1781. In that year he became Dean of Bristol, a position which he was to hold until 1799. He was successful and well-esteemed as Dean, and a contemporary wrote of him: 'He has by constant

4

residence and through his own example and interest in the Chapter, not only brought the choir service into so excellent order, that it is excelled by few others, but he has ornamented the fabric to so great a degree, by annually laying out considerably upon it'.[4] He was also described as 'a man of high character, and well-read in sacred and profane literature'.[5] He showed no desire for further preferment, and turned down the Bishopric of Chester when it was offered to him.

John Hallam was also a man of considerable substance which presumably explains his generosity in 'laying out' on the upkeep of the cathedral fabric. As his parents' only surviving son he had inherited at quite a young age his father's properties in and around Boston. Apart from three houses in the town itself, there were tenanted estates in the villages of Shirbeck, Leverton, Leake, Wrangle and Benington, which yielded substantial rental incomes.[6] He also owned property in West Bromwich, in Staffordshire, and inherited the neighbouring Charlemont Hall, 'a lofty, neat-looking house of brick, faced with stone, with iron palisades',[7] from his cousin, Elizabeth Lowe, in 1788. In 1806 John Hallam granted one of the West Bromwich properties to Henry, who inherited, after John's death in 1811, the rest of his estate, though he sold Charlemont Hall not long afterwards.

John Hallam's marriage, when he was well into middle age, was to Eleanor Roberts, daughter of William Hayward Roberts, a former Provost of Eton who had died three years previously. By a strange elision of generations, Roberts had become a King's Scholar at Eton in the same election as John Hallam. Like Hallam, he was subsequently a Scholar and a Fellow of King's, but then returned to Eton, first as an assistant master, then as a Fellow, finally, as a result of his acquaintance with King George III, becoming a rather unlikely Provost of Eton in 1781.[8] Although he had had a distinguished university career, and was a published poet and biblical scholar, he cut, as Provost, a rather comic figure in what now seems a very eighteenth-century way. He was described as 'a portly man and of much pride and state, and was used to have routs . . . in the college apartments, for card playing, which filled the college court with carriages and tumult, not much to the edification of a place of education.' His considerable girth, coupled with his Gloucestershire origins, earned him the nickname of 'Double Gloucester'. Fanny Burney (alias Madame d'Arblay)'s comments on him were rather more blunt: 'The provost is very fat, with a large paunch and gouty legs. He is good-humoured, loquacious, gay, civil, and parading.'[9] During his ten-year period as Provost, Roberts also managed to become extremely wealthy by drawing premiums when the leases of college properties were renewed.[10] He ensured that two of his three sons became masters at Eton and one of them, William, eventually became Vice Provost.

The lateness of the marriage between John and Eleanor Hallam precluded a large family and they produced only two children, Henry, the elder, and his sister Elizabeth, who became for many years a member of

Henry's household in London. Sir John Boileau, who drew up a biographical memoir of Henry Hallam shortly after his death, thought that Hallam had 'a deep affection for his mother and she was evidently a very "superior person", though "excitable in some things".' Boileau believed that Henry Hallam had inherited this characteristic from her.

But above all Henry Hallam inherited considerable intellectual gifts. Boileau relates that 'In childhood he manifested unusual talent, could read any book at 4 years old and wrote 8 or 10 several sonnets'.[11] As a schoolboy at Eton, as both his sons were to do, he quickly acquired a reputation for brilliance, though it was brilliance of a different sort from Arthur's. Where Arthur's abilities were inseparable from his 'undeviating sweetness of disposition', Henry's were altogether more severe. His studiousness earned him the nickname of 'the Doctor'[12] and, despite his early efforts in English poetry, it was in the much more rarefied (but much more highly regarded) area of Latin verse composition that he gained distinction. In 1795 *Musae Etonenses* was published, a three-volume collection of poems written in Latin by Eton boys, and including no fewer than seven poems by Hallam, written in either elegiacs or hexameters. They were all written during the academic year 1794–5. The subscription list shows that two copies of the collection were purchased in the name of Hallam, though the Dean of Bristol was in good company: two copies were also purchased by the Archbishop of Canterbury.

Although the Hallam family had an obvious dynastic affiliation to Eton, their university loyalties were rather more fickle. It might be expected that Henry Hallam would have followed in the footsteps of his father, grandfather and uncles, and been sent to Cambridge. Instead, in 1795 he entered Christ Church, Oxford. Although, under Dean Jackson, the college had become more intellectually distinguished, it was very much a Tory and High Church enclave, an unusual breeding ground for the man who was to become 'the father of Whig history'. Henry's later decision to send both his own sons to Cambridge thus becomes less surprising, though Henry, especially in his later years, was notably lukewarm about both the ancient universities. George Ticknor reported a conversation in which Hallam had expressed strongly the 'objection . . . that . . . With such great resources of property and talent they yet effect so little.'[13] Perhaps this explains Henry's involvement (not shared by Arthur, who was arrogantly contemptuous of it[14]) in the fledgling and initially highly controversial University of London, on whose Council he was to sit from 1828 to 1831.

Whatever the reasons for sending Henry to Christ Church, he settled himself very purposefully to work there, and was certainly a more conscientious undergraduate than his son Arthur ever became. He continued to justify the nickname he had been given at Eton. At Christ Church Henry laid the foundations for his subsequent scholarly achievements and began an academic régime of almost punishing diligence which was to be pursued for the rest of his active life. Although he was attentive to his formal studies in Classics and Mathematics and took German lessons three times a week, his reading was omnivorous, as his diary for 1797–8 shows. His programme of work for January 1797 was: 'Livy, Paley, Polybius, German Grammar, Paradise Lost, Butler's "Analogy"'. The following month's was 'Aenead, German, Chemistry, Pope.' He maintained a monthly register of his reading with the characteristic meticulousness that he extended to everything, including in due course his commonplace books, his travel diaries and his household accounts. In September 1797 he summed up his year's work:

> I find upon the whole not much cause for dissatisfaction. I have obtained in the first place some knowledge of Roman History, by reading Livy, Polybius, some lives of Plutarch, & some part of Appian. To this I have added some ideas of the Roman constitution: but in this I feel myself still being deficient.. I have learned the elements of Anatomy, of which I was wholly ignorant before, as also . . . of chemistry . . . I have acquired some knowledge of German, but not enough to enable me to read it with ease: in this I have much to regret . . . I have by reading, conversation, & thought made some little progress in physical inquiries: yet how much remains to be done, & how faint are the hopes of satisfaction in that most intricate of sciences! However I flatter myself that some light has been thrown on my mind in these points . . . The perusal of Smith's Wealth of Nations has given me some notion of Political Economy; a vast an important study in which I hope one day to make further advances. While I contemplate with some though not unmixed pleasure what I have done, I must not overlook what I have omitted . . . .nothing has been done in Mathematics and very little in modern history. Poetry has been unaccountably neglected, & with it all attention to style: I have written literally nothing . . . . In the ensuing year I am willing to hold out to myself the prospect of greater assiduity. Whether I shall be able to persist in my resolution, time must show.[15]

It has been necessary to quote this passage at length for a number of reasons. Firstly, its sentiments, and the gravitas with which they are expressed, do not sound like those of the usual twenty-year-old undergraduate. Henry Hallam had already aligned himself with that select band of men who choose not to live but know. His irritation at the thought of books unread and knowledge not gained is communicated very strongly. As much as a report on a year's reading, this passage sounds like the work of a Puritan examining his conscience in the knowledge that he can never meet the high standards which he feels are required of him. They also show the polymath's struggle to attain all the knowledge which he can. Henry Hallam belonged to the last generation of men for whom, if it was not possible to know everything, it was at least possible to aspire to. This compulsive and wide-ranging curiosity was to reach its apotheosis in 1839 when he completed his last and most ambitious historical work, the Casaubon-like *Introduction To The Literature of Europe in the Fifteenth, Sixteenth and Seventeenth Centuries.*

In the light of Henry's systematically industrious habits at Oxford, it is not difficult to understand the irritation he was later to show at what he thought were Arthur's frivolous undergraduate preoccupations at Cambridge. Arthur's mind was agile and speculative, spiced with more than a dash of the poet's imagination. His powers of assimilation were quick, and he also read widely, but in a way that inevitably struck his father as dilettantish. Arthur's lack of interest in university honours was also an irritant. If Henry's undergraduate life seemed compulsively driven, Arthur's, though in its own way no less energetic, became, after an uncertain start, much more enjoyable, despite Henry's occasional attempts to weigh down his son's university vacations with large doses of Blackstone and Justinian.

Henry Hallam's friendships at Oxford tended to be made with comparably earnest young men, all of whom were to die young. Apart from Henry Wintour (whose daughter Anna was for a time to figure prominently in Arthur's life), there was Peter Elmsley, subsequently Camden Professor of Ecclesiastical History at Oxford, and Lord Webb Seymour, a brother of the Duke of Somerset. Although Seymour has been unflatteringly described as 'a man of high thinking but small achievement . . . [a] laborious inquirer after truth, whose sole literary accomplishment was a few pages on geology',[16] he was a long-standing correspondent and confidant of Hallam. Although Henry was not outwardly warm-hearted in manner, his friendships were loyal and deep. Seymour stayed with the Hallam family in West Bromwich in the summer of 1799 (the year after Henry's graduation) and the two serious young men visited various 'manufactories' in the newly industrialised Birmingham, observing the largest steam engine in England and concluding that 'nothing can be more wonderful than the manufactories of this great trading town; the mind, especially of one unskilled in the arts & sciences connected with them is incompetent to apprehend every thing, or retain more than a very small part of what it apprehends.'[17] The following summer Hallam and Seymour visited Coalbrookdale, and Seymour reported that over the following weekend: 'Every interval . . . was employed in philosophical discussion, chiefly on metaphysical topics'. Hallam's correspondence with Seymour always retained its tone of high seriousness, even to the point of pomposity. In a letter of 1802, for example, after Seymour had gone to live in Edinburgh, Hallam bemoaned his lack of intellectual companionship as

> 'on philosophical questions, the powers of the mind are quickened and
> formed by collision with the minds of others . . . when I compare my

8

literary assiduity during the last three years, with my Oxonian life, I have no reason to regret a diminished velocity in the intellectual progression I have made.'[18]

Although he insisted that both his sons underwent legal training, Henry Hallam's entry to Lincoln's Inn (to which he was admitted on 26 June 1798) seems to have been his own choice. He had toyed with the idea of a career in politics,[19] but decided against it on the entirely characteristic grounds that he felt insufficiently well informed about issues and personalities. Nevertheless, as both his sons also did, he viewed the practice of law with some distaste. He spent seven years as a barrister on the Oxford circuit, though dealing only with relatively minor cases 'concerning, among other things, election petitions, unpaid rents, and other property disputes'.[20] He saved up most of his considerable intellectual energy for private reading, writing, and occasional journalism.

In 1806 he left the Bar and became a Commissioner for Stamps. Although such a post was not in theory a sinecure, in practice it had become one. Henry was one of seven Commissioners for Stamps employed at the Stamp Office in Somerset House. In general terms the Stamp Office was the predecessor of the modern Inland Revenue rather than of the Post Office, as the issue of stamps was still at this time an important means of tax-collecting. The range of items on which duty was payable had gradually increased since the Stamp Office's foundation in 1694 and by the end of the eighteenth century newspapers, patent medicines, hair powder, perfumes, items of clothing and country bank notes, as well as all legal documents, had to bear a government stamp to indicate that the duty had been paid on them. The administrative intricacies of the Office had become almost intolerable to those who needed to use it, especially to lawyers, and the institution eventually became the subject of a Special Commission of Enquiry which was extremely critical of it. The seven Commissioners were officially required to attend at the Office from 10.30 a.m. till 3.00 p.m. daily but in fact they seldom did, usually taking Mondays off and sharing the work between them for the rest of the week. Nor were the Commissioners noted for their harmonious relationships and, for some time at least, Hallam and the Chairman were not even on speaking terms.[21] Clearly the post was convenient for Hallam as, despite his complaints about its incursions into his time, it offered ample opportunity for his own reading and writing. It is probably not coincidental that he resigned in 1825 just after the first Commission of Enquiry report had been published, though he drew a pension of £500 per year until 1850.

Among Henry Hallam's friends at Eton had been Charles Elton, son of Sir Abraham Elton, Fifth Baronet, of Clevedon Court in Somerset, and, after a short engagement, in January 1807, at Clevedon Church, Henry married Elton's sister, Julia Maria. She was six years younger than her husband.

Although the Elton family had originated in Herefordshire, it had since the seventeenth century been very much associated with the City of Bristol; indeed the rise of the city and the rise of the family were very closely intertwined. In the seventeenth century Bristol was in the process of becoming England's second port and Abraham Elton, subsequently the first Baronet, who had started as an apprentice cooper, by dint of effort and acumen, turned himself into something of a merchant prince. He was twice Mayor of Bristol, as well as sitting as its (Whig) MP. He acquired Clevedon Court as his country seat in 1709 and his Baronetcy in 1722. His son, also Abraham, who succeeded to the Baronetcy in 1727, had trading interests which stretched as far as Turkey, Maryland and Virginia. He also served as an MP and as Mayor of Bristol. He was Master of the Merchant Venturers, but took more interest in Clevedon Court than his father had, and was responsible for much restoration work there.

Abraham persisted as a family name and Julia's father was the fifth bearer of it. He was, however, very different from his urban and mercantile ancestors. He was ordained in 1782 and was Vicar of West Bromwich, before inheriting the Baronetcy in 1790. He was of strongly evangelical persuasion and a friend and associate of the philanthropist Hannah More. He was also the first Elton to play the part of the country squire. As the family's historian writes: 'the Revd. Sir Abraham had a princely opinion of himself . . . He had discarded his clerical garb and dressed himself . . . in the finest of clothes, made frequent visits to Bristol, Bath and North Aston, and saw to it that his name was in Boyle's *Court Guide* when he took a house in London.' Social pride and evangelical rigidity proved a troublesome combination and he exhibited 'an autocratic will, a disposition to meddle, and an implacable determination to eradicate sin'.[22]

Clevedon Court, standing just outside the town from which it takes its name, is an attractive house in which the Elton family still lives. It dated originally from the fourteenth century. Its building had been extended, though it retained its original plan, with its great hall and family chapel. Julia's stepmother, who had a keen interest in landscape gardening, did much for the improvement of the grounds, so that Hallam's Cambridge friend, Charles Brookfield, could subsequently report: 'I am delighted with it beyond anticipation. Every delightfully old-fashioned room I saw. Every lovely bit of home landskip. Every quaint romantic terrace, every smooth shaven bit of delicate Ladyfoot grass plot'.[23]

But if the house's location was idyllic, life within doors was quite the opposite. It has been described as 'a joyless citadel'.[24] Although Henry Hallam's friend, Charles, the eldest son and subsequently sixth Baronet, had been educated at Eton, and, although he had literary and scholarly interests (he published volumes of poetry and translations from the classics), his dictatorial father forbade him a university education and sent him into the army, from which he eventually retired on half-pay to live a life of genteel poverty, receiving for a time financial assistance from his brother-in-law. The fact that Charles wished to marry a Unitarian, with whom he had to elope, caused him to be viewed by his father as a black sheep and for a long time he was not welcomed at Clevedon. The second brother, William, was also in the army and the youngest, Henry, had a distinguished naval career. Julia, as the only daughter, became 'the idol of my fond parents',[25] though her position even so was not an enviable one. Just as she herself was to fret almost pathologically about the welfare of her own children, so her father had been over-protective to her, believing her to have a delicate constitution, and dictating precisely what clothes she should wear and what food she should eat. Her father's evangelical views also cast a long shadow over her life which was always, in consequence, permeated by an acute and ingrained sense of original sin. The journals which she was to keep in the 1830s reveal a tortured spirituality which only just falls short of religious mania.

A direct consequence of this was that Julia was to take the religious education of her daughters very seriously. She presided daily over family prayers and the reading of psalms on Sunday. In their turn, the journals which her daughters kept at various times in their lives carry their own burdens of guilt, along with a sense of joyless suffering and self-sacrifice. To what extent she influenced Arthur's outlook is much more difficult to gauge. Julia's active concern for the spiritual welfare of her younger son, Harry, was undoubtedly a source of friction between her and her husband, as Henry maintained that the boy should be allowed to form his own opinions without undue interference from his mother.[26] Perhaps by that time Henry Hallam had seen what the unintended effects of his wife's piety could be. Arthur, when he suffered his mental breakdown in 1829, experienced an acute spiritual crisis too, but this took the form of grappling with atheism, rather than with feelings of guilt and sinfulness. The Christian faith which he subsequently professed and wrote about was of a much more orthodox and less personally anguished kind than his mother's. Even so, it is worth noting that in the poem which he addressed *To My Mother* in 1831, and which looked back on that spiritual crisis of two years earlier, he paid tribute to the comforting power of 'thy gentle faith' which 'would steal upon my heart' and which, having 'saved me from that utter scathe . . . I could not live apart'.[27]

The words on Julia's memorial tablet in Clevedon church which describe her as Henry's 'affectionate and cheerful companion' are misleading. She undoubtedly had a genuine affection for her husband, but in practice seems seldom to have been cheerful. Her thirty-three year marriage to Henry was in many ways a tragic one. She disliked the business of managing his household and dealing with servants and also found the obligations of playing the hostess at Henry's frequent dinner parties trying. The thoughts she confided to her own journals give the impression of someone who has long ago resigned herself to suffering in silence. Henry's letters to her, especially those written early in the marriage, are charmingly affectionate, and even as late as 1835 he could write 'how thankful should I be that you were proposed to me – the best & most indulgent of wives – your love is my best solace in declining years, and under many cares'.[28] However, it is doubtful if he ever fully understood the real nature of his wife's emotions or her recurrent bouts of depression and hypochondria.

In the interests of clarity, it has so far been convenient to speak of the four Hallam children: Arthur, Ellen, Julia (junior) and Harry, but Julia Hallam actually gave birth no fewer than eleven times. Even in an age in which the rate of infant mortality in all classes was high, it is difficult not to see the Hallams as having been dealt a particularly malign hand. The family historian offers the only explanations which are now plausible, either 'that [Henry and Julia] were genetically mis-matched' or that Julia 'may also have been the victim of obstetrical ineptitudes'.[29] Whatever the reason, Julia produced two sons (one named Charles William Waterloo, born in 1815 and the other Walter John) who both died in infancy. More significantly, she also suffered a series of miscarriages and stillbirths which inevitably took their toll on both her mental and physical health. When the deaths of Arthur at 22 and Ellen at 21 are taken into account, it is not difficult to understand the neurosis and gloom of her last years, nor her obsession with the welfare of Harry, who was to outlive his mother but himself to die at the age of only 26. A genetic predisposition to melancholy (inherited from her father) can only have added to the gloom of the Hallam family homes in London, and perhaps goes some way to explain Henry's habit of making extended foreign tours and frequently leasing houses outside London for long periods. His wife, after the death of her two eldest children, referred to their Wimpole Street house as 'our desolate home'.[30]

The Hallams' first marital home, however, was in Bedford Place, not far from the British Museum, where they lived for twelve years and it was during this period that Henry Hallam embarked upon his career as a man of letters, contributing reviews of History books to *The Edinburgh Review*. Although periodical journalism was still not thought a fit profession for gentlemen, Hallam's association with the *Review* was, at least with hindsight, an extremely opportune one.

The Edinburgh Review, under the editorship of Francis Jeffrey, had come into existence in October 1802, two years before Hallam started writing for it and from its very first edition it made clear that it was going to be a force to be reckoned with. Its initial *Advertisement* stated that it was 'to be distinguished rather for the selection, than for the number of its articles'; that it would appear each quarter rather than each month in order to ensure that the contents were as varied as possible and that its articles would, in general, be more substantial 'than is usual in works of this nature'.[31] Although Jeffrey himself was widely known to be personally gentle and unassuming, his fearsomely blunt reviews of new writing were what became the journal's best known feature. *The Edinburgh Review* rapidly became required reading for all those who wished to be informed about literary and political matters and its influence was even felt beyond British shores: Stendhal, Napoleon and Mme. De Stael were reputedly amongst its readers.[32] The *Review*'s political standpoint was Whig, though Henry Hallam was in due course to detach himself from this when he felt the journal had become too radical in its opinions. Although himself always associated with the writing of 'Whig history' and continuing to move in Whig circles, he was a Whig more by association than by profession.

An apparent error in a review of Payne Knight's *Inquiry into the Principles of Taste* brought Hallam publicity of a kind which he could hardly have relished. The review quoted some lines of Greek in the belief that Payne Knight had himself composed them. It complained of some inaccuracies in the lines. However, it was quickly pointed that the lines in question were actually by Pindar. This detail did not go unnoticed by Byron, who, having been himself unsympathetically treated by Jeffrey, countered with his *English Bards and Scotch Reviewers*. This satire, owing much to the rhetorical model of Alexander Pope, attacked the 'scribblers' of Grub Street, who were now plying their mercenary trade in Edinburgh rather than London. Hallam found his way into the poem, (though, it must be noted incidentally, that he did so in distinguished company: Southey, Scott, Wordsworth and Coleridge were also hauled over the coals). The poem made three references to Hallam, most famously in its evocation of him as 'classic HALLAM much renowned for Greek.' It also attempted to brand Hallam as a toady of the Whig grandee, Lord Holland: ('See honest HALLAM lay aside his fork,/Resume his pen, review his Lordship's work').[33] Hallam was, not surprisingly, hurt by these words. Byron's irony is gleeful, even if not particularly subtle, and Henry Hallam was properly proud of his learning. He was also seeking to make a literary reputation for himself. His subsequent remonstrations with Byron, however, bore fruit of a kind, as, unlike his stylistic mentor, Byron's hatreds were not visceral, and he was prepared to forgive his victims if necessary. He added a note to later editions of the poem, which, in apparently gentlemanly spirit, concluded: 'If Mr Hallam will tell me who did review it, the real name shall find a place in the text, provided nevertheless the said name be of two orthodox musical syllables, and will come into the verse.'[34] The fact that the review turned out to have been written by Dr. John Allen, himself a noted scholar and also a member of the Holland House set, duly exonerated Henry Hallam from charges of deficient classical scholarship. Arthur Hallam was in time to take the view that all literary publicity was good publicity, but Henry's association with Grub Street, incongruous though it was, had been too close for comfort.

Although Byron's suggestion that Henry Hallam was no more than a mouthpiece for Lord Holland is a gross distortion, Hallam, by virtue of his connection with *The Edinburgh Review*, soon became a member of the distinguished group of literati, intellectuals and statesmen who comprised what became known as the 'Holland House circle'. Lord and Lady Holland were prominent Whigs and closely involved with *The Edinburgh Review* whose proofs Lady Holland had been reputed to correct. Lady Holland was very much the dominant personality at Holland House. Her husband was charming and complaisant and often went down to dinner in the evening in complete ignorance of who his wife had invited to dine that night. Lady Holland was voluble, domineering and a great admirer of Napoleon. She has been described as 'the leading hostess in Europe'.[35] The Hollands generally held two or three large dinner parties a week in their grand dining room, and guests included a range of European intellectuals as well as political figures such as Grey, Melbourne and Palmerston, not to mention authors such as Samuel Rogers, Tom Moore, Wordsworth and Byron, the latter of whom, after burying yet another satirical hatchet, became a frequent visitor to Holland House and indeed first met Lady Caroline Lamb there.[36] There was no doubt that Henry Hallam had begun to move in the highest of social and literary circles.

Nor were his dinner appearances restricted to Holland House. He also became a regular guest at Bowood, the country seat of Lord Lansdowne near Calne in Wiltshire. Lansdowne was to become the godfather of the youngest Hallam sibling, Henry Fitzmaurice, who was named after him. Lansdowne had had a lengthy and distinguished career in public life, and was even invited to form an administration in 1855, an honour which he declined. In his youth he had met Boswell and Burke and had debated with Pitt.[37] He was a considerably more gracious host than the opinionated Lady Holland, though both the ambience and the clientele of his house parties were very similar to hers and at Bowood Hallam would again find himself in the company of Rogers, Moore and Macaulay. Mme. De Stael and Maria Edgeworth had also been known to visit. Arthur accompanied his father both to Bowood and to Holland House at various times, being remembered at the latter as a thirteen year-old Eton schoolboy.

Although social life to some extent rests upon personal obligations, it is unlikely that the Hollands or Lord Lansdowne would have invited Hallam to their tables if they had not enjoyed his company (and he was a guest at Holland House for over thirty years). Even so, Henry Hallam was not to everybody's taste. He was a controversial figure in every sense of the word, being known to possess 'a mind disputative and dogmatical in its natural bent',[38] and it is this side of his character which was often (and memorably) chronicled during his lifetime. After meeting him at a Holland House dinner, Lord Holland's son, Henry Fox, described Hallam as 'one of the most disagreeable members of society I ever have the misfortune to meet' and also as 'an odious man in society, very good in his books, I believe'.[39] Fox was only just turned twenty when he made these remarks so can perhaps be forgiven the arrogance of youth. But Sydney Smith was a completely different matter, and the fact that he and Hallam often dined together did not stop Smith in his turn from dining out on Hallam's reputation. If he is to be believed, Hallam in company was scarcely bearable and Smith was the origin of many of the stories which circulated about him.

It was Smith more than anyone who propagated the image of the disputatious Henry Hallam. Smith reported arriving late for a dinner party 'And there was Hallam, with his mouth full of cabbage and contradiction!'[40] Whether Smith was the originator of the description of Hallam as 'the bore contradictor' is unclear, but he was certainly responsible for describing the recently invented electric telegraph 'as a device that would enable Hallam to contradict somebody at Liverpool'.[41] Best known of all was Smith's party piece with which he was wont to set the London dinner tables in a roar by relating a story of Hallam, lying ill in bed with influenza, contradicting the night watchman every time he passed beneath the window to announce the time and comment on the weather. This story would clearly have lost nothing in the telling, though it bears all the hallmarks of the authentically apocryphal.

In an age whose dinner tables witnessed the brilliance of Sydney Smith and 'Conversation' Sharp, Henry Hallam was perhaps too much given to seriousness and his manner of speech, alternately 'precipitate'[42] and hesitant,[43] would not have made him easy company. Boileau tried to defend Hallam on the grounds that it was 'his love of truth and eagerness to ascertain it [which] made him appear contradictory & even contentious',[44] but Samuel Rogers once complained that, being placed between Hallam and Macaulay at Bowood , they 'wrangled and faught' over him 'as if I was a dead body'.[45] Those who knew Henry Hallam in later life reported that he had mellowed and the surviving portraits of him in middle age suggest a rather benign-looking figure. Even so it is clear that Hallam, however well-meaning in intention, was not the easiest of men, either in daily life or in social encounters. Those who wished to defend Henry Hallam's character inevitably pointed to his financial generosity, the happiness he gained from the long hours spent in his study, his moral uprightness and his generally liberal principles, but they were only part of the story.

Arthur Hallam inherited all of his father's tendency to disputatiousness, though he carried his arguments off with much greater *elan* and his performances were usually enjoyed rather than resented. Nevertheless, to be Henry's eldest son, however gifted, was a position which brought its own problems. In a passage which has often been quoted, Lloyd Sanders described Hallam senior as 'something of a domestic martinet inclined to be fussy over the cooking of whitebait, and of such fixed habits that when he travelled with his family they had to take surreptitious lunches by turns in the rumble of the coach'.[46] This sounds no more than mildly eccentric, but it conceals the fact that Henry's authoritarian ways extended well beyond merely dietary matters. He regarded it as his natural prerogative to direct Arthur's life as he chose and, while that was not unusual in the age in which he lived, Henry's interventions invariably seem, at least at first sight, stark and unsympathetic and they brooked no court of appeal. Henry thus determined (against Arthur's wishes) which university he should attend; he determined (against Arthur's natural inclination) what career he should follow; he forbade Arthur from publishing a joint volume of poems with Alfred Tennyson in 1830 (even though it was in proof) and he made almost insuperable difficulties over Arthur's engagement to Emily Tennyson.

None of these interventions were made out of deliberate malice, and they can all, as will be seen, be justified. Henry believed that he was working in Arthur's best interests, despite the latter's frequent protestations. Arthur learned to cope with his father by first seeming to acquiesce in his demands and then, as far as he could, going on in his own way. Henry understood well enough that his son was exceptionally gifted, though he never learned to live with the fact that Arthur's gifts were different from his own and that Arthur could not be moulded into a shape identical to his. Doubtless Arthur, like most sons, could be a source of anxiety as well as pride to his father. Indeed, a tone of mild exasperation marks the very earliest surviving comments that Henry made about him. Writing to Webb Seymour, Henry reports that 'Arthur comes on very rapidly, in bodily & mental vigour, but his genius seems to lie more towards horses than metaphysics'. A few months later he was making much the same point: 'Julia and Arthur are extremely well, but, alas for philosophy! the latter shews no taste but for living or delineated horses. I am sometimes afraid that the animal, which is very fine, will predominate over the speculative soul.'[47] Considering Arthur's subsequent interest in metaphysics and the tension that this was to create between father and son, Henry's comments are not without their irony, particularly as Arthur was only two years old at the time. It is not entirely safe to assume that Henry was joking: his expectations of both his sons were extremely high.

Nor is it difficult to understand why Arthur, after he had become friendly with Alfred Tennyson, enjoyed visiting the Tennyson family at Somersby Rectory in Lincolnshire. Although the remoteness of Somersby and the proneness of the Tennyson family to melancholy have often been emphasised, the eleven Tennyson siblings enjoyed an uninhibited, not to say Bohemian, existence which Arthur found instantly entrancing. The fact that there was a bevy of pretty sisters also helped, but, above all, Hallam, on his visits to Lincolnshire, must have found the free-and-easy atmosphere an exhilarating contrast to the earnest gloom of his own home. Throughout the early years of Arthur's life, Henry was at work on his first major publication, *A View of the State of Europe in the Middle Ages*. This proved a taxing and long-drawn-out project which occupied Henry for a decade and ultimately undermined his health. When to this is added his mother's gynaecological problems, frequent periods of illness, and moral earnestness, it is not difficult to see how Arthur's life as a child encouraged him in serious intellectual pursuits, but offered him less than his fair share of the happiness that children generally enjoy.

In December 1819, Henry Hallam moved his family to 67 Wimpole Street. This is the house which Arthur viewed as his home and which was in due course to be apostrophised by Tennyson as the 'dark house . . . in the long unlovely street'.[48] Tennyson's description of Wimpole Street is not unjust. Wimpole Street, then part of the Portland estate, is indeed a long, straight, street, which, as a result of the high buildings on each side of it, has an oppressive feel. There is little architectural harmony as, although both sides of the street are apparently terraced, the houses date from different periods and boast a variety of styles and facades. No. 67 is at the 'town' end of the street, being only five minutes walk from Oxford Street. It is a house of four storeys plus basement, now divided into apartments. It is stone-faced on the ground floor, with a brick elevation above. Apart from a fanlight, a foursquare and undecorated front is presented to the street. Nevertheless, despite the rather insistent angularity of Wimpole Street and its neighbourhood, the Portland Estate has always been a most desirable area. There is no shortage of blue plaques commemorating famous and distinguished inhabitants and visitors: Hector Berlioz, for example, is celebrated as having stayed just round the corner in Queen Anne Street.

Arthur's next youngest surviving sibling was Ellen. Although she was five years younger, they became and remained very close to each other. They shared the same Swiss governess (generally referred to as 'Madame') and, when at school and university, he often wrote to her. Her own precociousness meant that she was able to take an interest in Arthur's activities at Eton and he reported them without in the least writing down to her. Arthur was probably closer to Ellen than he was to his mother. The journals which Ellen kept after Arthur's death show that she never fully recovered from the shock of it, and also reveal that she had been very much taken into his confidence about his feelings for Emily Tennyson and the difficulties which had attended them.

Henry Hallam was an enthusiastic foreign traveller. As a means of recuperation from the rigours of his work on *A View of the State of Europe*, he undertook a major tour in the summer of 1818. Ellen was deemed too young to accompany the family, but, after some hesitation, it was decided that Arthur should join them rather than being looked after by his aunt. Although the ostensible purpose of the journey was to allow Henry to restore his health by taking the waters at Spa in Belgium, the itinerary also took the Hallams to Germany, Switzerland and Italy. The extent to which this tour was intended to have educative value for Arthur is uncertain. Subsequent foreign tours acted as clear punctuation marks in Arthur's career, occurring, for example, immediately before and immediately after his years at Eton, but Henry had mixed feelings about their educational advantages, believing on both occasions that, despite broadening his experiences, time spent travelling had distracted Arthur from serious academic work.

After spending time in the Belgian cities and visiting the site of the (then very recent) battle of Waterloo, the family journeyed by way of the Rhine valley to Heidelberg, Baden, Freiburg and the Black Forest. Although Henry could only bring himself to say that the Rhine 'may be compared to the Thames at Battersea', he found Germany in general agreeable in its 'comfort and prosperity'.[49] In Switzerland the Hallams stayed at first in Zurich. Henry then went on to Lucerne to walk in the Alps for a week, whilst his wife and Arthur stayed in Berne, and then in Geneva, whence Henry went off again, this time to Italy, with his old Oxford friend Peter Elmsley. In Geneva, rather than patronising an hotel, Arthur and his mother stayed *en pension* with 'a most respectable family'. Henry was very enthusiastic about the advantages of this kind of accommodation as it allowed Julia Hallam to mix with 'as much of the best society as the place could furnish'.[50] It also enabled Arthur to become a fluent speaker as well as an accomplished reader of French, though Henry was forced to admit that this was at the expense of his progress in Latin in which 'having gone through the elements . . . before this time . . . it was necessary to begin again with first rudiments which he mastered within the year'.[51]

The journey was less advantageous for Julia Hallam: she was pregnant. Although Henry on his return at first opined that 'her stay was perhaps rather imprudently protracted, [but] there seems no reason to repent of it',[52] she nevertheless shortly afterwards gave birth prematurely to a daughter who died.

Arthur's second foreign tour took place between the May and September of 1822. The itinerary of this trip was different from the sort usually favoured by Henry in that it concentrated less on visiting cultural sites and was largely spent in the Swiss Alps. From the very detailed journal which Julia kept it is possible to follow the places visited and learn about the conditions under which the family travelled. They went south through France as far as Lyon, and then stayed again in Geneva, where they twice visited the French historian Jean de Sismondi and his family. Arthur had been 'taken ill of the chickenpox' in Paris, but appeared to make a quick recovery, which was as well, as there was some quite rough terrain to be covered. In chronicling the daily progress from one Swiss town to another, Julia reports storms, flooded roads, and broken bridges, as well as time spent climbing mountains: 'scrambling up among rocks and sheeps walks, sometimes with scarce any path'.[53] It would be pleasant to think that this particular trip had been undertaken with Arthur's interests in mind as it certainly offered the kind of adventure which an eleven year-old would be capable of enjoying.

In due course, the more formal aspects of Arthur's education also needed to be considered. There had been some talk of sending him to a school in Beaconsfield in 1818 while his parents were abroad, though Henry's sister Elizabeth, who would have been his guardian, thought that Beaconsfield was too far away and worried for Arthur's health, offering herself to help out with teaching him Latin if necessary.[54] Although it was in practice possible for a boy to enter Eton as early as the age of eight or nine, it was far more usual to send a potential Etonian to a preparatory school at that age, in order to make sure that he acquired sufficient competence in Latin and Greek. Henry Hallam in the *Remains* comments briefly that 'In the spring of 1820, Arthur was placed under the Rev. W. Carmalt at Putney, where he remained nearly two years.'[55] Henry's wording seems to suggest that Carmalt's school might have been known to his readers. It was certainly different from a conventional preparatory school. Preparatory schools of this period generally consisted of a few boys who lived as boarders in the house of a clergyman who would take pupils in order to supplement his income. Standards in such schools were variable and boys were often poorly fed and cruelly treated. Given Henry Hallam's background and connections, he would be well placed to make a discriminating choice: Putney School was actually a large and thriving concern and its headmaster was an unusual man.

Putney was at that time still a village, though only four miles west of Hyde Park Corner. At the beginning of the nineteenth century 'the land was . . . mostly park or heath, with some arable and a little market garden and pasture'.[56] Putney School occupied a 'stately and imposing edifice' on the Upper Richmond Road, which had originally been the country house of the Duke of Hamilton.[57] It was apparently used as a school for about thirty years, during which time William Carmalt became a well-respected local figure. His name still lives on in Putney in Carmalt Gardens, the road which is named after him.

He originally came from Appleby, in Westmorland, but moved to London as a young man, having been promised a cadetship in the East India Company. As no preferment was immediately forthcoming, he took a post as an usher at Putney School on what he thought was a temporary basis. When it became clear that his hopes in East India direction had been dashed and that his future looked likely to remain that of a schoolmaster, he entered Queens' College, Cambridge and took a degree in order to allow him to proceed to holy orders, 'not' (his grandson remembered) 'because he felt any special vocation for the Church, but because in those days schoolmasters were usually clergymen.'[58] He must also have been a man of means as he acquired a riverside house known locally as 'The Palace' which had fallen into some decay. He destroyed what remained of it and rebuilt on the site (it is now part of a council estate). Despite his lack of conventional piety, Carmalt as a 'Vestryman of Putney' made lengthy representations to parliament on the question of poor-law reform.

What would appear to be the only extant document relating to

Carmalt's school is actually the work of Arthur Hallam himself. Preserved at Trinity College, Cambridge is a 'LIST OF PUTNEY SCHOOL BY A.H. HALLAM/ONE OF ITS MEMBERS'. From this (undated) document it is possible to discover that the school consisted of nine classes. The '1st class' containing three boys, was the most senior and the '9th'(or 'Chits' class') the most junior. Hallam himself was in the third class. Apart from being Hallam's earliest surviving work, this list is interesting in that it shows that some classes had as many as 17 or 21 boys in them, and that the whole school roll was 107. This was very large indeed for a school of this type and certainly confirms that it was a much more substantial concern than a mere run-of-the-mill coaching establishment.

Whether or not Arthur enjoyed his time at Putney School is not recorded, though two letters to his Aunt Elizabeth have been preserved. In view of the premature adulthood which posterity has tended to thrust on Arthur, it is refreshing to see him behaving as any other boy of his age might be expected to. One of the letters to his 'Dear Coddling Aunty' reports of his health: 'I am very well as to my arm, but for my cough it is not well.' The doctor has told him 'to stop a few days in on account of my arm'. Arthur then moves on to a more traditional schoolboy preoccupation in thanking his aunt 'for the eatables you sent me'. On another occasion, with the sublime inconsequentiality of childhood, he asks his aunt to send him a hoop as 'The boys are all playing with hoops here. I am not yet in the 3rd class, but in Greek I am two from the top & in Latin seven. All my cake is gone. Golding had two feasts at Michaelmas to one of which he invited me.'

Arthur's aunt Elizabeth Hallam was also the recipient of a sequence of letters written when he was fourteen, and by that time at Eton. In the summer of 1825, Henry Hallam took a holiday in Ireland. After visiting Dublin, he went on to Killarney, where he had the unexpected misfortune to fall from a rock, and, in the words of his doctor, 'fractured his leg and sustained other severe injury'[59]. Henry was bedridden for thirteen weeks, and his wife and Arthur were duly summoned to provide some highly necessary assistance and moral support. The family stayed in what sounds like very modest circumstances in a small cottage by Killarney's Lower Lake. Although Arthur bemoaned the lack of books, as he was often to do when away from home, he clearly made the best of a bad job, probably cheered by the fact that his return to Eton for the new term was inevitably postponed.

Arthur seemed to take well to the country pursuits he was forced to adopt. He watched a stag hunt which greatly excited him; he helped the gardener to dig an irrigation channel, and reported that 'I sally forth daily with a small gun to make havoc among birds and rabbits . . . I have made such proficiency in shooting since I have been here under William's tuition that I actually the other day shot at a rook, who very provokingly instead of being killed, flew away cawing.' Arthur's 'hebdomadal epistle[s]' (sic) to his aunt are particularly charming. He is both observant and witty. The child's freshness of observation is combined with a sophisticated prose style: the letters must have been a joy to receive. In one of them he outlines his daily routine: 'Get up very sleepy. N.B. Always am here! . . . My room is pantry, servants' hall, house-keeper's room & I know not what besides! . . . accompany the Mot. [his mother] out, who begins hoeing, while I assist in driving up the cows or paddle my white canoe at the mouth of the great Ditch . . . Lunch: either potatoes, chocolate, cheese or jelly. Sit a bit with the Pip [father] till dinner, read 20 pages or so of Quintillian with him' etcetera. Arthur also took a particular liking to a servant called Patrick, who had literary interests and was currently reading a novel 'by Miss Edgeworth'.[60] This unexpected period in the Irish countryside was also to bear some modest literary fruit in the poem *The Bride of the Lake* which appeared in *The Eton Miscellany* in 1827 and which shows that the topography of Killarney had continued to haunt him.

Despite the liveliness of Arthur's letters from Ireland, there had been genuine concerns about Henry's health following his fall. Not only had he been depressed but his recovery had been slow, and it was feared that he might be permanently disabled as a result of the injury: indeed he always walked with a limp thereafter.

The period in Killarney offers a last view of Arthur Hallam the boy. He had by that time been at Eton for three years and was just about to embark on the first stage of the exciting intellectual journey which comprised the rest of his life. Despite the superficial differences between them, Arthur was very much his father's son. Like Henry's, Arthur's life was also to be the life of the mind, dominated by books and ideas. His interests and values were not those of his father, and this would always be a potential source of friction, but restless mental energy, coupled with self-reliance and a remarkable intellectual confidence would henceforth, for both good and ill, become his hallmarks.

CHAPTER TWO

An Unreformed Education
Eton College, 1822–1827

William Ewart Gladstone, the future Prime Minister, became Arthur Hallam's closest friend at Eton. In his biography of Gladstone, Roy Jenkins dismisses the Eton of the 1820s rather tartly: 'Eton was not well run at the time, with too few masters, and those that there were of uncertain quality. Its main advantage was the opportunity to make influential friends'.[1] Nobody in Arthur Hallam's family would have seen the school in this way. Arthur was, after all, descended from impeccable Eton stock: his father and grandfather had both attended the school and his grandmother had been a daughter of the Provost and a sister of the Vice-Provost, though Arthur himself, particularly by the side of his close friends Gladstone and James Milnes Gaskell, was never unduly fulsome about the school (on one occasion he spoke of feelings of 'nausea' at the beginning of term[2]). Nevertheless there have been plenty of commentators prepared to see the Eton of Hallam's time, when it was under the leadership of the legendary Dr. Keate, as something of a golden age.

Whilst Eton would undoubtedly have viewed itself as a 'public school', it would have understood something different by the term than the later nineteenth century did. The public school as we have come to understand it is a mid-Victorian phenomenon, and indeed many of what are now Britain's established public schools were either Victorian foundations or re-foundations of older establishments, created with the purpose of providing a 'gentleman's education' to the sons of the middle classes. The public schools attended by boys of Hallam's generation were very different. They were 'public' in the sense that they drew their pupils from all over the country. Private schools (run by their owners) or grammar schools (local foundations) served smaller communities and were predominantly day rather than boarding institutions. Indeed, there were, in the early nineteenth century, very few schools that could properly describe themselves as public schools: Winchester, Eton, Westminster, St. Paul's, Merchant Taylors Harrow and Rugby; possibly Charterhouse and Christ's Hospital (they were charitable foundations for poor boys) and Shrewsbury which was just being rescued from a long decay under the headmastership of Samuel Butler.[3]

Eton had originally been founded jointly with King's College, Cambridge in 1440 by King Henry VI to provide education for poor scholars, but its charitable purposes had become considerably diluted over the centuries. Indeed in 1818 a Parliamentary Commission under Lord Brougham had been charged with investigating the extent to which the original statutes of Winchester and Eton were still being followed. Eton's Provost Goodall had put up a notoriously poor showing under questioning and the commission concluded that 'considerable unauthorised deviations have been made . . . from the original plans of the founders . . . these deviations have been dictated more by a regard to the interests of the Fellows than of the Scholars'.[4]

The connection with King's College, Cambridge had developed into a comfortable self-perpetuating machine. In accordance with its original foundation statutes, Eton continued to educate 'Collegers' who lived and worked together in the school's main building known as College. Collegers could be admitted to King's as and when vacancies occurred, irrespective of academic merit; students at King's could, in time, proceed to Fellowships, and Fellows of King's could in due course become Fellows of Eton (resident clergymen) or assistant masters there. King's College was devoted exclusively to the education of Old Etonians and existed as an entirely separate institution within Cambridge University, its students not being eligible for university degrees. This state of affairs did little for the intellectual standing of King's and less than it might have done for the intellectual standing of Eton.

Despite the amount that has been written about them, Collegers formed a minority of pupils (in Hallam's time they were outnumbered by about 8 to 1) and, although there was a greater social diversity amongst Collegers as a result of their subsidised fees (they received free board and lodging and paid tuition fees only for 'extras'), they were not, as they have subsequently become, especially distinguished by academic merit and the rough-and-ready nature of their communal existence in the infamous Long Chamber did not make a Colleger's life an enviable one. Those who were not scholars (and they included Hallam and all his friends) were known as Oppidans (Latin: oppidum = a town), because rather than living centrally in College, they lived in boarding houses run either by 'dames' or assistant masters in Eton town. The education of an Oppidan came rather more expensively than that of a Colleger, but the quality of his life was unquestionably more civilised, indeed enviably so.

W.D. Tucker who himself was a Colleger a few years before Hallam's time, wrote admiringly of the refined existence which an Oppidan could expect:

'[he] would be treated kindly, and as a gentleman's son. He would share a clean, tidy room with some one of his own standing . . . he might sit down to [breakfast] as comfortably, in its way, as he would at home . . .

> There was nothing in an Oppidan's house like continual or systematic severity or bullying . . . The fagging was almost nominal . . . When he reached the Fifth [form] . . . he would have a room to himself-carpeted, curtained, and fairly furnished . . . A room far more comfortable than his first chambers in the Temple, or the first lodging in his Curacy . . . He was free from interruption, and might lay out a course of reading if he so willed – and many did – wholly independent of school work.'[5]

It was in this atmosphere that Arthur Hallam managed to educate himself so effectively and, in time, to enjoy the benefits of civilised intercourse with a close circle of highly intelligent friends. Food was generally of a good standard in Oppidan houses and Gladstone's father was in the habit of providing his son with wine at the beginning of term and insisting that he drank it.

If all this makes Arthur Hallam's Eton life sound luxurious, it has to be pointed out that the drudgery of the schoolroom was considerable. The curriculum was narrow, the classes were large and the academic tasks were repetitive. Work done 'in school' (which is to say under supervision in class) was exclusively classical. Although private tutors existed for a range of subjects, including mathematics and modern languages, such tuition as they gave was extra-curricular and was paid for separately. Eton boys enjoyed a low standard of numeracy (never considered a requisite for a gentleman) and had no official acquaintance with geography, science or modern history. Hallam struggled with mathematics. He wrote to Gladstone during the Christmas vacation of 1826 that he had been 'in mental agony with sines, cosines, tangents &c'[6] and his relative ineptitude in this area was to be in time a problem at Cambridge and was to prevent him from taking the honours degree which his father had hoped for. Hallam's proficiency in modern languages was mainly the result of his travels in Europe, though his friend Gladstone attended French classes and read widely in French literature.

The processes of classical study were of three kinds. The first was the learning by heart of passages of Homer, Horace or Virgil. Boys aged 13 or 14 could be required to commit as many as 70 lines to memory per day.[7] They were also required to translate or 'construe' passages from these authors, being examined (or 'heard') on such passages orally. During their time at the school, boys might cover the entire *Iliad* and *Aenead* more than once, depending on how long they stayed. No other texts from Homer or Virgil were officially covered in school.[8] The third and most demanding activity was the composition of Latin or Greek verses on a given theme. Proficiency in verse composition was in the opinion of Henry Hallam: 'the chief test . . . of literary talent' at Eton, and, as has been seen, Henry had been particularly proficient at it himself, though it was never a task for which Arthur had much inclination.[9] The value which Henry Hallam set upon verse composition is illustrated by the fact that he

24

preserved several dozen examples of Arthur's efforts in Latin and Greek verse in his papers[10] and even included one of them (a translation from Dante into Sophoclean verse) in the *Remains*. In addition to the principal texts, boys were required to work at some rather threadbare anthologies of Greek poetry and Greek and Roman prose and oratory. These might be supplemented by work on Greek plays and other texts with individual tutors outside official school time. Boys' tutors would also 'look over' their verse translations with them and make corrections before they were finally shown to masters in school.

Henry Hallam rated Arthur as 'a good, though not perhaps a first-rate, scholar in the Latin and Greek languages' and attributed his relative lack of interest in the routines of classical study partly to the disruptions caused in his education by time spent abroad and partly to 'the strong bent of his mind to subjects which exercise other faculties than such as the acquirement of languages calls into play'. Henry was in due course to make much the same point about Arthur's indifference to classics at Cambridge. It should be added that, although Hallam never had much interest in the study of Latin and Greek *per se*, he had his favourite classical authors: Aeschylus and Sophocles, Lucretius and Virgil, though, according to Henry Hallam he never much cared for Euripides or Homer.[11]

Defenders of the classical curriculum could be found. Apart from the implicit approval of Henry Hallam, C. Allix Wilkinson believed that there was 'no better discipline for the mind'[12] than the composition of Greek and Latin verse and even a late twentieth century writer could claim that, through this strict classical training, 'A clever boy . . . [could cultivate] a powerful memory, a quick and orderly mind, an elegant and correct mode of expression, and build up a reservoir of quotable passages from the literature which was believed to be the sum of all that was wise and valuable in the history of human experience.'[13] Anyone who had had this kind of classical education could exist on terms of allusive equality with anyone else who had, as the classical references and quotations in Hallam's letters and debating speeches show. Unfortunately, in the case of boys who were not clever, the system simply became corrupt, and an idle boy need do very little if he so wished, having a range of survival strategies to choose from. The laxity of supervision meant that boys, asked to repeat the passages they had supposedly learned by heart, could get away with looking over the master's shoulder at his text; there was a trade in second-hand verses, and a stupid senior boy could often bully a clever younger one to do his translations for him.[14]

The prestige which Eton enjoyed at this time was largely the result of the Head Master, the redoubtable Dr. John Keate, who became a legendary figure both in Eton and beyond it and, in time, despite his extremely authoritarian regime, the subject of much mellow reminiscence by old boys. A scholar of Eton and King's (of which, like his father, he had been a Fellow), Keate was a distinguished classicist having, whilst at

Cambridge, won four Browne medals and a Craven Scholarship. He had made some important emendations to the text of Horace, though the demands of his work as a schoolmaster prevented him from publishing them in his own right.[15] By the time Hallam arrived in the school Keate had been Head Master for thirteen years. His authority by that time was formidable but it been significantly assailed on several occasions. Keate was the first Head Master of Eton in the modern sense of the term and it was his vision of what the school should be which prevailed over that of the comfortable, reactionary, Provost Goodall, his nominal superior. As A.C. Benson records, during the 25 years of his Head Mastership, 'Keate was Eton and Eton was Keate.'[16]

It has been Keate's fate, not entirely fairly, to be associated with the widespread and undiscriminating use of corporal punishment, or 'flogging' as it was invariably known. Although the early nineteenth-century public schools existed to educate the sons of gentlemen and thus perpetuate their caste identity, these gentlemen's sons had a highly developed sense of their own liberties and had no automatic respect for authority. Keate decided that the boys of Eton needed firm discipline and was, by the standards of his time, remarkably successful at administering it, but he was throughout his Head Mastership often resisted and undermined by the boys. Shelley's friend, Thomas Hogg, had said of Keate in his early days that 'His behaviour was accounted vulgar and ungentlemanlike, and therefore he was peculiarly odious to the gentlemen of the school',[17] and indeed Keate's reputation as a flogger had been largely forged in the face of some large-scale and public acts of disobedience by boys. These virtual rebellions had been met with mass floggings, which, on one celebrated occasion, had been administered well into the small hours of the morning. By Hallam's time large-scale disobedience had become rare but daily provocations persisted: gunpowder was regularly put into Keate's candle snuffers before late school on winter evenings;[18] he had been pelted with books and on one occasion a stone (to which, not surprisingly, he took particular exception). In school he himself taught all the senior boys together in one class, numbering up to 170, of whom there were always some who liked to challenge him: practical jokes, fights with bread pellets and outbursts of impromptu singing were not unknown. Keate continued to flog as and when he saw fit, and, as the only master allowed to flog, he frequently had to do the disciplinary work of his less effective subordinates. In time flogging came to be viewed as something of a spectator-sport. W.D. Tucker described it as 'rather a pleasant pastime than otherwise, from the ease with which it was incurred'[19] and Benson remarks that: 'To almost everybody concerned the whole thing was a gigantic joke.'[20] In practice it was a small group of recalcitrant malcontents, such as can be found in any school, who felt the sting of Keate's cane (actually a bunch of birch twigs). Most boys, including Hallam and his friends, avoided it easily enough and, despite Keate's harshness with the more commonplace schoolboy peccadilloes, his ability to turn a blind eye meant that bullying, fighting and drunkenness among the boys remained deeply embedded in Eton's culture.

Although a figure of 'offensive authoritativeness'[21] in public, Keate was not a cruel or vindictive man in his private life. His breakfast parties for senior boys were notoriously genial and civilised occasions and he was happily married with a family of seven children. Nevertheless neither Gladstone nor Hallam particularly warmed to him. Gladstone was capable of managing civil comments on Keate when the mood took him, but he did not forget him as 'A graceless, senseless, cruel little martinet'.[22] On other occasions Gladstone could be more dispassionate, writing to his father that

> 'His [Keate's] chief faults are, an extremely arbitrary manner, which does not show itself in words alone; and his partiality. The former may be in great measure excused, on account of the nature of his subjects whom he rules over; and of the various ways in which they elude or defy his authority. His *partiality* is only *partial* . . . as it is only in the case of noblemen, generally speaking, and of those he knows privately that he displays it.'[23]

Hallam was less forgiving. When Keate tried to control the activities of the Eton Society, the debating society in which Hallam and his friends performed and starred, Hallam wrote to his friend William Windham Farr, who had recently left Eton for Cambridge:

> 'we are in some fear of being blown up by a sudden explosion of the Little Doctor's spleen. [Keate was an exceptionally small man, scarcely 5ft in height and often ridiculed for this] You must know that he has for some time been chafing in secret at our fondness for political subjects . . . [he] flew off in a tangent, almost swore . . . that we had no right to debate anything subsequ[ent to the Revolution], adding by way of a soothing sequel that [he would] break up the Society all together!!! . . . the confounded little Autocrat.'[24]

Nevertheless it should be pointed out that, in general terms, Keate was highly supportive of the Society, just as he was to be of Gladstone, Hallam and others when they devised and published a journal called *The Eton Miscellany*. When Hallam left Eton, Keate asked him for his picture, and the portrait still hangs in the Election Chamber there.

Just as Hallam could not fail to be drawn into Keate's proximity, so he would have been witness to the lawlessness and violence that were part of Eton life. If Etonians were jealous of their liberties, they certainly had much more personal freedom than would be regarded as desirable today. There were lengthy breaks between lessons and in a typical week

27

Tuesday would be a whole holiday, and Thursday a half-holiday. Additionally, saints' days were whole holidays, and the eves of saints' days half-holidays.[25] Confirmation days were whole holidays too. Tucker writes:

> 'This perfect freedom . . . gave an inexpressible charm to Eton life – a charm that never dies, and remains in the memory through all the trials, troubles, happiness and hard work of after years . . . The Masters, from Keate downwards, never interfered or intervened in any way out of school. We were a self-governing Community.'[26]

This was the freedom that enabled Hallam, Gladstone and Gaskell to spend their time taking walks together, breakfasting together, discussing literature, politics and theology and planning meetings of the Society, but it is not in the nature of most adolescent males to be so high-minded and many Eton boys took their pleasures rather more roughly. Drunkenness was common (and partly connived at), and, although there was some provision for organised games, youthful energies were frequently channelled into less reputable activities. Fights often occurred. One of Gladstone's earliest letters home describes a fight between a fellow Liverpudlian, Kemp, and a boy called Bowring:

> 'the honour of Liverpool was bravely sustained by [Kemp] . . . who gave Bowring such a licking that he could not come into school – Kemp too was terribly knocked about, his whole face being dreadfully swollen and in some places the skin broken . . . There was another battle between a Colleger of the name of Voules and Oppidan of the name of Hallifax. To my great joy Hallifax licked him.'[27]

Fights took place in a corner of College Field, hidden from the gaze of those in authority but visible to passengers coming to Eton by the London coach along the Slough road. If there was a fight in progress it was not unknown for the coach to stop on the 'fifteen arch bridge' so that the passengers could watch it and even Keate himself was once heard to remark that he did not 'object to fighting in itself; on the contrary, I like to see a boy return a blow.'[28] Henry Hallam feared that 'bloody battles will make Arthur too much afraid', but saw nothing intrinsically wrong in institutionalised violence: 'when I was at school boys did not faint after fighting'.[29] During Hallam's time one celebrated fight even caused a fatality and attracted the interest of the national press. A number of different versions of the events have survived but the brute facts were that two boys, Ashley (son of the Earl of Shaftesbury) and Wood fought each other until Ashley collapsed and was taken back to his house where he later died. Hallam's friend James Milnes Gaskell provided his mother with an account of the fight, which he witnessed, and as Wood was in the same house as Hallam, Hallam must have known all about it too. What is particularly significant about the aftermath of the fight is that, although Wood was charged with manslaughter by Aylesbury magistrates, no further action was taken against him. Ashley's funeral was conducted by Keate in the school chapel and Lord Shaftesbury subsequently wrote a letter to him saying that he forgave the boys concerned and urged that no punishment be given to any of them.

James Milnes Gaskell's letters to his mother provide us with a considerable insight into the life of an Eton Oppidan at this time. A few months older than Hallam, Gaskell was a rather prim and priggish only child and, as such, he was a natural victim for bullies. His letters tell of violence and intimidation, in addition to the fagging (performing menial tasks for older boys) which was part of the lot of every junior boy at Eton. In his first term Gaskell wrote: 'I had to set the things, run down to Cripp's for ham, bacon, bread, chocolate, etc., then receive several blows from Morrell because I was not quick enough; then I had to boil eggs for Taunton, fetch up the rolls, butter, etc., and then I was generally employed in the servile offices of brushing Halifax's clothes and tying his shoes'.[30] The way in which Gaskell was treated by boys of his own age was no better. He was hissed at on entering the schoolroom because he refused to swear; his furniture and wallpaper were vandalised; his clothes were torn; his hat was used as a football; he was hit in the eye and stoned. 'I think how very fortunate I have been not to lose an eye. I hope I shall not be disfigured when you come to Eton',[31] he told his mother. Yet with the passage of time, cheered with the company of Hallam, Gladstone and the rest of the intellectual elite, he was able eventually to write: 'Why do you not congratulate me on the Elysian state of happiness that I in common with most other Etonians enjoy?'[32]

If Hallam was never on record as finding Eton 'Elysian', he was spared the worst excesses of fagging and bullying; at least references to such activities did not find their way into his letters home. The earliest surviving letter from his Eton days (Sunday 8 May 1825) shows a resigned tolerance of the routines of the place ('My tutor's remains just as it was'), together with the self-contained satisfactions of the bibliophile: 'I have bought a Byron's works in a beautiful green binding . . . My library is full and beautiful . . . [the Provost's lodging] contains lots of nice books.'[33] There is perhaps a touch more worldly wisdom in Arthur than in the priggish Gaskell, though, like Gaskell, Arthur was a precocious child and forced to develop his own *modus vivendi* in the company of potentially critical older boys. Perhaps his charm helped. His father certainly believed that he would 'please everybody – no boy was ever more likely to be popular – dear cub.'[34] He had entered Eton at the age of 11 which was not uncommon. Boys could enter as young as 8 or 9, but the majority entered at 13. The school list for 1823 shows that in his second year Arthur was in the Fifth Form, Lower Division, an advanced placement for one of his age, alongside Gladstone and William Windham Farr who were both two years older than he was.

Whilst the 1820s at Eton were undoubtedly 'the age of Keate', Hallam had the great advantage of coming under the influence of the man who was in due course to become Keate's successor. On the surface Edward Craven Hawtrey was just as much a product of Eton inbreeding as Keate had been. There had been connections between the Hawtrey family and Eton and King's for two centuries. In all other respects the two men could not have been more different. Where Keate was blustering and abrasive, Hawtrey was patient and humane: 'always on the look out for any bud which he could warm with a little sunshine'.[35] Having been bullied, almost literally, to death as a boy at Eton himself, he was particularly keen to discourage bullying both as master and as Head Master. Physically unprepossessing (his ugliness caused him to be known by the boys as 'Plug'),[36] he compensated for this with dandiacal manners, wearing scent and sporting flamboyant waistcoats. Although these foppish tendencies and a penchant for cultivating the sons of the aristocracy did not pass unnoticed by his critics,[37] he was absolutely the right man to be Hallam's housemaster (in Eton parlance 'My Tutor'). Hawtrey knew and respected Henry Hallam, was a dinner guest in Wimpole Street and was eventually to be responsible for installing a bust of Henry Hallam in Eton's Upper School Room after his death. Hawtrey looked back on his friendship with Henry 'as one of the most valued Honours of my life' and remembered Arthur and his younger brother 'not only with admiration but . . . affection'.[38] A good many of Hawtrey's tastes and enthusiasms were to be reflected in the boy who would ultimately become the best known of his pupils. Although inevitably required to concentrate on the teaching of classics during school hours, Hawtrey was proficient and widely read in modern languages, in particular French, Italian and German. He was to publish some translations from Goethe, at that time little read in English, not to mention supervising the production of *The Eton Atlas of Comparative Geography*.[39] His house was furnished with great taste, particularly in the matter of pictures and books, and he was generous both in loaning and giving books to his pupils.[40] He was the epitome of the dedicated bachelor schoolmaster and generations of those whom he influenced lived to tell the tale and to tell it appreciatively. Gerald Wellesley who had an adjacent room to Hallam's in Hawtrey's house remembered that:

'His house was extremely well managed, and, in the matter of food and attendance to all our wants, I could not find a fault. As a tutor, I shall always be grateful for Hawtrey . . . He took great pains with any boy that was disposed to read, gave excellent advice, encouraged private reading, and helped me immensely in preparation for Oxford. In fact, under his guidance, I read privately nearly all the books in which I was finally examined at Oxford.'

Similarly, his biographer explained how the Hawtrey ethos and values were disseminated:

> 'He would come round in the evening to our rooms – a remarkably upright, military figure – bearing a little lamp; would stand leaning against a bureau and discourse at length in a thoroughly friendly way with us, disarming us of all fear of him as a Master, and managing dexterously to introduce topics of high interest, so as to rivet our attention.'[41]

It is safe to assume that Hawtrey appreciated the special qualities of the young Hallam: his wide-ranging interests; his command of language (he had composed ten verse tragedies by the time he went to Eton); his outward confidence and self-sufficiency and the charm that could keep him on the right side of an authority which he did not entirely respect. Hallam's references to Hawtrey in his letters are not always reverential, for example, and on one occasion he 'went in a deputation' to Hawtrey 'to ask for more coals; but [he] looked sour . . . & declared that during twelve years of power he had never heard his coalscuttles impeached or his coals voted bad'.[42] Nevertheless Hawtrey was just the man to let Hallam develop his own interests, with care, but without too much inter- ference. Hallam's attractiveness to others has become the stuff of legend but he could be solemn and self-righteous too, acquiring for a time the nick-name 'mother Hallam'. He also brought the assumptions and manners of cultivated London society to an institution where such things were by no means possessed by everyone. He was in time drawn to the school's most brilliant intellectual coterie which he did as much as anyone else to dominate. Gaskell and Gladstone might have been the first but were certainly not the last of his school and university friends to be impressed by his distinguished background. Gladstone especially was, for the rest of his life, acutely conscious of his own social inferiority to Hallam. Gaskell first described Hallam to his mother as 'a son of the author of the 'Middle Ages', who is preparing another work for the press, which is expected to be very clever'.[43] Gladstone in a similar vein recalled 'He had evidently from the first, a large share of cultivated domestic education: with a father absorbed in diversified business.'[44] In addition to acquiring a reputation as Eton's leading poet, Hallam also impressed his contemporaries with his conversation and intellectual authority. Another of his Eton friends was Francis Doyle, a future Professor of Poetry at Oxford, who remembered that:

> 'We all of us . . . felt whilst conversing with him, that we were in the pres- ence of a larger, profounder, and more thoughtful mind than any one of us could claim for himself . . . his temper was so charming and his social qualities so delightful, that it would be difficult to say whether we admired or loved him most.'[45]

31

Gladstone never forgot that 'he was of the most tolerant temper imaginable',[46] whilst again joining the chorus of tribute to his intellectual gifts: 'it was of him above all his contemporaries that great and lofty expectations were to be formed'. To Gladstone, Hallam was the ultimate authority on literary matters among Eton boys, not merely on account of his own writings, but because 'there was no one upon whose taste and judgement I had so great a reliance. I never was sure that I understood or appreciated any poem till I had discussed it with him'.[47] In writing about Arthur Hallam there is an inevitable and recurrent problem in separating contemporary comment from sentimental hindsight but there is remarkable consistency to be found in the opinions of those who knew him as a schoolboy.

There can be little doubt that Hallam's Eton career really took off when he was elected to the Eton Society. Variously described as 'the Society', the Debating Society or (subsequently to the age of Hallam) 'Pop', its members were known as *Literati*. Keate had a slightly ambivalent attitude to the Society, according due respect to its members but insisting that, in the area of political debate, it restricted itself to events which had taken place over fifty years previously. Whilst this might seem an over-cautious position to adopt, it was not an unusual one in its time. Both the Cambridge and Oxford Unions imposed comparable prohibitions in an age when political convictions were often the result of atavistic and almost visceral party loyalties. Henry Hallam similarly wished to avoid unnecessary controversy when he stated in the preface to his *Constitutional History* (1827), that he would not cover the period after 1760, as he was unwilling 'to excite the prejudices of modern politics, especially those connected with personal character'.[48] John Burrow has pointed out how debates ostensibly devoted to historical subjects could easily bear on contemporary political developments and that

> 'It requires little imagination to conceive the excitement with which . . .
> in the mid-1820s just prior to Catholic Emancipation, the Eton Society
> of Gladstone's day must have debated whether the conduct of England to
> Ireland from . . . 1688 to 1776 was justifiable.'[49]

Keate in general was, however, a great encourager of oratory and required boys who had been promoted to the Sixth Form to make a formal speech for which he himself would take great pains to coach them. This, along with the daily oral 'construing' of classical texts in school, indicated the strength of Eton's valuation of the spoken word. Indeed, one historian of the school has pointed out that this training proved 'invaluable to [the boys] in their subsequent careers as statesmen, as preachers or as pleaders in the courts of law.'[50] More specifically, it pointed Hallam towards the world of the Apostles, the exclusive debating society in which he was subsequently to flourish at Cambridge and helped to form the basis of the vigorously dialectical prose style which is apparent not only in his letters (where on more than one occasion he apologises for lecturing his recipients) but also in the critical and philosophical writing which he was to produce as an undergraduate. Keate's Eton was not merely the barbaric and licentious place of legend: it offered genuine intellectual opportunities to those capable of taking them and it is unlikely that the Society ever enjoyed as much prestige as it did in this period.[51] Indeed as the nineteenth century moved on, 'Pop' developed in ways which Hallam's contemporaries would have scarcely understood. With time it moved from being a debating society for the school's intellectuals into being a society for the school's athletes who took upon themselves the responsibility of keeping discipline around the school but who remained self-electing for another century-and-a-half. The body still exists as an elite corps of school prefects who assist the Head Master and have a conspicuous role on most public occasions.

Meetings took place weekly during term-time. They were held at 4 p.m. on Saturday afternoon and the Society's minute book can still be read in the Eton College Library. Proceedings were formal, indeed quasi-parliamentary, in nature. By tradition meetings were relatively short, lasting less than an hour, though the eloquence of Hallam and Gaskell sometimes lengthened them. Speeches were made by 'honourable members' and were reported, usually with the utmost precision, by the Vice-President who was elected specifically for each meeting and who was assisted sometimes by two clerks, who were not themselves members. 'Strangers' were allowed to attend as observers, though not to speak, and they were required to leave at the end of the formal debate before the Society turned to its private business. Strangers are not recorded at every meeting so there must have been many occasions on which the society was, so to speak, debating to itself, with perhaps fewer than a dozen members present. Its methods of election (in which blackballing was possible) meant that numbers were purposely restricted. When Hallam became a member of the Society on 26 November 1825 ('without a single blackball', as he proudly told his father) membership appears to have stood at just eleven. Gladstone had been elected just over a year previously and Gaskell was to be elected on the 1st of July 1826. At the time of his election Gaskell put the number of members at twelve to fourteen, adding, with a pleasing absence of self-consciousness, that they were 'the only choice few, the only desirable associates'.[52] Numbers inevitably fluctuated as new elections took place and older members went off to the universities. Gladstone was proud that, at the time of his departure from Eton in December 1827 (the term after Hallam), he left the Society with a record number of twenty-one members. The Society was self-governing and self-sufficient. It enjoyed neither the patronage nor the intervention of masters in its affairs and, as Francis Doyle pointed out slightly more tactfully than Gaskell, 'it brought together many of the cleverer boys from their different forms, and . . . from every corner of the college as well. By this means, those who would otherwise have hardly known each other to speak to, were soon turned into intimate friends. They read with, or, as, Whigs and Tories, in opposition to each other, they discussed historical and literary subjects, they argued and split hairs, and walked together disputing about Shakespeare, Milton, the old dramatists, and so on.'[53]

The Society occupied its own premises, four rooms, situated rather modestly over a cookshop, including 'our little room of 6 feet square', as Hallam termed the room in which the debates took place.[54] In its own way it also aspired to the conditions of a gentleman's club, subscribing to a range of newspapers and journals, which were in those days relatively expensive items for purchase by individuals, and whose subscriptions themselves were the on-going objects of contention amongst members. Members could also be fined for non-attendance, if no explanation had been given, as well as for a range of other peccadilloes such as the use of inappropriate language or failure to write up the report in time. It is difficult not to see an element of schoolboy playfulness when we read that Gladstone had endeavoured to fine Hallam for throwing a piece of orange peel against a wall and staining it. Hallam defended himself by stating that he had thrown the peel against Pickering's head and that if Pickering had not ducked there would have been no problem. On another occasion Hallam was fined 'for not filing the papers.' It is also worth noting that the Society was not entirely without social conscience and that on 13 May 1826 Hallam supported a motion that subscription be raised in aid of 'the distressed weavers in the manufacturing districts.' Gladstone summed up the spirit of the Society best when he said: 'Our society are great politicians in a small way; that is, they are wont to dispute with great vehemence and little knowledge.'[55] Gaskell was generally regarded at the time as the most political beast of them all. Although his subsequent political career as an MP (he was the Tory member for Wenlock in Shropshire for over 30 years) did not begin to rival Gladstone's in prestige, his enthusiasm for politics at this time verged on the obsessive. As Doyle wrote: '[he] was a very curious specimen of a boy. He had fed upon politics and House of Commons details until he became a sort of walking Hansard . . . he had got acceptance from the various door-keepers as a sort of honorary MP'[56] Gladstone remarked that 'Gaskill [sic] was 'a great politician, but as far as I have seen, a very pleasant fellow.'[57]

Following his election in November 1825, Hallam's first recorded intervention in a debate was on 4 February 1826. The question was: 'Is the character of Archbishop Cranmer blameable or praiseworthy?' Although this was described as 'an eloquent maiden speech', Hallam's real debut came two weeks later when he opened the debate on the question 'Had Shakespeare any equal among the Poets, ancient or modern?' The

Society's debates usually comprised two main speeches, often (*pace* Gladstone) of some length and sophistication, one member 'opening' by proposing the motion, the other replying with a speech which opposed it. Members could then intervene with their own comments before the question was put to the house and a final vote taken. Hallam's speech in praise of Shakespeare argued that Shakespeare had had few advantages of birth or education and that he was thrust on the world at a tender age. He went on (according to the Vice- President's account) to assert that 'some others might admire the grandeur of Milton, the originality of Homer, the delicate pathos of Virgil – but that in Shakespeare – we saw the various poets combined and brought to perfection in one harmonious and magnificent whole . . . he was sorry for the want of taste and sensibility of those, if indeed there were any such who were dead to the beauties of those works which must ever remain the object of the admiration of posterity, the ornaments of English Literature.' These are noble sentiments from a youth barely fifteen years of age, though the ease with which Hallam consorts with the great figures of literary history does not conceal the fact that he was making a little go a long way, and defending his own position by patronising those likely to disagree with him. He won the debate by one vote.

The following week, the question concerned the fall of the Roman Empire. Gladstone thought it was a 'Capital debate . . . Hervey-Selwyn-Farr-Hallam-Doyle & I spoke – Hervey & Farr, beside myself, a second time.'[58] 'Mr. Hallam,' in his contribution 'espoused and eloquently supported the cause which Mr. Selwyn had adopted'. Hallam shared Gladstone's enthusiasm, writing to his sister Ellen: 'We have had a better debate today than has been known for a long time; an hour minus a few minutes', adding, 'I know you love the society and all that belongs to it'.[59] Ellen was barely ten at the time, but she was Hallam's closest sibling, in intellect as well as years, and was clearly in awe of him. Her interest was a genuine one and not mere wishful thinking on her brother's part.

Although the questions for debate were occasionally on literary and aesthetic subjects, the Society was essentially a forum for argument about more modern and recent history with an emphasis on issues relating to the seventeenth and eighteenth centuries. This inevitably contributed to the development of party-political, which is to say Whig or Tory, sympathies. When Hallam complained that 'we are dreadful Tories in the Society',[60] he was not including himself. His own politics at this time were, following family tradition, unreconstructedly Whig, and the fact that he was in a minority in holding and defending his views merely added fuel to his rhetorical fire. He was, after all, Henry Hallam's son and had inherited his full share of the paternal disputatiousness. Indeed, although he was to change his political stance significantly at Cambridge, it is difficult not to think that there was an element of family pride involved in his debating performances at this time. Although Henry Hallam's

Constitutional History had not yet been published, it is a safe assumption that Arthur would have had some awareness of its contents and his repeated assertions of the Whig position are informed and authoritative, though more explicitly partisan than his father's. He argued in favour of the execution of King Charles I, the republican politics of Milton, the Hanoverian succession, the ministry of Walpole, high levels of individual liberty and emancipation for Roman Catholics. 'A Whig', he epigrammatically opined, offering his own version of one of Henry Hallam's most famous definitions, 'was a lover of liberty, without abandoning monarchy; a Tory a lover of monarchy without abandoning liberty'. His defence of the treatment of the Whigs in the reign of Queen Anne was a particular *tour de force*, even though Farr, his opponent, carried the day with a speech of comparable length, less wit, but more precision. It is difficult to resist the sheer exuberance of Hallam's declamation ('we breathe the same air as those noble men breathed: we tread the same soil, we love the same freedom, we fight for the same privileges which the Whigs in that period contended for. . . . a Brunswick Sovereign of Liberty, against a descendant of the House of Stuart, with the sword of Bigotry in the one hand & a French pension in the other. . . . . . Swift . . . dipped his pen in gall to bespatter names, which I trust, will long outlive his own). Whilst there is undoubted force and spirit in these political certainties, of a kind which only a fifteen year old can have, it was Farr who 'sat down amidst considerable Applause, which his admirable vein of eloquence so justly elicited from the House'.

Despite Keate's embargo on the debating of contemporary political issues, the Society habitually debated and divided on party lines and many of the questions were clearly posed with that outcome in mind: indeed it is difficult finally to know to what extent the members' politics at this time were determined by the subjects of debate, or to what extent the subjects were determined by the members' politics. It would be wrong to see Hallam as being always on the losing side. At the beginning of the summer term of 1826 he was victorious when the question was put: 'Was Queen Elizabeth justified in her persecution of the Roman Catholics?' Hallam argued that she was not, and Gladstone reported enthusiastically, that 'Hallam-Pickering minor-Doyle & Farr spoke – at considerable length. Debate on whole excellent . . . Moved also that any member throwing about – striking with, or using in any offensive manner any property of the Society, or any other property in Society room, be liable to a fine of 2s 6d.'.[61] Hallam also informed his sister that this had been a particularly good debate.[62] His rising status in the Society became noticeable as both the frequency and substance of his speeches increased. Hallam continued to report enthusiastically about the debates during the rest of the summer term. Subjects included whether the disarming of the Scottish Highlanders was laudable; whether 'Athens or Lacedaemon' should be preferred; and whether the Polish government was justified in excluding protestants.

The range of the subjects chosen for debate by this group of adolescents must strike any observer as impressive, particularly when it is remembered that the historical knowledge required to make any kind of informed contribution to the questions being considered could come only from private reading and reflection, as there was no provision for the systematic study of modern history within the school curriculum. The Society did not merely allow its members to enjoy the sounds of their own voices but to educate themselves in the process. Henry Hallam recorded that Arthur's 'being led away . . . from the exclusive study of ancient literature', provided time for wide reading, particularly of 'The poets of England' and 'the older dramatists'. He had the confidence to follow his own literary interests, acquiring a particular enthusiasm for Fletcher and a wide knowledge of Shakespeare: 'He knew Shakespeare thoroughly; and indeed his acquaintance with the early poetry of this country was extensive'.[63] A great deal of self-education must also have been the result of the amount of time that Gladstone, Hallam and Gaskell spent in each other's company. Gladstone records patterns of activity which were to remain as long as Hallam was in the school: tea, walks, 'Wine & fruit', not to mention private debates about contemporary political issues which took place in Gaskell's room. On Sundays discussions were wont to take a theological turn. On the 14 May 1826 Gladstone reported: 'stiff arguments with Hallam, as usual on Sundays, about Articles, Creeds, etc'.[64] Hallam never entirely lost his taste for theological debate.

Another means by which Gladstone and Hallam cemented their friendship was the river. Eton had an ambivalent attitude towards boating: it had not always been an officially sanctioned activity. Sculling was a common pastime, though, and Gladstone often refers to sculling Hallam 'up to Shallows' or beyond. Hallam himself sang the praises of sculling (or, more accurately, of being sculled): 'You don't know & never will know the delight of sculling up to the shallows or Boveney', he wrote to Ellen, '& floating down, lying at the bottom of the boat with the sun shining full in your face & the birds chirping all round'.[65] He was also at this time an enthusiastic swimmer, according to school tradition having once leapt into the river from Eton Bridge. His mother's considerable apprehensiveness about these activities did not prevent him from pursuing them, and he pointed out to her that 'The idea of swimming constituting exertion & as such being to be deprecated in this hot weather . . . is ridiculous . . . The more one exerts in the water, the cooler one is.'[66] Julia Hallam always suffered agonies about her children's well-being but she had good cause for anxiety. A few years previously, her brother Charles's two sons had been drowned when they were swept away by the tide in the Bristol Channel. Additionally, on 21 June 1826 Gladstone sent to his mother details of the drowning of a boy called Deane, a member of Hallam's house: 'Keate, Hawtrey . . . and others were on the spot and several medical men . . . I saw him carried into the house . . . they let his head hang down backwards.'[67] Drownings were common occurrences at this time but, despite the physical risks inherent in life at Eton, the summer term of 1826 was, for Hallam and his friends, an especially enjoyable one, at times almost lyrically so. Election to the Society at the age of fourteen had been a sign, in Eton terms, of a coming-of-age, and there is no doubt that Hallam's friendship with Gladstone strengthened and solidified in this period. Gladstone had to go home before the end of the term as his sister had been taken seriously ill. Nevertheless he was to write that the term was 'independently of state of health at home, by far the happiest I ever spent at Eton'.[68] Hallam's presence obviously had a great deal to do with this.

For the summer months Henry Hallam, as he always did if not travelling abroad, took his family out of London to more healthy surroundings, on this occasion to Sutton Court near Epsom in Surrey, where they remained until it was time for Arthur to return to Eton at the end of September. Although he was not in general given to enthusing about life at Eton, Hallam was clearly bored at being separated from his newly-made friends over the summer. He complained that there was no river for bathing at Epsom, so was spending time riding instead and, not for the first or last time, he found himself short of books.[69] He sustained himself by writing to Gaskell and Gladstone, and, though he beseeches Gladstone to write ('I had begun to fear you had reasons for not doing so of some unpleasant nature'), he suggests that there should be 'A truce to politics: write me word at your leisure all sorts of news'.[70] Gladstone did write at length to Hallam twice in August though, as might be expected, politics would keep on breaking in. As Hallam reported to Gaskell: 'I heard from Gladstone . . . a long and very orderly epistle, as you may suppose, full of lamentations about Liverpool, [Lord Liverpool, The Prime Minister] the country, the ministry'.[71]

The topics covered in these letters were those which preoccupied Hallam for the rest of his time at Eton and until a year travelling in Europe broadened the range of his interests. They can be seen as an extension of his debating activities. In looking forward to the next term's Society meetings, Hallam hopes for a series of debates about Charles I, about whom he was clearly spoiling for a fight. To Gaskell, *a propos* the coming term's debates, he writes: 'Pray take up Charles's side: it is sweetly untenable and I shall have the luxury of beating you down with fair sheer argument . . . We shall meet again, and in arms . . . I will raise the lofty banner of Whiggism in the society and who shall view it unmoved?'[72] To Gladstone he bemoans the years of Tory party rule 'which have brought England to the verge of a precipice'.[73] He supports the cause of parliamentary reform (though like his father, he would eventually come to oppose it) and even more strongly the cause of Catholic emancipation in Ireland, which was the biggest political issue of the day and the one that he felt most passionately about. In short, as he subsequently wrote to Farr, he was spending the summer 'breathing politics at every pore & anticipating a glorious session [i.e. of the Society in the coming term]'.[74]

Some brief respites from the daily routines of Sutton Court took place: a trip down the Thames to the Kent coast, where he particularly appreciated the scenery, and a visit to the home of his Eton friend Pickering in Clapham. Hallam much valued the entertainment he received there: 'a pretty good house . . . a glorious dinner, a very agreeable party . . . I fear my powers of entertainment will fall short of his'. Clearly the young men packed in quite a lot of activity. There was riding, and also a visit to 'a large public bath at Camberwell', though it was stagnant and green. Pickering's father, a barrister, ('a sensible though not a very liberal man and strongly anti-Papistical') was tolerant enough to allow himself to be lectured by Hallam on the subject of Catholic emancipation.[75]

Hallam's letters of this period reveal a mixture of adult sophistication and an adolescent love of furious partisanship and commitment to a cause. The subject of Catholic emancipation roused him very quickly. Writing to Farr during the first week of the autumn term, 1826, he says:

'for God's sake, reflect for a moment: think how England stands with respect to *Ireland* . . . do you think *when a war comes* & come it will and must . . . that the Irish millions will let slip the opportunity? . . . Secure the Catholic Clergy, by making them dependent on the State for their subsistence: disfranchise the 40s Freeholders who are the instruments of bigotry: give Catholic Peers & Gentry seats in Parliament, for we have tried *their* loyalty & found it pure . . . grant Emanc:ion & you paralyse the blow of bigotry, you save us from the awful depth of ruin..beware how your voice is added to the cry of No Popery. Beware how you write with those who have not acquired audacity of assertion from profundity of thinking! You have all the o[ld] women, all the stupid, all the foolish on your side.'[76]

It always said much for Hallam's personal warmth of manner that he was able to keep the loyalty of those friends whom he could so enjoy provoking in debate or just generally haranguing.

In view of the high hopes which he expressed for the new academic year, the autumn term of 1826 was something of an anti-climax. In November Hallam wrote to Farr that he was 'sincerely sick of this term & long to breathe the invigorating air of Bowbells. Our debates have been on the whole good this time: but we have not yet managed an adjourned one'.[77] On 30 September the question was 'Was Richard I King of England or Charles XII King of Sweden the finest [sic] character?' The comparison between these two monarchs was not a purely arbitrary one: it had originally been made by Burke, hence, presumably, the interest in the subject. Hallam, unpatriotically, and with an entirely conscious iconoclasm, argued for Charles, and was defeated by 6 votes to 1 for his pains. He found the medieval world of Richard I and his crusades rebarbative:

> 'that Coeur de Lion was actuated by any religious feelings or any desire to recover the Holy Sepulchre from the grasp of an infidel, his actions, I think, do not give us any sufficient proof . . . I hold the atrocities of Richard to be of a deeper dye than those of the Swedish Hero. Richard was cast nigh – true Chivalrous character but like most of the heroes of those dark ages; was by turns generous & cruel, bigoted and unenlightened . . . irascible, haughty & vindictive.'

His speech is much more effective in attacking Richard than it is in defending Charles. Gaskell, who opposed him, was actually much more rigorous and meticulous in examining Charles's record, though Gladstone described Hallam's speech as 'brilliant and plausible.' Brilliant plausibility was again in evidence two weeks later when the question was 'Was the Political Conduct of Milton deserving of praise?' This was a question tailor-made for Hallam's interests even though again he failed to secure a majority in the house: 'It would be a dereliction of those political principles wh. I have been wont from childhood to revere . . . if I were to stamp with censure the conduct of John Milton.' Once more we see Hallam saving the best of his oratory for the condemnation of those of whose conduct he disapproved, such as 'that odious prelate, who had the effrontery to assert, that it was an acceptable thing to the God of mercy, that our fellow creatures be tortured because they did not kneel in a particular fashion'. Gladstone as Vice-President was responsible for writing up this debate for the minute book and his account ran to forty-four pages of which twelve were devoted to Hallam's speech. The subject certainly brought the giants face-to-face with each other: Hallam and Doyle spoke in favour of Milton, and Gladstone, supported by Gaskell, violently opposed him. Gaskell, who was less magnanimous than Gladstone in his views of Hallam at this time, claimed that Hallam 'flew away upon the wings of "liberty" "equality" and every kind of name, invented by the radical for a colouring to those measures which tend to destroy it'.

It is always the case in a close-knit community that friends will talk (or write) behind each other's backs. Gaskell clearly felt closer to Gladstone than he did to Hallam, telling his mother at the time of his leaving Eton that 'idea of being separated from Gladstone is really distressing to me, in fact, writing upon the subject is enough to make me melancholy'. Gaskell thought that Gladstone was 'the individual . . . to whom I should first turn in an emergency'.[78] For Gladstone, however, it was Hallam who was to be particularly and repeatedly singled out. In his diary entry for 24 September 1826, Gladstone wrote: 'Breakfasted with Hallam [shortly after this time they were to start breakfasting with each other daily as a matter of course]. Walk with Hallam. I esteem as well as admire him.

Perhaps I am declaring too explicitly & too positively for the period of our *intimacy* – which has not yet lasted a year – but such is my present feeling.'[79]

Gladstone was not in the habit of recording very much personal information in his diaries of this period and the confessional nature of this particular entry is, in its context, therefore, unusual. Gladstone seems to be registering some embarrassment at raising the question of his '*intimacy*' with Hallam at all, even privately to himself. Gladstone's high estimation and admiration for Hallam was to be reiterated until the very end of his own life, despite a long subsequent history of disagreement and difficulty between them, but a genuine friendship at the time they undoubtedly had. Gladstone, for example, was extremely attentive to Hallam's physical well-being. By the side of Gladstone's innate robustness of constitution, Hallam's relative frailty was noticeable. Hallam did not participate in games, hence Gladstone's taking the initiative in sculling him on the river. When Hallam was confined to his room with illness (Gladstone described it as 'earache', though Hallam hinted at something more serious),[80] Gladstone 'sat with' him each day. When, on Sunday, 5 November 1826, Hallam was 'called out of Church, on account (I believe) of his grandmother's sudden & dangerous illness' (in fact she died on that day), not only does Gladstone's diary record the matter but there is a fretfulness that Hallam has still not returned to school the following Friday.[81] Gladstone's sensitivity to Hallam's signs of ill-health forms the source of one of his most revealing observations about him: ' . . . it was probably a forecast of the mournful future, that if ever I entered Arthur Hallam's room after he had been closely engaged in work, I used to find him flushed up to the very eyes, in a way quite beyond his usual colour, which was always high'.[82] Francis Doyle noticed these things too: 'he had suffered much at intervals from serious head-aches. His Eton and Cambridge friends, naturally enough, thought them headaches and nothing more'.[83] Both these comments were made in the light of Hallam's early and sudden death, though in fact neither high colouration nor a tendency to headaches need be symptomatic of anything other than themselves.[84]

But there is another side to Gladstone's friendship with Hallam. Gladstone's feeling of social inferiority as a Liverpool businessman's son has already been mentioned but his sense of personal inferiority to Arthur himself was always there: 'I had the sense enough to regard [the friendship] all along as a high privilege though one which I found it impracticable to turn to adequate account. But to this hour I am unable to conceive how on his side he could have found for it any sustaining amount of *pabulum*. It was without doubt the zenith of my boyhood, and it must have been the nadir of his . . . [he] had over me the advantage of an immense moral superiority both original and acquired'.[85]

Encountering Arthur Hallam, as most people do, through Tennyson's *In Memoriam*, the lineaments of Gladstone's friendship with him are familiar ones: above all else is the perception of human gifts of an almost transcendental order, representing more than ordinary manifestations of intellectual ability or good nature. Hallam, especially after his death, was regularly represented as charismatically attractive both to men and women, and a large part of this attractiveness lay in the fact that he was unaware of it. He tended to find his friends less attractive than they found him. His own feelings about Gladstone were equivocal and his letters often betray an unease in his relationship with him. Sometimes he seems to go to uncomfortable lengths to praise and flatter Gladstone. At other times he seems thin-skinned and prickly. In talking of Gladstone to other people, Hallam is certainly capable of praising him: 'Whatever may be our lot, I am confident *he* is a bud that will bloom with a richer fragrance than almost any whose early promise I have witnessed.'[86] But this does not conceal a satirical, almost patronising, edge to some of Hallam's other remarks. On Gladstone's re-election to the Chairmanship of the Society in March 1827, he remarks to Farr: 'I suppose Gladstone will be re-elected Chairman: Prime Minister of England not quite so certain.'[87] Similarly, when talking about Gladstone's success as a student journalist he again refuses to take his friend entirely seriously: 'we used to set poor William Ewart down for nothing but Methodist hymns'.[88] The often rather detached attitude which he takes to his friends (he talks, for example, of 'walking out a good deal, & running the changes on Rogers, Gladstone, Farr and Hanmer'[89]) shows Hallam keeping others at an arm's length, as if he is exploiting rather than reciprocating the warmth of their regard for him. Although Hallam was often to be found at the centre of a social circle, his feelings of being deprived of genuinely close friendship lasted until well into his time at Cambridge.

It was the beginning of the Easter term of 1827 which prompted Hallam to write to Farr of 'the nausea which always attends a return to Eton & which indisposes one for everything; the horrors of a four exercise week to begin with & the more serious business of preparing for a Confirmation which is to take place the day after tomorrow'.[90] The confirmation in question was conducted by the school's official Visitor, the Bishop of Lincoln, who, Gaskell reported, confirmed 'the whole school with the exception of very, very few indeed'.[91] Gaskell himself was not confirmed but Gladstone was. The ceremony took place on 1 February so if Hallam was one of the confirmands that day, he would have been so on the day of his sixteenth birthday. Sadly, as Hallam noted in a letter to his Aunt Elizabeth, the bishop died a few days later.[92]

The Society continued in its business. The previous Saturday, Gaskell, not without self-congratulation, reported a 'capital debate . . . upon the conduct of England to Ireland. Hallam and I were upon the same side. He spoke uncommonly well; but the cheering they gave me was tremendous, considering the thinness of the assembly'.[93] Debates took place that term on, among other subjects, the character of Augustus; on Sir Robert

Walpole's ministry (again); on Herodotus' and Xenophon's accounts of Cyrus; on Wat Tyler, Lord Bute, and a comparison of the men of the reigns of Queen Elizabeth and Queen Anne. Also 'Mohammed, is he to be admired?' Hallam believed he was: 'because I think the gentleman much calumniated, & a great man for his times & country: I was however left in a minority of 3.'[94]

On 20 February Gladstone was promoted to the Sixth Form, an important rite of passage at Eton. The Sixth Form consisted of about two-dozen boys, roughly equally divided between Collegers and Oppidans. Certain small rituals were involved: distributing almonds and raisins amongst one's fellow sixth formers and making a speech in front of Keate. Gladstone appeared to thrive on his newly acquired status, finding the sixth form 'much more pleasant than any other part of the school. It certainly affords greater opportunities for improvement in classics; Keate treats one with much more civility'.[95] Hallam observed that 'Our friend Gladstone . . . is dignified towards lower [i.e. junior] boys, a species of rigor which is nowadays most rare, as the inferiors are more presuming, & the superiors more lax than ever I reme[mber].'[96] Hallam's elevation followed in May, having been delayed because of an incident in which one of his contemporaries was discovered drunk. Keate postponed the promotion of all the other candidates as a result, though, when the time came, Hallam was suitably blasé about the experience, seeing it more as a chore than a privilege:

'The first great plague of getting in will be the sending round *Almonds & Raisins* to all the 6th form: the second will be the being tormented into good, or rather bad speaking by Keate [Hallam, according to Gladstone, did in fact make a speech 'in school' on 4 June, subject unrecorded]: the first great pleasure will be the exercising penal rigor towards the unfortunate lower boys: the second – oh I have no time, or patience to go on to the second & perhaps there is no other.'[97]

This is typical of Hallam's lack of interest in the minutiae of school life. Where both Gaskell and Gladstone record in letters and journals facts and impressions of daily life at Eton, Hallam's tendency to solipsism generally restricts him to mentioning only those activities (the Society and later *The Eton Miscellany*) in which he himself took an active part.

The fact that the summer term of 1827 was Hallam's last at Eton meant that decisions about his future must already have been taken. In the absence of entrance or leaving examinations, boys were free to join or leave Eton as their parents chose. The fact that, at the age of sixteen, Arthur had attained the top form in the school meant that the next stage of his education could be planned. It was not unusual for Collegers to remain at school longer, while waiting for a vacancy at King's to occur, and Gladstone, though older, was also to remain in the school for a term longer than Hallam did. In Hallam's case, particularly given his rather cool feelings towards Eton, there was clearly little reason for him to remain there any longer. Gaskell, who left at the same time as Hallam, and who was less directly affected by paternal interference than Hallam was, agonised for some time as to whether Oxford or Cambridge University was to be preferred. He eventually, like Gladstone and Doyle, went to Christ Church, Oxford, believing

> 'that at Oxford a man is much more independent than at Cambridge; that at Cambridge there are few intermediate grades between hard reading and dissipated men; secondly the debating club at Oxford is respectable, gentlemanly etc, whereas the Union is the contrary . . . Gladstone tells me that he thinks I have no chance of distinguishing myself at all at the Cambridge Union, because my opinions are much too moderate.'[98]

Hallam, too, had his doubts about the Cambridge Union. Although he encouraged his friend Farr's activities in it, he was less enthusiastic about it in his comments to Gladstone:

> 'He [Farr] seems mad after the Union but . . . the account he gives of it is not inviting! The tumult, clapping, cheering & hissing is so constant & their expressions of disapprobation given so "con amore" that "one must have the courage of an imp of darkness to make head in such a Pandaemonium".'[99]

Most certainly the rough-and-tumble of a university debating chamber must have been very different from the lively but ultimately self-congratulating coterie of the Eton Society. Hallam took some interest in the Cambridge Union when he was at the university, but the more enclosed and precious atmosphere of the group known as 'The Apostles' better answered to his taste and experience.

The question of why Hallam attended Cambridge rather than Oxford is an interesting one. As he was not a Colleger, he was not eligible for a place at King's; as an indifferent mathematician, he was an unlikely candidate for Cambridge, where mathematical studies carried the highest prestige. Oxford would have seemed a much more likely destination for him, as it did for many Etonians at this time. His father had been at Christ Church. Perhaps Hallam's account of his working hard at mathematics during the Christmas vacation of 1826 is an indication that decisions favouring Cambridge had by then been made, though Gaskell in the following May says that he is still to discover which university Hallam is intended for. Certainly by July 1827, Hallam was writing to Farr that

> 'I shall come up to Granta [i.e. Cambridge] next October year . . . What do you think as to the propriety of going into the Union – is it really what

44

some people represent it, very plebeian, or is it the thing? I know my father will want me to sap [Eton slang for 'work hard']; so I shall probably be obliged, when I start freshman, to abjure the sweet sin of politics altogether.'[100]

Hallam did indeed turn his attention to matters other than politics at Cambridge, though it was the influence of friends rather than a dedication to academic study that caused him to do so. His interest in politics quickly withered on its stem.

That Henry Hallam wanted Arthur to 'sap', and that he had not been entirely approving of his son's dissipation of energies into the frivolous area of political and philosophical debate, have been the reasons generally given for Arthur's being sent to Trinity, the most illustrious college in Cambridge, rather than to Christ Church, its Oxford equivalent. It seems scarcely credible that Henry could have viewed the likes of Gaskell, Gladstone and Doyle as undesirable influences who might distract Arthur from the primrose path of academic achievement and it has been suggested that there were more important considerations in Henry's mind than simply separating Arthur from his friends.[101] It is possible that Henry's negotiations with Christ Church, undertaken as long ago as 1823, had proved unsatisfactory. A new Dean at Christ Church in 1824 had made clear that he felt no obligations towards promises of places made by his predecessor, at a time when the number of applications to the college had significantly risen. Indeed, Christ Church's popularity at this time meant that it actually had a waiting list.[102] This meant that Henry Hallam was faced with the option either of making representations to the new Dean, or of sending Arthur to Cambridge (lesser Oxford colleges presumably being out of the question). Given the closer association of the Hallam family with Cambridge than with Oxford, Henry's decision was less surprising than it might at first seem, though it may have led to the deferment of Arthur's entry to Cambridge by a year. Whatever the explanation, Arthur was not enthusiastic about Cambridge, either in prospect or in reality:

'It is my destiny, it would seem, in this world to form no friendship, which when I begin to appreciate it, & hold it dear, is not torn from me by the iron hand of circumstance. The friends whom I loved at Eton I shall not see at Cambridge.'[103]

Fortunately for Hallam, and for English literature, there were friends at Trinity to be found in due course, though it would take him some time to discover them.

Hallam's final months at Eton were lived out in a fever of excitement about national political developments. The hero of the young political Turks at Eton was George Canning, the 'great commanding luminary of the twenties', as Gladstone had called him.[104] Canning himself was an Old Etonian, and his third son, Charles, was a contemporary of Hallam's at the school and a great friend of Gaskell's. Born in 1770, Canning had been an MP since 1794 and had witnessed all the political upheavals of the period in a career that had not itself been without controversy. For five years he had been Foreign Secretary in Lord Liverpool's Tory ministry, but this was to change when Liverpool suffered a stroke in February 1827. After lengthy negotiations with King George IV, Canning was eventually asked to form a new ministry in April. However, shortly before Liverpool became incapacitated, Canning had attended the funeral of the Duke of York in Windsor on a very cold night (visiting his son at Eton and actually staying overnight with the Provost), and had caught a chill from which he never properly recovered. Additionally, the ministry which he led was particularly fraught. Canning's own sympathies were strongly pro-Catholic (this explains his popularity with Hallam and his friends) but such sympathies were not widespread in the Tory party and Canning found it impossible to form a ministry without including some sympathetic Whigs in it. Conspicuously, the two most prominent and gifted Tory politicians of the day, Peel and Wellington, refused to serve, so Canning's job was not an easy one.

The Easter vacation of 1827 saw Hallam acting as a parliamentary reporter to Gladstone who was at home in Liverpool, far away from the action, though Liverpool at the time was well-served by newspapers. Hallam had been prevented from attending the House of Commons to hear the motion proposing the creation of Canning's ministry by one of his father's 'awful' dinner parties. Nevertheless, he assured Gladstone that 'Nothing but the Ministry is talked of in society, as well by Ladies as Gentlemen'.[105] He was able to attend a Commons debate a few days before returning to Eton for the summer term, where, he told Farr, he had been 'highly delighted' to hear Canning, Brougham, Peel and Burdett speak. He was especially taken by Brougham's eloquence (he had spoken for an hour). He was convinced that those members of the Whig party who had joined Canning's ministerial team were doing so from the highest of motives: 'I don't agree that the Whigs have scrambled for place: no man with an honest heart, or a sound pair of eyes, could say so *seriously*: more disinterested conduct *on all sides & from all parties* has seldom, I should think, been known.'[106]

Returning to Eton, the Society's activities continued throughout the summer term, though the atmosphere of its meetings became less harmonious, and internal squabblings broke out. Hallam wished to see the powers of the chairman increased, so as to suppress unruliness in the debates. He also feared that it was becoming '*the spoutingclub of a faction*'.[107] In other words, he was failing to dominate the proceedings as much as he would have liked. Debates took place that term on the comparative merits of Clarendon and Hampden, and of Leo X and Lorenzo de

Medici, on the Duke of Montrose, Elizabethan drama, Queen Elizabeth and Queen Mary, and Strafford. Gladstone was able to report that 'The society gets on very well',[108] but Hallam's interest in it seems to have waned. The factionalism had increased, he writes on 26 May: 'Our hostility is now much more personal, than it used to be: I don't mean that we quarrel, but that the division is much rather *Gaskell & Anti-Gaskell*, than *Whig & Tory*,' and the following day he wrote rather sourly to his sister that 'we had a bad debate yesterday & a bad debate the Saturday before: & that we anticipate bad debates for the next two Saturdays.'[109] Perhaps Hallam's loss of enthusiasm for the Society was mirrored in his performances in it, as Gladstone wrote at this time that he thought Gaskell rather than Hallam had emerged as the Society's best speaker.[110]

The fading of interest in the Society can also be explained by the fact that it was giving way to a new and more exciting activity. There was a tradition of schoolboy journalism at Eton. Winthrop Mackworth Praed and his associates had been responsible for producing a much-acclaimed journal, *The Etonian* in the early 1820s. Consciously seeking to emulate this, and largely as a result of Gladstone's initiative, *The Eton Miscellany* came into existence during Hallam's last term at school. Gladstone's organisational skills were given free rein and he recruited the leading lights of the Society to his editorial committees of which there were to be two, a general committee of about twelve members and a select committee of four. Gladstone's plans were grandiose: 'We shall endeavour to secure all the fittest persons in the school . . . Several contributions have been received, and many more are in their authors' hands'.[111] Gladstone, as editor, took the pseudonym of Bartholomew Bouverie and he put great efforts into the production of the journal throughout his last two terms at Eton, as well as over the summer vacation. His diaries report editorial meetings, visits to the printers and late night sessions correcting articles and reading proofs. This intensity of effort was necessary as the journal, each number containing 48 pages, was to appear fortnightly. Gladstone recorded happily of the first edition, published on 4 June (the birthday of King George III, always kept as a festive day at Eton): 'sale very great and very rapid-opinions of course various'.[112]

Altogether ten numbers of the *Miscellany* were published: five during June and July in 1827 and a further five in October and November, after Hallam had left. Contributions were received from thirteen boys. Gladstone was responsible for the largest number of articles (thirteen), George Augustus Selwyn for ten and Hallam and Doyle for eight each. Gaskell made two contributions. In keeping with the journalistic convention of the day, all the contributors were, as Hallam reported to his father, '*bound, by promise,* not to tell the author of each article, and I believe none except Hanmer and Doyle are known with the least certainty'.[113] The whole thing was much applauded by Keate who took the view that it was 'a good way for the boys to employ their time', which,

:ad Master at the end of a long summer term, it undoubtedly must
~een.[114]

Hallam, writing to elicit Farr's support in Cambridge at the end of
May, came nearest to providing (however ironically) a prospectus for the
Miscellany:

> '*The Eton Miscellany* will go forth to battle in the name of all the Etonians
> of the rising generation . . . it will consist of miscellaneous articles, some
> in the shape of essays (a la Spectator or Microcosm), some in that of
> reviews, or humorous pieces (of which latter we have one instance so
> exquisite by Selwyn that, if it does not make people laugh, when printed,
> as much as it has us . . . I shall be very much out of humour with the inven-
> tion of printing); interspersed with poetry &c & the whole got up under
> the supposed superintendence & editorship of Mr *Bartholomew Bouverie*
> . . . I suppose we may depend on you for procuring us an extensive sale
> at Cambridge & for spreading the intelligence far and wide over the habit-
> able globe.'[115]

These sentiments may seem less hubristic when it is remembered that
The Etonian, whose successor the *Miscellany* saw itself as being, had sold
widely in Oxford and Cambridge, whence it had drawn a number of its
contributors. Indeed Hallam's letter to Farr clearly had the purpose of
eliciting such contributions itself, as it goes on to say that he has spoken
to John Frere (who in fact was not enthusiastic about the project) 'as
wishing to secure Tennyson & others, who were friends of his & by no
means untried in composition'.[116] The Tennyson in question was
Frederick, eldest brother of Alfred, and the only one of the family to attend
Eton. Although he was four years older than Hallam, he had left Eton for
Cambridge only the previous year and had been a member of the Society.
There is no reason for thinking that he and Hallam had known each other
well at Eton, but it is a reminder that the name of Tennyson would have
been familiar to Hallam when he reached Trinity.

The Eton Miscellany is very much a miscellany. Clearly Gladstone
allowed his contributors complete freedom to submit exactly what they
wanted. There is no sense of a manifesto or overall design, the whole
project seems to have been to encourage the *Literati* of Eton to indulge
such talents as they had and to enjoy the privilege of appearing in print
in a publication which had actually to be purchased by its readers. The
Miscellany with its anonymous or (more frequently) pseudonymous
contributions has a mildly eighteenth-century, Scriblerian, air to it, not
least in one of its satires on pedantry. The 'exquisitely humorous' piece
by Selwyn, does, in fact, owe a great deal to the Scriblerian mythology of
'dulness'. It is called *The Eton Dull Club* and would clearly afford entertainment to those capable of enjoying its essentially private jokes and
innuendos, though Selwyn, its somewhat incongruous author, was ulti-

mately to become the most sanctimonious of Hallam's Eton contemporaries. He rowed in the first university boat race, became Bishop of New Zealand and then of Lichfield, and had the distinction of having a Cambridge college named after him. Among the rest of the *Miscellany*'s contents there were examples of Gladstone's own rather heavy-handed humorous writing, several letters to the editor, aiming to show that the journal was at the centre of controversy on a range of issues, and also a fair amount of dull and competent versification. Some of this was by Francis Doyle who, with a characteristic lack of false modesty, was happy to inform his readers in his autobiography of sixty years later, that he himself was considered a better poet at Eton than Hallam.

Hallam's contributions included a humorous article *On Names* in which he argues that the great figures of history have only become so because of the appropriateness and attractiveness of their names. He also provided two pseudonymous letters to the editor, two poems, and three sets of *Remarks* on Gifford's edition of the plays of John Ford. Both of the published poems have Irish settings. *The Battle of the Boyne* is (as might be expected) a pro-Orangist, Whig poem, praising 'The orange standard's chivalry', and written under the pseudonym of 'Roland'. The other poem *The Bride of the Lake* is more ambitious, but is, from its title onwards, clearly inspired by Scott. It is written in heroic couplets, and manages its own kind of Celtic dreaminess, recalling the lake of Killarney, where Hallam had stayed two years previously:

> While o'er the foam, that wreathes in smiles thy wave,
> Varies the magic light his parting radiance gave
> And distant chimes, heard thro' the twilits grey
> Swell the sad note, and mourn th' expiring day.[117]

Rather surprisingly, perhaps, Henry Hallam, although declining to publish these lines in the *Remains* still felt moved to remark that they bore 'very striking marks of superior powers'.[118]

Of considerably more substance are Hallam's three essays on the plays of Ford, which not only stand out for their scholarly seriousness amidst the inevitable ephemera of a school publication, but give some insight into the range of Hallam's reading and thought at this time. His enthusiasm for what was then described as the 'early' English dramatists has already been noted. The first essay offers some general remarks about the author:

> 'We were always very partial to John Ford. He was, we believe, the last of those potent enchanters, who, in the days of Elizabeth and James, awoke the dormant spirit of our literature into gigantic strength.'

The second essay reminds us that Hallam was dealing with an author who, at this time, was far from fashionable, or indeed universally accept-

able on grounds of taste. Hallam devotes most of this essay to an examination of 'that painfully-interesting play' *'Tis Pity She's a Whore*, from
which he quotes two scenes in their entirety, making a comparison
between one of them and Desdemona's death scene in *Othello*. The third
essay ends with an eloquent tribute to the poetry of the Elizabethan age
which:

> 'bears the same resemblance to that of the succeeding age, as the free and
> mountain torrent, exulting in the grandeur of its liberty, bears to the
> inclosed waters of the fountain, leaping but to a certain height, and recur-
> ring with an eternal monotony of sound to the marble basin which
> imprisons it.'[119]

Hallam had acquired a reputation as a poet at Eton, and, in addition
to those pieces which found their way into *The Eton Miscellany*, one or
two other fragments from this period remain. They do not in general
constitute complete poems, often containing corrections which suggest
early drafts. There is an untitled poem of spiritual self-reproach, which
begins rather arrestingly:

> Scorner, there's woe upon thy soul,
> Tempter of God.
> In vain thou raisest now the empty scoff,
> The bitter laugh . . .

There is also a fragment of a verse drama about William Tell, a fluent
love poem to an unspecified (probably imaginary) recipient, an *Ode to
Freedom* ('Hail, Goddess of the sea-girt shore') which reflects Hallam's
political partialities in celebrating 'The great Hampden' whose death on
Chalgrove Field is alluded to. There are also some pencilled musings about
war, which seem to owe quite a lot to *Macbeth*. Although these poems
are all clearly experiments, they show an interesting diversity of interests,
styles and influences and are significantly bolder than most of the poems
by other hands which found their way into the *Miscellany*.[120]
Despite the energy which went into the production of *The Eton
Miscellany*, the journal's life was, inevitably, a fleeting one. Hallam,
Gaskell and Selwyn departed at the end of the summer term, leaving
Gladstone to soldier on alone. He was particularly sorry to lose Selwyn
'a most valuable working man,' though he confessed that he had been
'generally disappointed' in Hallam as a contributor.[121] Hallam's own
enthusiasm subsided over the summer and he counselled Gladstone to
'give up' the *Miscellany* rather than produce sub-standard work: 'Nothing
could be more lame than a breaking down after your second, or third
number: nothing so unworthy of ourselves, as to carry it on feebly, and
prolixly, and languidly, and with no zest or spirit'.[122] Although Hallam

had undertaken to write an article on 'the Lake poets', he never completed it. Perhaps this final act of dilatoriness was what provoked Gladstone's disappointment. The *Miscellany* had doubtless been fun while it lasted, but its editor was to have the last word on it in due course: 'the design was rash and reprehensible, the execution extremely imperfect . . . there are few things in it that rise above mediocrity, and many which sink below it.'[123] Few modern readers would dissent from this view.

Hallam and Gaskell's leaving Eton at the end of term was celebrated in the Society by a vote of thanks from Gladstone. Traditionally these votes had been delivered by letter, but, as both Gaskell and Hallam were expecting to go abroad, Gladstone decided to perform *viva voce*. He spoke of Hallam's

'great, eminent and continued services to this society . . . I remember not only the ability which my honourable friend has displayed, not only the unwearied industry with which he has promoted the interests of the Society, but also the length of time during which that ability and that assiduity have been manifested and exerted.'

The Vice President was forced to confess that he could not provide a verbatim account of Hallam's reply because 'it was accompanied by the loudest and warmest of cheering', though he did note that 'The honourable member was evidently much affected . . . He sat down amid the most marked and gratifying testimonies of approbation.' Hallam's emotions seem more than merely the stuff of a rhetorical flourish, as Gaskell added that Hallam had 'alluded to the hours he had spent there [i.e. at the Society] as the happiest ones of his life'.[124] Gladstone thought that Hallam and Gaskell were 'both great losses to us & I fear not soon or easily to be repaired'.[125] The following day, at an Oppidan dinner, a toast was drunk to *The Miscellany*, and on Election Monday, 30 July, at that time Eton's principal festive day, Hallam, alongside Gladstone, Hanmer, Pickering, Law and Selwyn performed at 'Speeches', Hallam and Law declaiming passages from Virgil. Hallam was critical of Gladstone's abilities in classical recitation, telling his father that 'though he speaks very gracefully in the Society, where he can go on rapidly with a "tonens dicendi copia" he sings dreadfully when obliged to speak slow in school'.[126]

A long-standing Eton custom was that when boys left the school they presented their friends with books. Hallam had already received one from Gladstone and believed that he was to receive another. He consequently thought hard about what it would be appropriate for him to give in return and asked his father if he could supply a copy of his *Constitutional History*, then very hot from the press (it had appeared only the previous month). Henry Hallam duly obliged, though Gladstone's gift to Hallam was even more generous: he presented him with the complete works of

Burke, which ran to six volumes, the first of which contained the inscription 'A.H. Hallam from his friend W.E. Gladstone. Eton July 1827. Donum et Exemplar'.[127] If Hallam's gift might, superficially at least, seem paltry by comparison, it was nevertheless a gift which Gladstone always valued, pointing out, at almost the end of his life, that its three volumes were among his oldest books, and that its donor had been 'at that time my dearest friend'.[128] Hallam's Burke volumes are lost.

Leaving Eton after five years was obviously a significant moment in Arthur Hallam's life, but he would probably have liked to have left school with as little sentimentality as possible and no overt display of emotion. Nevertheless he had to admit to some pangs of feeling when the time came and he wrote to Farr:

> 'Leaving Eton is a horrid bore just at the moment. The "antique towers" look more agreeable, than they ever did before: and the Playing-fields, one finds out, are very pretty, pleasing and inviting, just when one presses them for the last time. Keate was civility personified, and asked me for my picture. My tutor [Hawtrey] too grinned as gracious a grin, as his native ugliness permitted.'[129]

He was more open about his feelings in a later letter to Gladstone, admitting to feeling emotional when the time for departure came: 'though you used to accuse me of want of feeling on the subject, I assure you I was very uncomfortable when I took my last walk round the Playing-fields an hour before I left'.[130]

Although the course of Arthur's next year had already been set out by Henry Hallam, who had planned a lengthy tour through France and Italy, Arthur was far from exhilarated by the prospect of another continental trip presided over by his father. The previous foreign tours had been extended summer holidays: this one was scheduled to last for the best part of a year. Hallam had written baldly and without relish to Farr on 17 July: 'in another fortnight I shall have left Eton for ever, and in another after that, shall be crossing the seas to Calais. I shall not come back for a year'.[131] In the intervening weeks he continued to write to Gladstone, literally until the eve of his departure on 20 August. There is no sense of impending adventure in these letters. Even though he had been finding London 'a desolate, dreary place . . . in August', the prospect of foreign travel did not cheer him. 'It is a melancholy thing to leave England for any length of time . . . I have been suffering much from headaches, and sometimes, when in low spirits, anticipate being laid up at some informal posthouse'.[132] He added that their walks together to Salthill had been a better experience than he imagined sight-seeing in Europe would be. This was the third European tour the family had made in Arthur's lifetime and it is not surprising that he saw it as a disruption rather than as an adventure.

Hallam's continued correspondence with Gladstone during the last weeks before his departure to the continent was clearly a sign of his unwillingness to let go of his chief confidant but was also the result of developments on the national political scene. At the end of the parliamentary session in July, Prime Minister Canning, ill and worn out, had been invited by the Duke of Devonshire to recuperate at Chiswick House. By the beginning of August it became known that he was mortally ill, and indeed Gaskell visited the Canning family at Chiswick only days before his friend's father died, and saw him 'lying upon that couch upon which he was about to die, and from which he never rose'.[133] The element of personal concern shared by these young men for the fate of the Prime Minister seems scarcely conceivable until it is realised that before the days of film stars, popular musicians and sportsmen, politicians came the closest to providing those heroes and role models that young men have need of, particularly those who live close to the seats of power. Gladstone's first biographer appreciated this when he wrote that 'The most moving public event in his [Gladstone's] school-days was undoubtedly the death of Canning, and to Gladstone the stroke was almost personal.'[134] When it was known that Canning seemed unlikely to survive his illness, Hallam's surprisingly fogeyish view was that 'Should the Tories come in, [i.e. as the result of a new Ministry] it will be time to pack up one's things and be off to America.'[135]

Two days later, Canning was dead and Hallam was writing, in a letter to Gladstone, his own obituary notice for him: 'As a man, and as a man of genius, all parties can hardly help lamenting him; unless indeed those who are irremediably blinded by the bad passions of bigotry'.[136] Hallam's tribute is appreciative, eloquent and expressed with the judicious formality of a public speech. The fact that it is difficult to believe that this was written by a sixteen-year-old boy who had just left school is a tribute to Hallam's rhetorical prowess. It is also a tribute to the education which he had received over the previous five years at Eton. Although the curriculum was narrow, the teaching nugatory and the texture of daily life often brutal, the opportunities for personal intellectual development were considerable for those boys who chose to take them. If Arthur Hallam did not leave Eton as a minute classical scholar on the Keate model (as his father would have liked), he had been able to sharpen his wits in debate with members of the school's intellectual elite, and he had been able to read avidly and write as much as he chose. Unreformed Eton permitted many boys to pass through it and learn next to nothing. For the able and the confident it provided boundless intellectual freedom of which Arthur Hallam was a conspicuous beneficiary.

Hallam's last letter to Gladstone before leaving London was written on Sunday, 19 August 1827. The following day, after some fear that the departure might need to be postponed as a result of his and his father's illness, he left for Calais on the first stage of a lengthy journey that was

to have important and irreversible consequences, not least for his relationship with Gladstone, who was shortly to return for what must have
been an anti-climactic final term at Eton without his closest friends. What
Gladstone could not have realized was that he and Hallam would by slow
degrees go their separate ways, and would meet again only on brief and
fleeting occasions. Hallam wrote at length to Gladstone during the early
stages of his European tour, but the correspondence lapsed and was only
partially resumed after Hallam went up to Cambridge. The tour marked
the end of their period of real intimacy.

Hallam's letters to Gladstone from Italy in the autumn and winter of
1827–8 (the last one was written on 2 January), though affectionate in
tone, present a picture of a young man happily assimilating new experiences and hastening to draw a line under older ones which he feels he is
beginning to outgrow. He wrote from Florence on 30 October: 'I am very
sensible, that I have not profited from your friendship as much as was
reasonably to be expected from the excellence of your character: but
should it please God that we should ever be intimate again, as we have
been intimate, I hope I may prove more worthy of such a friend'. These
are generous words, but Hallam does not express any great conviction
that the friendship will be resumed. Likewise, although he apologises for
his failure to contribute as much to the *Miscellany* as Gladstone would
have liked him to, he is not ultimately repentant: 'Does the Miscellany go
on? I am conscious I have not behaved well towards you on that score, by
not writing: the fact is, I did write at some length, but burnt it not liking
what I had written, & postponed further employment foolishly to Paris,
where I found . . . no spare time . . . I am heartily ashamed of the trash of
which by far the greater part of my contributions to the first volume
consisted'. The Society, too, was also soon found wanting: 'I believe the
habit of studying politics, & much more the habit of speaking upon them,
before they are well matured by the reflection, is injurious, inasmuch as
it gives a dogmatic turn to the character: & the impressions received in
early youth are so fearfully profound!'[137]

Gladstone's best-known and most frequently quoted reminiscences of
his friendship with Hallam were written much later in his life and
contributed significantly to the development of the Hallam mythology. In
1829, two years after his departure from Eton, Gladstone's feelings about
Hallam were still peculiarly intense, as an entry in his diary for 14
September of that year shows. Gladstone himself was at the time staying
with Gaskell at his home in Yorkshire and had recently written to Hallam,
whom he had at that time not seen for over two years. Unbeknown to
Gladstone, Hallam was actually replying to his letter on the very day that
the diary entry was made. Gladstone sounds wounded and betrayed. The
entry is embarrassed and oblique, its subject remaining anonymous
throughout, though easily identifiable. Gladstone seems to be confronting
a series of emotions which he would otherwise prefer to evade:

The history of my connection with_____is as follows
It began late in 1824, more at his seeking than mine.
It slackened soon: more on my account than his.
It recommenced in 1825, late, more at my seeking than his.
It ripened much from the early part of 1826 to the middle.
In the middle_____[Farr?] *rather* took my place.
In the latter end [of 1826] it became closer & stronger than ever.
Through 1827, it flourished most happily, to my very great enjoyment.
Beginning of 1828 [Hallam] having been absent since he left Eton, it varied but very slightly
Middle of 1828 [Hallam] returned, and thought me cold. (I did not increase my *rate* of letters as under the circumstances I ought to have done.)
Early in 1829, there was friendly expostulation (unconnected with the matter last alluded to) and affectionate reply.
Illness in [spring and summer of 1829]
At present, almost an uncertainty, very painful, whether I may call [Hallam] my friend or not.

Tennyson's biographer Robert Bernard Martin was firmly of the opinion that these words resulted from Gladstone's jealousy of Hallam's (by then) developing friendship with Alfred Tennyson. Either way, their foreshadowing of certain features of *In Memoriam* is uncanny. Whilst obviously accepting that Hallam is still alive, Gladstone's prose-poem is elegiac in tone. Like Tennyson, he traces his relationship with Hallam through the course of recent years. Like Tennyson he feels bereft and the past tense predominates. The Arthur Hallam of this passage, like the Arthur Hallam of *In Memoriam*, is known and loved, but elusive and never-to-be possessed, something of which Gladstone remained conscious for the rest of Hallam's life.

CHAPTER THREE

A Farewell to the South
Italy, 1827–1828

'The fire of my wrath burns fiercely against that old constitutional clod for taking Hallam to Italy before he sent him to Cambridge.' Thus wrote Francis Doyle, Eton friend and London neighbour, shortly after Hallam's return from his travels in the summer of 1828. He remarked, shrewdly: 'I am rather afraid Hallam will not do a great deal at Cambridge. He cannot recall his spirit from Naples to Trinity, from the Tiber to the Cam'.[1] Foreign holidays with Henry Hallam (Doyle's 'old constitutional clod') were serious undertakings and it is likely that Henry saw this particular tour as being the means by which Arthur would acquire at least some part of a gentleman's culture and sophistication. Additionally Ellen Hallam, only slightly less precocious than her brother, had now reached the age of eleven and was deemed old enough to benefit from the cultural delights which Europe had to offer. Nevertheless Henry Hallam was candid enough to admit with hindsight, and in terms similar to Doyle's, that, as a means of preparing Arthur for the next stage of his academic career, the tour was a failure, having above all else stunted the growth of that proficiency in 'the learned languages' which would be needed at university. Indeed it was Henry's view that Arthur's 'mind had been so occupied by other pursuits, that he had thought little of antiquity even in Rome itself.'[2] When he came to edit his son's *Remains*, Henry also took pains to suppress nearly all of the poems which Arthur had written whilst in Italy, particularly those which cast direct light on his emotional life. Both psychologically and artistically, Arthur's travels in Europe had a significant effect on him and he was himself acutely aware that he returned from them, still only seventeen, but as something rather more than just a talented schoolboy. By that time Hallam had become sufficiently worldly to find the prospect 'entering on a College system of life' at Cambridge a far from appealing one.[3] Not only had he seen the sights of Italy, he had mixed with the cream of English and Italian society, explored the galleries and museums and become fluent in the Italian language. He had also fallen in love for the first time. It is not surprising that he found his return to England in June 1828 emotionally disorientating.

In his enthusiasm for travel Henry Hallam was very much a man of his time. Continental travel had become easier after the end of the Napoleonic Wars. There had been an increase and improvement in the quality of accommodation available, new roads had been constructed (or old ones re-surfaced), and all were now generally free of *banditti*. Also, as Marianna Starke, the writer of the standard guidebook for European travellers, pointed out, the development of street lighting in cities made them safer and put a stop 'to the dreadful practice of assassination'.[4] Well-established support-systems for travellers existed. There were some scheduled carriage services from London to European destinations, and a variety of modes of horse-drawn transport available on the European mainland once the traveller had arrived there. The Hallam family would have either hired or purchased their own carriages. Although it could be expensive and complicated to take a carriage across the channel, it was very cheap to acquire one on arrival in France.[5] The Hallam entourage included the parents, Henry's sister Elizabeth, Arthur, Ellen and servants, though not the two youngest children: Julia was nine and Harry only three years old at the time. They stayed with their grandparents at Clevedon Court.

The Hallams' itinerary followed the pattern adopted by many English tourists. Italian tours generally ran from September of one year to May or June of the next, thus avoiding the height of the summer. This arrangement also fitted in with the timing of the London season and the general fear of catching malaria when abroad in the hot summer months.[6] It was usual to visit Florence first, in the autumn, arriving at Rome for Christmas, and, after a brief respite in Naples, to return to Rome for Holy Week, before going on to Venice. The Hallams deviated slightly from this plan, by remaining in Rome till Easter and visiting Naples later. Rome was the city to which tourists, especially English ones, flocked in the early nineteenth century. It was seen as the foundation as well as the centre of European culture, truly the city to which all roads led. Again, Miss Starke, whose guide book Hallam almost certainly read and whom he met in Rome, set the tone. Rome was:

'the most magnificent city of Europe, and the unrivalled Mistress of the Arts . . . The society at Rome is excellent; and the circumstance of every man, whether foreigner or native, being permitted to live as he pleases, without exciting wonder, contributes essentially to general comfort. At Rome, too, every person may find amusement: for whether it be our wish to dive deep into classical knowledge, whether arts and sciences be our pursuit, or whether we merely seek for new ideas and new objects, the end cannot fail to be obtained in this most interesting of cities, where every stone is an historian.'[7]

Additionally, during the carnival season in the period immediately before Lent, an estimated 5,000 people might attend masked balls each evening. There were also the festivities of Holy Week, which were the chief tourist draw, though Hallam, like many English observers, was unimpressed by them. Even France paid homage to what it saw as the cultural superiority of Rome: young artists and musicians saw the highest honour that they could aspire to was the much esteemed and rigorously contested *Prix de Rome*, which granted them three years of study in a city thought to offer the ultimate in cultural and aesthetic stimulation. The city was also home to a large colony of émigré painters and sculptors from England, Germany and America.

The English tourists of the early nineteenth century were the heirs of the grand tourists of the eighteenth. Where the earlier travellers had been aristocrats, by the 1820s English visitors to Italy were more likely to be middle class. Their enthusiasm for art and culture was genuine but they were also keenly aware that they could live much more cheaply in Italy than they could at home, and, in their large numbers, not all of them were popular with their hosts. There had been complaints made in Rome that English tourists were prone to get drunk at lunch-time and they had also been known to eat their sandwiches in the Sistine Chapel, leaving chicken bones on the pavement.[8] Whilst it would be inappropriate to make comparisons with modern package-tourists, it is certainly true that, in setting off for Rome in 1827, Henry Hallam and his family were following a well-worn path.

The details of this path can be traced most easily in the journals kept by Ellen and Henry. Although only parts of these journals survive, Ellen's manuscript covers the period from their departure on 20 August 1827 until their arrival in Rome in December; Henry's journal gives a characteristically punctilious account of their homeward itinerary. The writing of travel journals was a common activity at this time: Samuel Rogers's *Italian Journal* has been published and to some extent defines the genre. The existence of a small notebook bearing the names of Arthur, Ellen and Julia Hallam, and dated three days before their departure, seems to suggest that some sort of joint journal had been mooted, but in the event Arthur's reactions to what he saw and experienced on the tour find their way into letters to friends (to begin with, chiefly Gladstone). Despite the vividness of Hallam's writing, these do not amount to a systematic treatment of his life abroad and the letters grow less frequent with time.

Once having arrived at Calais, there were several possible routes that could be taken overland to Italy and the Hallams took the quickest and the most scenic one, even though Miss Starke recommended it only for the physically robust. From Calais they travelled to Paris where they remained for ten days. They went on to Dijon, through the French Alps to Geneva, doubling back into France, and then via the Simplon Pass into Italy, before moving on to Turin and Genoa, where they stayed for a few days before travelling to Pisa and Florence. They then spent just over five months in Rome, visiting Naples after Easter.

As has been seen, Hallam, whose mind, to begin with at least, was still full of English politics and his Eton friendships, did not embark on this journey with any enthusiasm. He also knew that travelling with his father, who took his pleasures seriously, was a demanding business, requiring energy and dedication. He could not have been anticipating much personal freedom and he was determined to be unimpressed with Paris, which, admittedly, in the 1820s was far from enjoying the reputation for sophistication and delight that it acquired later in the century. Miss Starke described it as a sober and rather dispiriting place in which 'social intercourse is almost destroyed . . . *gaîeté de coeur* . . . has given place to thoughtfulness, reserve, and discontent'.[9] Hallam too was dismissive of the social life, writing that '*nobody* who is *anybody* was [there] at so unfashionable a season' and he distanced himself from 'All the plebeians' who rushed to see one of the first two giraffes in Europe, recently imported to the Jardin des Plantes, and which he thought looked decidedly unhealthy.[10]

Nevertheless Ellen Hallam's journal presents a different picture, suggesting that their period in Paris was both busy and varied. They stayed at the *Hotel Aubin* in the Rue de Rivoli, which had 'very good apartments indeed, and magnificent bedrooms'.[11] Apart from visits to the Tuileries Gardens, Le Palais Royal, the Place de Vendome, and the Louvre (which even Arthur had to admit was interesting), two evenings were spent at the theatre and calls were paid to various family friends and acquaintances in the city. There were several dinner parties.

Hallam's spirits as well as his descriptive powers were improved by the time he reached the Val de Suzon ('the first morsel of fine country one meets with'[12]) and the French Alps, which he viewed with as great a sense of exhilaration as any Byronically-inclined observer might. It has been suggested that the typical English traveller of this period took a 'somewhat bookish approach to the countries he travelled through'[13] and Hallam's letters to Gladstone exhibit a self-conscious, though spirited, enthusiasm which often makes them sound like carefully crafted extracts from a guide-book. Foreign travel always stimulated Hallam to literary exuberance and when writing to Gladstone from France and Italy he was as happy to take on the role of the travel writer as he was for Emily Tennyson when he wrote to her from Austria in the summer of 1833. An important facet of this European tour was its influence on Hallam as a writer, for his descriptions of his travels, as well as being more-or-less faithful pieces of travelogue, are also the work of a gifted young author flexing his literary muscles. It is difficult not to feel that Hallam was aware that he was outstripping his friend at Eton who was still stuck in the *Miscellany*, as he wrote of the Jura:

'It is one thing to ascend amidst bold rocks & fearful precipices, to the summit of a lofty range; and another to make the same ascent amidst the added beauties of innumerable pinetrees, enveloping in one black mass the crags around us, scarce deigning to move their foliage to the blast, that sweeps thro' their recesses & standing in such still, erect, changeless, sublimity, that they would seem to have experienced no alteration since the first hour of creation. I broke my way into one of these deep forests; & had the satisfaction of being for some minutes remote from everything human.'[14]

Alpine travel was popular at this period not only for the spectacular natural sights that it provided but also for the feats of road building and civil engineering which now enabled the Simplon Pass, for example, to be negotiated, where the newly built road passed through 'a continued series of serpentine galleries and grottoes, rising one above the other, and united by stupendous arches of the most chaste and elegant construction.'[15] Hallam was also impressed by the new road from Turin to Genoa from which the Ligurian port and the Mediterranean could be seen in splendid prospect.

Although Turin was not deemed worthy of a lengthy stay, Genoa was, and the Hallams spent a week there from 20–27 September. Arthur appreciated the city's location in its amphitheatre-like site high above the Mediterranean, though its steep, narrow streets made sightseeing an exhausting business. In keeping with Henry's general pattern, visits were made to galleries, *palazzi* and churches (four of them in one day on Saturday, 23 September). On the Sunday, they were able to witness the procession, known to the locals as the *Casacci,* which only took place once every two years. They watched it by torchlight from the balcony of a palazzo. Hallam reported that 'it consists in carrying imm[ense] crosses of massive silver, images &c. with innumerable lights & grotesque dresses thro' the streets at night . . . The ancient nobility of *Genoa* are said to pay largely to its continuance. Poor wretches!' In keeping with other British travellers of this period, Hallam was critical of the various absolutist political regimes to be found in Italy but he was not alone in deploring the fact that England, after the defeat of Napoleon, had connived at the suppression of the independent Italian republics and supported the return of despotism ('Would she have done so, had *Canning* then sat at the helm? Surely not.')[16] Genoa was currently under the sway of the unpopular and reactionary King of Sardinia, Charles Felix.

Hallam was greatly captivated with 'the exquisite beauty of the new road, across the Apennines from Genoa to Pisa' which formed the next stage of their progress towards Florence:

'you can have no idea of the rich outlines of the distant hills, the bold forms of those more near, the delicious clearness of the atmosphere . . . the luxuriant vegetation of olives, & canes . . . intermixed with pendant festoons of vines from tree to tree, the picturesque villas, & still more picturesque towns . . . It is a country one would wish to crawl thro' in a wagon rather than gallop with posthorse rapidity.'[17]

Not surprisingly Florence, where the family arrived in early October, instantly beguiled Hallam. If there was an educational purpose in Henry Hallam's programme of travel, there is no doubt that Arthur benefited hugely from it in Florence where he began for the first time to acquire the sensitivity both to visual art and to Italy's Renaissance culture which were to form such a significant part of his intellectual make-up. The 'Etrurian Athens' afforded splendours on every side and Hallam encountered enthusiastically the work of 'a certain set of painters of the very highest order' in which he included del Sarto ('a painter of great tenderness') Fra Bartolomeo, ('exalted and sublime') Titian and Raphael. Although Hallam was often fickle in his enthusiasms, these were to last. He found the Venus de Medici possessed 'every trace of divinity', and thought Byron mistaken in Canto IV of *Childe Harold's Pilgrimage* in finding it too voluptuous.[18] Henry Hallam acknowledged the importance of this period in developing Arthur's taste and eye: 'His eyes were fixed on the best pictures with silent intense delight. He had a deep and just perception of what was beautiful in this art', though, 'To technical criticism he made no sort of pretension; painting to him was but the visible language of emotion.'[19] Ellen Hallam, too, had a very good eye, and wrote comprehensively about the pictures which she saw. In particular she reported a visit made to the Pitti Palace on 11 October, selecting two paintings for particular mention. These were Raphael's *Madonna del Gran Duca,* and Michelangelo's *The Fates*. There was clearly some empathy between brother and sister where these paintings were concerned. Hallam was sufficiently taken with them to make them the subjects of what are effectively his first two 'mature' poems (even though Henry Hallam included only one of them in the *Remains*). In writing about the Michelangelo painting, Hallam's representation of the eternally frozen moment captured by the work of art, shows that Keats was an influence as well as Byron:

None but a Tuscan hand could fix ye here
   In rigidness of sober coloring.
Pale are ye, mighty Triad, not with fear,
   But the most awful knowledge, that the spring
Is in you of all birth, and act, and sense.
   I sorrow to behold ye: pain is blent
With your aloof and loveless permanence,
   And your high princedom seems a punishment.
The cunning limner could not personate
   Your blind control, save in th'aspect of grief;
So does the thought repugn of sovran Fate.

Let him gaze here who trusts not in the Love
Toward which all being solemnly doth move:
More this grand sadness tells, than forms of fairest life.[20]

By the side of the poems which survive from Hallam's Eton days, this shows much greater technical assurance: it assimilates its Keatsian influences with care and, for the first time, shows Hallam dealing with a subject which genuinely interests and challenges him.

Hallam continued to write to Gladstone during the closing months of 1827, though his letters intersperse descriptions of places seen and visited with more parochial matters relating to events at Eton in which Gladstone was naturally still involved. There was no shortage of Etonian company in Italy. In Florence Hallam reported the presence of '*Coxe, & Lord Alexander*' in the same hotel that he was staying in, as well as '*Antrobus, Trench and Balfour*' nearby.[21] More significantly Hallam was shortly to encounter James Milnes Gaskell who provided him with the companionship he needed and gave him opportunities to escape from the oppressive presence of his father.

Travelling via Siena and Vitérbo, the Hallams reached Rome on Monday 5 November. Their first resting place was Balbi's Hotel ('newly set up' in Ellen Hallam's words) but, in keeping with the general custom of English travellers, they ten days later found a house for themselves, *Casa Sebastiani*, 43 Via de Greci. This was located near the Piazza di Spagna which was the area most favoured by English tourists (it was known locally as the *Ghetto degli Inglese*). Apart from being easy of access to travellers approaching Rome from the north, it was viewed by the English as most fashionable part of the city, largely, it would seem, because so many other English tourists could be found living there, thus affording congenial company.[22]

The presence of familiar faces, the relative comfort of travelling *en famille* and the exhilaration of encountering new places and experiences might make Hallam's life at this time seem an enviable and privileged one. But, as often with Hallam, there were darker and more worrying undercurrents and he seems to have experienced not only bouts of physical illness but also of depression. These things presumably explain the sporadic nature of his correspondence. He told Gladstone that he had been 'not . . . altogether in health' in Paris and, after reaching Florence, he was 'miserably unwell', suffering from 'that destroyer of all strength, and damper of all happiness, ill health'. From Rome he wrote of 'the precarious state of health I had for two months . . . & the occasional despondencies which, maugre all philosophy, and what is worth more than philosophy, would sometimes take hold of my mind'.[23] The language in which the early nineteenth century discussed illness, as well as Hallam's own vagueness, makes it difficult to understand exactly what he had been suffering from, and Ellen's journals make no mention of it at all. However

there seems little doubt that Hallam was experiencing an early manifestation of the serious depression which was to overshadow his first year at
Cambridge. Even amongst his family Hallam felt isolated and there is a
surprising absence of reference to other family members in any of his
letters. The emotional distance between himself and his family which this
suggests and his very great pleasure when eventually he met James Milnes
Gaskell in Florence ('Gaskell's coming has given an impulse to my spirits,
which has nearly made me, what I used to be'[24]), point to a deep and
largely unassuaged loneliness. Hallam's precocious psychological and
intellectual self-sufficiency, on the surface so impressive, was actually
rather brittle. James Milnes Gaskell's arrival in Rome thus proved not
only therapeutic but providential.

Gaskell, travelling with his parents and his own personal tutor,
Richard Rothman, had reached Italy by much the same route as the
Hallams had taken a few weeks before. He had written to Hallam to
inform him of his movements so their meeting in Rome, whilst not having
been specifically planned, was certainly not a chance occurrence. Hallam
immediately took a great liking to Gaskell's parents (he was subsequently
to visit them in England more than once) even though he was quite blunt
about the fact that Mrs. Gaskell was the dominant force. Benjamin
Gaskell, James's father, had been a Whig MP whom Hallam found to be
'a quiet little man, very goodnatured, & simple, almost, as a child; with
very little conversation in him, and much laudable desire of seeing everything that is to be seen, & doing everything that is to be done to the last
iota.' Mary Gaskell, his wife, was 'remarkably pleasant, and
wellinformed, but withal most singular . . . both as to her conversation,
and other points; not without a wish to be listened to, and admired, yet
rather shy, than otherwise, and therefore more effective in tete a tete, than
in a large party. More civil people . . . I do not recollect to have ever seen.'[25]
They were also more enthusiastic participants in the social life of Rome
than Hallam's own family were. Henry Hallam was dismissive of the
generality of English tourists whom he found frivolous and ill-informed
and feared would be a bad influence on his son:

> 'To enjoy . . . Rome, one should exclude the modern – but above all, one
> shd. Exclude English society – he who comes hither with a true Roman
> feeling shd. keep his countrymen at a distance, even the number . . . of
> those who can distinguish between the eternal city, & Brighton . . . It is
> therefore a very bad place for a young man, & tho' no one can behave
> better than Arthur, he is of course not free from the contagion.'[26]

Henry's judgement is harsh in that it is hardly excessive for two young
men such as Hallam and Gaskell to set about enjoying themselves in
Rome, discovering in the process that there was more to the city than its
classical remains. In fact Arthur made his opinion of these rather clear:

'who can sympathise with two feet of broken wall, or the separated base of an unknown column? The Forum is choked up nearly with mud, disfigured with hovels, and deprived of all effect by piles of dirty linen, hung out to dry!!'[27]

He did, though, persevere with learning Italian in which he received tuition from the Abbate Paulo Pifferi. His natural facility meant that he made quick progress, far outstripping Gaskell, who, despite the presence of his own tutor, was unwilling to make much effort, either in language or in sightseeing. Henry Hallam believed that Arthur learned to speak the language 'with perfect fluency', though with (apparently) a Siennese accent. Pifferi encouraged Arthur not only in the study of the language but also in the writing of Italian verse in which he was greatly impressed by his pupil's accomplishment. During his time in Italy Hallam composed seven Italian sonnets in the manner of Petrarch, thinking highly enough of two of them to have them published in Cambridge in due course. Henry Hallam also included them in the *Remains*. Although Henry had doubts about their suitability and merit, he consulted Sir Anthony Panizzi, the librarian of the British Museum, whose view was that they were 'much superior not only to what foreigners have written, but to what I thought possible for them to write in Italian.'[28] Another Eton contemporary called Beresford, who was in Rome at the time, remembered that after six weeks he himself was still struggling with elementary translation but that Hallam had moved on to reading Dante, the discovery of whom was the most significant literary experience of his life.

But intellectual pursuits by no means took up all Hallam's time and there was plenty of time to enjoy Rome's social delights. The friendship between Hallam and Gaskell gradually became closer, with Hallam remarking early in January that he and Gaskell were 'scarce a day' out of each other's company. They had known each other at Eton largely in the context of the Society where there had been an element of rivalry between them. Hallam thought that Gaskell's removal from the world of Eton debating ('where he was far too much flattered') had done him good and remarked, a trifle primly:

'Not a little quiet good sense, real good nature, and unaffected simplicity are to me as evident, as agreeable in his disposition: there is talent, too, though certainly not of an extraordinary kind: nor can any thing, I should conceive, be more pernicious to Gaskell's success in future life, than teaching him to consider himself as a prodigy. How many have been ruined by that infatuation?'[29]

Hallam and Gaskell's sojourn in Rome included the two great festive periods of the Roman year: the Carnival and Holy Week. Pre-Lent carnivals existed in all the major Italian cities and in theory the Roman one lasted from Christmas until Shrove Tuesday. It was during that period that the theatre and opera seasons were licensed, though what might be thought of as the Carnival proper took place in the week before Lent began. It was at this time when, according to one contemporary observer, the normally grave and sombre Romans, whose 'faces . . . are rarely lighted up with smiles' suddenly

'become the most wild and extravagant people in the creation. It seems as if some sudden delirium had seized them . . . They assume rich, picturesque, grotesque or buffoon costumes, according as it is their object to excite admiration, laughter or love.'

All social classes were involved, the lower orders and servants attending public masked balls, or *Festini* (where 'the company is not very select'),[30] whilst the middle and upper classes attended balls and parties held in private houses. Hallam and Gaskell entered fully into the spirit of things in ways that Henry Hallam doubtless found easy to disapprove of. At one masked ball Gaskell went dressed as a Turk and Hallam as a Greek, and on another occasion Hallam, with some ingenuity, donned the guise of an astrologer, only to be told by Gaskell that he looked ridiculous. It is clear that they had entrees to the most distinguished of addresses, having received invitations, for example, from the celebrated banker Giovanni Torlonia. Torlonia, who was to die the following year, had risen from humble origins and had purchased the title of Duca de Bracchiano, and had 'fitted up the Palazzo Nuova di Torlonia, with all the magnificence that wealth can command; and a marble gallery, with its polished walls, lofty columns, inlaid floors, modern statues, painted ceilings, and gilded furniture'.[31]

Hallam estimated that there were about 1000 English tourists in Rome in January 1828 and 'Our [protestant]chapel is crowded to excess every Sunday'.[32] The Holy Week celebrations in Rome were elaborate, spectacular and long drawn-out. They were dependably offensive to protestant sensibilities, though they drew crowds of English observers nevertheless. For a week Rome was full of pilgrims, processions of penitents and bewildered peasants, thronging the streets and piazzas. The festivities were ultimately a spectator sport, beginning on Palm Sunday when the Pope blessed the palms at the Quirinale. Each day crowds squeezed and pushed their way into the Sistine chapel (for which tickets were required) in order to hear the choir sing Allegri's *Miserere*. Good Friday witnessed the ritual of the *Tre Ore*, representing the three hours of Christ's agony on the cross, and the annual ceremony of the Conversion of the Jews, in which a few token infidels (usually in practice Turks) were baptised. After the resurrection service on Easter Saturday there were peels from all the church bells, which had been silenced for three days, together with the beating of drums and the firing of guns. The whole week was rounded off with a spectacular firework display on Easter Sunday evening. Hallam's attitude to Catholicism itself differed little from that of his English contemporaries. He thought that it was characterised by 'superstitious frivolity, and intellectual degradation',[33] and he was subsequently to be dismissive of the 'Papal Hierarchy with its pomp of systematised errors.'[34] However he was not sympathetic to the rather parochial views of those who wore their protestantism on their sleeves and who voiced their disapproval of what they saw as Catholic excesses in such a way as to wound 'the feelings of the inhabitants of Rome. Nothing can be more right, than that such heedless flippancy should be interfered with.' He thought that the protestant fear of the Pope's potentially 'dangerous influence on distant countries' was exaggerated and naive.

If Henry Hallam was disappointed in his son's lack of enthusiasm for Rome's classical heritage, Arthur was not short of interest in the more modern buildings and galleries: 'Grand, & imposing churches – superb collections . . . open before us with endless profusion, till the brain reels with the intoxication of beauty.'[35] Something that was part of every English tourist's programme whilst in Rome was a visit to the Protestant cemetery, about which more than one author had grown lyrical.[36] It had been a place of pilgrimage even before the time when it contained the graves of Keats and Shelley. However it was these relatively recent additions which drew Hallam to the site and which also stimulated him to verse. His *Two Sonnets, Purporting to be Written in the Protestant Burial-Ground at Rome by Moonlight* carried, when they were printed in his 1830 *Poems*, a quotation from Walter Savage Landor:

> 'If any thing could engage me to visit Rome, to endure the sight of her scarred and awful ruins, telling their grave stories in the midst of eunuchs and fiddlers; if I could let charnel-houses and opera-houses, consuls and popes, tribunes and cardinals, orators and preachers clash in my mind, it would be that I might afterwards spend an hour in solitude, where the pyramid of Cestius points to the bones of Keats and Shelley.'

Hallam devotes a sonnet each to the graves of Keats ('Young bard, whose lay was of Endymion,/ Here is thy rest: the world has done its worst) and Shelley ('spirit of light, and love, Creative emanation from the Mind').[37] In a city crowded with antiquities, it is significant that Hallam chose to celebrate the contemporary, or near-contemporary: two poets whose work was at that time all but unknown and unread in the country of their birth.

In addition to the cultural satisfactions on offer, it is not surprising that two young men-about-Rome such as Hallam and Gaskell would at some point find someone to fall in love with. What was more surprising was that they both fell in love with the same woman. More surprising still was that this love served to strengthen rather than destroy their own friendship. But that is what happened, and, easy though it is to be patronising about Hallam and Gaskell, and treat the whole business as no more than youthful infatuation, Hallam's attraction to Anna Wintour was deep and genuine, and, despite what he would one day say to his fiancée, its memory cast a long shadow over the next year of his life. Anna Wintour dominated Gaskell's life for even longer. Not only did he remember her in his will but his daughter married her nephew.

Anna Mildred Wintour was seven years older than Hallam. She was the daughter and youngest child of Rev. Henry Wintour, who had been a close friend of Henry Hallam's at Eton and Oxford, but who had died of consumption shortly after Anna was born, leaving her, her mother and two brothers in a precarious financial state. Mrs Wintour had been reduced to living on charity. Henry Hallam had, with characteristic generosity, offered her financial assistance on at least one occasion, and the self-pitying letters which she often sent him seem to hint that further help would also have been welcomed.[38] Although Hallam was to associate Anna with the glamour and romance of Rome, it is highly unlikely that she participated much in the glittering social life which Hallam and Gaskell enjoyed. She was in Rome with her mother and her aunt less to enjoy the season than to find somewhere cheap to live: after the death of her husband, Mrs Wintour had lived the characteristically peripatetic life of the widow in straitened circumstances. Nevertheless it is clear that Anna was something of a cynosure, and that Hallam and Gaskell were but two of the young men caught up in her aura. There was certainly no shortage of gossip about her: it tended to be malicious and it presumably originated in social snobbery. Thus 'Mr. Brooke, a fine young man, was sent to Europe to be cured of his love for her, and a few years ago, all Cambridge was set on fire by her beauty.' Another observer remarked, even more tartly, that Hallam and Gaskell 'were both desperately in love with the same woman, who refused them both and made a new bond of friendship between them. The woman, who was utterly commonplace, married a boozy Yorkshire yeoman.'[39] Gaskell's son Charles Milnes Gaskell, who had access to his father's journal, wrote, more judiciously, that 'both the Eton friends, amongst many other older and wiser than they fell deeply in love. She accepted their homage, little aware no doubt that the impression she produced was likely to be so deep.'[40]

There is no evidence that Hallam had met Anna before but it is not impossible. Mrs Wintour had struck up a friendship with Hallam's mother and had written of Arthur and Anna in a way which unintentionally prefigured their meeting in Rome: 'I have never seen so far fine a boy as Arthur, therefore it is no disrespect to him, but I cannot help wishing that Mrs. Hallam may have the blessing of a daughter, in everything except her birth & fortunes resembling my heavenly tempered Anna.' She was also aware not only of Anna's attractiveness, but the dangers that such attractiveness carried with it: 'she will never I think be vulgar, but her beauty has been much over-rated & fortunately she never heard of it.'[41]

Precisely when Hallam's interest in Anna began is not clear but it is certainly the case that he gave her a copy of a poem, which he entitled *O che bel riposo*, in February 1828. The poem was subsequently included by Hallam (entitled *Song Written at Rome*) in his 1830 volume, though its sensuous tone disqualified it from inclusion by Henry Hallam in the *Remains*. It was Hallam's best poem to date, and is reminiscent of those fleet but flimsy poems to young ladies, real or imagined, that Tennyson was writing at much the same time:

> Blest be the bower, where
>   Nina reposes;
>   Blest be the roses
> That Circle her round!
>   Bright tho' the rose blush,
>   One blush is brighter:
>   Sweet tho' the violets
>   Perfume the ground,
> Something more sweet, more lovely is found!
>   Blest be the bower, where
>   Nina reposes:
>   Blest be the roses
> Circle her round!
> Soft breath of twilight,
> Move o'er her slumbers:
> Wooer of numbers,
>   Say, who so fair!
> O were I like thee,
> Child of the morning,
> How would I linger
>   Murmuring there!
> How would I wave my light wing of air!
> Soft breath &c.[42]

As well as the poem, there was the gift of a volume of Dante. Gaskell followed suit with a volume of Petrarch. Anna was the subject of nearly a dozen more poems by Hallam. These testify not only to the extent of her influence over him but show how essentially *literary* the relationship was: Anna could not be quite separated in his imagination from the distantly adored Beatrice and Laura.

Both Hallam's and Gaskell's itineraries involved moving on from Rome to Naples. Gaskell left first, in February, and Hallam found himself writing coyly allusive letters to his friend on the subject of Anna. Apart from informing Gaskell of a potentially dangerous riding accident ('my horse, being blind of one eye, and probably not seeing too well with the other . . . precipitated himself on his head, and me over it on mine. It was not the most agreeable thing . . . to ride home a matter of ten miles with twenty candles before one's eyes'),[43] he talks of a visit made with Anna, her mother and his Etonian friend Beresford to the studio of the Danish sculptor Thorwaldsen. Thorwaldsen was something of a cult figure in Rome at the time, enjoying a particular prestige among the English community who found his neo-classicism much to their taste and saw him as at least the equal of the generally more celebrated Canova, a visit to whose studio was generally considered a necessary part of any sojourn in Rome.[44] Hallam also recounts that he has received a promise from '*La Bella Stagione*' (i.e. Anna) 'to join our riding party . . . I have had two rides to which all others, even the most pleasant, are as the dull and noxious weed to the brightest floweret that freshened the bowers of Eden'. He also enjoys titillating Gaskell ('I can fancy your eyes glistening at the very idea') with the prospect of repeating the trip the following Saturday. Gaskell had already opened his heart to Hallam about his own feelings for Anna, as Hallam remarked, *a propos* Gaskell's letter to him, that 'A more decided case of "over head and ears" I do not remember to have witnessed.' He accepts that what he himself writes could well 'give you [i.e. Gaskell] over to the "green-eyed monster"'.[45]

Hallam does not seem outwardly to have acted in other than a mildly flirtatious way and his consciously provocative comments to Gaskell seem to be made only on the assumption that they will not be taken too seriously. Even so, when he had to leave Anna his feelings of dejection were acute. It was particularly painful to leave Rome, knowing that Anna would be remaining there. 'I leave Rome,' he wrote, 'with much regret, having passed a most delightful winter here, and formed several friendships the renewal of which hangs on a thread of fortune too frail not to inspire me with uneasiness and regret.'[46] There is a fragment from a letter to Anna, written at this time and containing the copy of Dante, which makes clear that Hallam had not simply been a passive observer of her beauty:

'As your plighted word is of course irrevocably sacred I may hope you will accept this pocket Dantino from me . . . I am at a desperately low ebb of spirits this morning, & am at this moment breakfasting on your exquisite music of last evening, which if I live to the age of Methuselah, will still glitter like the morning star on the misty horizon of my early years.'[47]

If this writing cannot ultimately escape the charge of mawkishness, it is still genuine and eloquent. After an eventful winter in Rome, Naples, for all the fact that it was described in Miss Starke's guidebook as 'the most captivating City of Italy',[48] meant separation from Anna and the tantalising thought of leaving her behind him to be squired by Gaskell. There seemed little chance that he would see her again, as, although the Hallams' stay in Naples was a brief one (less than a month), their departure from it marked the beginning of their homeward journey which would include only a swift passage through Rome, before going on to Venice (where the Hallams and the Gaskells would coincide again).

Hallam's short period in Naples marked the beginning of another new friendship. He encountered a family called Robertson, 'delightful people'.[49] They were Scottish, with a country house at Glenarbach, just north of Glasgow, and were, like the Wintours, already acquaintances of Henry Hallam. The Robertsons had become near-permanent residents in Italy, returning to Scotland only for short periods. There were three daughters and a son, Robert, who was to become a regular correspondent and friend. He, like Hallam, was destined for Trinity College Cambridge, though his matriculation there was delayed for a year by illness. There was also Anne, the second of the three sisters, who, like Anna Wintour, knew both Hallam and Gaskell, and enjoyed their affections. In this case Hallam's were the more enduring: he subsequently wrote several poems to her and was clearly captivated by her company at Glenarbach when he and his father visited Scotland in the summer of the following year.

But it was Anna Wintour who continued to dominate his thoughts and his writing, even though Gaskell, 'over head and ears', was both physically and psychologically closer to her. Gaskell had had more time in Rome to spend in Anna's company and the fact that he remained in Italy after the Hallams had returned gave him more opportunity to pursue his suit. It is surprising, but undeniably true, that Hallam, although he was unhappy with this state of affairs, suffered no jealousy for his friend. That he was himself strongly attracted to Anna there is no doubt, but he was less adroit than Gaskell at pursuing his interest, a fact which rather surprised him, as he made clear to Gaskell when he wrote: 'you are decidedly the last person – *literally the last* – that six months ago I should have fixed upon as likely soon to experience the influence of the archer god'. Hallam was always capable of offering his friends powerful admonitions when the mood took him and he lectured Gaskell on the potential embarrassments of the current situation:

> 'I hear so much of your desperate state of love-sickness at present . . . that I am in sober sadness afraid you are laying up for yourself a store of future discomfort and unavailing regret . . . I should not, I think, be dealing rightly with you did I not urge you to moderate a little the vehemence of that adoration which may (I speak advisedly) tend to make you a butt to those whose esteem you ought to command.'

He then went on to tell Gaskell that these rather harsh words had been 'written in the calm sincerity of friendship . . . For Gaskell, I am firm in hope that, however superficial our intimacy at Eton may have been, we are now real friends for ever. We have been thrown together for the last few months in a way that cannot but cement unto durability that friendship.'[50]

They were able to discuss these matters further, and *tête-à-tête*, when they met briefly in Venice in May. Gaskell reported that 'I was closeted with Hallam from about ten o'clock until one talking, not upon the subjects but subject which mutually interested us and time flew away imperceptibly whilst SHE was the subject of our thoughts.'[51] Hallam made clear exactly what the importance of these thoughts was to him when he wrote that

'I . . . still look back to the happy days I have spent in her society with feelings much stronger than words can express. They are the brightest days in my life – they were the principal means of rescuing me from a drooping state of mental misery'.[52]

Gaskell's imagery was similar, though his claims more intense, when he wrote in his journal: 'She is a perfect being . . . a steady and shining light to guide and direct my course . . . I will guard with pious gratitude to her the flame of genuine affection; the fire from heaven, of which she is the holy depository'.[53]

For Hallam, Anna's most vivid existence was in his imagination and memory, though when he said that words could not express his feelings he was being disingenuous for he wrote about her repeatedly and at length. She became the subject of the most substantial poem he ever wrote. *A Farewell to the South*, composed in the summer of 1828 at the time of his return to England, runs to 693 lines. Yet again the poem was quietly forgotten by Henry Hallam when he put together the *Remains*, and before long it came to be a source of embarrassment to Arthur also. It seems likely that it was this particular poem that was in Hallam's mind when, having published his *Poems* in 1830, he said of the volume that it contained 'enormous faults of conception & expression, and, what is worse, of morbid feeling, which one has no right whatever to send afloat in the world.'[54] The poem is private and highly coded. Like Hallam's other long poem, the Cambridge prize entry *Timbuctoo* of the following year, its expansiveness largely serves to make its contents seem diffuse and obscure. Hallam, the born prose writer, seems shackled by the medium he has chosen, rather than being emancipated by it, though his editor reminds us of the poem's precociousness and also its modernity when he says:

'The impulse which led a boy of seventeen thus to analyse his first love affair was purely romantic and Wordsworthian, though preceding

Hallam's ardent admiration for Wordsworth by almost a year.'[55]

In that the poem is directly autobiographical, the Wordsworthian comparison is just, but, in all honesty, it is difficult to find much emotional sophistication in *A Farewell to the South*, not least in the poem's reliance on the unmediated 'I'. This is the 'I' of the adolescent, not of the egotistical sublime.

Hallam describes the experience of falling in love:

> 'Twas an eve of Spring,
> And the quaint triton curled his frolic water
> In odorous thraldom to a zephyr's wing:
> Near that cool influence we stood. I brought her
> To the proud palace, where th'aspiring Dane
> Outsculptures him of Venice, and th'Avatar
> Of the chaste muse is visible once again,
> Who at his call deserts her starry clime. (443–50)

The poem's tone and imagery tell us a great deal about how Hallam wishes to represent his Italian experiences. It shows how the relationship with Anna develops (if that is the word) against a background of aesthetic sophistication. The love that is described is inseparable from the works of literature and art among which it was played out:

> The glory of the look of her devotion,
>   Likest those matchless Sibyls', which approve
> Rafael, the prince of limners, such emotion
>   Kindled within my bosom, and I knew
> A power, upraising thought, as winds the ocean,
>   Within me, but not of me: for it grew
>   Unto my spirit, striking root, as moved
>   By some supernal influence, breathing through
> The medium of the being that I loved! (480–88)

The poem is the fruit of Hallam's first love for a woman and he consequently finds himself trying to define what the special nature of womanhood is:

> how mild
> Their eyes are, when they speak of woman's spirit,
>   Knowing its tempering rare, and what a shield
> Of exquisite creation we inherit
>   In her, who gives and shares and glads our life! (560–4)[56]

If Hallam grew to believe that passages such as this exhibited 'morbid feeling', a more detached reader can take a less extreme view. The poem describes the process of Arthur Hallam's discovery of his sexuality: it grapples with the experience of falling in love for the first time. The embarrassment that both father and son in their own ways felt about *A Farewell to the South* comes as result of the self-exposure which the poem cannot avoid, even though Hallam is honest enough to accept that the relationship with Anna, notwithstanding its importance to him, was doomed to end in separation: ('from thine imaged aspect I can have/Delight and vantage, though far hence is seen/Thy corporal presence' (644–6)). The poem is a *Farewell* not only to a time and a place but also to the relationship which gave rise to it. Hallam's love for Anna Wintour was a product of the warm south, and the poem is clear-sighted enough to accept that *amours de voyage* do not tend to survive their original circumstances. His friendship with Gaskell is the one which would last longer, even though the memory of Anna was a difficult one to repress. It was inevitably to Gaskell, who was still abroad, that Hallam would write from Dover immediately and at length on his return to England on 25 June 1828.

Innocent though Hallam's interest in Anna Wintour might seem to us, it continued to be viewed with some suspicion by the Hallam family (especially Henry, who avoided all references to it in the *Remains*), and also in due course by the Tennysons. The fact that Anna's situation in life, as the daughter of an indigent widow, was not entirely respectable, presumably contributed to this, as also, on Henry's part, did the fact that she was the daughter of a man who had been one of his closest friends and whose memory needed to be treated with respect. The relationship thus became a victim of the Victorians' desire to possess only edited and sanitised versions of the lives of those they had loved.

There is a gap of just over two months in Hallam's published correspondence, between mid-April 1828 (when he left Naples) and late June (when he returned to England). There are a number of possible reasons for this. Firstly, he had clearly run out of things to say to his hitherto chief correspondent, Gladstone, whose interest in the detail of his itinerary must by that time have been limited. Nor did he, quite understandably, wish to make Gladstone party to his feelings about Anna. These feelings, coupled with his tendency to melancholia, deprived Hallam of much enthusiasm for sight-seeing or for the return journey through Germany and Belgium, which must have seemed anti-climactic after the delights of Rome. Although he met Gaskell again in Venice, Hallam left no record at all of his impressions of that city, where the family remained more than long enough for all the important sights to be seen. The only document which Hallam left from this period is a poem which now bears the rather incongruous title *Lines Written in Dejection at Tunbridge Wells*, but which was originally dated 'Innspruck, May 1828' (the Hallams stayed there on 26 and 27 May). The reasons for the dejection are not hard to find. Hallam cherishes a ring which 'Nina' (Anna) gave him, but inevitably finds it a poor substitute for Anna herself:

> Nina, the ring thy finger prest,
>   Now closely linked to mine,
> Can calm to peace this throbbing breast,
>   And bid each thought be thine!
>
> Let Siren pleasure idly sing,
>   And wreath her flowers in vain:
> Few, few can tell the joys that spring
>   From Memory's soothing pain.
>
> No guilty wish, no coward fear,
>   May dare this breast to move:
> I moisten with affection's tear
>   The talisman of love![57]

From Innsbruck the Hallams crossed into Germany. Travelling via Munich, Stuttgart, Heidelberg and Frankfurt, they reached the Rhine valley at Bingen on 15 June. Henry Hallam yet again found the Rhine less than impressive, recording in his journal that he found 'the windings of the river . . . rather too frequent in this more admired part, there is more beauty to me beyond Coblentz'.[58] The shortcomings of the Rhine were yet again to be a subject of complaint four years later when Hallam visited Germany with Alfred Tennyson. There was a stop in Cologne to look at the cathedral, after which the party made its way to Brussels, Antwerp and Ghent, before sailing from Calais on 25 June. After a night at Dover and a few nights' stay at Hatchett's hotel in London, where Hallam complained of the heavy and fetid air, so different from 'The glorious King of light, whose sovreignty in the South is supreme',[59] the Hallams took up residence for the rest of the summer at 14, Albion Place, Ramsgate, as their Wimpole Street house had been let until October.

Hallam returned to England in an intensely emotional state. His travels had undoubtedly provided him with a sentimental education of an almost text-book kind. The 'grand tour' which young men had undertaken in the previous century had been an important rite of passage in the journey from boyhood to manhood and Hallam's tour shared a number of features with it. Obviously the presence of his parents had limited the opportunities for that scattering of wild oats which typified the traditional grand tour, but the experiences that had the greatest effect on Hallam were of broadly the same sort that the grand tourists went in search of. There had been the exposure to the culture of the Italian renaissance; to the social delights of Europe's most sophisticated and cosmopolitan city; to adult company, to the Italian language, and to the *bouleversement* of first love. Hallam never visited Italy again, but he could say a year later that, blotting out the period of depression which he suffered at Florence, 'I was happy there: and I have never been happy since . . . My soul was dawning then, and the sky, all but the little black cloud in the horizon no bigger than a man's hand, was very clear: now the dayclouds have settled down on it.' It is not surprising that Hallam found England drab and the prospect of Cambridge uninviting. On the very day of his arrival at Dover he wrote his lengthy letter to Gaskell. There was nobody else with whom he could share the mixture of exhilaration and regret in contemplating his recent experiences. Only Gaskell could understand, and perhaps pardon, the lengthy self-analysis which Hallam's letter contained. Whether Hallam perceived the presence of the seeds of his subsequent psychological illness is harder to tell, but a reader quickly appreciates the narrow path which this letter treads between self-analysis and a more pathological self-concern, a self-concern of which he was clearly aware, when he wrote: 'I am quite ashamed of writing anything so egotistical. I have spoken of nobody and nothing but myself. Pardon me, Gaskell; my heart was full, and I wrote from its impulse.'

The letter covers five closely printed pages in the collected *Letters*. It flies off in a number of almost simultaneous directions in which his friendship with Gaskell is fused with memories of Italy and of Anna Wintour, and which cause Hallam to ponder the nature of memory and at the same time to examine the roots of his own desire to succeed as a poet:

> 'There are moments when I feel lifted above myself, when something speaks within me that is worth more than myself; when I burn with the intense longing to make the name I bear honoured in a second generation-to create something – to find something in the mingling, combining, colliding fantasies of my brain, that may be a worthy and a public offering at the altar of Truth. In such moments as these I write poetry . . . Again I ride by *her* along the bank of the Tiber – turn to catch the sunset over St.Peter's – see the Monte Mario with its crown of cypresses, and the Ponte Molle . . . again I enter Torlonia's gaily-lighted rooms-press through the crowd, make my way to *her*, take my place with *her* . . . Again I listen to her conversation, trembling on the musical sounds of that voice which fell on my ear'.

He tells Gaskell that he has been reading Madame de Stael's novel *Corinne* (subtitled *Or Italy*). As its 1807 English translation is called *Corinna*, it seems likely that Hallam had read it in French. The novel tells of a young Scotsman's travels in Italy and his sojourn in Rome and Hallam's exaggerated praise of it clearly comes from his total identification with its central character. Hallam's responses to literature are very rarely couched in such overtly emotional terms as these, when he says: 'I shed tears over its pages – insomuch that I was obliged to read the most powerful parts in solitude, that my emotion might not be observed. Are such tears childish?'

Aware of the tumultuous nature of his current thoughts, he considers how to cope with the necessarily more mundane life he will be leading on his return:

> 'Solitude and a long journey through a comparatively uninteresting country had worked up my thoughts to a state of fever. But repose may do much, and I shall fling myself headlong into study, in order to modify, at least, if not to change my present constitution of mind.'[60]

Hallam's apologies for the egotistical nature of this letter are in a sense well made, for they disarm immediate criticism. The Hallam who emerges from the pages of this letter may well, like the narrator of Tennyson's *Locksley Hall*, embody 'young life, its good side, its deficiencies and its yearnings'.[61] But the letter betrays other and more important aspects of Hallam's character, aspects which those who have only met him through Tennyson's *In Memoriam* and other works of tribute would never be aware of. In insisting that Gaskell is the only recipient this letter could have, Hallam again draws attention to his own psychological isolation. As previously noticed, he writes as if he has undertaken the Italian journey entirely on his own. He craved a spiritual companionship which nobody but Gaskell at that time could even come near to providing. One of Henry Hallam's most quietly revealing comments in the *Remains* shows that he had noticed the profound effect which Arthur's travels had had upon him, believing that they had 'sealed . . . the peculiar character of his mind, and taught, too soon for his peace, to sound those depths of thought and feeling, from which, after this time, all that he wrote was derived.'[62]

Soon after Hallam's return communication with Gladstone started again, though Hallam's letters to him are less eloquent and more parochial than those to Gaskell and most of his Italian experiences are left undescribed. At no point in his correspondence with Gladstone were Hallam's powers of self-censorship more apparent than now. He acknowledged the fact that he had 'been, I believe, somewhat changed since I last saw you; I have snatched rather eagerly a draught from the cup of life, with its strange mingling of sweet, & bitter', though he gives no specific illustration as to why or how the change has taken place and Gladstone could hardly be expected to know exactly to what he was referring. Hallam also unwittingly echoes Francis Doyle's view that his travels had, in a sense, been premature, that a certain kind of adulthood had been forced upon him too early: 'all this should rather have come after my three years of College, than before, but nothing can cancel it *now*, and I must on in the path that is chalked out for me.' His absence of enthusiasm at the prospect of Cambridge, both intellectually and socially, caused him to claim that, although he had 'no aversion to study' his 'ideas of the essential do not precisely square with those of the worshipful Dons of Cambridge'.

Socially, he found the prospect particularly bleak:

> 'It is my destiny, it would seem, in this world to form no friendship, which
> when I begin to appreciate it, & hold it dear, is not torn from my by the
> iron hand of circumstance. The friends whom I loved at Eton I shall not
> see at Cambridge.'[63]

Hallam's communication with Gladstone again revealed their friendship's underlying tensions. When Hallam referred to the 'inveterate
pugnacity'[64] which existed between them, he was not merely referring to
the rather synthetic world of the Eton debating society. When their letters
crossed, Hallam became petulant, and, without considering their effects
on Gladstone's sensitivities, he made some forthright criticisms of the later
numbers of *The Eton Miscellany* that he had been able to see in Italy.
Given the comments that Hallam had already made to Gladstone about
the *Miscellany,* he clearly felt that he himself had outgrown it. He was less
thoughtful than he might have been about the fact that, while he had been
enjoying the delights of Italy, Gladstone in Eton had continued to produce
numbers of the journal and, not surprisingly, felt proprietorial about
them. Hallam was not afraid to sit in judgement:

> 'there was a certain monotony in the general spirit of the articles, which
> must very much have destroyed the effect of the better portion. Changes
> are rung upon the same key from No 1. to No. X: and people who laughed
> at the one, are but too apt to yawn at the other.'

Nor is Hallam afraid to speak *ad hominem*: 'Your eulogy on Canning
I liked very much; I mean that in prose; the verse you must pardon me for
not liking at all'.[65] Hallam was also less than enthusiastic about
Gladstone's wish to reprint a collected edition for general sale, though he
offered to make a financial contribution if Gladstone needed it.

Gladstone had clearly been offended by this and Hallam was forced to
write defensively about his earlier impatience at what he thought was
Gladstone's dilatoriness. Clearly Hallam's comments about being friendless had been misconstrued as well and he apologises if 'in the hurry of
letter-writing I let my pen outstrip my judgement.' Nor, with hindsight,
was his encomium on Gaskell tactful either: 'I have been much thrown
into his society during those happy months I spent in Italy: and it has much
endeared him to me. He has been an excellent friend to me'.[66] Gladstone,
as will be seen, was always particularly susceptible to feelings of personal
inferiority where Hallam was concerned, and Hallam was certainly not
above patronising him. An interesting side-light on Gladstone's view of
Hallam can be found in his correspondence with his two older brothers
who had been in Rome while Hallam was there and who had met him.
Gladstone had warned them in advance of their meeting that 'He has some

vanity', and afterwards was sorry to hear that 'Hallam has not pleased you. I have always known him to be vain, but I must confess I know of no other fault in his composition. The vanity may indeed have become a prominent feature now; & brought forth among other fruits that of affectation'.[67]

Ramsgate was an inevitable anti-climax and Hallam found it 'most *boring* of places'. The wet and blustery weather, he wrote, rather superciliously, 'is an enigma to one, who has been accustomed, like myself, to a Southern temperature.' Nevertheless the dullness of the place and the weather combined to provide him with the opportunity to read for 'six or seven hours a day.' Some of this reading seems to have been directly focussed on preparation for Cambridge, and, when Mathematics reared its unwelcome head again, it is not difficult to feel the influence of Henry Hallam behind it. 'I am not to be envied. I think I grow more stupid as to Mathematics daily.' He also complained that he had 'been tormenting myself with Euclid for the last five years'. Fortunately there was also time for more congenial reading. He had been studying the Greek orators and their background ('a study much more to my taste'), particularly glorying in Demosthenes ('the very prince of good fellows'). He was a child of his time in having a decided preference for Greek over Roman culture and indeed he talked of the Greeks as if they were his bosom friends: 'how much more at home one feels when walking with the old Grecians, than with their rivals . . . [the Romans] whose oligarchical, gladiatorial, blood-drenched, tyranny-seared spirit was one, and indivisible'. Amongst contemporary authors, he had read Coleridge's *Aids to Reflection* which he found 'somewhat appalling . . . at first sight, but amply rewarding a deeper search', and also *Biographia Literaria*, some of which at least he admitted to finding 'entertaining'. He noted that Coleridge's comments on Wordsworth's poetry 'considering the way in which the world usu[ally] clubs them together', were 'free' and wide-ranging. He also devoured seven volumes of Scott

> 'which I think bad: the world I understand, thinks it good . . . but I shall hold to my opinion notwithstanding . . . In Italy, France, & Germany, his works, either in the original, or in some vile translation, form the staple of every bookseller's shop. I wonder how the translators deal with his Scotch!'[68]

Hallam, the youthful iconoclast, doubtless felt that Scott was fair game but he must have moderated his language when, in company with his father, he met the great man himself in Scotland the following year and indeed wrote a poem about the occasion.

Ramsgate, wet English weather, the memory of a love affair and the impending tyranny of mathematics did not do much to raise Hallam's spirits over the late summer of 1828, as he contemplated 'entering on a

College system of life': 'volumes might be written on our baneful system of education – and they will be written, before the world is fifty years older'.[69] Hallam's prophecy was not entirely accurate, though one of the people who did write in defence of the 'baneful system' was William Whewell who was, in a few months' time, to become Hallam's tutor at Trinity College, Cambridge.

CHAPTER FOUR

'Cambridge I hate intensely'
Trinity College, 1828–1829

Arthur Hallam is an eternal undergraduate. It is as a Cambridge student that he was most vividly recalled and evoked in the years after his death. James Spedding, in his reminiscence which formed part of the published *Remains*, presents a vignette of Hallam 'in some friend's room, reading or conversing . . . He could read or discuss metaphysics as he lay on the sofa after dinner, surrounded by a noisy party'.[1] Richard Monckton Milnes, wrote that 'he really seems to know everything, from metaphysics to cookery'.[2] To Tennyson, he was, 'the master-bowman,' always victorious in debate yet spreading 'seraphic intellect and force' in whatever company he found himself.[3]

These descriptions have common features. Hallam embodies that effortless brilliance which undergraduates have traditionally valued above all else. He is also pictured indulging in the most idealised forms of undergraduate behaviour: sparkling conversation, wit and good-humoured sociability. Yet this persistent feature of the Hallam legend cannot go unquestioned as it conceals a great deal about Hallam's own reactions to Cambridge and particularly to his extremely fraught and unhappy first year there: a year that was ultimately curtailed by both physical and mental illness. His first year was a trial. His Etonian friends were at Oxford where he would have preferred to have been himself. He was embarked on a course of study for which he had little aptitude (Gladstone remarked that Oxford would have been 'more propitious to[his] mind'[4]), and he was always conscious of his father's high academic expectations. He was still nurturing tender but wounded feelings for Anna Wintour, and his mind could hardly detach itself from those scenes of cosmopolitan excitement which he had experienced during his months in Italy. In short, sending Arthur Hallam to Trinity College, Cambridge in October 1828 looked like a mistake.

As with Eton, it is very easy with hindsight to be critical of the education which Cambridge University offered (or indeed failed to offer) at this time, and for some of the same reasons. Its curriculum was narrow and old-fashioned; its teaching methods inefficient; and its students frequently lax and dissolute in their habits. It was possible to remain a number of years at Cambridge and learn very little and there was no compulsion to read for a degree. No lesser figure than Macaulay could comment that many Cambridge students, even with honours degrees, would 'enter into life with their education still to begin'[5] (much the same had been said about Eton). A significant number of undergraduates treated the university as a finishing school which offered leisure for drinking, gaming and whoring, before they went on to inherit their fathers' estates. There was a crude but accepted division of undergraduates into 'rowing' and 'reading' men. The word 'rowing' rhymed with 'ploughing' rather than with 'going', and denoted not so much an inclination to athletic exercise as a desire to get drunk in very public ways. 'Reading men' kept quiet hours, dressed always in their black academic gowns even when they took country walks, and worked for honours degrees, usually as a means to entering the church. It is a strange comment on this division that Arthur Hallam, for all his intellectual energy and distinction, could not technically be described as a 'reading' man, as his own interests had little in common with the formal academic requirements of the university.

Apart from 'fellow-commoners', young men who could prove noble descent and who were rewarded with honorary degrees (as well as the right to dine with the College Fellows), other students read either for pass degrees or for honours. Hallam was a 'pass degree' or 'poll man' (deriving from *hoi polloi*). Honours graduates read for the 'Tripos', an examination, which originally could be taken only in Mathematics. A Classical Tripos had been introduced in 1822 but as an addition, not as an alternative, to mathematical studies. Indeed, its introduction had been opposed by mathematicians jealous of their hitherto privileged position within the university. Only those who had already taken honours in the Mathematical Tripos were eligible as Tripos candidates in Classics. The Mathematical Tripos was a daunting affair. In 1827, for example, it involved 23 hours of examinations, and lack of ability at Mathematics had regularly proved a stumbling block to some otherwise distinguished scholars. Macaulay managed to be elected a Fellow of Trinity despite having effectively failed in the Mathematics Tripos, though this was a very rare (and possibly unique) occurrence.

If the addition of the Classical Tripos might have seemed a welcome and appropriate innovation, its content was not inspiring. J.C. Hare, who was Hallam's Classical Tutor, noted that it consisted of 'classical philology, of a somewhat meagre kind, hardly rising beyond grammatical criticism, and the minute details of archaeology'.[6] It was also only comparatively recently, too, that the Mathematical Tripos had been modified to include study of new continental developments in algebraic analysis, as opposed to traditional Newtonian calculus (or fluxions, as Newton had called it). The greater sophistication of Mathematical study had tended to mean that the teaching of the subject lay beyond the expertise of the average college Fellow and in consequence a number of private tutors, younger men with more up-to-date knowledge, were employed to teach undergraduates. Hallam, for a brief spell in his first year, was taught by one of them, John Hymers.

Other subjects could be taught and studied, though not for degrees.[7] There were professorships, prizes and medals, and college teaching and examining, but no means by which these other subjects could be formally examined for the Bachelor of Arts degree. It was possible to become a Bachelor of Law, Divinity or Medicine, but these degrees were taken by very small numbers of students and were viewed as greatly inferior to the degree of Bachelor of Arts. Professors of Law lectured on the subject, but colleges did not generally provide teaching in it. Only twenty or so students a year read Law and they tended not to be the most distinguished ones, which is significant in the light of the fact that, after the church, the law was the most favoured professional destination of Cambridge students at this time. In general they preferred to graduate as BAs and to study Law subsequently (as Hallam did).[8] Medicine had been taught at Cambridge since the Middle Ages, but, again, to very small numbers and nowhere near on the scale in which it was taught in the Scottish and European universities. Science lectures were given by Professors, but not examined formally until the Science Tripos came into existence in 1848. Modern History, in which the Regius Professorship had been set up in 1724, was viewed with suspicion. The professor's lectures were limited to certain periods in the academic year and undergraduates were not encouraged to attend them for fear that they might interrupt their 'real' work, whatever that may have been.[9] Nevertheless, for an undergraduate with an enquiring mind and a desire to benefit from what was on offer, it was possible to study (or at least to dabble in) a range of subjects. Hallam's friend Richard Monckton Milnes proudly announced to his sister at the beginning of the Michaelmas Term 1828 that he was 'attending lectures on [anatomy], and a man comes down from town to be cut up next week'.[10] A year later he told his father 'what I mean to do for the month – Political Economy, Italian, German, speaking, and a little Metaphysics, lectures on Geology, which cost nothing, and the College of Astronomy on Newton'.[11] Milnes liked to assure his father that he was working hard but, given his compulsive sociability, it was perhaps unlikely that these noble educational aims would be fulfilled. They do not quite have the ring of Henry Hallam's programme of study at Christ Church thirty years previously.

Despite the opportunities which existed for institutionalised idleness, for those undergraduates with any pretensions at all to academic success examinations loomed large. Hallam complained of 'the primum mobile of emulation',[12] which pervaded the academic atmosphere. The course of study for the BA was usually of ten terms' duration. In Hallam's case, that would be, in practice, from October 1828 to January 1832. In their fifth term students sat the 'previous' examination, in which they would be examined on one of the gospels or the *Acts* in Greek, Paley's *Evidences of Christianity* (generally much derided as old-fashioned), and a Latin or Greek set text. Although this was certainly 'not a very demanding test',[13] it did serve to separate sheep from goats and failure in it could spell the end of some undergraduates' careers. One of the less agreeable consequences of taking university examinations in January was that students could suffer from frozen fingers and be rendered incapable of writing their papers because of the icy conditions in the unheated University Senate House.[14] Apart from official university examinations, Trinity College itself had a long history of setting examinations for its own undergraduates which were taken in each of their three years.[15] The original purpose of these examinations was to test Mathematics, though by Hallam's time Classics had crept in, too, and each candidate was examined on classical texts. These examinations, although they often tested not much more than an ability to regurgitate, could be stressful. Henry Alford wrote at the end of his first year at Trinity that 'Our college examination was a very tough and fatiguing one, being for five days, eight hours a day',[16] and the ubiquitous and generally rather insouciant Monckton Milnes was overcome in mid-examination, 'became excessively faint and giddy, and could hardly see before me . . . I lost all self-possession and rushed out of the hall in a most miserable state, and cried myself to sleep on my sofa.'[17] But he still managed to pass.

It is interesting to speculate whether Gladstone's comment about Oxford's being 'more propitious' to Hallam's mind would have proved accurate. Certainly there was much less mathematics studied at the older university (though this did not prevent Gladstone himself attaining the distinction of a double first in Classics and Mathematics), and although the emphasis on Classics was exclusive and much criticised, Oxford's classical curriculum itself was broader, involving both literary and philosophical studies. Gaskell's assertion (previously quoted) that Cambridge undergraduates were more starkly divided into the studious and the dissipated had some foundation. Oxford undergraduates were becoming generally more academic and purposeful at this time but there were still large numbers of them who did not read for degrees, only about 20% taking honours.[18]

Although not the most venerable of the Cambridge colleges, Trinity was at this time the most distinguished, outstripping in terms of both intellectual and social distinction its formidable next door neighbour, St. John's.[19] Founded by King Henry VIII in 1546 (the same year as Christ Church, Oxford), Trinity had grown not only in prestige but in size. In 1828, the year in which Hallam matriculated, he was one of 133 new entrants. The total undergraduate population was between 300 and 400 altogether. One of the first things which the Master, Christopher Wordsworth, had done on his election in 1820, was to build New Court in order to house the increasing number of undergraduates. Many of these, especially the poorer ones (and these included the three Tennyson brothers), chose to live out of college in nearby lodgings, but Hallam throughout his time had his rooms in this New Court (No. 3 on Staircase G).The court was indeed very new, having been completed only three years previously. Little kudos attached to this building, however, as it had, by the standards of its time and place, been jerry built: 'the windows showed a sham quality, for their elaborate Gothic frames were made of cast iron . . . .this addition to the college buildings was not regarded with any pride by the undergraduates of Trinity . . . [it had been built] with an economy which was thought shameful'.[20] Nor was a student's life unduly rich in creature comforts. Although dinner was taken each afternoon in the grandeur of the college hall, beneath portraits of Newton, Bacon, Cowley and Dryden, the only means of heating the hall was a large brazier which stood underneath the lantern which was kept open in order to allow the fumes to escape. This meant that much of the hall could be very cold indeed during the chilling East Anglian winter, though the heat was over-powering for those sitting close to the brazier and there was smoke everywhere.[21] Diet was simple and monotonous: at dinner, the staple fare was a large joint of meat from which students hacked their own portions much as the Collegers did at Eton.

As Master of Trinity, Christopher Wordsworth, youngest brother of the poet, has not generally received a good press. He was an unusual candidate for the post, as he had, at the time of his appointment, been away from Cambridge for sixteen years. Although he had been elected a Fellow in 1796, and had published six volumes of *Ecclesiastical Biography* in 1810, he was thought largely to have owed his Mastership to nepotsim, having been Private Chaplain to the Speaker of the House of Commons, and had, as a result, been recommended for the post by the Prime Minister, Lord Liverpool. His associations were Tory and High Church, in a college whose traditions had been predominantly Whiggish. He was a widower, which meant he did not entertain and therefore seemed remote from the general life of the college. Monckton Milnes spoke for the younger generation when he described Wordsworth as 'an old man . . . who had not recommended himself to the undergraduate mind by any exhibition of geniality or especial interest in our pursuits, our avocations or even our studies'.[22] His absence of geniality extended to the more senior members of the college as well. The longer Wordsworth remained as Master, the more dictatorial he became. Indeed the word 'monarchical' has been used to describe his manner of conducting college business in his later years. William Wordsworth is known to have visited Trinity twice, once in 1820 and again in 1830, meeting undergraduates on both occasions, but the brothers were not particularly close, and although Christopher's children enjoyed staying with the poet's family at Rydal Mount, William complained that when he stayed at Trinity, he found his brother often preoccupied and remote.[23]

Nevertheless, Christopher Wordsworth had some real achievements, particularly during the earlier part of his Mastership. Although he himself felt that, widowed and worn down by his long years of clerical effort, he would not be strong enough to do the job for long,[24] he at first showed himself to be a reformist and a vigorous political operator who was uncowed by opposition. His decision to extend the residential accommodation at Trinity, for which he gained support from the King, was in response to his genuine fears that the large number of undergraduates who lived in lodgings led idle, dissipated and undisciplined lives which he wished to improve. He thought the best way to do this was to make the student body an entirely residential one.[25] Likewise, the reason that he was instrumental in creating the new Classical Tripos was because those undergraduates who were not reading for honours degrees often found themselves working at a very low standard. Trinity had the highest standing as a classical college at this time, judged by its success in university prizes and competitions, and as a result Wordsworth's proposed innovations were seen as self-interested, particularly by the formidable phalanx of St. John's mathematicians. But Wordsworth persisted, and, although he was forced to make compromises, the new Tripos came into existence even though it was not, as Wordsworth had hoped, made compulsory for those seeking honours.[26]

The prestige of Trinity College did not rest on size and buildings alone, or indeed solely on Classics. Whatever Henry Hallam's reasons for sending Arthur to Trinity, he could not have been unaware that the college enjoyed intellectual distinction across a range of subjects, even if these did not form part of any systematic or integrated undergraduate curriculum. The Trinity Fellows of the 1820s included distinguished men who had a significant influence on the university's intellectual life as a whole.[27] Their academic disciplines included Geology, Mathematics and Astronomy. Herschel and Faraday were both Fellows, though undoubtedly the most gifted and influential member of the Fellowship was William Whewell, who, in due course and at Wordsworth's request, succeeded Wordsworth as Master and upheld with great distinction the absolutist traditions of the post.

William Whewell, known to generations of undergraduates as 'Billy Whistle', because, as Hallam noted, his name was 'more easily whistled . . . than pronounced',[28] was in many ways a prototype of the modern academic. He was the power behind Wordsworth's throne and was undoubtedly the most substantial academic figure in early nineteenth-century Cambridge. At a time when college fellowships were generally part of the career structure of the Church of England and often occupied as sinecures until their holders married, Whewell taught, researched, examined and published across an unexpectedly wide range of subjects. Indeed his reputation was so formidable that it had the honour of being skewered by Sydney Smith, who remarked of him that 'science is his forte and omniscience his foible'.[29] Born the son of a carpenter in Lancashire, Whewell acquired only rudimentary social skills and had the physique and bearing of a prize-fighter rather than a scholar. His achievements were many and varied, and though ultimately celebrated as a scientist (a word which he coined), he had, as an undergraduate, won the College Declamation Prize (in Latin) at Trinity in 1813, and the Chancellor's Medal for English Poetry in 1814. He had been President of the Cambridge Union in 1817. Whewell became a Fellow of the Royal Society in 1820, and, two years after his ordination in 1825, preached both the Commencement and Commemoration sermons in the University. He held at different times the Professorships of Mineralogy and of Moral Philosophy, and published treatises or books on English Philology, Architectural History, Astronomy and Natural Theology, as well as a substantial *History of the Inductive Sciences*, and although very much an early nineteenth-century figure by formation, he lived long enough to be associated with Prince Albert and the Great Exhibition of 1851. He was also an enthusiast for the poetry of William Wordsworth with whom he was acquainted,[30] and on at least one occasion, after Arthur's death, was a dinner guest of Henry Hallam in London.[31] His reputation for omniscience was not entirely unjustified, though his research and publishing inevitably made it difficult for him to balance the demands of teaching and administration (as he often complained). It is not surprising that his pupils found him 'neither sympathetic nor readily accessible',[32] though he was fair-minded 'and received the opinions of young and insignificant persons with remarkable courtesy'.[33] Whilst being of firmly traditional views about teaching, discipline and such things as compulsory attendance at college chapel,[34] he was a significant university reformer, being instrumental in broadening the academic curriculum through the establishment of the Moral Sciences and Natural Sciences Triposes in 1848. He defended firmly the concept of the 'Liberal Education' (i.e. one which was not related to future employment), not merely as a kind of eighteenth century social polish but because he thought it encouraged 'the cultivation of the basic faculties of the human mind'.[35]

In Hallam's time Trinity was divided into three tutorial 'sides', which is to say that each undergraduate was assigned to one of three tutors. Hallam was assigned to Whewell and attended his mathematics lectures. Hallam was not easily impressed by his elders but he did go so far as to describe Whewell, rather patronisingly, as 'a very consummate man . . . and far from a mere geometer'.[36] Tennyson also got on well with him, despite being of the general opinion that in Cambridge '"there was a great gulf fixed" between the teacher and the taught', though Tennyson's view was not shared by all Whewell's pupils.[37] The tutorial system of teaching which has come to be generally associated with Oxford and Cambridge universities, and which is characterised by tutor and student working closely together, did not yet exist, and teaching was done almost entirely through the medium of lectures. Whewell's responsibilities towards his students were thus more administrative than pastoral. Indeed the only surviving correspondence between Hallam and Whewell concerns the payment of a college bill.

A typical student's day would begin with compulsory chapel at 7 a.m. It would then, theoretically at least, be followed by lectures from 8 a.m. till 10 a.m., free time for reading until 2 p.m., dinner at 3 p.m., then evening chapel, tea and work, for those inclined to it. However, as Robert Bernard Martin has pointed out, undergraduate existence was an incongruous mixture, 'compounded of rules for the guidance of the adolescent and a freedom that often verged into licence'. The chapel rules at Trinity had been revised as recently as 1824, as a means of ensuring that students got up early in the morning and could also be checked up on later in the day, but they did not prevent those who chose to live that way turning up in the evening 'the worse for drink, but drunkenness was generally held to be a lighter offence than missing chapel.'[38]

Wordsworth and Whewell were both obsessive about compulsory chapel and in general Fellows in Cambridge had to take Anglican orders within seven years of election (though at Trinity there were two positions for lay fellows). It was also the case that candidates for a degree had to profess allegiance to the Church of England, and when Connop Thirlwall went so far as to suggest that dissenters should be allowed to take degrees, he was hounded from his fellowship at Trinity by Wordsworth. It might thus be assumed that the Cambridge of Hallam's time cherished spiritual values but this was not so. Compulsory attendance at chapel was a highly contentious issue, being opposed as much by the religious as the irreligious. John Sterling, as an undergraduate a few years before Hallam, and himself an extremely devout man, was affronted by 'these statutory genuflexions . . . At these seats of sound learning and religious education, the students indeed kneel, – to discuss the boat-race, or the cricket-match; – and read the prayer-book, – to make it the subject of profane parodies and ribald comments'.[39] Likewise Hallam's contemporary and friend, the extremely pious Henry Alford, who eventually became Dean of Canterbury, recoiled from 'being constantly brought into contact with men who live without God in the world, and in the chilling effects of study on the religious affections and communion with God in prayer, and in being surrounded with professors of religion who are, many of them, neither moral nor religious.'[40] A significant contributing factor to Hallam's mental breakdown in 1829 was religious doubt and struggle, and, robbed of the Anglican certainties of such friends as Alford and others, and unsupported by any strongly institutionalised religion, he was forced to deal with these doubts very much unaided.

By sixteenth-century statute, the Michaelmas, or Autumn Term at Cambridge officially began on 10 October, which in 1828 fell on a Friday.

It seems likely that Hallam went into residence sometime during the next week. Although he reported that he had 'been in so constant a state of bustle, & worry, and perplexity, that I have hardly found a minute's leisure to think', he seemed irritated rather than stimulated by this necessary busyness. He refused to be impressed, referring to Cambridge as 'this odious place'. Indeed, he seemed determined to dislike it at all costs. Letters written to a variety of recipients all tell the same tale, and tell it with considerable bluntness. Writing to Gladstone, three weeks after his arrival, he says: 'My chance of success here is *next to nothing*. I come up, naturally deficient in the first place in those mental faculties, which are indispensable to a course of study here, *Attention*, and *Memory:* secondly, my tastes & feelings are all at variance with the methods of acquiring knowledge here . . . the whole mode of existence here – its society, as well as its midnight lamp – its pleasures as well as its compulsions are alike in my eyes odious.'[41] This is a surprisingly comprehensive denigration of Cambridge for one who had been in residence for so short at time, though Hallam's analysis of his own intellectual shortcomings was to be echoed by his father some years later when he attributed Arthur's lack of formal academic success to the fact of his not having a good memory.

Although he was careful to keep his criticisms of Cambridge away from his father, he was still unenthusiastic at the end of term when he wrote to Ellen that: 'There is nothing in this college-studded marsh, which it could give you pleasure to know; or I would tell it you.'[42] Writing during the Christmas vacation to Robert Robertson, who would go up to Trinity the following year, Hallam, although admitting that his time had been 'completely filled', distanced himself from the academic pursuits of the university, particularly as understood by 'reading' men: 'I understand completely its [i.e. Cambridge's] good, and its evil, I am disposed to think it is a very pleasant, and for those whose equable minds take things as they find them, a happy life . . . I have never taken the least interest in mathematical science. I shall study it to a certain degree in order to discipline my mind to evidential reasoning, and nerve it thereby against morbid sensibility. But I can never make it a prime object . . . I long for repose – I long for leisure to exert my mind in calmness, not under this universal pressure, I long in short for Italy [where Robertson was still living], for the friendliness of gentle society, for all the glorious Past'.[43]

Hallam's first term at Trinity was not entirely nugatory, however. His classical lecturer was Julius Hare, a conscientious man who, rather like Hawtrey at Eton, took a personal interest in his students and encouraged their reading.[44] He subsequently left Cambridge to spend the rest of his life as Rector of Herstmonceux in Sussex. Hallam thought Hare was 'a man of great talent, but not, I think, of genius. His lectures are admirable and so copious that I should think they very nearly exhaust the subject'. The Greek texts which Hallam studied with Hare offered an enjoyable contrast to his mathematical labours under Whewell. He worked on

Aeschylus' *Eumenides* 'which . . . forms unquestionably one of the grandest performances of the human intellect.'[45] So enthusiastic was he at the prospect of studying Book Seven of Thucydides' *History*, that he prepared himself for it by reading the whole of the work first. Indeed his enthusiasm for Greek remained undiminished, and he continued to sing the praises of its language: 'I love it for the swell and the majesty and interminable melody of its diction . . . for the grandeur of the associations that cluster and play around it like the Multitudinous starlight along the clear deep azure of heaven.'[46] In other areas, though, his tastes were (characteristically) fickle when, in dissenting from what he saw as current Cambridge fashion, he declared : '*Shelley* is the idol before which we are to be short by the knees. For my own part . . . I cannot bring myself to think *Percy Bysshe* a fine poet.'[47] This was an opinion that was very soon, and very significantly, to be revised.

Hallam's jaundiced view of Cambridge and its institutions extended to the Union, to which it was inevitable, given his interest in debating, he would be drawn. Although the Cambridge Union was 'a training ground for budding politicians',[48] it did not enjoy the prestige of its more venerable counterpart in Oxford, having had a shorter and less illustrious history. A dispute about the debating of contemporary political issues had led to the Union's closure for four years, and during Hallam's time, for all its 'green baize table loaded with tumblers and water decanters',[49] its premises comprised, according to Monckton Milnes, a 'low ill-ventilated, ill-lit apartment, at the back of the Red Lion Inn – cavernous, tavernous – something between a commercial room and a district branch meeting-house.'[50] Even so, its weekly debates held on Tuesday evenings could sometimes draw audiences of up to 200, though the debates themselves, for all their self-conscious rhetorical performances, were often drunken and raucous occasions. Hallam noted that the union's 'influence' was 'very much felt . . . even among reading men', though he disliked (it is tempting to say, of course) much of what he heard: 'The ascendant politics are *Utilitarian*, seasoned with a plentiful sprinkling of heterogenous Metaphysics. Indeed the latter study is so much the rage, that scarce any here at all above the herd do not dabble in Transcendentalism, and such like'.[51]

As has already been seen, Hallam had rehearsed the pros and cons of being active in the Union before he left Eton, the subject figuring prominently in his correspondence with Farr. It is characteristic of the various disappointments of his first term that he was to find that Farr himself had, with time, become much less congenial company: 'His mind seems pitiably vacant; his talents, and wit, smouldering day by day. His talk is exactly the same highflown, unreflective talk, which it used to be . . . He lives almost entirely in a small set of drinking High Tories'.[52] It was Gladstone's view that Farr had been made too much of at Eton and had sunk into intellectual torpor in Cambridge as a result. He was clearly too dissipated to make any kind of mark in the Union. Hallam found the general standard of speaking at the Union 'at a lamentable ebb',[53] though he was greatly struck on his first visit to a debate on 4 November by the performances of Sunderland, Kemble, Milnes and Trench. The subject of the debate had been the character of Voltaire. He found Sunderland 'wonderfully fluent', Kemble 'a great blackguard according to most accounts', though still found him the 'Pericles, or rather Cleon in the Union' and Milnes 'not so fluent . . . [but possessing] more materials of a speaker in him than even Sunderland.'[54] It is interesting that before long all these names would become real people and figure prominently in Hallam's life. Blackguard or no, John Kemble, even more than Milnes, would in time become a close and valued friend.

At both Eton and Cambridge, Hallam had no difficulty in attracting acolytes but was slow to find and make friends himself. Although there were several members of his circle from Eton at the university at this time, they do not seem to have figured prominently in his life. Although Farr had clearly moved off into other orbits, Pickering, Hamilton, Frere and Wellesley were all in residence. Only Frere 'one of the best of breathing things',[55] seems to have figured very much in Hallam's life at this time. Hallam was always complimentary about Frere. His presence in Hallam's life often seems peripheral, but he and Hallam spent quite a lot of time in each other's company during Hallam's first term, and Hallam reported that he had dined three times with Frere's uncle who was Master of Downing College. Apart from the Union, Hallam also attended meetings of other debating societies though he dismissed them as being mere vehicles for those who wished to show off their 'effervescence of talent'.[56] Debating was such a popular activity that, quite apart from the Union, there were numerous smaller, private debating societies which existed in individual colleges. Milnes once claimed to have attended three debates in one day. Hallam and Milnes both belonged to at least one of these groups, as Farr reported to Gladstone: 'Hallam was in a Private debating Society . . . they are innumerable here . . . and was to make his debut on the Catholic association suppression question, on *Sunday* night'. Milnes thought that Hallam's speech on this occasion was 'capital'[57] and looked forward to a debate on Rousseau the following week. Hallam was trying to find the right forum for himself. Disliking as he did the rough-and-tumble antics of the Union, he was searching for something which would recall the more refined and inward-looking spirit of the Eton Society. Early in the following term Hallam was elected President of a private debating society called Rochfort's. Although he described it as 'not very prosperous', he believed that 'more sense is talked there, than at the Union; and it contains a very fair Florilegium of University talent'. It would certainly have provided opportunities for discussion of those political and literary topics that Hallam favoured: debates were held on 'the characters of Milton, of Burke, & of Johnson', and also (amongst others) on the relative value to the world of poetry or science, in which, unsurprisingly, Hallam argued for poetry.[58] In general, though, Hallam was critical of the intellectual level of those around him, as he told Robertson of the undergraduate fondness for 'communicating a highly metaphysical tone to conversation and an ardent enthusiasm for certain Poets and Philosophers and consequently for certain *schools of poetry* and *systems of philosophy* . . . It shall be my endeavor to seek out Truth patiently and desiringly, sifting out the chaff from the grain day by day.'[59]

If Hallam was unenthusiastic about his first term at university, his Christmas vacation did not provide too much relief. Henry Hallam (despite his disparaging remarks about the place when he was in Rome) had moved the family to Brighton for the winter, installing them in a house at 24 Old Steyne. Arthur, of course, found Brighton 'dull, dull, dull, even to nausea'.[60] Although Brighton still enjoyed a reputation as a fashionable and sophisticated resort, Hallam found the social scene tedious and preferred walking alone on the Downs and communing with nature, 'a method of glorifying the animal part of our nature in order to calm, & harmonise the intellectual'. He looked forward to escaping to London as soon as he could.

Also, those underlying difficulties between father and son which were never to be entirely resolved, surfaced particularly bitterly at this time. Henry had never been happy about the bent of Arthur's intellectual interests. He had brusquely dismissed his philosophical and poetic leanings at Eton, and was far from pleased that these interests were still dominating his son's mind at university. To Henry, discussing metaphysics whilst reclining on the sofa did not constitute the academic life: it smacked of dilettantism. Although Arthur undoubtedly possessed a quick and penetrating intellect which could dazzle his contemporaries, and although Milnes had offered testimony to the range of his knowledge, Arthur's mind did not take easily to the sober intellectual pursuits which had characterised his father's undergraduate years. It is impossible to imagine Arthur keeping commonplace books and painstakingly acquiring mastery of all the major branches of learning. Whilst Arthur could indulge in lengthy self-analysis when necessary, nothing in his writings equates to the young Henry Hallam's painful annual summaries of what he had learned and read, and how he proposed to remedy the gaps in his knowledge. In particular, Arthur's lack of interest in minute, philological, classical scholarship, in the Keate and Cambridge mode, seemed to Henry a dereliction. There was also a clash of generations. Henry Hallam had been formed in a different intellectual and literary culture from that in which his son now lived. Henry knew Scott, had dined with Byron and Wordsworth, and had read Coleridge. Nevertheless, as his *Introduction to the Literature of Europe* repeatedly shows, Henry saw literature in eighteenth-century, neo-Johnsonian terms, though he wrote about it without Johnson's brusque individuality. Of the authors whom Arthur devoured and admired Henry was disapproving: he thought Coleridge was meretricious. He was also disparaging about the designs of Arthur's able and respected Classical tutor, Hare, himself an enthusiastic disciple of Coleridge. Writing to Frere on the evening of Tuesday, 23 December, Hallam mimics the domineering voice of his father:

> '"I always thought the man [Hare] an impostor! and now I'm sure of it. He has cheated himself with words, and now he is going to cheat other people! That's just the way with Coleridge & the rest of them: they spin a spider's-web of language to catch foolish flies, who think that this mysticism is originality of thought! Read Paley; if he is not deep, which he often is not, he is always clear: his understanding is of the same kind with ours. Read Locke; read Bacon; but these never *will* be read, when Coleridge, & Shelley are: such authors, as favorites, must deprave the mind . . . As for this Hare, he is trying to found a school: and, mark what I say, his school will be a bad one." I am resolved – neither my father, nor anyone . . . shall influence my metaphysical creed.'

Although the tone of this letter clearly suggests a tongue in the cheek, there is no reason to doubt that Henry Hallam meant everything he said and that Arthur is reporting his words as faithfully as he could, though the exhortation to 'read Paley' must have occasioned particular mirth, considering the poor reputation which he had amongst Cambridge undergraduates at the time. Despite Arthur's resistance, Henry did not compromise in the demands he made on his son and was quite explicit in his requirement that Arthur's priority should be to work hard at the subjects of the official university curriculum, just as Arthur had previously predicted. Henry insisted that he should sit for a Craven Scholarship the following term. Arthur's fears that this exertion would 'grind me into powder'[61] were not heeded and Henry, at least in his son's eyes, was completely impervious to reason on the subject.

Craven Scholarships were among the highest Classical honours that could be gained at either of the two English universities. Founded as long ago as the seventeenth century, they had been augmented in both number and value over the years and were worth £50 a year in Hallam's day. In 1829 there was only one scholarship available, so the field was a highly competitive one. Examinations began on Monday, 26 January, two weeks after Hallam had returned for the new term, and Hallam wrote to his aunt that he was working hard ('that is, speaking relatively to my usual quantum of industry'.[62]) The examinations lasted from Monday to Saturday, the whole process illustrating the delight in gruelling competitiveness that Cambridge could exhibit when it chose. For a week the candidates settled down to a veritable orgy of translation from and into the ancient languages. Hallam wrote to his father after the first three days' worth of papers that, among other things, he had made translations into

English from various Greek authors. Part of 'Lady Macbeth's sleeping scene [had] to be translated into Greek Trochaics'. Thomson's *Liberty* had to be translated into Latin hexameters and 'a page of Hume into Latin prose'. Additionally, there was 'a Chorus from the Hercules Furens, to construe which would have been superhuman.' Although claiming to be 'indignant' at the unreasonable demands of the examination, he concluded that 'Upon the whole I am satisfied with what I have done.' He told his aunt that, although the examination was easier than he had expected, 'some of the papers were very severe, and indeed ought never to have been set'.[63] The final three days included a translation of a chorus from Euripides into Latin Alcaics as well as into English prose. Extracts from Cicero, Tacitus and Livy had to be rendered in English, a section of Bolingbroke translated into Greek. Herodotus, Plato and Thucydides had to be construed, and, as light relief, the potential scholars had to write original Latin hexameters on the subject of ice-skating. It is difficult not to feel that a limited number of skills were being tested *ad nauseam* and that ultimate success depended as much on stamina ('hard buffeting' as Hallam called it) as on linguistic dexterity. Hallam was sufficiently proud of his hexameters to send his father a copy of them, but the scholarship was won by Christopher Wordsworth (junior), son of the Master of Trinity. This did not come as a surprise to anyone, as Hallam had already noted that he was the favourite, so there was no nepotism involved.

For all the satisfaction which Hallam expressed about his performance in the Craven, he was clearly never a contender for the prize and felt little personal disappointment in failing to achieve it. His failure was an honourable one in the face of stiff competition, and he received a generous mention by the examiners.[64] Nevertheless it was a decisive moment in his academic career in that it marked the point at which his aspirations (or more accurately lack of them) became clearly defined. Whatever Henry's wishes, Arthur knew that his future at Cambridge was not going to be spent in pursuit of recognised academic success. He made his position clear in the very careful letter which he wrote to his father on Sunday, 15 February. The letter is clearly calculated to disarm, if it can, possible opposition or criticism from Henry. Arthur begins, with commendable tactical skill, by informing his father that he has taken care to provide himself with a private tutor in mathematics, John Hymers 'a clever man . . . and a driller of long standing.' However:

'That he will be able to drill me into any mathematical knowledge, I am strongly inclined to doubt. Certainly if Nature ever gave a person warning that the gates of some science were barred to him, she would seem to have done so in my instance. My memory in many things serves me well: in some I can even remember continuously, link after link: but as to all figure and number I lie under an interdict. It has always been so, since I first was informed that two, and two make four. And yet labour has not been spared with me; nor have I spared it myself. Hence it appears to me doubtful whether it be possible for me at eighteen, I do not say to read Mathematics to any extent, but to *get them up*, in Cambridge phrase, with all their minutiae, and, which is much more concerning, with that combining, and applying, and deducing faculty, without which the bare understanding of the characters, expressions, as they appear in some particular instance, is for any University purposes worth nothing at all.'

Despite his assurance to his father that he has acquired a competent private tutor in Mathematics, this was, in fact, the point at which Hallam abjured the serious study of Mathematics, and in so doing distanced himself from the quintessential feature of a Cambridge education, the feature that had probably been crucial in Henry's decision to send him there in the first place. Henry stuck firmly to the view that a grounding in mathematics was a necessity in forming Arthur's mind for the legal career which he wished him to pursue. Perhaps he also felt that the subject might have value in balancing Arthur's tendency to 'morbid sensibility.' However, Arthur then went on to consider in his letter how, as a result of his experiences in sitting the Craven, he rated himself as a student of the classics. To apply himself to both mathematics and classics, would be self-defeating in that it would prevent him from gaining distinction in either subject:

'I feel confident that it [i.e. the study of Mathematics] could never take place compatibly with my reading Classics to any extent, or any other reading at all. When I say to any extent, I mean – so as to attain any Classical honor. For the University Scholarship has done me this good, that it has shewn me how I stand with respect to my competitors; and it is not now difficult for me to take a full survey of the field . . . Now I know from the examination I went through, that a great deal of careful, and attentive reading in various quarters, but all Classical, must be pursued by me in the course of the next year, if I would read for the purpose I mentioned.[65]

Continuing to mollify his father as best he could, Hallam moved on 'to more cheering topics', in which he mentioned his search for success in two other areas of competition. He intended to submit a Greek Ode for the Browne Medal and had already written a poem 'in a fit of enthusiasm' for the Chancellor's Gold Medal for English poetry. Both these examples were presumably intended to convince Henry (rightly) that Arthur was not spending his time frivolously and that he had also taken a firm decision about where he thought his real abilities lay. It seems reasonable to conclude that Henry, at least for the moment, took Arthur's statement of intentions philosophically, though equally, the sense of disappointment which breaks through in his preface to the *Remains*, shows that it was a state of affairs which Henry never entirely accepted and goes some way to explaining the very high expectations which he was to place on his younger son, Henry, in due course.

Despite his shows of hostility towards the Union, it was inevitable that Hallam would make his debut there before long. His maiden speech, delivered on 25 February, showing a speedy tergiversation from the Whiggish views held at Eton, opposed the decapitation of King Charles I. Whether or not Hallam spoke with conviction or was merely adopting a debating position, Milnes (who opposed him and therefore could hardly be objective) reported that 'he did not succeed very well'.[66] The following two weeks' meetings of the Union were devoted to debating the Catholic question. Hallam strongly supported emancipation and was pleased that the motion was carried in its favour by a majority of 46. He had originally hoped to speak, but in the end decided not to as so many other people wished to have their say. It is easy to see why the Union did not entirely enjoy official approval (Monckton Milnes thought it was in danger of being closed again) when Hallam reports: 'we divided; one party filing out at one door; and one at the other, which made us meet in the innyard below. The scene was really picturesque. Three hundred men, with scarcely room to move, waiting in breathless expectation for the announcement of the numbers from a window above, and the silence frequently rent with proposals of "Three cheers for Mr. Peel!" or from the enemy "for Lord Eldon!" . . . The cheers were tremendous, and must have been highly distressing to the Master, & Co.'[67]

Although Hallam was still claiming to have found no 'true friend' at Cambridge, apart from Frere whom he had already known at Eton, his various activities in debating societies clearly give the lie to the impression that he was aimless and unnoticed. To Gladstone, he wrote at the end of February: 'I live here principally in what may be termed the "metaphysical set", many of whom are men of great talents, but in none of whom . . . except Frere . . . have I found a *true friend*. There are many, very many, whom I like, and esteem: but in the higher point I am difficult to please.'[68] This was always true of Hallam, though he was cultivated by those of his contemporaries who were more outgoing than he was. Monckton Milnes was an obvious example and, at the beginning of the Michaelmas term, he had told his father that, among the new intake of undergraduates 'there is Sutton, the Speaker's son, very gentlemanly, and Hallam, the son of the historian'.[69]

There is little doubt that Milnes took an instant fancy to Hallam. Educated privately because of delicate health, Milnes had entered Trinity in 1827, the year before Hallam did. He was a cousin of Hallam's Eton friend James Milnes Gaskell, though he does not seem to have been particularly close to him. As a Fellow Commoner he enjoyed the privileges of dining with the Fellows at high table, and wearing a blue and silver-lined gown, and was unique among Hallam's circle in enjoying this status. His mother had watched him from a gallery on his first night in college and was delighted that he 'seemed as much at home among all the dons as if he had been there for years.'[70] Milnes had crushes on people, and at the time of Hallam's arrival had been much taken up with another man in his own year, Augustus Fitzroy, though the friendship does not seem to have survived for long. Later he took up with Stafford O'Brien, who responded to Milnes's warmth of manner, by telling him that 'I have never seen anyone at all like you, and I am quite provoked when I hear anyone compared to you'.[71] Although he eventually married, Milnes had, in modern parlance, a camp manner. Despite his portliness, he donned veil and petticoats to play Beatrice in a college production of *Much Ado About Nothing* and liked to boast of his attractiveness to other men, once asserting that 'I think Goethe would have fallen in love with me; and I am not sure that Platen didn't.'[72] Later in life, as Tory MP for Pontefract, he claimed that he always liked 'the attention of young M.P.'s as an old coquette does those of the sons of her former lovers.'[73] He was affectionate, gregarious, and quick to throw his arms round his friends, of whom there was always a large number. He also had a reputation as a brilliant conversationalist, which earned him the nick-name of 'the Bird of Paradox'. Although it is difficult not to see him as a charming dilettante, he had serious literary interests and was a prolific poet, widely read and published in his lifetime. The elegy which he wrote on Hallam's death is not a negligible piece and it almost certainly influenced Tennyson in Section VII of *In Memoriam*. Milnes was also (as Lord Houghton) to become the first editor of Keats's poems and letters and was an enthusiastic propagator of the works of Wordsworth and Shelley when they were far from fashionable.

Milnes was impressed from the moment he met Hallam. 'I have a very deep respect for Hallam. Thirlwall [Fellow of Trinity] is actually captivated by him'. Eschewing false modesty, Milnes found him 'the only man here of my own standing before whom I bow in conscious inferiority'.[74] It was inevitable, given the overlap between their political and literary interests, that Hallam and Milnes would come to enjoy each other's company, though as debaters they were competitors also, just as Hallam and Gaskell had been at Eton. Although they remained regular correspondents for some time, Hallam's feelings for Milnes were more equivocal, and his comments on him could be patronising, describing him to Gladstone as one 'of our aristocracy of intellect here; [a good] & kindhearted fellow, as well as a very clever one, but vain, & paradoxical'.[75] Milnes found Hallam rather difficult and distant to begin with, but friendship of a kind developed between them, even though Milnes was not really the sort of friend Hallam was looking for. Indeed, he was to find no great difficulty in terminating the friendship when the appropriate moment came.

Hallam at this time had too many preoccupations of his own to readily enjoy friendship. Although his letter to Henry had been an attempt to clear the air on academic matters, the issues which it had raised did not go away: indeed they continued to plague him. He was pleased to hear of Gladstone's 'incessant reading' at Oxford, but had to admit that

> 'For my own part the horizon grows blacker, and blacker: the elements of mathematical science, instead of becoming easier by practice, increase in difficulty: and I utterly forget what I have repeatedly acquired. In Classics I might partially succeed . . . but the consequences of suffering mathematics to encroach on that kind of knowledge which is most congenial to my mind will, I am convinced, be such as to shipwreck the whole concern . . . I care not a snap of a finger for the bubbles, called by courtesy "University honors" . . . I know that the work of deterioration is going on; that the chain, which binds me to this my dungeon, is rotting into my soul: but I have still a resource in my favorite metaphysical and poetical speculations, and I throw them up as a bulwark.'[76]

Conscious as Hallam was of disappointing his father, he was surely conscious also of disappointing himself. Although he could fall back with an assumed undergraduate airiness on the excuse that he cared nothing for the 'bubbles' of academic success, it was a severe bruise to the ego of a hitherto precocious young man, of whom much was expected, to have to admit to intellectual failure in an area which was proving too much for him. The disappointment which he felt in being unable to master his academic work would continue to haunt him for some time.

There were 'crushing cares' in more personal areas too. A letter from Robert Robertson in Rome had reopened the matter of Anna Wintour, and Robertson had, whether intentionally or not, acted rather provocatively in professing that he, too, had fallen in love with Anna. ('Oh, Hallam, what loveliness there is in her face, what sweetness, what delicacy'). Hallam's response to this was rather tart: 'I can never be sorry to hear that truth repeated, but I cannot see what business it has to come from Robertson's lips.'[77] Hallam had also, it seems, managed to lose the ring which Anna had given him, which caused him some distress and he was further dispirited to hear the news that Anna and her mother proposed to remain in Italy, possibly for a few more years, thus depriving him of the meeting with her which he had been expecting in the summer.

The cold Cambridge spring took its toll on Hallam's health. He was taken ill in early March with 'An influenza [which] seems to be going about here; most people of my acquaintance have been unwell.'[78] He assured his father that 'I have no cough, nor have had. I had some feverishness with my cold some weeks ago: but that went away: and since that time I have had only recurring headaches, and a sort of langour, which I find most men here complain of, more or less, and generally attribute to the air.'[79] Hallam's attempts to underplay the seriousness of his illness by asserting that everyone else was suffering from it do not entirely convince. He himself was particularly prone to influenza-like symptoms and also to severe and recurring headaches. Physical illness with Hallam often had a psychological basis too, and when he wrote to Gladstone again in mid-March he was clearly in a very disturbed state of mind. The self-absorbed excitement which had manifested itself, for example, on his return from Italy the previous summer, emerged again now though its tone is very different. Hallam was later to declare more than once that he feared insanity, and, given the intensity of his broodings at this time, it is easy to see why. The immediate reason for his writing to Gladstone was the death, after a long illness, of Gladstone's sister, Anne, which Hallam had only recently heard about. Hallam wrote that 'to contaminate so pure a thing [as Gladstone's grief] with my own dark & wayward griefs, would be an atrocious sacrilege'. Gladstone had evidently drawn a parallel between the sufferings of his sister and Hallam's own 'crushing cares and occupations'. Gladstone's hope that Hallam might be 'transfigurated by the faith of one pure soul into joy', was unfortunately a vain one, and Hallam moved on to a passionate analysis of his own struggling spiritual state, a state which could conceive of few easy solutions to its anguish. Hallam's language was forceful, passionate and agonised, as he wrote of himself as 'a seared, rent, jarring soul, in which ardent aspirations for good co-exist with domineering influences of sense, and the link is broken, which should connect devotional sensibility with moral firmness.'

He went on to outline a guilt-inducing crisis of faith in which he had set his will, 'my perverse, corrupt, natural will against the will of the Supreme Reason, and in the words of [Jeremy] Taylor "turned my back on the sun to dwell in the dark, and the shadow." . . . From that first I did not awake till sickness was on me, and everything I saw of beautiful, or dreaded of calamitous, conspired to purify me through agony into faith'. He saw these signs of purification as 'proofs that the Divine Idea is not altogether obliterated from my mind, that there yet inheres . . . a seminal principle . . . that shall one day thrill my whole Being by the intimacy of its presence . . . Meanwhile the crisis is tremendous.' He quoted the passage from St Paul's *Epistle to the Ephesians* about wrestling with the forces of darkness and spiritual wickedness. Gladstone had offered Hallam the suggestion that (quoting Milton) '"this is a trial to be endured for purification"', which Hallam rejected as too simple ('it leaves me weak and sickly'). He likewise found that the 'toil of mathematics', to which he had been much exposed, did nothing to help him make sense of the world. He felt that he could only do this through 'Metaphysics, & Poetry . . . it is my firm conviction that these are not only the surest pillars, but even the constituting elements of the Christian Scheme . . . If this seems wild, & mystical, I can only beg of you to suspend your judgement till some future occasion when we may speak on the subject with that calmness, & earnestness, which it amply deserves.'[80]

Hallam was neither the first nor the last Cambridge undergraduate to experience a crisis of faith. Others amongst his own circle also did. What is particularly striking about this letter is its unexpected intensity: it does, for example, consist of just one fevered, almost breathless, extended paragraph, whose tone is very different from that of the letters preceding it and whose completely unexpected change of mood makes Hallam's fear of insanity seem entirely justified. The self-loathing which Hallam's spiritual doubts provoked is also illustrated in a poem which he wrote at this time, which provides both a gloss upon and an extension to the emotions expressed in the letter. It is a frank and a disturbing poem which hints at psychological depths of which many of his later Cambridge friends would remain unaware:

Lines Written in Great Depression of Mind

I have lived little on this earth of sorrow,
Few are the roses I have watched in blooming;
         Yet would I die!

Visions of beauty are, which never reached me,
Hills, which my mind's eye straineth to behold now;
         Yet would I die!

Intimate feelings, presences of grandeur,
Thrills of sweet love for God and man await me;
         Yet would I die!

I have known such, and deemed they made my being;
Now their place knows them not in my heart's chambers;
         Oh let me die!

Evil bides in me, evil bides around me;
More is this torture than the bliss of old days:
         Oh let me die!

I should mistrust a rush of new enjoyment:
Beauty will aye be other than it has been:
         Oh let me die![81]

As much as Tennyson's better known poem *The Two Voices*, this poem could bear the sub-title 'Thoughts of a Suicide'. It was the most powerful poem Hallam had yet written, and it marks the start of a poetically prolific period. Poetry was inevitably the medium most answerable to the expression of his thoughts and emotions at this time. Gladstone, certainly, was a close enough friend to receive confidences about Hallam's spiritual state, but there were few enough other people amongst his correspondents at this time, least of all his father, who would be capable of responding to him with understanding, let alone sympathy, though Hallam, it is true, did warn his father that he had 'a great deal to talk to you about' during the Easter vacation.[82] The sequence of poems which he subsequently wrote (and published) virtually constitute a diary for the rest of the year. A poem which Hallam's editor entitles *A Confession and a Prayer* also related closely to the spiritual struggles described in the letter to Gladstone, especially in its desire to form a true relationship with God, involving a subjugation of the self's rebellious impulses. Arthur Hallam's faith was precariously held:

Oft have I worshipped thee, and still I bow,
With reverence, and a feeling, like to hope,
Tho' something worn in th' heart, by which we pray.
Oh, since I last beheld thee in thy pomp
Right o'er the Siren city of the south,
Rude grief and harsher sin have dealt on me
The malice of their terrible impulses . . .

Yet is thy bondage beautiful: the clouds
Drink beauty from the spirit of thy forms,
Yea, from the sacred orbits borrow grace
To modulate their wayward phantasies.
But they are trifles: in thyself alone,
And the suffusion of thy starry light
Firmly abide in their concordant joy,
Beauty, and music, and primeval love:
And thence may man learn an imperial truth,
That duty is the being of the soul,
And in that form alone can freedom move.
Such is your mighty language, lights of heaven:
Oh, thrill me with its plenitude of sound,
Make me to feel, not to talk of sovranty,
And harmonize my spirit with my God![83]

Despite Hallam's real, oppressive and ongoing psychological problems, he had managed to undertake another, and more significant, poetic project, though one of a markedly less personal kind. Hallam had already mentioned to his father his entry for the Chancellor's Gold Medal for English Poetry, and had begun work on his poem immediately after the Craven Scholarship examinations. The poem had certainly been submitted well before the end of the term, despite the emotional difficulties that Hallam was experiencing. On 13 December 1828, the annual advertisement had appeared in *The Times*, announcing that a prize was to be offered for 'the best ode, or the best poem in heroic verse . . . not to exceed 200 lines in length.' The closing date for entries was 31 March 1829, the winner would be announced in June and the subject was *Timbuctoo*. Superficially, this might not seem a very helpful subject, but it was in the best traditions of this university genre. (When Whewell had won the prize back in 1814, the subject was *Boadicea*; the following two years' subjects, for which Hallam also submitted entries, were *Byzantium* and *The North West Passage*.)

Whilst these subjects initially suggest a panel of examiners plucking titles randomly from the air, Timbuctoo was in fact very topical and something of a talking point. The eponymous city on the edge of the Sahara had been first settled in the eleventh century and was subsequently famed for its legendary wealth. It was a Moslem stronghold and its inhabitants were very hostile to Christians. For this reason, European attempts at exploration had been generally doomed to failure. Mungo Park had set out for Timbuctoo but failed to reach it. In 1824 the Geographical Society of Paris announced a prize of 7,000 francs for the first person to visit Timbuctoo and return. This provoked a certain Anglo-French rivalry and two English expeditions were also undertaken. One of them failed to reach the city, but the other, led by Major Alexander Gordon Laing, did actually reach Timbuctoo, though Laing was murdered when he refused to renounce his Christianity.[84] News of this reached London in 1828, though the previous year a Frenchman, René Caillié, had set off for the ancient city dressed as a Muslim servant. He lived to tell the tale and was honoured by the French government on his return. He published an account of his travels in 1829, which appeared in an English translation in 1830. Unfortunately Caillié's expedition had proved an anti-climax as all he found were ruins, 'the most monotonous and barren scene I ever beheld.' Nonetheless his journey and experiences had been received with interest in academic circles.[85] The subject thus offered a greater range of imaginative possibilities than at first might have seemed the case. It was also responsible for initiating a friendship between Hallam and another young Cambridge poet, Alfred Tennyson.

It is not absolutely clear when Hallam and Tennyson first met. Tennyson was in the year above Hallam and did not live in college. Trinity was a large college anyway, and neither of the young men was particularly outgoing. Although Hallam and Tennyson submitted entirely separate entries for the competition, there is evidence of collusion of a kind between them. Hallam, entirely without bitterness, subsequently maintained that Tennyson had borrowed his main idea from him. Tennyson's poem won the prize (he had failed the previous year) and was subsequently much read and admired in Cambridge. The reason that the rivalry between the young poets remained a friendly one is that neither of them took the competition particularly seriously. For a start they both broke the rules: neither poem was 'in heroic verse'. Tennyson wrote in blank verse, Hallam in *terza rima*. Tennyson exceeded the stipulated number of lines, by writing 248 rather than 200. Hallam's poem ran to 198 which possibly explains its rather abrupt ending. Hallam's poem never actually mentions Timbuctoo at all (without its title, no reader would be able to guess its subject) and Tennyson's was largely and quickly pirated from an earlier unpublished poem called *Armageddon*, in response to his father's insistence that he should enter the competition. Tennyson also provocatively prefaced his poem with a spurious quotation from Chapman. Neither poet was actually present on the day on which the winning poem was declaimed. Hallam was by then ill and being nursed at home and Tennyson, probably to avoid the exposure of a public performance, claimed illness also ('a determination of blood to the Head . . . I am far from well'.[86]) Charles Merivale read Tennyson's poem instead. Equally, both poets wasted little time in dissociating themselves from their efforts. Hallam was subsequently to describe his poem as 'my queer piece of work about Timbuctoo. I wrote it in a sovereign vein of poetic scorn for anybody's opinion, who did not value Plato, and Milton, just as much as I did. The natural consequence was that ten people out of twelve laughed, or opened large eyes; and the other two set about praising highly, what was plainly addressed to them, not to people in general . . . My friend Tennyson's poem, which got the prize, will be thought by the ten sober persons afore mentioned twice as absurd as mine'.[87] Tennyson never included *Timbuctoo* in editions of his own works, and, when it was printed in a volume exclusively devoted to Cambridge prize poems, he wrote to the editor that 'Prize poems . . . are not properly speaking "Poems" at all and ought to be forgotten as soon as recited. I could have wished that poor *Timbuctoo* might have been suffered to slide quietly off, with all its errors, into forgetfulness'.[88]

Even so, both poems provoked interest, and even superlatives, amongst the 'poetical set' in Cambridge, and Hallam's poem had its partisans. William Bodham Donne thought it was superior to Tennyson's, and Milnes thought it 'the finest thing that has been produced since the days of Shelley.'[89] Even though Hallam had no particular regard for this work, he asked for twenty-five copies of it to be published in pamphlet form in Cambridge (in fact the printers produced fifty). The rules of the competition required of its entrants a lengthy discursive poem. In Tennyson's case, this stipulation tended to suppress the poet's individual voice, and, in comparison with his other verse of the period, *Timbuctoo* seems self-consciously literary and derivative. Milton's influence is pervasive. Hallam's poem is derivative also, even to the point of actual quotation, from Wordsworth. Aidan Day remarks that that Hallam's *Timbuctoo* is 'laboured and derivative . . . His composition reads like a versified treatise on the imagination and we should be hard pressed to recognise in it that "vital union" between language and figure which we take to be a distinguishing feature of the fully realised Romantic poem'.[90] While

Tennyson presents his imaginary journey to Timbuctoo as ultimately disappointing, just as Caillié did (though he could not have known this as Caillié's account was not published until the following year), Hallam meditates on the city as a vision of an ideal and permanent world: 'Symbol of Love, and Truth, and all that cannot die':

> Thy Palaces and pleasure-domes to me
>   Are matter of strange thought: for sure thou art
>   A splendour in the wild: and aye to thee
> Did visible guardians of the Earth's great heart
>   Bring their choice tributes, culled from many a mine,
>   Diamond, and jasper, porphyry, and the art
> Of figured chrysolite: nor silver shine
>   There wanted, nor the mightier power of gold:
>   So wert thou reared of yore, City divine!

Timbuctoo is a Utopian dream also:

> Methought I saw a nation, which did heark
>   To justice, and to Truth: their ways were strait,
>   And the dread shadow, Tyranny, did lurk
> Nowhere about them: not to scorn, or hate
>   A living thing was their sweet nature's bond:
>   So every soul moved free in kingly state[91]

Hallam offered a number of explanatory notes to the poem when he published it in his 1830 volume. This is partly to acknowledge influences and allusions, but also, it must be admitted, to help the reader through a poem whose direction is not always clear and whose allusions do not necessarily serve to clarify. Hallam was certainly aware of this problem, as, when sending his aunt a copy of *Timbuctoo,* he told her that she would need 'a running commentary in order thoroughly to comprehend the thing itself. At least parts are somewhat mystical'.[92] Where Tennyson's poem is *about* disappointment, the end of Hallam's poem merely disappoints. Hallam seems uncertain how to end and comes to rest beneath a quotation from Wordsworth's *Tintern Abbey,* which attempts to celebrate the state of mind in which the glories of Timbuctoo can be contemplated, rather than those glories themselves. The poem duly received censure from Henry Hallam, who was moved to uncharacteristic levity by 'the extremely hyperbolical importance which the author's brilliant fancy has attached to a nest of barbarians'.[93]

Looking at Hallam's poetic output during the early part of 1829, it might seem that he was developing into a significant literary figure in Cambridge. He was also becoming known in the university in general. This could not, however, conceal the fact that his mental state was visibly deteriorating in a way that gave rise for concern amongst his friends. He had told his aunt in March that was 'by no means well in health, or indeed in spirits'.[94] After he had returned to Cambridge for the summer term, Pickering wrote to Gladstone that 'Hallam has, I am sorry to say, been quite unwell lately. He has certainly been in low spirits since he has been at Cambridge, & I fear he has rather encouraged, than attempted to remove them. I sincerely hope however that they will improve with his health, for it is a sad thing for one of his age and talents to indulge a melancholy, which leads too soon to philosophy and retirement'.[95] Pickering, like Hallam's father, and even Hallam himself, saw Hallam's philosophical interests as a cause rather than a consequence of his depression. The poems which Hallam wrote during the Easter vacation continued to show the results of painful introspection. One of them, addressed to James Milnes Gaskell makes a painful contrast between them:

> In sooth I envy thee: thou seemest pure:
> But I am seared

'Seared' was the very word that Hallam had used to describe himself in his letter to Gladstone, and in this poem as in the letter, Hallam attributes his spiritual distress to the devil ('coiled around the fibres of my heart . . . with his serpentine, thought-withering gaze').[96] Another poem of this period yearns to be again in the presence of Anna Wintour.

Henry Hallam, in his preface to the *Remains* did not gloss over the details of Arthur's mental and physical health at this time:

> 'In the first year of his residence at Cambridge, symptoms of disordered health, especially in the circulatory system began to show themselves; and it is by no means improbable that these were indications of a tendency to derangement of the vital functions, which became ultimately fatal. A too rapid determination of blood towards the brain, with its concomitant uneasy sensations, rendered him frequently incapable of mental fatigue. He had indeed once before, at Florence, been affected by symptoms not unlike these. *His intensity of reflection and feeling also brought on occasionally a considerable depression of spirits, which had been painfully observed at times by those who watched him most, from the time of his leaving Eton, and even before.*' (my italics)[97]

It was this latter state to which Hallam referred when later in the summer he told Robert Robertson: 'you . . . can have no adequate idea of the miseries I suffered in mind . . . the most abject despondency mixed with vague dread and strong remorse. Oh my God! I hope never to know such days as those again.'[98]

In the middle of May, Hallam suddenly left Cambridge, being forced to go home, obviously seriously ill. He was forbidden to return for the rest of term, was 'kept within gates'[99] in Wimpole Street and, not surprisingly, was gloomy at the prospect of forthcoming 'dreary' months which he would have to spend as an invalid. He had been ordered not to strain his eyes and a gap in his published correspondence until 6 July was the result of his having been also forbidden 'to handle a pen.' He claimed he was well enough to receive visitors and hoped that Milnes would call on him when he was in London, though there is no evidence that he did. One of the more bizarre deprivations which Hallam suffered at this time was that of witnessing Milnes taking to the sky in an air-balloon. Accompanied by a Mr. Green 'the well-known aeronaut' and another undergraduate, George Wyndham Scott, Milnes's ascent was a sufficiently unusual event to merit coverage by the local newspaper. It was also an occasion for a rare show of wit by William Whewell, who, when Milnes asked his permission to undertake the flight, provided him with a chit containing simply the words 'Ascendat Mr. Milnes'. These were the words used in the university degree ceremonies to invite graduands to receive their degrees from the Vice Chancellor.[100] Whewell presumably thought the occasion was an opportunity for scientific research, rather than (as one suspects it was) an elaborate undergraduate prank. Milnes, in mid-air, could not resist writing a note to Hallam, which he had originally had the fancy of tying to a stone and dropping from the balloon. A fragment survives which reports flying at a height of 2,000 feet and looking down on the town of St. Neot's. Milnes thought the countryside looked like 'a beautiful model', but feared that the descent would be 'rather dangerous'.[101] In the event all passed off without mishap. Hallam, probably breaking doctor's orders, could not resist penning a reply to 'the prince of all Aeronauts . . . Henceforward I shall look on you with much increased reverence.'[102]

As it turned out Hallam was confined to his parents' home for less time than he had feared, and the summer in fact proved to be a refreshingly peripatetic one. The month of June found him, for the first time in his life, following his own nose, 'a few days-on a sea-breeze speculation' in Brighton before 'the whim . . . came into my mind to glance aside to Normandy . . . on a speculation of bettering myself, mind and body, by a change of scene.'[103] During the seond half of the summer he made an extensive tour in Scotland (described in more detail below) with his father, from which he returned to England in late August to join the rest of the family in Great Malvern.

Precisely how long Hallam stayed in Normandy is not absolutely clear, but he was certainly back before 25 June, when Gaskell reported to his mother that Hallam had returned. The one poetic memento of this trip seems to corroborate Gaskell's view. It is a happy, song-like little poem, not in Hallam's usual vein, *Stanzas Written at Caudebec in Normandy*, of which the first verse makes rather light of recent sufferings:

When life is crazy in my limbs,
   And hope is gone astray,
And in my soul's December fade
   The love-thoughts of its May,
One spot of earth is left to me
   Will warm my heart again:
'Tis Caudebec and Mailleraie
   On the pleasant banks of Seine.[104]

No fewer than twelve poems follow the route of Hallam's subsequent Scottish journey, and help to plot the course which he and his father took throughout July and August. The poems offer Hallam's responses to Edinburgh, Lanark, the Pass of Glencoe, Ben Lomond, the Banks of the Tay, Fingal's Cave on the Island of Staffa, The Pass of Killiekrankie, Loch Katrine and Melrose Abbey. Hallam's reactions to mountain scenery and wild nature clearly owe much to Wordsworth whom he claimed at the time was his favourite poet. Motter also notes the similarity between the poem *Written in View of Ben Lomond* and Section CXXIII of Tennyson's *In Memoriam* in their contrast of the transitoriness of human life with the permanence of nature:

Mountain austere, and full of kinglihood!
Forgive me if a child of later earth,
I come to bid thee hail. My days are brief
And like the mould that crumbles on thy verge,
A minute's blast may shake me into dust;
But thou art of the things that never fail.
Before the mystic garden, and the fruit
Sung by the Shepherd-Ruler vision-blest,
Thou wert; and from thy speculative height
Beheld'st the forms of other living souls.[105]

Hallam travelled from London to Edinburgh by steamboat, which took two days, and arrived in the Scottish capital at 11 p.m. on Friday, 3 July. It was his first visit to Edinburgh, and, despite the rain and mist, he was impressed by the city. He liked the roads and the hills though he claimed that he would have preferred the houses in the New Town to be higher. He was able to report to Robert Robertson that although he was 'somewhat altered' in appearance since they had last met 'I am much better. I see my way out of my glooms when they come upon me, and I despair less of ultimate peace of mind.'[106] Henry Hallam, as a former contributor to *The Edinburgh Review*, had an entree into Edinburgh literary society and so Hallam met 'Jeffrey, Napier, Scott, & sundry worthies of this sort'. He was pleased to have met 'such stars' as these, but complained that in general travelling with his father brought him much into the company of bores. Francis Jeffrey, as editor of *The Edinburgh Review* had been notably hostile to Wordsworth, though Hallam found him surprisingly agreeable: 'the most benevolent, to all seeming, of literary men. How so douce an animal could have written that critique on Wordsworth I cannot imagine'.[107] Hallam was not alone in reacting to Jeffrey in this way. Lady Holland, for example, found him 'a very dear little man, who has the best heart and temper, although the authors of the day consider him their greatest scourge.'[108] On his first meeting with him in Edinburgh, Hallam found Sir Walter Scott dull, though he accepted that the encounter had provided him with a couple of good stories to tell when he got back to Cambridge. Henry Hallam had known Scott for some years but to Arthur he was very much one of the old guard, a world away from Wordsworth and Coleridge and Shelley.

Hallam was looking forward to seeing Robert Robertson again, not only for his own sake, but as a means of reopening his acquaintance with Robertson's sister, Anne: 'I need not, I am sure, express the delight I shall feel in meeting with her especially and thus having an opportunity, though it be for a little while, to cement what she will perhaps allow me to call our old friendship.'[109] Hallam had proved almost as susceptible to Anne Robertson in Rome, as he had to Anna Wintour, and indeed had probably found her a more responsive object of his attentions than the much-courted Anna. It even seems likely that he had unburdened himself to Anne about his feelings for Anna when they were all in Rome. He remarked to Robert that 'the influence of your Sister's conversation on my character, at a very critical moment of its development, will never I hope, believe, and pray, cease to work in me for good'.[110] It is not too fanciful to believe that Anne consoled Hallam, calming him down when he fretted about Anna. He seldom wrote to Robert during this period without referring to her, though a poem written about her at Glenarbach, the Robertsons' house, shows that he was not above lecturing her when the moment arose. *Wordsworth at Glenarbach: An Episode* recounts a rebuff which Hallam received from Anne after trying to convert her to Wordsworth. The poem is clearly written in part-flattery of Anne ('That winsome Lady sitting by my side,/ Whom still these eyes in every place desire',).

> I spake of Wordsworth, of that lofty mind,
> Enthronized in a little monarchy
> Of hills and waters, where no one thing is
> Lifeless, or pulsing fresh with mountain strength.

But Anne remained resolutely unmoved and Hallam, at first offended by this, eventually decided that he had no good reason to be so and that Anne's views were to be respected:

I prayed that she,
Whose face, like an unruffled mountain tarn,
Smiled on me till its innocent joy grew mine,
Might ne'er experience any change of mood[111]

It was clearly a happy time. Glenarbach was an attractive house, standing in an estate of sixty acres and situated on the northern bank of the Clyde about twelve miles from Glasgow and offering views of the river on one side and Ben Lomond on the other. It had previously belonged to Henry Hallam's friend Lord Webb Seymour. When the time came, unwillingly, to leave, Hallam wrote *A Farewell to Glenarbach*, commemorating this visit, and particularly Anne, whom he hoped to see again but in fact never did.

In early August Henry and Arthur Hallam met Scott for the second time when they visited Abbotsford, an event which was deemed sufficiently important to merit a reference in J.G. Lockhart's life of Scott. Lockhart wrote that 'Sir Walter received this summer a short visit from Mr Hallam, and made in his company several of the little excursions which had in former days been of constant recurrence. Mr. Hallam had with him his son, Arthur, a young gentleman of extraordinary abilities, and as modest as able, who not long afterwards was cut off in the very bloom of opening life and genius.'[112] Clearly by 1838, when Lockhart's biography was first published, the lineaments of the Arthur Hallam legend were in place, though his 'modesty' would have been very necessary when in Sir Walter's company as a means of concealing his less than reverential attitude to the novelist's reputation. One of the excursions undertaken was to Melrose Abbey, which Hallam commemorated in a poem, *Stanzas Written After Visiting Melrose Abbey in Company of Sir Walter Scott*. On this occasion, Hallam is much more charitable about Scott and writes respectfully of the ageing author, sensing that he was, perhaps, nearing the end of his life. Scott was in fact to suffer a stroke the following January:

Then ceased I from my envying state
    And knew that aweless intellect
Hath power upon the ways of fate,
    And works through time and space uncheckt.
That minstrel of old chivalry
In the cold grave must come to be,
But his transmitted thoughts have part
In their collective mind, and never shall depart.[113]

Returning to England, both father and son were guests of the Gaskells 'for a few days in late August' at Thornes House, near Wakefield. As always, Hallam enjoyed the company of Mrs. Gaskell whom, he told Gladstone, he found 'clever, very agreeable, and withal rather singular . . . her exceeding kindness, and friendliness will grow on your perception the longer you know her'.[114] However, a letter to Milnes from York on 15 August had shown that his feelings of depression were still recurring: 'I am as miserable, if not more so, than ever. I really am afraid of insanity . . . Do you ask what is the matter? I cannot tell you: I am not master of my own mind; my thoughts are more than a match for me; my brain has been fevering with speculations most fathomless, abysmal, ever since I set foot in Scotland.' But there had been moments of 'sunshine' also, in which 'my poetical faculty has developed itself marvellously: it burns now within my heart: God grant me, if I am to have a Poet's destiny, at least a Poet's power! I have sat within the voice of cataracts, & looked on the silent faces of hills'. He also judged that his 'verses lately have had more of a Wordsworthian cast', and he included the Ben Lomond poem in the letter.[115]

Whilst staying with the Gaskells, Hallam had the unusual experience of visiting a local lunatic asylum. It was a ritual which Gaskell inflicted on several of his guests at this time. The visit produced what is perhaps Hallam's most interesting poem of this period. *Lines Addressed to Alfred Tennyson* is a misleading title, since it seems to suggest that it was another of those social and occasional poems which Hallam's Cambridge circle liked to address to each other. The poem is more substantial than this. It is addressed to Tennyson because Hallam has a strong urge to share this, to him, far from ordinary experience of 'general life, the stern, the real' with his fellow poet. The poem's central image is that of one particular mad girl:

> The vision clings upon my brain
>   Of her flushed cheek, and eye's quick gleam,
> And that dread sense of doubting pain,
>   That seemed to wrap her, like a dream
>   Whose bounds, we guess, engird us fast,
> Yet hate we that dim thought, and struggle to the last

Unusually for Hallam, this poem presents an encounter with what Wordsworth would have called 'common life'. If Hallam's imagination at this time had a tendency to be haunted by sounding cataracts, this poem is Wordsworthian in another way: in its sympathetic identification with a suffering and marginalised figure:

> Ask ye the cause that she was there?
>   No tale have I of sweet love's pity:
> For all I know, though she was fair,
>   She ne'er shed tear for amorous ditty:
> But general life, the stern, the real,

Lay iron on a heart so tender and so leal.
The world so cherished grew within,
    A glorious world of clear delight;
But nought external seemed akin,
    So pined the maiden day and night.
    Thought staggered in its own dark mesh;
And there she sits alone like one without a wish.[116]

The month which Hallam then went on to spend at The Lodge, Great
Malvern, with the rest of his family was the final stage in what might be
termed his psychological rehabilitation, though the weeks did not pass by
entirely without their dark moments. Malvern he liked: 'just the place for
philosophizing and poetizing, the only two studies to my mind worth the
trouble of thought.'[117] He returned to an active intellectual life. He wrote
eleven poems and spent his mornings reading philosophy. In the evenings
he was teaching himself German, reading Schiller with Ellen, and hoping
to be able to manage Kant and Goethe within a year. There were also
frequent rides 'through this magnificent country'. His only complaint was
against the local vicar 'Dr. Card . . . a conspicuous person among the thir-
drate writers of the day',[118] despite his being a lover of Shelley. All these
pastimes were conducive to a greater sense of serenity and it certainly
seemed as if Hallam was capable of taking a more objective and less
fevered view of his mental condition. Although he repeated yet again to
Frere that: 'I believe I have a tendency towards insanity', he added that 'I
am for the present *quite well,* but cannot flatter myself that the natural
liability to disorders in the head, which are half the effect, & half the cause
of a morbid disposition of mind should be removed so quickly.'[119] To
Robertson he admitted that 'my mind has been calmer since I reached
Malvern, than for months before. I cannot expect to change the habit of
my soul in a moment. Perhaps it is God's will that I should never change
it; my natural mood has been always melancholy.'[120] But it was Milnes,
holidaying in Italy, who received the fullest and most explicit account of
Hallam's mental condition as it had been over the previous weeks and
months. Writing to him on 1st September, Hallam emphasised the spiritual struggles which had taken place within him: 'though I have been the
creature of impulse, though the basest passions have roused themselves in
the dark caverns of my nature, & swept like storm-winds over me, lest
the glory of the majestic Imagination should make me free, I will struggle
yet, and have faith in God, that when I ask for bread I shall not receive a
stone . . . I had many grapples with Atheism, but beat the monster back,
taking my stand on the strongholds of Reason. But my present convictions are decidedly opposed to all Formal Religion.'[121] By mid-October,
when he again wrote to Milnes and was preparing to return to Cambridge
for the new academic year, Hallam offered his final comment on his
mental state: 'I have in truth been calmer since I settled down to my books

at Malvern: I have linked some reasonings, which afford me a resting place, on some highly important subjects . . . But . . . a little gust would upset me quite . . . My dark hours are less frequent, but they come.'[122]

Whatever the nature of Hallam's previous and subsequent misgivings about Milnes, the correspondence of this period shows that Milnes was Hallam's closest confidant in the late summer of 1829, just as Gladstone and Gaskell had been before him. This is evident not only in the confessional nature of so much that Hallam wrote to him, but also in the way he viewed Milnes as a fellow-poet. His letters to Milnes include samples of work-in-progress (or recently completed) as well as poems specifically addressed to him: a light-hearted *Chanson à boire* ('I'll pledge thee in this bloodred wine/Tho' thou art far away') and also a sonnet addressed to him on his return from Italy of which Milnes thought sufficiently highly to include it in a letter to his father.

It was to Milnes that Hallam also relayed the fact that his own father had accidentally come upon some of his poems and had 'read several pieces that assuredly I never dreamt he should see.' A 'long, but unsatisfactory conversation'[123] followed, in which Henry, in as well-meaning a way as he could, suggested that Arthur's interest in poetry and metaphysics was unhealthy and had probably contributed to his recent depressive illness. As always when this particular matter was discussed, Henry's words went largely unheeded, though his own position never changed, as Arthur was to discover the following year when Henry forbade the publication of the joint volume of poems which he and Tennyson projected. Milnes had obviously been trying to get in on this publishing venture as well, though Hallam's tactful absence of enthusiasm for it was made clear when he wrote to Milnes in October: 'You have my free vote for publishing along with Tennyson, and myself: but mine alone is not enough, and, as he refused his brother on the score of not wishing a third, some difficulty may lie in your way.'[124] No more was heard about Milnes's involvement in the project.

The fact that Hallam was feeling in much better health by the autumn undoubtedly enabled him to deal with a shock which might otherwise have overwhelmed him. In September he heard the news that Anna Wintour had become engaged to George Healey, a Yorkshire squire. It seems unlikely that Hallam knew Healey, but he wasted no time in voicing his disapproval of him. He turned to Gaskell for some anguished soul-bearing on the subject: 'There are certain circumstances connecting that man and myself in a way that will render it the last thing possible for me ever to see him . . . of his character I know little or nothing, though certainly my impression of the man is not that I had desired to receive from the chosen partner of the woman I had loved . . . it is an awful thing to me that I . . . who would now coin my heart's blood to do her any service, should alone, of all the world, be separated from her by a destiny for ever.'[125] Anne Robertson, too, was again called upon to offer comfort and succour to her susceptible friend and would-be lover. By the time he wrote to Gaskell, Hallam had clearly taken Anne into his confidence and she had counselled forbearance: 'a few tones from a gentle womanly voice strike on the soul, like the irresistable force of music . . . Some persons, I know, dislike counsel or even conversation on matters of that high and absorbing interest: to me, there is nothing more welcome or more sacred'.[126]

It has been said that Hallam was a demanding friend and certainly in the summer and autumn of 1829 he made considerable inroads into his friends' powers of sympathy and tolerance. They had to accept the near-solipsism of his letters and their tendency, aided by his naturally vivid pen, to emotional exhibitionism. During the earlier part of the summer, when his distress was at its most acute, correspondence had stopped altogether for some time, but the autumn was a time for reopening communication with friends: Frere, Gaskell, Robertson and Milnes in particular. September also saw a rapprochement with Gladstone after many months. Gladstone had written to Hallam on hearing of his illness in the spring. In apologising for his considerable delay in replying, Hallam acknowledged that it was more than two years since they had last met, and proposed to take the opportunity of visiting Gladstone in Oxford before his own term started at Cambridge. Hallam again hoped that the worst of his mental struggles were behind him, and that he was now much calmer. He confided in Gladstone a desire for fame, though not of a specifically academic sort: 'If it please God that I make the name I bear honored in a second generation, it will be by inward power, which is its own reward: if it please him not, I hope to go down to the grave unrepining, for I have lived, and loved, and been beloved.'[127]

At the time Gladstone unexpectedly received this 'very gratifying letter from Hallam',[128] he was staying at Thornes House with the Gaskells. The letter must indeed have been gratifying for Gladstone, as it was only the previous day that he had made the diary entry (already quoted in CHAPTER TWO) in which he chronicled what he thought was the end of his friendship with Hallam. He enthusiastically took up Hallam's suggestion of a meeting and accepted an invitation to Malvern. Hallam then accompanied Gladstone to Oxford, where he was briefly reunited with Gaskell and Doyle. As always, though, Gladstone's touchiness about Hallam had some justification. Robert Bernard Martin reminds us that while Gladstone was at Malvern, Hallam 'talked much of the time of Tennyson and read *Timbuctoo* over and over to Gladstone.'[129] It is not difficult to see why Gladstone became uncomfortable about Hallam's friendship with Tennyson.

There is no doubt that Hallam, despite his original misgivings about Cambridge, was perfectly reconciled to returning for a second year and by October the threads of his life had been sufficiently drawn together to make the return seem logical and timely. There were good reasons to think that the next academic year would be better than the last. There was the friendship with Alfred Tennyson, which the summer's events had unavoidably put on hold. Also on 16 May, shortly before his enforced departure, Hallam had been elected a member of The Cambridge Conversazione Society, better known to posterity as 'The Apostles.'

On Thursday, 22 October 1829, Hallam began his second year at Cambridge. Milnes wrote home that 'Hallam is looking very well, and in full force; his marvellous mind has been gleaning in wisdom from every tract of knowledge.'[130]

CHAPTER FIVE

Living Awfully Fast
The Apostles and Somersby,
1829–1830

I feel as if I had lived awfully fast-in everything been premature-ran round, as it were, the whole circle of this life's opinions & sensations, before my nineteenth summer has past from over me.
HALLAM TO GLADSTONE, 14 SEPTEMBER 1829

Alfred Tennyson had entered Trinity College in November 1827, a month after the university term had started. On his first evening he had hovered outside the college hall and seen the assembled undergraduates at dinner. He was so frightened by the sight that he turned and fled. Nevertheless he had stayed long enough for W. H. Thompson, a fellow student (later to become Master of the College) to catch sight of him and to exclaim 'That man must be a poet!'

Thompson spoke more than he knew, of course. Most certainly Tennyson looked the part. Although he was yet to acquire the shaggy beard and sombrero, he was of commanding height, swarthy, shambling and unkempt, with a far away look in his eyes, the result of acute short-sightedness. He had been a poet for virtually all his life. His earliest surviving manuscript dates from his eighth year, though he had probably been writing odd lines since the age of five. By the time he was ten he assured his younger brother, Arthur, that 'I mean to be famous'. He had written epics in the style of Scott and lengthy heroic poems in the manner of Pope. At age fourteen he had composed three acts of a comedy *The Devil and the Lady* and four years later published *Poems by Two Brothers,* ostensibly a collection of poems written by himself and his elder brother Charles, though it also contained contributions from his eldest sibling, Frederick.

Like Hallam, Tennyson was slow to adjust to living in Cambridge. Although Frederick and Charles were both in residence with him, the sense of family solidarity did little to reconcile him to the place. Alfred shared rooms with Frederick and Charles at 57 Corpus Buildings, Trumpington Street, a little way from his college and though in later life he tried to dissociate himself from his critical poem *Lines on Cambridge of 1830*, he wrote, shortly after his arrival to his aunt: 'I feel isolated here in the midst of society, the country is disgustingly level, the revelry of the place so monotonous, the studies of the university so uninteresting, so much matter of fact – none but dry headed calculating angular little gentlemen can take delight in it'.[1]

Tennyson's family background was both provincial and unorthodox. The third of eleven children, his father was Rector of Somersby, a tiny village in Lincolnshire. This might sound eminently respectable, but George Clayton Tennyson's history verged on the bizarre. Although he was an elder son, his own father had taken an intense dislike to him and had made his duller but more amenable younger son, Charles, his heir instead. George had been educated at St. John's College, Cambridge, but he had been given little option other than to enter the church, for which he had no particular vocation, and a parish in Lincolnshire had been earmarked for him even before he went up to university. By the time that his three eldest sons had arrived at Cambridge, George Tennyson had degenerated into alcoholism and was given to outbursts of extreme bad temper, often accompanied by swearing and threats of violence, and his physical health had become increasingly precarious. One of his brothers-in-law had attempted to have him certified as insane and for a time in 1829, while Alfred was at Cambridge, his wife had engineered a trial separation, taking herself and the younger children off to the relative safety of lodgings in Louth. George was twice sent off abroad: partly to leave his family in peace, and partly in the hope that he could recover health and stability there.

What made George's life the more tragic (and he was keenly aware of this) was that he was a man of considerable abilities: a scholar with a wide range of interests, including oriental languages and science, a musician and also a writer of verses. He had a library of over 2500 books. He had taken the degree of Doctor of Civil Law at Cambridge in 1813. He proved a severe but capable tutor to Alfred, who had disliked his formal schooling in Louth, and there is no doubt at all that Alfred benefited considerably from having access to his father's books. Dr Tennyson, though bearing no overt grudge against his brother, had a keen sense of his own status as a gentleman and had sent his eldest son Frederick to Eton, where he had had a distinguished career as both scholar and sportsman. Dr Tennyson sent Charles and Alfred to the most prestigious college in Cambridge (even though he himself as an undergraduate had once fired a pistol shot through its chapel windows), to which Frederick in turn migrated from St. John's. Although he was respected by his parishioners, Dr. Tennyson was not by conventional standards a conscientious pastor. His sermons generally went considerably over the heads of his small agricultural congregation and he had been known to take snuff in the pulpit. After a particularly violent domestic outburst on one occasion his wife had complained of his using the kind of language that was highly inappropriate in one of his calling.

Life in Somersby Rectory clearly had considerable tensions and Alfred had suffered from them as much as anyone. There was a family predisposition to mental instability and melancholia. Tennyson at times feared for his own sanity, and two of his younger brothers showed clear psychotic symptoms. Those who have wished, in the tradition of Harold Nicolson, to paint Tennyson as 'the black, unhappy mystic of the Lincolnshire wolds',[2] have found most of their evidence in his early years, despite the fact that life in Somersby (especially when Dr. Tennyson was away) was often enjoyable for the Tennyson children. They had a great deal of freedom to wander at will through the neighbouring countryside whenever they chose and were sufficiently uninhibited to enjoy music-making and dancing both indoors and out. They were a good-looking and attractive family who entranced Hallam when he met them and whose generally emancipated air offered the most appealing of contrasts to his own buttoned-up existence in respectable Wimpole Street.

It is easy to emphasise the differences between the Tennyson and Hallam families and to forget their similarities. Most certainly Hallam as a Cambridge undergraduate enjoyed a higher personal standard of living than Tennyson (who had to be assisted by a small allowance from an aunt) and Hallam's father was famous, well-connected, and married to the daughter of a Baronet, but even in age that was finely tuned to social gradations, it is possible to exaggerate the gap between them. Hallam had known of Frederick Tennyson at Eton and Tennyson's grandfather, although starting out as a solicitor in Market Rasen, owned a number of properties in Lincolnshire, just as Hallam's father did. Tennyson's mother was a niece of a Bishop of Lincoln, and both his uncle and grandfather were or had been MPs. If the Tennysons were provincial rather than metropolitan and bohemian rather than conventional, their differences from the Hallams were in the end superficial ones. Both families were cultured and *au fait,* and it is a safe assumption that Dr. Tennyson's library could more than bear comparison with Mr. Hallam's.

It was poetry which first drew Hallam and Tennyson together. The way in which their *Timbuctoo* poems arose collusively has already been described. But they are not the only evidence of collaboration. A sonnet *To Poesy* exists in copies by both Tennyson and Hallam, Hallam's manuscript containing the note: 'N.B. I had some hand in the worst part of this Sonnet'.[3] That they were planning a joint collection of their poems within a very short time of their initial acquaintance indicates just how much they were stimulated by their common interest, and Hallam's sonnet *To A.T.*, dating from May 1829 bears witness to its author's awareness that this friendship was a significant one (though Hallam at different times wrote sonnets to several of his other friends, including Gaskell, Milnes and Charles Tennyson):

Oh, last in time, but worthy to be first
  Of friends in rank, had not the father of good
  On my early spring one perfect gem bestowed,
  A friend, with whom to share the best and worst.
Him will I shut close to my heart for aye.
  There's not a fibre quivers there, but is
  His own, his heritage for woe, or bliss.
  Thou would'st not have me such a charge betray.
Surely, if I be knit in brotherhood
  So tender to that chief of all my love,
  With thee I shall not loyalty eschew.
And well I ween not time with ill or good
  Shall thine affection e'er from mine remove,
  Thou yearner for all fair things, and all true.[4]

That his abilities were noticed and appreciated can be seen in the fact that, not long after Tennyson's arrival at Trinity, Charles Merivale had described him as 'an immense poet, as indeed are all the [Tennyson] tribe',[5] and in due course he was elected to the exclusive Cambridge society known as 'The Apostles' in October 1829, five months after Hallam. This society, which continued to exist well into the twentieth century (and has been rumoured still to do so) was in relative infancy during Hallam's time, and had only recently acquired its characteristic identity. Officially known as 'The Cambridge Conversazione Society', it had been formed in 1820, at a time when there were many private discussion and debating groups in Cambridge. The society was happy to accept and use its nickname 'The Apostles', but it seems likely that the name itself had been originally applied critically. The society did not restrict its membership to twelve, but it did quickly gain the reputation (truer in the mid 1820s than later) of taking itself very seriously. The double-edged nature of the nickname can also be gauged by the fact that the twelve students who gained the worst degrees in the Tripos examinations were known as the Apostles. The group's own members referred to it, as members of the Eton Society had also done, simply as 'the Society'. It had originated at St. John's College, but after a few years it was monopolised by Trinity men and had effectively become a Trinity College society, though it never found room either for Edward Fitzgerald or W. M. Thackeray, both of whom were resident there in Hallam's time.

Its earliest members had been a rather austere group of Tory Evangelicals, but by the late 1820s, its religious and political flavour had become more liberal, and however earnest the spirit of the debates may have been, the Apostles of Hallam's generation knew how to enjoy themselves as well. On at least one occasion, the Dean of Trinity called at Hallam's rooms during a wine-party to tell his Apostolic friends to make less noise. Such frivolity as this would have been anathema to the man who had a few years previously stamped a decisive image on the society. The serious and austere F. D. Maurice, did not see the Apostles as a social organisation in any way. For him the society existed for the pursuit of truth and he defined its agenda. Although Hallam never met him, he held Maurice in the highest regard, on one occasion urging Gladstone to become acquainted with him, on the grounds that 'The effect which he has produced on the minds of ma[ny] at Cambridge . . . is far greater than I can dare to calculate.'[6] Maurice came from a dissenting background and much of his life was given up to spiritual struggle, as he was unable, whilst at Cambridge, to profess allegiance to the doctrines of the Church of England and was thus unable to graduate. After a few years living a literary life in London, he eventually embraced Anglicanism and matriculated at Exeter College, Oxford to continue his education there.

The other significant Apostle of the generation immediately before Hallam's was John Sterling. Although he had resigned from the society in December 1827, his influence remained a pervasive one, not least through his friendship with several of Hallam's contemporaries. Carlyle later wrote Sterling's biography and said of his undergraduate life that it 'seems to have been an ardently speculating and talking one; by no means extensively restrained within limits . . . Sterling and his circle . . . were in all things clear for progress, liberalism; their politics, and view of the Universe, decisively of the Radical sort'.[7] Sterling's radicalism was particularly directed towards Cambridge University itself and indeed one of the Apostles' defining features was its opposition to many aspects of the university's organisation. In this respect Sterling's views chimed sympathetically with Hallam, who had been sceptical of Cambridge's educational purpose ever since he arrived. Sterling and Maurice were both involved in writing for the journals *The Literary Chronicle* and *The Athenaeum* in the late 1820s and Sterling's articles included criticisms of the Cambridge curriculum, the privileges granted to fellow commoners, the Previous examination, and the reduction of much of the so-called academic activity to pieces of 'dead task-work.'[8] John Kemble, who became a close friend to both Hallam and Tennyson, expressed the view that the prime function of the Apostles was actually to supplement the very narrow education which the university provided: 'Its business was to make men study and think on all matters except Mathematics and Classics, *professionally* considered . . . To my *education* given in that Society, I feel that I owe every power I possess, and the rescuing myself from a ridiculous state of prejudice and prepossessions with which I came armed to Cambridge.'[9]

Nevertheless, the Apostles' radicalism was not without its contradictions. Isobel Armstrong has described it as 'conservative anarchy . . . a conservative position which [the Apostles] conceived of as revolutionary'.[10] Part of its defining outlook lay in a rejection of prevailing Benthamite notions. Its gods were the poets not the utilitarian philosophers. R.C. Trench described the Apostles (disapprovingly, as it happened) as a 'Wordsworthian-Germano-Coleridgian' group. The Apostles belonged to the first generation who venerated Wordsworth and Coleridge, particularly the former, as teachers. Maurice had seen materialistic thought as schematic and superficial, not in essence at all altruistic.[11] Wordsworth, looking for truth within himself, was seen as the best kind of agent for political and institutional reform. The atheism of Shelley was assimilated as a form of religion, and he was also installed, slightly uneasily, in the Apostles' pantheon, though his revolutionary politics were ignored. The Apostles' enthusiasm for the work of Tennyson was influenced by their desire to produce from their number a great poet who would regenerate the nation through literature. They wished to see a better Cambridge, and by extension a better society, though they thought that this would be brought about by a kind of mental purification. They were deeply opposed to most forms of direct political action, especially to parliamentary reform, though, as will be seen, they were capable of taking political initiatives themselves when they thought the circumstances merited them.

Above all else, truth was to be approached through debate, through self-examination and the examination of others' opinions, through what Peter Allen calls ' a programme for personal growth through the free interchange of opinion.'[12] The seriousness with which ideas and opinions were entertained and argued about inevitably brought the Apostles into close personal friendships which extended well beyond the bounds of their weekly meetings and became, effectively, a system of mutual support, the effects of which were expected to be life-long. Kemble's view was that 'No society ever existed in which more freedom of thought was found, consistent with the most perfect affection between the members; or in which a more complete tolerance of the most opposite opinions prevailed . . . very few of the distinguished Cambridge men of our time have not been members of it'.[13] Of Hallam's contemporaries, it is perhaps Charles Merivale who most fully sums up what membership of the Apostles meant to those involved with it (and he was not blind to its less fortunate consequences): 'I am sure we all have ever felt and still feel a certain freemasonry of sympathy which binds us implicitly to one another as brethren of one family. Our common bond has been a common intellectual taste, common studies, common literary aspirations, and we have all felt, I suppose, the support of mutual regard and perhaps some mutual flattery. We soon grew, as such youthful coteries generally do, into immense self-conceit. We began to think we had a mission to enlighten the world upon things intellectual and spiritual. We held established principles, especially in poetry and metaphysics, and set up certain idols for our worship. Coleridge and Wordsworth were our principal divinities.'[14]

Few things are more effective in fostering a sense of solidarity than ritual, and the society was rich in this. Election was secret, members only being informed if the outcome was successful. Kemble described the process: 'No one ever knew that he was elected till every actual member was agreed that he should be elected. Temper, moral conduct and good feeling were quite as essential as brilliant acquirements. And at one time the Apostles were by no means distinguished in the University pursuits. One black ball was fatal'.[15] There were only a few vacancies in any given year and often potential candidates were mulled over for months before an official election took place. The society had little formal organisation. The elaborate record-keeping of the Eton College Society was alien to the Apostles. Papers were kept in a chest called the 'ark', but there was no detailed minuting of meetings. Members were fined for non-attendance. Meetings took place on Saturday evenings in the room of the member who was to read the paper and who was given the title of 'moderator'. Before the proceedings started, the oak (ie outer door) would be sported (locked) to prevent intruders. The speaker would stand on the hearth-rug before the fireplace. Discussion of the issues raised by the paper would follow, with each member speaking in turn, the order having been decided by lots taken beforehand. At the end of the evening a question was formulated and entered into the Society's record book, and each member signed his name as either agreeing with the question, disagreeing, or abstaining. Refreshments consisted of 'Whales' (anchovies on toast), taken with coffee. When an Apostle left Cambridge he became an honorary member but could continue to attend meetings (which many did) and there was an annual dinner to which both past and present members were invited.

The society also had a private language, largely rooted in an extended metaphor which suggested that its members were born and not made: possible members were 'embryos' who were discovered by means of 'propagation'; their sponsors were 'fathers', and their first meeting was their 'birth'; upon leaving the society they 'took wings' and became 'angels'. Other linguistic conventions prevailed too. The university of Oxford was 'oxford' with a lower case, and the philistines, those beneath contempt (i.e. presumably most non-members), were known as 'stumpfs'. Doubtless these indications of supercilious clannishness made the Apostles an easy prey to potential critics, as did their belief that they would inevitably make a mark in the world: the signs that this was being done were known as 'footprints'.[16]

The scantiness of the society's records makes it more difficult to appreciate the tone and tenor of its debates than was the case with the Eton Society, but Henry Sidgwick, who was an Apostle in the mid-century, compiled, in order to assist Hallam Tennyson's *Memoir* of his father, a list of the questions discussed at meetings between 1829 and 1831. In true Apostolic tradition, Sidgwick was keen that Hallam Tennyson should not reveal too much, explaining that the information should be used as 'material . . . for *general* statements', but that it was not the wish of the society that details should be published.[17] In Hallam's first term, five meetings of the society were held. The subjects for discussion were, for the most part, such as any debating society of the time might consider. At Hallam's first meeting on November 7 the question was 'Whether the clergy of the established church should be allowed to sit in the House of Commons' (Hallam voted 'no'; Tennyson was fined five shillings for non-attendance).The following Saturday found the Apostles discussing 'Whether the present law of libel[was] calculated to allow freedom of discussion combined with the necessary protection of individuals' (Hallam again voted 'no'). On November 21, the question was 'Whether the poems of Shelley have an immoral tendency' (Hallam and Tennyson both said 'no'), and the following week it was 'Whether there is any rule of moral action except general expediency' (Hallam and Tennyson voted 'aye'). Signifcantly, Hallam raised the philosophical level of the society when he read his first essay at the final meeting of the term on the question 'Whether the existence of an intelligent First Cause is deducible from the phenomena of the universe' (Hallam and Tennyson voted 'no').[18]

It has often been pointed out that the 'footprints' left by the Apostles of Hallam's generation were less extensive than they anticipated, and their subsequent careers did not in practice differ dramatically from those of any other group of early nineteenth-century Oxford or Cambridge undergraduates. Their subsequent achievements were in general estimable rather than brilliant. Several of Hallam's contemporaries in the society (Alford, Blakesley, Merivale and Trench) were eventually to occupy Deaneries, and Trench the Archbishopric of Dublin; John Kemble was to produce the first English edition of *Beowulf*; James Spedding was to devote himself to the editing of the works of Bacon, and Milnes was to become the first editor and biographer of Keats. Alford, Kemble, Milnes, Spedding, Sterling and Trench (as well as Hallam and Tennyson) were to publish poetry, but if the Apostles can thus be seen as a nest of singing birds, it has to be admitted that their songs were not always memorable ones, and it is ironic that their most significant poet turned out to be insignificant as an Apostle. The society was not Alfred Tennyson's natural *milieu* at all. Where Hallam flourished in metaphysical speculation and debate, Tennyson was tongue-tied, his natural conversational manner being hesitant to the point of gruffness. He was never at home when writing prose, being, for example, a notoriously reluctant letter writer. It is hardly surprising that when his term came to read a paper (he chose the subject of 'Ghosts') his nervousness of public performance caused him to tear up his effort before it was read. He subsequently resigned, though his presence was more than tolerated and he continued to be treated as the Apostles' pet genius. Indeed it has been suggested that one of the reasons for his life-long hypersensitivity to criticism was the result of the adulation in which he was held at this time.

The best guide there is to Hallam's state of mind during the autumn term of 1829 comes in a letter which he wrote to Robert Robertson in

December. The fact that this letter was written in reply to one which Robertson had sent Hallam as long ago as 20 October indicates that the term had been a busy one. Hallam was obviously happier: 'This odious place has been less odious to me this term than before, yet I fear I have purchased my increase of pleasurable excitement by a diminution of thoughtful habits and energies . . . A little metaphysics – a little modern poetry rather less ancient, and a minimum of mathematics have passed into my mind since I last wrote.' It is also noticeable that the Hallam who had seemed aloof and friendless in his first year at Cambridge now seems to be positively revelling in friendship, giving Robertson character sketches of Milnes, Leighton ('who within the first half hour will kill you dead with laughing at his jokes'), Tennant, Monteith and Garden, quite apart from Tennyson and his 'beautiful poem, which was this year dishonoured by a Cambridge prize'.[19]

Hallam is much clearer about what his own priorities have become and there is little sense of guilt in his admitting to having been enjoying himself at the expense of his academic work. He is also more confident about standing up to his father. A letter from early in the term showed that the skirmishes between Henry and Arthur had continued with neither side making any concessions. In this letter Arthur informs Henry of what texts he has been reading (Theocritus and Aristophanes, much preferring the former) but he promptly moves on to a defence of his own interests which is assertive in tone, almost to the point of petulance: 'I am sorry you should think my fondness for modern poetry so excessive as to militate against correctness of general views, or the formation of other literary tastes . . . I shall hardly be persuaded to think I have done wrong in feeding myself with Wordsworth or Shelley. "Misty metaphysics" is soon said; but that phrase in my opinion will apply with far more distinct, & weighty meaning to the works of Lord Byron, than to those of his great contemporaries'.[20]

Immersion in the world of the Apostles and encountering Tennyson again for the first time since May, meant that Hallam's interest in poetry was now more than a matter of vague preference. The autumn term of 1829 was the one in which he most firmly nailed his poetical colours to the mast, and started out on the first of those acts of literary entrepreneurship which would characterise the rest of his life. 'Percy Bysshe' had now been restored to the pantheon after his demotion twelve months before and was granted equality with Wordsworth and Coleridge. The air was full of the discussion of modern poetry. On 8 November Hallam spoke, albeit briefly, at the Union on the question: 'Is Wordsworth or Lord Byron greater poet?'. His fellow speakers were Milnes and Blakesley. Hallam had the always stimulating experience of being defeated (50 votes to 23) and as James Pope-Hennessy writes 'this was merely the opening battle of a long campaign',[21] and Hallam, though in a minority was nonetheless in good company. Julius Hare thought the vote for Byron too large because there was not a sufficient number of men in the house worthy to be called Wordsworthians, though Milnes wrote to his mother that 'Our debate . . . went off very ill. I spoke for an hour and twenty minutes – they tell me, very fluently . . . Hallam spoke well, but shortly; he would be a splendid speaker if he had more nerve'. But Hallam was not an enthusiast for the Union style of debating and he admitted afterwards that he had spoken 'merely to oblige Milnes.'[22]

Even more significant combats were in the offing. After the Apostolic debate on 'Whether the poems of Shelley have an immoral tendency', Hallam and his friends, so to speak, took Shelley on the road. It seems likely that the Oxford versus Cambridge debate which took place in Oxford on 26 November had been hatched when Gladstone was staying with Hallam at Malvern in the summer. Hallam, along with Milnes and Thomas Sunderland, took the coach to Oxford on a snowy day to argue the case for Shelley's superiority to Byron. This debate became the stuff of legend and was much recalled by its participants in later years. One of these participants was the future Cardinal Manning, then an undergraduate at Balliol College, with a high reputation as a debater, who reminisced nearly forty years later that 'We Oxford men were precise, orderly, and morbidly afraid of excess in word or manner. The Cambridge oratory came in like a flood into a mill-pond. Both Monckton Milnes and Arthur Hallam took us aback by the boldness and freedom of their manner. But I remember the effect of Sunderland's declamation and action to this day. It had never been seen or heard before among us: we cowered like birds and ran like sheep.'[23] Milnes was characteristically more *insouciant* about the whole business, seeing it, rather like his ascent in the hot air balloon, as yet another adventure. He liked to say that he been granted permission to be away from Cambridge by Christopher Wordsworth largely because he had intimated that he was going to Oxford to speak in defence of the poetry of his brother William. He also claimed that the Oxonians were so ignorant of Shelley that he had made up some of the quotations he used and indeed it is quite likely that he had substituted some extracts from Tennyson. Milnes was also the source of the attractive but probably apocryphal story that the Oxonians had been under the misapprehension that the Cambridge party had come over to defend the claims of Shenstone, causing one undergraduate to assert that the only line from the poet that he could call to mind was: 'My banks are well furnished with bees'.[24]

Hallam and his friends were, perhaps inevitably, yet again defeated, by 90 votes to 33 (a very large turnout), though neither party seemed unduly concerned by the voting as 'Both . . . cheered loudly, as both were quite satisified with the result'.[25] If the Oxonians were impressed by the quality of the Cambridge oratory, the Cambridge group granted that the Oxford Union itself was superior to their own. Even though Milnes thought that their speaking was 'wretched', he noted with approval 'The contrast from our long, noisy, shuffling, scraping, talking, vulgar, ridiculous-looking kind of assembly, to a neat little square room with eighty or ninety young gentlemen sprucely dressed.' He was also impressed by the performance of Gladstone, 'The man that *took* me the most . . . I am sure a very superior person.'[26] It was agreed that, of the Cambridge speakers, Hallam had performed most successfully, a fact that Milnes attributed to Hallam's being among friends, not only Gladstone, but Doyle and Gaskell as well.

Despite their differences of character, Hallam and Milnes were on close personal terms at this time, though Hallam was not above, in the sonnet which he had written to him the previous summer, exhorting his friend to take life more seriously:

> Enough of flickering mirth, and random life!
>   Yearnings are in thee for a lofty doom:
>   Trample that mask; a sterner port assume,
> Whether thou championest th'Uranian strife,
>   Or marked by freedom for her toged array,
>   Reclaim'st thy father's soon abandoned bay.[27]

Hallam's other companion in the debating match was a man of a very different kind. Hallam had been much taken by Thomas Sunderland's performances at the Union during his first term at Trinity, just as Manning was when he heard him in Oxford. Although Sunderland made more than 35 speeches at the Cambridge Union between 1826 and 1831 and had been elected to the Apostles in his first term at Trinity, his presence among them was a divisive one. He was supercilious and demanding and he clearly thought Milnes was a lightweight. Milnes, whilst appreciating Sunderland's gifts as an orator, disliked him intensely: 'he is a man whom I cd. Never make a friend of . . . His self-conceit & contempt of all others except the oligarchy of his momentary admiration, will stand in his way.'[28] He was the subject of Tennyson's poem *A Character*, where he receives significantly short shrift:

> Most delicately hour by hour
> He canvassed human mysteries,
> And trod on silk, as if the winds
> Blew his own praises in his eyes,
> And stood aloof from other minds
> In impotence of fancied power.[29]

Sunderland provides a telling insight into the hothouse atmosphere surrounding the Apostolic set in Cambridge at this time. Shortly after he left the university he started to suffer from delusions. Whilst on holiday in Switzerland he threw overboard a boatman on Lake Geneva whom he believed was being paid by the British government to spy on him, and subsequently imagined himself to be an illegitimate son of the Duke of York. He was unable to pursue the promising career that seemed to lie before him and Milnes's biographer claims that the Apostles 'never heard of him again' until 'a brief announcement of his death' at the age of 39 appeared in *The Times* in 1867.[30]

It is at this time that Hallam's life acquired the momentum which would henceforth define it. Quite suddenly he had become very busy – largely in the service of literature – and he would remain so for the rest of his time at Cambridge and after. The autumn of 1829 witnessed another, and a more significant, publishing venture.

Sometime during his Italian travels of two years previously, Hallam had acquired a copy of Shelley's poem *Adonais*. Exactly how he came by it is not certain, but it was believed that he had found it in Rome. As its original place of publication had been Pisa, which Hallam had also visited, it is equally possible that he had found it there. Strange as it may now seem, there was no text of *Adonais* easily available in England at that time. Shelley had originally had the poem printed when he was living in Pisa in 1821, and, though he had made efforts to have a version printed in England also, this version had sold very badly (probably fewer than 100 copies) and had received only three reviews, of which two were highly critical (the third, by Leigh Hunt, was more enthusiastic). The ignorance of Shelley reputedly shown by the Oxford students is less surprising when it is remembered that copies of Shelley's poems were very hard to come by in England. Galignani had just published in Paris a collection of poems by Coleridge, Shelley and Keats ('which are now for the first time given to the public'), but anyone else who wished to read Shelley in England in the 1820s had to do so in pirated editions, of which two were published by William Benbow in 1826. A copy of one of the Benbow editions had been given to the fourteen year-old Robert Browning, who, never having heard of Shelley before, was instantly overwhelmed and consequently renounced God and the eating of meat for a time. Hallam's reactions were more measured, but it is easy to see why Henry Hallam would look askance at Arthur's enthusiasm for Shelley, who was far from respectable: atheist, adulterer, republican, and only available in underground editions.

Hallam and Milnes arranged (and presumably paid) for 500 copies of *Adonais* to be 'Printed By W. Metcalfe And sold by Mssrs. Gee and Bridges, Market-Hill', as a pamphlet with a green paper cover. The title page goes on to inform the reader that 'The present edition is an exact reprint (a few typographical errors only being corrected) of the first edition of the "Adonais" – dated Pisa, with the types of Didot, MDCC-CXXI.' In fact, the text which Hallam and Milnes produced differs from the Pisa edition more than this comment suggests, though Milnes in old age claimed that he could not remember exactly who had been responsible for the editing.[31] There are no records of how the poem sold, though the claim has been made that this edition 'was chiefly responsible for the first general enthusiasm over Shelley' in England.[32] It is interesting that the one copy which survives bears the inscription 'to S. Rogers Esq. With Mr. A. Hallam's compliments'. Rogers was well-chosen as a recipient, being not only a member of Hallam's father's circle, but one who had in his youth been a friend of Byron and was considerably more sympathetic to modern poetry than Henry Hallam was.

Towards the end of the term Hallam took Charles and Alfred Tennyson to London, where he introduced them to some of his Eton friends, including Francis Doyle, who claimed to find Alfred Tennyson likeable but odd. Hallam managed somehow to pick up James Milnes Gaskell on the way, who accompanied them back to Cambridge to hear a Union debate about Milton, but Doyle remained in London and in consequence 'received a severe row from the Heroic Hallam which I cared very little about'.[33] Gaskell remained in Cambridge for three days, and left on 19 December when Hallam and Tennyson departed homewards also.

It is necessary to examine the events of the Christmas period 1829 with some care, as it has long been thought that this was when Hallam made his first visit to Somersby and met Emily Tennyson. As Jack Kolb points out,[34] if Hallam left Cambridge for London on 19 December, there would have been precious little time for him to have made a round trip to Lincolnshire before Christmas, and as he had been in Tennyson's company right up to the point of his departure, there would have been little reason either. A letter to Milnes written early in the new year, full of details about mutual friends whom Hallam has recently encountered, makes no reference to Tennyson or to Somersby. Hallam's own subsequent references in letters to Emily about the length of time he had known her seem to point to their first having met the following April.

Hallam in fact enjoyed an extremely sociable Christmas in London, followed by a visit with his father to Lord Lansdowne's country seat at Bowood in early January. The details of this visit are not recorded: Hallam informed Milnes that he had 'sundry things to say'[35] on the subject, but that they could wait until they met. Bowood was described as 'the most finished or (to borrow the French expression) best-mounted house in Europe'.[36] It was home to a very fine collection of paintings and Lansdowne himself was a notably gracious and attentive host who 'took care that all should share in the conversation . . . He talked delightfully, and he listened as well as he talked'.[37] It is a pity that Arthur left no account of this occasion. It was not the first time that he had accompanied his father to a distinguished dinner table, though the fact that he had been included in Lord Lansdowne's invitation shows that, socially, he had come of age.

J. W. Blakesley reported to Tennyson that their friend had been 'submitting himself to the influences of the outer world more than (I think) a man of his genius ought to do'.[38] Hallam had been doing a great deal of theatre-going and had been much taken by the actress Fanny Kemble, sister of his Cambridge friend John Kemble. Although far from being a belle, Fanny Kemble was enjoying a reputation as a celebrity and a pin-up girl. Her debut, as Juliet at the Covent Garden Theatre, had taken place only the previous October.[39] Hallam became caught up in the general enthusiasm for 'the divine Fanny', as he called her, seeing her not only as Juliet, but also, in Doyle's company, as Belvidera in *Venice Preserv'd*. Doyle complained that Hallam could not keep his eyes off Miss Kemble, was unwilling to surrender his opera glass, and 'went raving home to write two sonnets about her.'[40] The two sonnets would seem to be *To An Admired Lady*, and 'How is't for every glance of thine I find'. The feeling of worship – from – a-distance recalls *A Farewell to the South*:

> Who in my Sais-temple wast a light
> Behind all veils of thought, and fantasy,
> A dim yet beautiful Idea of one
> Perfect in womanhood, in Love alone,
> Making the earth golden with hope and joy?
> And now thou com'st embodied to destroy
> My grief with earnest eyes and music tone.[41]

Both Hallam's editor, Motter, and Sir Charles Tennyson believed that this sonnet had been written to Emily Tennyson, which caused Charles Tennyson to conclude that 'that winter saw the final extinction of his passion for Anna [Wintour]'.[42] This was not, in fact, yet the case. Hallam was still blissfully unaware of the existence of Emily Tennyson; he continued in his own way to feel possessive about Anna, and was disappointed when, having understood that the Wintours might be returning to live somewhere near Cambridge, he discovered that they were not and that he would therefore have 'no hope of renewing our intercourse'.[43] Writing to Gaskell in March 1830, he could still not let the matter of Anna drop: 'I have little to boast of in the way of moral firmness; yet were I again to see her, live near her, often converse with her, the effects on my mind might, for all I know, be as strong and vivid as on your own.'[44]

March 1830 saw Hallam's enthusiasm for the theatre take a new turn. On the 19th of that month the 'Cambridge Amateur Dramatic Club', mounted a production of *Much Ado About Nothing*, largely conceived by Milnes, who presumably saw it as his Cambridge swan-song before he left the university the following month. Not only did Milnes act as stage manager and produce an epilogue, he also played 'a somewhat portly Beatrice and, as he delivered the words, "He is no less a stuffed man, but for the stuffing – well, we are all mortal," fell through his couch to the floor of the stage, and before he was buried beneath his petticoats uttered an ejaculation entirely out of keeping with the character he was playing.'[45] Hallam found his level as Verges to Kemble's Dogberry, and Robert Tennant reported that the whole thing had caused him to fear that his companions in the audience 'would have died with most wicked laughter.' It is more than likely that, in the traditions of student drama produced for domestic consumption, the laughter resulted largely from the actors' ineptitude, though the occasion yet again illustrates that Hallam's undergraduate life was not all Apostolic solemnity. Even so, Milnes's epilogue was Apostolic in so far as it had its own expectations of the cast members' posthumous celebrity:

> But, ere our artless pageant disappear,
> We ask one boon – if in some after – year
> In evening hours your eye should chance to light
> On any name you recognised tonight –
> On some brief record of their mortal lot –
> Married, or murdered, ruined, or what not? –
> While natural thought returns upon its track,
> Just pause and murmur ere you call it back,
> With pleasant memory, sipping your liqueur –
> 'Yes, yes, he was a Cambridge Amateur.'[46]

Hallam's involvement with Tennyson and his family was growing during the first half of 1830, though to begin with the involvement was purely literary. The year 1830 was a notable one for the production of slim volumes of verse. In March, Charles Tennyson published a collection called *Sonnets and Fugitive Pieces* which, according to his namesake's biography of Alfred, 'was not a very striking production and did not receive much notice elsewhere than at Cambridge.'[47] It is difficult not to think that, in planning to publish a joint volume with Hallam, Tennyson had rejected the notion of a second cooperative effort with his elder brother in favour of someone whose work he thought superior, even though Tennyson in later life was to insist that he did not think of Hallam primarily as a poet.

In the event, however, Tennyson's *Poems Chiefly Lyrical* was published by Effingham Wilson in June without any contributions from Hallam. Throughout the spring, the two young poets had worked on the joint volume: the poems had been selected, proofs printed and a preface written. Tennyson was surprised and disappointed when, at the beginning of the summer term, Hallam announced that he was pulling out of the project. Whether Hallam explained his true reasons for this to Tennyson at the time is not known. He subsequently wrote to Tennyson's mother of 'the growing conviction of the exceeding crudeness of style, and in parts morbidness of feeling, which characterised all my earlier attempts'.[48] This made it sound as if the decision not to publish had been entirely his own, but it is very clear that the main reason he withdrew from the joint project was that his father had forbidden it, Henry's view being that the poems were 'unfit even for the limited circulation they might obtain, on account of their unveiling more of emotion than, consistently with what is due to him and to others, could be exposed to view.'[49]

Harsh and sudden as Henry's intervention might seem, it is not difficult to follow his reasoning. The longest poem in the collection describes the experience of a Dante-besotted adolescent falling in love in Rome with a woman six years older than himself. Despite his lack of sympathy with modern poetry, Henry cannot entirely be blamed for seeking to suppress what must to him have seemed no more than a lengthy exhibition of adolescent self-indulgence. Although the Hallam family's long-lasting squeamishness about publishing anything which related to Anna Wintour might seem excessive, it would have been plain to any reader of his son's love poems that Arthur and Anna were not, and could never be, Dante and Beatrice, or anything approaching them. The poems which Arthur had written to date had been almost uniformly poems of self-revelation and, for all their fluency and resource, they were often blatantly immature. It is easy to see Henry Hallam's wilful obstructiveness as yet another stage in the on-going battle to deflect Arthur from what he saw as his own chosen path, but we must also acknowledge the wisdom of the stand which he took. Arthur, of course, responded to his father's intervention in characteristic fashion: he ignored it as best he could, and had his poems printed privately in May, a few weeks before Alfred Tennyson's volume appeared.

If Hallam put on a bold face in response to his father's discouragement, it must have been in the growing knowledge that, in terms of joint production, he and Tennyson were not equal partners. The British Library copy of Hallam's volume runs to 168 numbered pages, though the original version was said to contain 174, which would have included advertisements and additional endpapers. It contains no title page, though a later handwritten note in the flyleaf says that there are copies containing the half-title: 'Poems by A.H.Hallam, Esq.' 'Printed by Littlewood & Co.'[50] This, it must be emphasised, like Tennyson's 1827 *Poems by Two Brothers*, was a printing rather than a publishing venture, so circulation was never going to be wide. Twelve copies of the book are known to have existed, but there were probably more and it is likely that further copies were distributed after Hallam's death. The first poem which the reader encounters is *A Farewell to the South*, which runs to 40 pages. This is followed by six *Meditative Fragments* (a collective title for a number of poems written in 1828–9) which occupy a further 20 pages. *Timbuctoo* comes next which runs to 14 pages. Hence the initial impression given is of substantial work. Altogether there are 49 poems, including seven sonnets in Italian and three translations from Schiller.

In terms of quantity, Hallam's contribution would have been much the same as Tennyson's, whose volume runs to slightly fewer pages but contains more poems. When Hallam sent a copy of his book to William Bodham Donne, he said that he also hoped to send him, as soon as it was available, the volume by Tennyson 'whose genius, I do not doubt, you will admire as fervently as we do. Friendship certainly plays sad pranks with one's judgement in these matters; yet I think if I hated Alfred Tennyson as much as I love him, I could hardly help revering his imagination with just the same reverence . . . Charles, though he burns and shines, is a lesser light than Alfred.'[51]

Like Hallam, Tennyson quickly grew dissatisfied with some of the poems in the collection, which he did not subsequently reprint, and it must be confessed that a number of them are undeniably trivial. It is not hard to see how some of the more lightweight and fanciful of the poems could contribute to the reputation which Tennyson gained for 'effeminacy' among his early reviewers. Even Tennyson's own friends in the years to come would urge him to engage with what they saw as larger, more significant subjects. In comparison with some of the poems which appeared only two years later, in 1832, we are aware of a Tennyson not yet at the height of his powers. Nevertheless, the collection does contain his earliest canonical poems: *Mariana* and *The Kraken,* along with *The Dying Swan, The Owl* and *A Spirit Haunts the year's last hours.* The two most substantial poems are *Supposed Confessions of a Secondrate Sensitive Mind Not In Unity With Itself* and *Recollections of the Arabian Nights.* Of the two poets, Hallam sometimes seems the more outwardly ambitious. It could be argued that the scope of his work at this time was greater. But he is the more derivative of the two, where Tennyson is more obviously experimental. There are imaginative limitations in Hallam: his poems are almost uniformly self-centred, and can make little sense if the reader does not understand the immediate circumstances from which they arose. Hallam's poems rarely move beyond those bourns of time and place which Tennyson's generally transcend, not only by a considerable power of observation, but by an ability to appropriate and modify other voices, narratives and mythologies: to take imaginative flight, in fact.

It says something for his literary judgement, and even more for Hallam's magnanimity, that he was as aware as anyone of the difference between himself and Tennyson as he made clear to Mrs. Tennyson: 'He [Tennyson] is a true and thorough Poet, if ever there was one; and though I fear his book is far too good to be popular, yet I have full faith that he has thrown out sparks that will kindle somewhere . . . No labour on my part shall be wanting to bring his volume into general notice'.[52] In the matter of attempting to further Tennyson's reputation, Hallam was to prove as good as his word, though his caveat about the likely limits of the poetry's popularity was a shrewd one. The audience for published verse was at this time small, and the fact that Tennyson still owed Effingham Wilson £11 three years later suggests that not too many copies of his book had been sold.[53]

Most people's knowledge of Hallam derives from reading *In Memoriam,* a poem which necessarily focuses on the relationship between

Hallam and its author. It is consequently very easy to forget that Hallam's involvement with the Tennyson family increasingly centred on Emily rather than on Alfred. The many letters which from this time onwards he wrote to Emily, as well as the poems which he wrote to and about her, reveal that she was absolutely central to his affections in the way that nobody else in his life ever was. Indeed, his love for her, and the emotional and practical complications which resulted from it, henceforth figure as prominently in the narrative of his life as his literary activities do.

It all began in April 1830, when Hallam was invited to Somersby for the first time.

Despite the difficulties of life at Somersby, and the highly overcrowded Rectory (Tennyson's father had once claimed that 23 people slept there each night, including servants), Alfred obviously felt confident enough to invite his sophisticated London friend to stay during the Easter vacation, though the fact that Dr. Tennyson was abroad must have made the decision easier. It was an inspired one. Hallam was entranced, and fell in love with Somersby at first sight, just as, one of the Tennyson sisters later said, Somersby fell in love with him. Hallam wrote to J.W. Blakesley (who was in Cambridge) on 13 April: 'my life here has been one of so much excitement . . . If I die I hope to be buried here: for never in my life, I think, have I loved a place more. I feel a new element of being within me . . . I have floated along on a delicious dream of music and poetry and riding and dancing and greenwood-dinners and ladies' conversation till I have been simply exhaled into Paradise . . . I shall return [to Cambridge] about the beginning of next week, and expect to be very miserable all next term.'[54]

Although Somersby was by any standards remote, it was, and is, a delightful spot, especially when enjoying fine spring weather as it did while Hallam was there. The Rectory was actually a large private house. It was owned not by the Church of England but by the Burton family who lived next door to it in Somersby Grange, an even more imposing eighteenth century Vanbrughesque building. To the south of the Rectory were Holywell Wood, and the brook celebrated by Tennyson in more than one of his poems. By Lincolnshire standards the village of Somersby stands high, its position on the Wolds affording wide views across the fields to the coast. Although it was by no means a large place, its population was three or four times what it is today, and the village possessed its own school, bath house and constable.[55] To Hallam, its association with Emily inevitably compounded its attractiveness, as he made clear in the poem which he wrote about it (despite his noting that he thought the poem seemed 'rather a mistake'):

Dear village home of her who is to me
    As the life current of my eddying thought;
    Calm to all toil, sunset of every doubt,
    Yet source of many an anxious agony:

Elms, full with voice of stately winged rooks,
  Slim cherry trees wall propped for lack of power,
  And you, ye blackthorns with your jubilant flower
  Silvering for her the green of quiet nooks –
Old Church where I have knelt beside my love,
  And watched her face of prayer; old curious cross,
  That from the porch no ill hand dares remove,
Tho' time hath spoiled its beauty – I your loss
  Parting deplore, but ye joy on, and ever
  Feed with still influxes her being's river.[56]

To one as susceptible as Hallam, the 'ladies' conversation' clearly added much to the charms of country existence at Somersby and this Easter holiday proved immensely significant for the emotional lives of both Hallam and Tennyson. Although Hallam was vague about when his attraction to Emily Tennyson seriously began, it is certain that the planet of love was on high at Somersby during the three weeks which Hallam spent there in April 1830. Hallam reminded Emily later of encountering her walking in Holywell Wood: 'I came to a wooded glen among wolds, where I saw a being more like Undine than I had ever thought to see.'[57] Other house guests at this time included two sisters, Emily and Anne Sellwood, daughters of a solicitor in the neighbouring town of Horncastle. On another walk through the enchanted wood, Hallam was with Emily Sellwood when Tennyson, wearing a long blue cloak, came upon them and asked her: 'Are you a dryad or a Naiad or what are you?' Tennyson's subsequent courtship of Emily Sellwood was a fraught one, and their marriage did not take place for another twenty years, but it is a significant fact that Tennyson and Hallam met their fiancées at the same time and in the same place, and, it appears, addressed them in much the same words. Sixty-five years later Emily Sellwood (then Lady Tennyson) remembered playing 'The Emperor of Morocco is Dead' and that 'Arthur Hallam was pleased with me because I went through the trying story between my two big candles with so much gravity.' Anne Sellwood made pencil sketches of Hallam and Tennyson, and Tennyson kept the Hallam sketch on his mantelpiece for the rest of his life.[58] The fact that Emily also knew and liked Hallam goes a long way to explain why the first time that Tennyson visited Hallam's grave in Clevedon was when he and Emily were in the West Country on their honeymoon.

Hallam clearly found these three weeks emotionally exhilarating in every way. His friendship with Alfred had been enhanced by the presence of Alfred's extremely attractive sister, and by the local landscape, which seemed, even to one as widely travelled as Hallam, an enchanting contrast to London. He was stimulated to verse, completing during the months of April and May almost twenty sonnets. These sonnets are dominated by Emily and many of them are addressed directly to her. It is no exaggeration to say that they are the best poetry Hallam had written so far. It is an interesting, almost paradoxical, coincidence that these poems should have been composed at almost the same time that the slim volume of *Poems* appeared, for they far surpass the latter's contents in quality. The intensity and directness with which Hallam expressed his love for Emily provides the neatest illustration of why Henry had been disparaging about the poems previously addressed to Anna Wintour. Whilst Hallam's repeated use of the sonnet form might seem unambitious, there is no doubt that it gives a force and precision to his writing which marks a considerable advance on the formlessness of many of the 1830 *Poems*, and in due course Henry Hallam was to have no qualms in letting several of these sonnets (though by no means all of them) see the light of day when he came to print the *Remains*. Hallam's own manuscript notebook divides them into two groups: *Somersby Sonnets*, dated April, 1830 and *Sonnets Written After My Return from Somersby* from the following month.[59]

The sonnets do not form a sequence in the Elizabethan or Dantean sense, in that they are not bound together by any underlying narrative structure. Rather, they chart individual real-life moments in a developing relationship. It is unlikely that Emily was aware of the sonnets' existence during Hallam's lifetime, but she did subsequently make copies of many them, probably late in 1834.[60] She would have found them poignant, if not tragic reading, as it is still possible to do:

> Oh Emily, my life, my love, my rest,
>   Thy look is on me, and my soul is blest.
> How strange it seems but a few weeks agone
>   I knew no glance of thine and thought of thee
>   Dim in the distance with no hope or fear[61]

Emily was now effectively Hallam's muse, and one of the consequences of his poetic engagement with her was an increasing assurance in his handling of the sonnet form. He was also able to modify the sense of brute egocentricity which had made some of his earlier poems seem gauche. Although Hallam seldom eschews the narrating 'I' altogether (he was probably incapable of it), Emily challenges and stimulates him into a more resourceful language and a parallel reduction in adolescent solipsism. Emily herself, for example, becomes a real presence in the Somersby poems ('the full music streams/rise from her lips to linger on her face):

> Why throbbest thou, my heart, why thickly breathest?
>   I ask no rich and splendid eloquence:
> A few words of the warmest and the sweetest
>   Sure thou mayst yield without such coy pretence:
> Open the chamber, where affection's voice
>   For rare occasions is kept close and fine:

Bid it but say, "sweet Emily be mine,"
   So for one boldness thou shalt aye rejoice.
Fain would I speak when the full music-streams
   Rise from her lips to linger on her face,
Or like a form, floating thro' Rafaelle's dreams,
   Then fixed by him in everliving grace,
   She sits i' th' silent worship of mine eyes.
Courage, my heart: change thou for words thy sighs.[62]

The reference to Raphael in this poem (just as the references elsewhere to Dante and Petrarch) reminds the reader that Hallam still tended to apprehend life through art; that his perceptions were coloured by the Italian culture in which he was so fully immersed (and which itself consciously idealised the female as Hallam does in these sonnets). But there is a real confessional intimacy here, which is also reflected in the poem 'Still here – thou hast not faded from my sight' and, more revealingly, in 'Speed ye warm hours' which shows a particular sensitivity to time and place, fusing Emily with her own natural surroundings:

Speed ye, warm hours, along the' appointed path,
   Speed, though ye bring but pain, slow pain to me;
I will not much bemoan your heavy wrath,
   So ye will make my lady glad and free.
What is't that I must here confined be,
   If she may roam the summer's sweets among,
See the full-cupped flower, the laden tree,
   Hear from deep groves the thousand-voiced song?
Sometimes in that still chamber will she sit
   Trim ranged with books, and cool with dusky blinds
That keep the moon out, there, as seemeth fit,
   To sing, or play, or read – what sweet hope finds
Way to my heart? perchance some verse of mine –
Oh happy I: Speed on, ye hours divine![63]

The occasionally (and consciously) mannered language of this poem ('My lady'; 'that I must here confined be'), does not detract from its real power as a love poem and its delicate capturing of Emily 'ranged with books and cool with dusky blinds'. Hallam's experiences at Somersby produced a more careful perception of detail: a heightened responsiveness to the particularly charged moment. The full-cupped flower, the laden tree and the deep groves would not have been such easy and unobtrusive presences in the poems of the 1830 volume.

Emily's influence on Hallam's poetry was important in two almost contradictory ways. Not only did she provide him with a real and developing subject, but she also domesticated his poetry, removing it from a desire to make big gestures and to strive for more self-consciously 'significant' themes. Her presence in the poems checks Hallam's tendency to discursiveness, which weakens and obscures *Meditative Fragments, A Farewell to the South* and, especially, *Timbuctoo*. Nor is it fanciful to suggest that Hallam's ability to handle emotion with more sensitivity and to register a more immediate reaction to the natural world was the consequence of his, by now, considerable familiarity with the writings of Alfred Tennyson. Literary history has long concluded that Hallam had a considerable influence on Tennyson; that an influence could pass in the opposite direction also needs to be acknowledged.

The positive Tennysonian influence which produced the ability to settle on particularities of time and place and to draw out the essentials of the momentary experience can be seen in the sonnet 'Lady, I bid thee to a sunny dome', the prompting for which was Hallam's encouragement of Emily's studies in Italian language and literature. Tennyson was subsequently to mention either this or a similar occasion in *In Memoriam,* when he speaks of Hallam, at Somersby, reading 'the Tuscan poets on the lawn'.[64] In this poem Hallam extends and explores that moment, celebrating his vision of Italy, which becomes the more wonderful when he can share it with 'An English maiden and an English wife':

Lady, I bid thee to a sunny dome
   Ringing with echoes of Italian song:
   Henceforth to thee these magic halls belong,
And all the pleasant place is like a home.
Hark, on the right with full piano tone,
   Old Dante's voice encircles all the air:
   Hark yet again, like flute-tones mingling rare,
Comes the keen sweetness of Petrarca's moan.
Pass thou the lintel freely: without fear
   Feast on the music; I do better know thee,
   Than to suspect this pleasure thou dost owe me
Will wrong thy gentle spirit, or make less dear
   That element, whence thou must draw thy life; –
   An English maiden and an English wife.[65]

But Hallam's poems of this period are not exclusively devoted to the subject of his love for Emily. 'The Garden trees are busy with the shower' is an interesting poem in that it seems to have been written in response to a challenge from Tennyson, who provided its opening words (in quotation marks below) and bade Hallam to complete the poem.[66] If this poem is compared with *To Poesy* Hallam and Tennyson's only other acknowledged collaboration (in 1828) it is easy to see how far both poets had travelled technically in the intervening years:

'The garden trees are busy with the shower
  That fell ere sunset'; now methinks they talk,
Lowly and sweetly as befits the hour,
  One to another down the grassy walk.
Hark the laburnum from his opening flower
  This cherry creeper greets in whisper light,
  While the grim fir, rejoicing in the night,
Hoarse mutters to the murmuring sycamore.
What shall I deem their converse? Would they hail
The wild gray light that fronts yon massive cloud,
  Or the half bow rising like pillared fire?
  Or are they sighing faintly for desire
That with May dawn their leaves may be overflowed,
And dews about their feet may never fail.[67]

This poem offers a detailed description of a natural scene, a genre much beloved of nineteenth-century poets, much of whose work it is worthy to stand beside. The poem has a self-sufficiency which it took Hallam a long time to achieve. It requires no autobiographical gloss to make it comprehensible. Despite or because of Tennyson's contribution to it, it has a strong claim to be the best poem which Hallam wrote and it is ironic that Hallam should shortly afterwards have renounced the writing of poetry at the very time when he was doing it most successfully.

Back in Cambridge for the summer term, Hallam (with no obvious sign of the misery which he predicted) had the pleasure of seeing first his own and then Tennyson's poems appear. One of the friends to whom Hallam sent a copy of his volume was Gladstone. His generosity was to have unexpected results. Gladstone, as might be expected, duly replied to Hallam to thank him for the gift, though the letter clearly caused him considerable pain to write. Gladstone noted in his diary that he 'wrote and wrote over a letter to Hallam',[68] and the surviving letter certainly bears many marks of having been 'written over'. The number of cancellations which the text contains, as well as its postscript, seem to suggest that Gladstone was in a state of acute embarrassment and uncertainty about what exactly he felt he ought to say to Hallam. The letter starts conventionally enough by thanking him for his gift, 'a book in which there is so much to admire: and what is more than that, in which there is so much to instruct and elevate . . . I am more particularly delighted with the development of your "imperial truth" and your views of Nature in all its parts and all its laws as the mirror of man'.

Then follows a very halting paragraph in which the bulk of the 'writing over' occurs to the point where it seriously affects the letter's coherence. (Brackets indicate cancellations).

'With reference to writing I do not know what to say. Perhaps I had better not speak at all, for believe me I have neither the intention nor desire to give you the smallest pain:<Only this>Pity<sacrifice>alone <to self> will I <make> sacrifice to self much-do not suppose <me> that I am silent because <I am> indifferent.'

He then quotes in a rather garbled fashion, four lines, as if from one poem, though actually comprising two lines from Hallam's *Meditative Fragments II* followed by a further two from *On My Sister's Birthday* (both poems, of course, being in the collection):

"For as I gaze old visions of delight
That died with th'hour their parent
There [sic] mind is now on loves grown cold
On friendships falling slowly away

It seems as if Gladstone, despite Hallam's gesture of friendship, can only see this friendship as a thing of the past, and himself as no longer a fit recipient of Hallam's affection. The long-standing sense of his own inferiority is now something which Gladstone, out of both sorrow and anger, cannot repress, though he is aware that giving expression to it might seem to go beyond the bounds of tact. He was presumably not blind to the implication, in the sonnet addressed to Alfred Tennyson, that he, Gladstone, the 'one perfect gem' of the poet's 'early spring' had been superseded:

'I . . . beg you not to communicate to me heights & depths to which I am unequal, nor to enter into commerce when there is nothing to return: for this I have the smallest <grain> title to expect: but in any hour when the sunshine of your soul is dimmed and even the poorest may offer something, then to remember me . . . if ever you should be reduced to such destitution as to have need of intercourse with such as me, not to shun it because the interval has been long and the heart grows cold in spite of itself and its long but unaided strivings. Be assured that I do indeed and from the bottom of my soul believe I have no right to complain of the cessation of intercourse: None: I never had a right to the enjoyment of it: that was a gift, unmerited, <and> perhaps unappreciated . . . May God bless you with light the highest of all blessings save one: and may he crown it with that one-love.' To which a postscript then reads: 'Whether I have written wisely or not, I cannot tell: I have written truly.

'That I much regret not having heard from you it would be vain to deny: at the same time let me assure you that I do not conceive I ever was properly qualified for intercourse with you – therefore it was not my legitimate passion – therefore I have no right to desire its restitution . . . my ardent hope [is..] that <..if> any day shall come to dim the Sunshine of your intel-

lect and heart, you will remember me as one desirous according to his
ability of being your friend. Meantime May God bless you.'[69]

Hallam wrote back to Gladstone by return. In comparison with
Gladstone he sounds in control of the situation, despite the shock which
the letter must have occasioned:

'I am somewhat surprised, but more grieved, that you should consider the
state of our intercourse requires the tone you have taken. I have always
found you a true friend, and have always wished to prove the same to
you. Never, since the time when I first knew you, have I ceased to love &
respect your character . . . Never, most assuredly . . . will I arrogate to
myself "a level" above the interchange of human sympathies, on any
fancied ground of intellectual superiority. I am utterly unworthy of the
admiring sentiments you express; every day brings me stronger evidence
of my own weakness & hollowness . . . Circumstance, my dear Gladstone,
has indeed separated our paths, but it never can do away with what has
been. The stamp of each of our minds is on the other . . . such intercourse
as we had at Eton is not likely again to fall to our lot, this is undoubtedly
a stern truth. But if you intimate that I have ceased, or may cease to
interest myself in your happiness, indeed, Gladstone, you are mistaken,
however culpably I may have behaved in neglecting to give you an
outward sign of it by letterwriting.'

Hallam then goes on to raise three other points. He says of his poems
themselves:

'I am glad you find anything in them to like; for my own part I have very
much outgrown my parental partiality, and they are very discordant with
my present views of what poetry ought to be. However I value them as
the record of several states of my mind, which may all be comprehended
in a cycle out of which I fancy I am passing.'

He also urges Gladstone to make the acquaintance of F.D. Maurice
who was by that time in Oxford, but then 'By the bye' adds what must
have been, albeit unwittingly, the unkindest cut of all and which probably
undid all the diplomacy of the rest of the letter, an exhortation to 'buy &
read Alfred Tennyson's poe[ms] . . . I am sure you will perceive their extraordinary merit.' He then says that he will be leaving for Normandy in a
few days.[70]

Hallam could not have realised that the apparently innocent puff
which he had just given to the poems of Tennyson would hurt Gladstone
considerably and add weight to the very point which Gladstone had been
trying to make. It was by Tennyson, above all others, that Gladstone felt
he had been superseded in Hallam's estimation. This was not, as

Gladstone seemed to suppose, absolutely the end of the friendship between them as they met twice the following year. But from Gladstone's point of view Hallam was by now set on the course which would ultimately cause him to prove much more satisfactory as a memory than he ever was in the flesh.

Hallam was right, of course, to point out that the intimacy which he and Gladstone had shared at Eton was hardly likely to be re-established, especially as Hallam's circle at Trinity was widening. Milnes and Tennyson both figured prominently in the narrative of Hallam's Cambridge life, but other members of the Apostles began to play important roles too, particularly given the various events which unfolded during the second half of 1830.

John Kemble has already been mentioned. He belonged to the famous theatrical family, being the son of the actor Charles Kemble, and brother of the 'divine Fanny', Hallam's favourite actress. Kemble was a popular, even charismatic, figure among the Apostles, and he, like Milnes, illustrated the fact that the Apostles were by no means always austere and ratiocinative. Kemble was extrovert and multi-talented (though not perhaps as much so as either he or his family believed). When taking his degree examinations he had disconcerted the examiners by writing an attack on Paley's *Evidences* rather than offering the conventional critical analysis which was required, and the examiners consequently deferred his degree until such time as he felt able to reconsider his position. He had been president of the Union in 1828, and, despite his hostility to Paley's apologetics, did, for a time, consider taking orders. He was a great enthusiast for the German philosophers and he was responsible for kindling a more fitful enthusiasm for things Germanic in Hallam, who for a time at least, took the view that 'Their [i.e. German] literature has of late mightily and nobly influenced our own'.[71] Hallam contemplated spending time 'at Bonn, Heidelberg or such like fine place', as Kemble himself had done earlier in the year, though Hallam was doubtful that his father would approve of such a course. Kemble could veer from the depths of melancholy to the heights of exhilaration, complaining on the one hand that 'If I could read mathematics with Blakesley or sleep on the sofa with Hallam or Donne in the day-time, I might be a happier man',[72] but on the other, making the most Apostolic of assertions that 'The world is one great thought, and I am thinking it.'[73] Although he eventually settled down to serious scholarship in the field of Anglo-Saxon and produced the first English edition of *Beowulf* in 1833, he never really fulfilled his promise, and caused Charles Merivale to write about him, rather smugly: 'very clever, very confident, very wayward; one who took the lead among his companions but did not long keep it. He . . . died in middle life, broken down in prospects and in health . . . he came . . . a very fair scholar, with good prospects before him; but he was bitten with politics, devoted himself to the Union and the cultivation of oratory, gave up all his time to newspapers and political essayists'.[74]

A rather incongruous friendship existed between Kemble and Richard Chenevix Trench (another former Cambridge Union president). Where Kemble was lively and wayward, Trench, future Dean of Westminster, Archbishop of Dublin, theologian and published poet, was earnest, socially aware, and not entirely attuned to the 'Platonico-Wordsworthian-Coleridgean-anti-Utilitarian' bias of Apostolic thought. Despite this, Tennyson, for example, always believed that it was 'impossible to look on Trench and not to love him, though he be . . . always strung up to the highest pitch'.[75] Where Kemble was interested in things Germanic, Trench was an enthusiast for Spanish culture, having written a tragedy on the subject of *Bernardo del Carpio* and having travelled for several months in Spain during 1829. Despite his eventual career in the church and distinction as a theologian, as an undergraduate he was tormented by depression and religious doubt.

A less outwardly conspicuous, though certainly no less important, friend to both Hallam and Tennyson was James Spedding. Tennyson described him as 'our Pope', and to some extent Spedding was to take over, after Hallam's death, his position in Tennyson's life, advising him on his poetry, and writing a substantial review when Tennyson's 1842 volume appeared. His friends agreed on his wisdom, Edward Fitzgerald declaring that he was the wisest man he had ever known 'and not the less so for the plenty of the boy in him.'[76] He was free from the spiritual upheavals which tended to beset the other Apostles, and was quick to return the affection which his friends gave him. He felt particular warmth towards 'the lordly-browed and gracious Hallam', and wrote some lines about him, which he included in a letter to W.B. Donne:

I love his voice, that falls upon my ear
Like a lonely leaping fountain.

Eyes of joyful grey, lit up
With summer lightnings of a soul
So full of summer warmth, so glad,
So healthy, clear and sound, and whole.[77]

Spedding's love and admiration for Hallam were able to take a more permanent form when Henry Hallam invited him to contribute his recollections to the memorial volume which would eventually be published as the *Remains*. It is this essay by Spedding, more than anything else (to be discussed in CHAPTER SEVEN), which evokes the charm, the dynamism and the dialectical brilliance which so characterised Hallam as an undergraduate. Spedding never sought worldly honours and devoted his life to editing the works of Bacon ('gnawing on that bare bone' in the opinion of G.S. Venables[78]). He was a generous host in his London home, and also entertained Fitzgerald and Tennyson at his parental home in the Lake District, where he probably engineered a private meeting between Tennyson and Wordsworth.

The effect which Hallam could have on his friends can be seen in the journal of Henry Alford, later Dean of Canterbury. Alford yet again illustrates the variety of personalities and outlooks that the Apostles contained and the caution that needs to be exercised in categorising them too easily. Alford, also a published poet, was a pious evangelical, his vocation for the church already determined by the time he entered Trinity. He had matriculated in the same term as Hallam and wrote to his cousin at the end of that term: 'Now that my first term is passed, I can look back with cool reflection . . . I know two or three good men. How very refreshing is Christian communion of this sort!'[79] Alford was elected to membership of the Apostles on 30 October 1830 and his hitherto rather earnest journal shows a palpable lightening of spirit as a result. Alford suddenly feels himself transported to a higher order of existence, writing of a visit to Tennyson's rooms to hear him read his latest poems, but more especially recording the educative value of getting to know Hallam, of whom he was considerably in awe: 'I have been able to unbosom myself more to Hallam and Tennant than to any men I have known here; full of blessings, full of happiness, drawing active enjoyment from every thing, wondering, loving, and being loved . . . At night Hallam came full of love and happiness, sat up with him till four a.m.'[80]

A common thread which linked the Apostles was an unquestioningly high mutual regard, a regard which manifested itself not simply in such acts as appreciating Tennyson's poetry or talking philosophy with Hallam through the night, but in a desire to work together for some kind of common good in a world which they felt they were well placed to serve, if not save. In the summer of 1830 the Apostles acquired a cause, albeit (as they themselves came to appreciate) an ultimately forlorn one.

John Sterling's father was a friend of General José María Torrijos, a Spanish exile, and a compelling figure with an impressive military record. He was the most prominent personality among what was quite a large colony of Spanish *émigrés* in London at the time. After the collapse of the Napoleonic empire, Spain, like other former European kingdoms, returned to the hands of its absolutist monarchy. King Ferdinand VII, having been restored, revoked the Spanish constitution and even went so far as to re-introduce the Inquisition. In 1820 opposition from liberals within the country had forced him to abandon his absolutist policy and to restore the parliament and the constitution, but three years later an alliance of France, Austria, Prussia and Russia (which is to say all the most powerful European states except Britain) had compelled the king to restore absolutism as a result of which savage recriminations against the liberals had followed. Many Spanish constitutionalists fled to England as a result, where, in Carlyle's memorable description, they could be observed in the squares of Camden: 'stately tragic figures in proud thread-bare cloaks.'[81] Trench had been taught Spanish by one of them before he went off to Spain in the summer of 1829, from where he had sent the direst reports of the plight of those constitutionalists who remained in the country. He wrote to his brother that 'They [the constitutionalists] now have their passions exasperated by persecutions . . . There are three Constitutional colonels now working as galley-slaves, with chains on their legs . . . They are a part of two thousand galley-slaves contained in this province.'[82] To Donne, he had written: 'I do not think Spain has any chance of escaping a bloody and terrible revolution.'[83]

It was this revolution which John Sterling, in a sense, now wished to precipitate, and a strategy was hatched. He and his cousin, Robert Boyd, who had recently acquired a small legacy, bought and equipped an old gunboat, which was to take Torrijos, along with Sterling, Boyd and a crew of about fifty Spanish émigrés to Gibraltar, from where they would join with local liberals to form a revolutionary force which would make its way northwards through Spain. Substantial reinforcements were expected to be on hand once they reached the country and intelligence indicated that the liberals would move into action as soon as Torrijos arrived. Unfortunately, the English authorities became aware of the plot, and Boyd's ship was impounded. The English force, along with Torrijos, consequently had to make their own way to Gibraltar as best they could. Sterling found himself unable to leave England, but Boyd, Kemble and Trench all in due course departed. The future Archbishop of Dublin, with a mixture of political commitment, self-sacrifice and a scarcely concealed desire for excitement, informed Donne when he and Kemble were about to embark that '[we] are wanted in Spain. The possibilities are that we shall be both hanged . . . You will say that all this is very foolish, but it is action, action, action, that we want.'[84] Kemble left England on 7 July, having told his parents that he was going to spend the summer in Norfolk studying theology.[85] Both Trench and Kemble duly reached Gibraltar, where, with Boyd and Torrijos, they happily bided their time in the belief that the revolution could be neatly arranged to take place over the Cambridge summer vacation. In this respect, as in so many others, affairs turned out very differently from what was expected.

Hallam and Tennyson were unlikely players in this revolutionary scenario, but they did acquire walk-on parts. By no means all the Apostles were as enthusiastic about Spain as Trench and Kemble were. Maurice, although a public supporter of the constitutional cause, argued strongly against direct action and Milnes perciently pointed out that Torrijos' political views were actually quite the opposite of those held by the Apostles. Hallam, nevertheless, had contributed money to the campaign and doubtless enjoyed doing something of which his father would be bound to disapprove. To Tennyson, this revolutionary activity offered his first opportunity for foreign travel, and perhaps Trench's admonition that 'we cannot live in art' spurred the poet to mix with action rather than wither in his garret.

There is not much evidence to suggest that Hallam and Tennyson's contribution to the Spanish revolution was a particularly important one, nor that they took it particularly seriously. Rather like something from a boys' adventure story, they were charged with taking money and coded letters, written in invisible ink, to a revolutionary group stationed in the Pyrenees. There does not seem to have been much urgency in the commission as Hallam and Tennyson were clearly incorporating it into a European tour. The first part involved travelling to Paris in the company of Frederick Tennyson, and also of John Rashdall. Rashdall seems to have originally been a friend of Frederick Tennyson and was an undergraduate at Corpus Christi College. He was of a pious temper and subsequently took orders. Quite how he came to attach himself to the Tennyson/Hallam circle is not clear, though he was to make a significant reappearance in Alfred Tennyson's life in Lincolnshire three years later. The return journey would involve falling in with Robert Robertson and his cousin who were then also in France. Tennyson stayed with the Hallams in Wimpole Street for a short time (thus enabling him to be vague to his family about where exactly he was going), before setting off on 2 July. When they got to Paris they met the statesman Guizot, a long-standing acquaintance of Henry Hallam, by whom they had been given a letter of introduction. They recited a poem to Guizot which they had jointly composed in French, beginning 'O Fontainebleau! O Fontainebleau!', though Guizot had to point out to them, somewhat humiliatingly, that they had failed to observe that the word, when scanned in poetry, had one more syllable than they had allowed it, thus rather spoiling their effort.[86] From Paris they went south to the Mediterranean coast, though had to delay their journey for five days when Tennyson fell ill.

Eventually, arriving in the Pyrenees, they had a rendezvous at Pont d'Espagne, near Cauterets. There they met the leader of the local revolutionary force, Ojeda, in order to hand over their money and documents. Ojeda turned out to be rather different from the handsome and courtly Torrijos, and his force, dispirited, and riven with internal jealousies, seemed hardly likely to make much headway once it crossed the border. Tennyson took an instant dislike to Ojeda, especially when he discovered that Ojeda's purposes were as much anti-clerical as constitutionalist and that his chief stated aim was to slit the throats of all the priests. Once Hallam and Tennyson had performed their allotted task, they retreated to Cauterets to allow Tennyson, who was still feeling ill, the opportunity to convalesce. So ended their brief careers as revolutionaries.

Hallam's attitude to the expedition was an ambivalent one. He rejoiced in his father's disapproval of his activities, reporting to Charles Tennyson in September that 'My father's letters have been more & more urgent for my return',[87] and later to Alfred that 'I cannot find that my adventures have produced quite the favourable impression on my father's mind that his letter gave me to expect . . . and he does not seem quite to comprehend that after helping to revolutionize kingdoms, one is still less inclined than before to trouble one's head about scholarships, degree, and such gear'.[88] Likewise when he came to write to Trench later in the year, he seemed fully aware of the incongruity of the expedition which he and Tennyson had undertaken: 'Alfred went . . . with me to the south of France, and a wild bustling time we had of it. I played my part as conspirator in a small way'. He also realised more or less immediately that the cause was a doomed one, opining to Trench, who was still in Spain, that: 'I had hoped and believed till the very last for the success of the noble cause for which you were struggling; but in spite of Kemble's sanguine letters, I can hope and believe no longer. The game is lost in Spain.'[89]

Hallam was right. Torrijos, Boyd, Kemble and Trench remained in Gibraltar through the autumn of 1830 and into the winter. Trench eventually returned in February 1831, and Kemble, much to his family's relief, in May. It was believed that in the following October junior officers in the Algeciras garrison would mutiny against senior officers and light beacons as a sign to attract Torrijos and his followers to join them. This did not happen. Other liberals on mainland Spain had been captured, and eventually Torrijos' boat was placed under guard by English officers from Gibraltar, who wished to avoid an international incident. In January 1831, Torrijos tried again to land at Algeciras but was driven back by Spanish government forces. In November 1831, eighteen months after their initial landing at Gibraltar, Torrijos and Boyd were ordered to leave by the Governor, who had been put under pressure by the Spanish government. Torrijos was encouraged to sail to Malaga, where it appeared the Governor there would be sympathetic, but on arrival Torrijos discovered that this was in fact a trap and he was forced to surrender. The 53 members of his party, including Boyd, were all promptly executed by firing squad on the esplanade at Malaga.[90]

Although Hallam made light of the Spanish affair, it was a tragic and ill-conceived undertaking, about which Sterling, for the rest of his life, felt acutely guilty, claiming that he could 'hear the sound of that musketry; it is as if the bullets were tearing my own brain.'[91] Neither he nor Trench ever spoke much of the tragedy if they could possibly avoid it. Trench's biographer sought to represent his involvement as a manifestation of 'his poetic and chivalrous imagination',[92] but Trench himself in later life spoke of it as 'misguided and inglorious . . . but . . . not unheroic.'[93] For him it was an incongruous episode in an otherwise impeccably respectable career. Both the Hallam and the Tennyson families found it best to forget, or at least downplay, the incident. Henry Hallam makes only an oblique reference to it in the *Remains* ; Hallam Tennyson sketches in the historical background and offers a few facts in his *Memoir*, but then comments brusquely (and inaccurately): 'No further information on this business has been preserved'.[94]

While their friends were quartered in Gibraltar, anticipating action, Hallam and Tennyson remained in France until the beginning of September. It had originally been planned that they would join Frederick Tennyson again at Bagnères, but when they arrived, Hallam was mildly offended to discover a letter from Frederick 'cool almost to effrontery, desiring us to hasten after him on a wildgoose chase to Paris.'[95] So they lingered at Cauterets instead. Both of them were impressed by the landscape around this remote little spa town, at the top of its valley in the Pyrenees, echoing to the constant sound of a mountain torrent, which Tennyson was to recall thirty years later in his poem *In the Valley of Cauteretz*. It was just the kind of scenery which Hallam had always been enthusiastic about, though it was Tennyson who made poetry out of it. Hallam wrote of 'precipitous defiles, jagged mountain tops, forests of solemn pine . . . waters, in all shapes, and all powers, from the clear runnel bubbling down over our mountain paths at intervals, to the blue little lake whose deep, cold waters are fed eternally from neighbouring glaciers.'[96] Tennyson's response to this landscape quickly found its way into *Oenone* and *The Lotos Eaters*.

Whether Robert Robertson and his cousin joined Hallam and Tennyson on their expeditions is not clear, but they did all travel back together, taking a steam packet, *The Leeds* from Bordeaux on 8 September and arriving in Dublin four days later. The sea had been rough to start with and Hallam had kept to his cabin with sea-sickness, but in due course he surfaced and found some congenial travelling companions. A Mr and Mrs Harden were on board with their three daughters. They were neighbours of the Spedding family in Cumberland, so a friendship was easily struck up. One of the daughters, Jessie, later reminisced about the voyage:

'Our fellow-passengers were four gentlemen – two of them Mr. Robertson, of Glasgow, and his cousin, of whom we knew something through my mother's relatives, and two others, who were none other than Mr. Tennyson and his friend Mr. Hallam. The weather was fine, and we were sitting on deck. Mr. Hallam was a very interesting delicate-looking young man, and we saw nothing of him the first day; he was in the saloon. The second day was warm, and he came on deck, and kindly read to us some of Scott's novels . . . . . We were all much charmed with our group of fellow-passengers.'[97]

The young people spent convivial evenings on deck, playing games and singing, and Mr. Harden made sketches of Tennyson and Hallam, Tennyson having 'a large cape, a tall hat, and a very decided nose'. Hallam is only pictured from the back, his face being invisible.

The *Leeds* duly docked in Dublin, from where Hallam and Tennyson crossed to Liverpool. It has been confidently stated by more than one of Tennyson's biographers that he and Hallam then travelled on from Liverpool to Manchester on 20 September by the first passenger train that ran on the newly opened Liverpool and Manchester Railway and that they were therefore present when William Huskisson, Liverpool's MP, fell beneath the wheels of Stephenson's *Rocket* and was fatally injured. However, the first train ran on the line on Wednesday 15 September, and it was on that day when the accident occurred. As the opening of the line was a festive occasion at which Wellington, the Prime Minister, among many other distinguished guests, was present, tickets were not on sale to the general public and the line only started normal passenger services between the two cities the following day. We know a great deal about the events on the fateful first journey from an eye-witness account given by none other than Fanny Kemble who was on the train, but we know nothing of Hallam and Tennyson's presence there. According to Robert Bernard Martin, Tennyson liked to tell in old age how he had been present on the day Huskisson was killed,[98] but, alas, this seems unlikely to have been the case, and if Hallam and Tennyson used the railway as a means of getting back to their respective homes, they must have done so on another day, thus avoiding witnessing the accident and thereby spoiling Tennyson's story.[99]

Hallam spent the few weeks, before the new academic year started, at Forest House, at Leyton in Essex. Forest House was the home of Samuel Bosanquet, Governor of the Bank of England and his sons. Hallam told Tennyson that he found the house 'a very pleasant place, an old country mansion, in the depths of the Forest, with cedars in the garden . . . and a billiardtable within doors, by dint of which I demolish time pretty well.' Clearly Henry was now imposing penalties on Arthur as a result of his two-months' not particularly educative absence. A visit to Somersby was out of the question, and 'six books of Herodotos' were prescribed, making Hallam wistful for 'the ferment of minds, and stir of events, which is now the portion of other countries. I wish I could be useful'.[100]

Hallam's desire to be useful persisted through the ensuing term. Along with many of his Cambridge contemporaries, Apostolic and otherwise, he believed that England was in an 'awful state . . . The laws are almost suspended; the money of foreign factions is at work with a population exasperated into reckless fury.' Although Hallam did not 'apprehend a revolution'[101] such as had broken out in France in July, men of more apocalyptic temperament did. There had been unrest among farm labourers in Cambridgeshire the previous year. Ricks had been burned as a demonstration against low agricultural wages. A petition from the farmers of Ely to parliament had stated that the labourers were 'no longer able to maintain themselves by the sweat of their brows' and had to seek 'the scanty pittance derived from parish funds', though more cynical observers thought that the peasantry had been turned militant by the greater avail-ability of beer.[102] Disturbances started again in the autumn of 1830, particularly in the southern and eastern counties of England, which caused fear of revolution in London. The unrest was believed to be orchestrated not by the labourers themselves but by groups of politically motivated artisans. As one of their chief grievances was the paying of tithes, demon-strations often took on an anti-clerical flavour, with farmers supporting, rather than opposing, their labourers' demands. The figure of 'Captain Swing' was invented, whose name would be appended to an otherwise anonymous letter, threatening imminent action. It would be delivered to a farmer in the morning by a mysterious figure in a green carriage. That night his ricks would be burnt.

On the evening of Friday, 3 December, it was possible to see from the courts of Trinity College that the sky was alight with flames above the neighbouring village of Coton, where a farmhouse had been set on fire. Charles Merivale was in Hallam's rooms where, at 'about half-past six, we heard a considerable row in the court, and, immediately after, that Trinity lane was crowded by hundreds. Out we sallied some half-dozen, with single-sticks and such weapons, and had just reached the great gate quite ignorant of what was going on, when on turning round we saw a general red glare hanging steady and still over the Master's Lodge. In a few minutes half Cambridge was in arms (in sticks, that is) and on the road to Coton. There was no dwelling-house burnt, but according to accounts to-day, twenty-three ricks – I should have thought more.'[103] There was a genuine fear that Cambridge itself was to be attacked the next day, which was market day[104] and, although the students' actions sound almost grotesquely hasty and improvised, the extent of the fear can be gauged when we hear that in Trinity 'Peacock [one of the college tutors] assembled the men in the cloisters and organized us in bodies of ten or eleven, in case of an attack on Cambridge which is meditated.'[105] Meanwhile, Merivale on returning to his own college, St. John's, found himself at a 'meeting among ourselves in College . . . [which] elected six captains, of whom I am one, each of whom is to bring a troop of ten men to begin with.'[106]

Merivale's belief that no residential property was affected by the fire does not seem to be quite true. When the undergraduates reached Coton (with Tennyson in charge of the fire-engine) they found that the fire had spread from the ricks to the stables and the farmer's house. They managed to save the latter, but only after the farmer had restrained them from trying to pull the whole place down.

The sheerly bizarre nature of all this activity was not entirely lost on some observers. The urbane Spedding spoke of the 'Corps of Poets & Metaphysicians, – & visions of broken heads & arms, scythes & pitch-forks disturbed the purity of our unselfish contemplations, & the idealisms of our poetical imaginings',[107] while Henry Lushington and G.S.

Venables celebrated the occasion in a comic poem, entitled *Swing, at Cambridge:*

> Scholars threw by their Grecian lore,
> The algebraist worked no more,
> One primal science thrives;
> Deep thinkers left their whys and hows,
> And stood prepared to solve with blows
> The riddle of their lives . . .
>
> So, all looked gladly for the morn,
> And yet I know we did not scorn
> The hungry multitude;
> Or hate them, that their evil chance
> Of want and woe and ignorance,
> Had made them fierce and rude,
>
> But doubtful in our dazzling prime
> We watched the struggle of the time,
> The war of new and old;
> We loved the past with Tory love,
> Yet more than radicals we strove
> For coming years of cold . . .
>
> Alas that night the winter sky
> Beheld no town more peaceful lie
> Through England broad and wide,
> We found it all in vain to look
> And sadly turned to desk and book,
> And laid our arms aside.[108]

Despite its conscious flippancy, this poem tells us a lot about the incident and pinpoints the major features of it: that a group of privileged young men felt moved to intervene in an uprising by local agricultural workers; that they were not clear about their ideological position (Tories behaving like radicals) or who exactly they were supposed to be helping; that their belief that Cambridge would be attacked was alarmist and entirely mistaken; and that (as the final stanza of the poem has it) 'We could not choose but smile.' In short it was best in the end to view it as a joke.

Although the events of early December 1830 involved more than just the Apostles, the similarity between the events in Cambridge and those in Spain are striking. In both cases we see a taking up of arms against ill-defined foes; a looking for a conflict which was not in the end provided; an uncertainty (at least among some of the participants) about the seriousness of what they were doing; and, somewhere beneath it all, a

148

vaguely-directed respect for liberty. As Spedding perhaps realised better than anyone else, there was something inherently self-contradictory in the Apostles' involvement in political affairs, however much they claimed to care about the state of the world. Both in Spain and in Cambridge, the participants were blithely unaware of the potential dangers in which they could place themselves and others. In Cambridge they had been playing with fire in a quite literal sense.

By the time Hallam came to write to his father on 13 December, he was able to report that 'All alarm had now ceased . . . and indeed there seems every reason to suppose that a great deal of it originated in hoax and humbug. Our swords are now turned into ploughshares; not that our rather hasty equipment was distinguished by a great number of actual blades: the principal weapon was . . . an ashen or oaken stick, of over-whelming thickness at one end, and terribly feruled into a point at the other'. Against whom these sticks were intended to be used was perhaps not clear to anyone and it is fortunate they remained purely symbolic. Hallam also asked his father for permission to visit Somersby for a few days when term ended 'as I have been much pressed to do so for a long while by the old Tennysons.' He claimed that one reason for his wanting to go was that the Tennysons might be leaving Somersby soon. As there is no evidence that this was the case, it is tempting to believe that Hallam was making it up. Deviousness towards his father was a regular and neces-sary feature of his courtship of Emily Tennyson and it is also relevant that the 'old Tennysons' would, on this occasion, include Dr. Tennyson, whom Hallam had not yet met, but whose approval he would undoubtedly need if his relationship with Emily was to be put on a firmer footing.[109]

Henry Hallam was agreeable to his son's visit to Lincolnshire and Arthur spent some days there between 16 December, when the university term ended, and 22 December, when he was back in Cambridge. The last day of the Michaelmas Term was celebrated as Commemoration day in Trinity and as part of the festivities the winner of the College Declamation Prize was required to read a speech in chapel before the Fellows, Senior Wranglers, senior medallists and other guests. James Spedding, who had won the prize the previous year, delivered the speech on this occasion (it was subsequently published in Cambridge). Hallam, as a competitor for the current year's prize, was also required to perform. Tennyson and Lushington were both present, as also, among the distinguished guests, was William Wordsworth, who was making one of his rare visits to his brother. It was reported that 'it was verily splendid to see the poet Wordsworth's face . . . kindle' as Hallam read it'.[110]

Three prizes for declamation, bequeathed by a Dr. Hooper, were awarded each year in the form of silver goblets, the first prize being worth £20 and other two £10 each. The subject of the declamations was restricted to English history. This explains Hallam's choice of topic: the conduct of the Independent party in the English Civil War, which seems something of a throwback to the preoccupations of his Eton days. Certainly the subject matter of this declamation stands rather at odds with Hallam's other intellectual interests at this time. The 'Independent Party' of Hallam's title refers to that group of men who, though supportive of the Parliamentary cause in the 1640s, were opposed to the establishment of an English church on Presbyterian principles. Simply speaking, they could have been described as Republican moderates and Hallam believed that the most illustrious man among them was Milton. It does not seem that Hallam had much interest in this declamation. Unlike most of his writings, he made no effort to have it printed, and, indeed, it was long believed to have been lost. However, a manuscript copy of it survives in an exercise book which Henry Hallam preserved and which is amongst his papers in Trinity College library.

The full title of Hallam's declamation is: 'Was the Independent party justified in seizing the government and putting force on the legislative body in the year 1648?'. The declamation is thus addressing itself to a very specific historical question, though it is a declamation first and a historical essay second. It was judged on the force of its rhetoric and the clarity of its argument rather than on its contribution to knowledge. If its subject matter is reminiscent of Hallam's debating speeches at Eton, so also is its style. Rhetorical elaboration abounds, as when the Presbyterians ('Whose hands were wet with the blood of Laud') are described as 'a faction, more intolerant than the prelates, more grasping than the cavaliers . . . The Church of Christ they maintained was one, & could have but one faith . . . etc.'. Against the Presbyterians are set the Independents, 'this firm band of patriots', wedded firmly to their country's good. Although Hallam's own political views had moved from Whig to Tory by this time, the declamation in fact presents a very Whig view of political history, stressing the significance of a 'continual development of [political] intelligence.' That the conduct of the Independent party can be celebrated when it is judged by Whig tenets, makes, of course, for a neat argument, and the forcefulness with which Hallam pursues it explains why he won the first prize. Although very much a debating-chamber kind of performance, it again provides convincing evidence of Hallam's much admired resourcefulness as a disputant.

Unfortunately Hallam's departure for Somersby prevented any further contact with Wordsworth who, on the following Sunday evening, met a group of undergraduates in Spedding's rooms. Alford, Blakesley, Brookfield, Tennant and Thompson were present and Tennant subsequently wrote to Tennyson that Wordsworth 'was in good talking but furiously alarmist – nothing but revolutions and reigns of terror and all that . . . But upon the whole, although he said nothing very profound or original, yet I enjoyed his talk till 1 o'clock in the morning; he was also pleased with his hearers'.[111] Henry Alford wrote a much more detailed account in his journal from which it is clear that Wordsworth's talk

New Court, Trinity College, where Hallam lived throughout his time at Cambridge (courtesy of The Master and Fellows of Trinity College, Cambridge)

Hotel Goldene Birne, Landstrasse, Vienna, where Hallam died. The building no longer exists (courtesy of The Master and Fellows of Trinity College, Cambridge)

Left:
Arthur Hallam,
at the time he
left Eton in
1827, by Sir
Martin Archer
Shee, the
portrait which
A.C. Benson
thought made
Hallam look
'beery'
(courtesy of
The Provost
and Fellows of
Eton College)

Right:
Henry Hallam
(1843) by
George
Richmond
(© The
National
Portrait
Gallery)

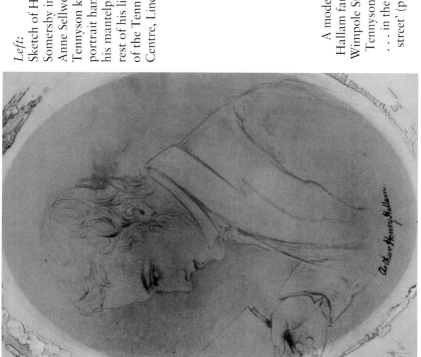

Left:
Sketch of Hallam at Somersby in 1830, by Anne Sellwood. Tennyson kept this portrait hanging above his mantelpiece for the rest of his life (courtesy of the Tennyson Research Centre, Lincoln)

Right:
A modern view of the Hallam family home, 67 Wimpole Street, London, Tennyson's 'dark house . . . in the long unlovely street' (photo by Philip Busgith)

Right:
Sketch of Hallam at Cambridge, by James Spedding (courtesy of the Tennyson Research Centre, Lincoln)

Left:
Posthumous bust of Arthur Hallam by Sir Francis Chantrey (courtesy of The Master and Fellows of Trinity College, Cambridge)

ranged more widely than Tennant's summary suggested.[112] If Hallam and Tennyson had been in Cambridge they would surely have been invited to join the party. Tennyson's shyness might have tempted him to make excuses, but Hallam would have felt no such inhibitions, and his name, presumably would not have been unknown to the older poet. Wordsworth and his wife had dined at least twice a few years previously in the company of Henry Hallam, on one occasion actually at the Hallams' house in Wimpole Street.[113]

> 'This has been a very eventful term: I have been on the whole in better spirits, and in a more settled & quiet temper of mind, than I remember myself for some time. I have been reading too, as much as the disturbed state of things would permit a man . . . Next term I hope will be quieter.'

These were the words with which Hallam concluded the 13 December letter to his father, and, while there is no reason to doubt the sincerity of them, it is an interesting paradox that the chief psychological benefit of an extremely eventful term appeared to be greater mental peace. The words could, of course, equally apply to the whole of the previous year. Hallam had indeed been busy: since the publication of *Adonais* twelve months before there had been the publication of his own poems, and of Tennyson's. There had been the 'wild and bustling' trip to the Pyrenees, there had been the witnessing of apparently revolutionary activity in Cambridge, and there had been the discovery of Somersby and the young woman who would become his fiancée. Yet again it is difficult to believe that these experiences had actually been those of a second year undergraduate who was not yet out of his teens.

CHAPTER SIX

A Young Man of Letters,
1831–1833

PART ONE   *The Last of Cambridge*

Hallam was reported by Robert Monteith at the beginning of 1831 to have 'recovered his amiability of late. He is not so dissatisfied with *himself*, not so morbid as he used to be and therefore more in possession of his naturally exuberant loving kindness towards others.'[1] On the surface the reason for this newly regained amiability is not hard to find. He was in love, and could write confidently to Emily in a poem entitled *To the Loved One*:

> Even now begins that holy life,
> For when I kneel in Christian prayer
> Thy name my own, my promised wife,
> Is blent with mine in fondest care.
> Oh pray for me that both may know
> That inward bridal's high delight,
> And both beyond the grave may go
> Together in the Father's sight.[2]

Both the assumption that Emily was now his 'promised wife', and the poem's imagery of earthly and heavenly companionship, were sadly premature. Whatever impression Hallam had made upon Dr Tennyson at Somersby before Christmas (and it is unlikely to have been a bad one), the Doctor was not willing to permit the engagement of his nineteen-year-old daughter to a young man whom she had only met on two occasions and who was but a few months older than she was. Nor, unsurprisingly, was Henry Hallam any more enthusiastic. In addition to the obvious accusation that Arthur was acting rashly, there was the distinct likelihood that Henry had only very recently heard of the Miss Tennyson in question and must have been aware that Arthur's last visit to Somersby had been undertaken for reasons quite different from those expressed to his parents before he went.

The result was a concordat between Henry Hallam and Dr Tennyson: Arthur was to make no more visits to Somersby until he came of age in

February 1832. This was a stark and uncompromising prohibition, showing little obvious sympathy on the part of either of the fathers. Fortunately it contained loopholes which Arthur could exploit and which other members of the Tennyson family could connive at. Henry's words did not explicitly forbid correspondence between Arthur and Emily (though he himself thought this was understood), nor for that matter, if interpreted literally, did they prevent Arthur and Emily meeting somewhere other than Somersby, should circumstances allow this. Mrs Tennyson certainly knew about and tolerated the correspondence between the lovers, even though in all probability she did not encourage it.

A further blow occurred in February, when Frederick, Charles and Alfred Tennyson were called home to what was obviously their father's death-bed. Dr Tennyson's always precarious physical and mental health had declined suddenly, and he died on 16 March. Alfred Tennyson had been suffering from a recurrent problem with his eyes (he had a great fear of losing his sight altogether at this time), and had been reputedly hoping that this condition might persuade the university authorities to grant him an aegrotat degree. It certainly seems as if he had given up hope of acquiring a BA by conventional means as James Spedding, reporting on Dr. Tennyson's illness, wrote that: 'Alfred will probably not return to Cambridge; Charles will take his degree next term.'[3]

Spedding's prediction turned out to be correct, so that Hallam was deprived of his most cherished points of contact with the Tennyson family and was faced with what must have seemed like an interminable length of time before they could be renewed. The Tennyson brothers' last night in Cambridge was spent in the company of Spedding and Thompson, with whom, after a late and lengthy dinner, they danced quadrilles until the coach left at 2.30 a.m. Tennyson afterwards recalled that his last sight of Cambridge was of Thompson's face caught under a street lamp. Hallam was not present, as, ironically, he was in London arguing with his father about Emily.[4] Relations between father and son were, yet again, tense, as, in addition to Arthur's love life, there had been a disagreement over that perennial issue of student existence: money. On 20 February, Arthur had been forced into writing a letter of self-justification as a result of Henry's taking exception to paying an outstanding Tutor's bill of £53. Arthur falls back on some predictable lines of defence, assuring Henry that the following term's bill will be smaller, because expenditure in the summer term is always less. Arthur claims that he runs up more modest bills than his friends, and that he intends to live more strictly, but that 'in a most expensive University . . . everybody remarks that money goes without one's knowing how'.[5]

It is not exactly clear when Hallam heard of Dr. Tennyson's death. In the week in which it occurred he was writing to Alfred, anticipating Charles's return to Cambridge the following month and reporting ongoing 'warfare' in Wimpole Street where he was proposing 'to fight like a true knight, though Emily's eyes will not be there to "rain influence"'.[6] His letter of condolence, addressed to Emily at her grandfather's house in Louth, is dated 30 March, exactly two weeks after Dr. Tennyson's death. Hallam wrote with sympathy for Emily and the family, expressing inevitable frustration at not being able to be with her at this time, though it is clear that he had been taken into the family's confidence about the less agreeable aspects of Dr. Tennyson's character: 'I would fain write as a comforter, but my own mind has been so stunned by all these dismal circumstances that my thoughts cheat my wishes . . . I know he was an affectionate father, and his violence was the result of those unhappy accidents which combined to shatter his frame, while his tenderness was native to the heart, and flowed from it abundantly to the last . . . I shall have no peace till I know how far the mischiefs of this horrible crisis in your family have extended. Dearest, forget anything rather than that I am your passionate and constant lover.'[7] Hallam assumed, as others did at the time, that Dr. Tennyson's death would mean the family's moving from Somersby, a place which, in his next letter to Emily, he predicts will become a spot beloved of literary tourists: 'many ages, after we have all been laid in dust, young lovers of the beautiful & the true may seek in faithful pilgrimage the spot where Alfred's mind was moulded in silent sympathy with the everlasting forms of nature. Legends will perhaps be attached to the places, that are near it. Some Mariana, it will be said, lived wretched & alone in a dreary house on top of the opposite hill . . . Critic after critic will track the wanderings of the brook, or mark the groupings of elm & poplar in order to verify the Ode to Memory in its minutest particulars.'[8]

In his letters to Somersby of the next few weeks Hallam did not dwell unduly on the family's bereavement. Indeed, back in Cambridge in mid-April, he expressed some irritation that Frederick and Charles had not yet returned. He had heard from their landlady, Mrs Gibson, that they were expected, and had apparently been sitting up waiting for them. 'Pray tell them I cannot continue for ever sitting up beyond all natural times of rest for the mere chance, and the sooner they let me know, when they mean to appear, the better for my temper and their welcome.' The general tone of this letter to Emily is sanguine. There is further lyrical praise of Somersby: 'not . . . the home of my childhood: but oh, while the pulses beat within my veins, those forms will stand up clear before my memory, wearing the light of your presence.' It is in this letter that Hallam suggested that he did not think there was any prohibition of his and Emily's writing to each other. Whether he genuinely thought this, or merely felt that it was something which they could get away with, is not clear: 'We may write to each other, Emily: we ought to write to each other . . . My father has given an implied consent to it. Your mother, I am sure, has no objection'. He was also, for the moment at least, confident about the future of their relationship: 'my late visit to London has fully confirmed me in the opinion I expressed to you before, that nothing stands in the way of our union but time, and that perhaps shorter than we had imagined.'[9]

Something else which Hallam's letters reveal at this time is a growing acceptance of the comforts of Christianity. Rather than the anguished and self-lacerating doubts which contributed to his mental breakdown of two years earlier, Hallam could write to Alfred Tennyson that 'I have derived lately much consolation and hope from religious feelings. Struggle as we may Christianity draws us all within its magic circle at last.'[10]

In his letters to Emily over the ensuing months Hallam shows a much greater willingness to discuss spiritual matters with her, and indeed often seems to take on himself the role of spiritual guide. He felt a growing need to explore and reconcile his own nature with Christianity, though it was Christianity of a very different sort from his mother's. He did, for example, attend with Milnes a service at Edward Irving's church in Regent Square in May 1831. Irving, whose 'Catholic Apostolic Church' encouraged millenarianism and speaking in tongues, was a figure of some fascination to the Apostles, though Hallam himself was not impressed. Religious exhibitionism never stirred him. More significantly, the paper which he delivered to the Apostles the following October was on the subject of ' the existence of moral evil [being] absolutely necessary to the fulfilment of God's essential love for Christ' and was subsequently printed as *Theodicaea Novissima*.

Although Merivale had written to John Frere in February that Hallam was 'reading for a scholarship and philosophizing on the minus sign',[11] there is in general very little evidence to suggest that he was devoting much time to official university study. He was increasingly living in his own literary world, also claiming that it was only when he got out of Cambridge that 'I seem to breathe freely; the use of my natural faculties returns to me; I can read, and I can think . . . I am glad that my Academical time draws to a close.'[12] Emily Tennyson was an obvious distraction, of course, as was his continued promotional activity on behalf of Alfred's poems, by the side of which he himself felt 'as Pisgah to Canaan'.[13]

In January 1831 a very favourable review of Tennyson's *Poems, Chiefly Lyrical*, had appeared from an unexpected quarter. *The Westminster Review* was an explicitly Utilitarian journal, and the author, W.J. Fox, was a Unitarian minister of radical political views. He wrote from a standpoint very different from that of the Apostles, being frankly progressivist in tone. The opening sections of his essay do not seem propitious, or indeed remotely Tennysonian, when he writes: 'The great principle of human improvement is at work in poetry as well as everywhere else . . . the real science of mind advances with the progress of society like all other sciences'.[14] Nevertheless, he shows a keen appreciation of the originality of the 1830 poems: 'Mr. Tennyson . . . seems to obtain entrance into a mind as he would make his way into a land-scape . . . In the "Supposed Confessions of a Second Rate Sensitive Mind" . . . there is an extraordinary combination of deep reflection, metaphysical analysis, picturesque description, dramatic transition and strong emotion . . . He can cast his own spirit into any living thing, real or imaginary', and he goes on to praise *Mariana* as 'altogether, the most perfect composition in the volume. The whole of this poem . . . is gen-erated by the legitimate process of poetical creation . . . There is no mere amplification; it is all production; and production from that single germ that must be a rich intellect, in which thoughts take root and grow.'[15]

It is not certain what Tennyson thought about this review, or even if he read it, but Hallam was clearly fired by it and it encouraged him into even more vigorous action on his friend's behalf. In January he had writ-ten, out of the blue and 'as a perfect stranger to you', to Leigh Hunt, literary critic, former friend of Keats and Shelley, and at that time, briefly, editor of the *Tatler*. He included copies of the poems of both Charles and Alfred Tennyson, which he hoped Hunt would be interested in and might wish to publicise. Of Alfred's poems he said, 'you will, if you peruse this book, be surprised & delighted to find a new prophet of those true principles of Art, which, in this country, you were among the first to recommend both by precept, & example.'[16] Hallam's flattery of Hunt more than paid off. Hunt wasted no time in reviewing both vol-umes, and concluded that 'the more closely we have become acquainted with Alfred Tennyson's poems, the more the author has risen upon our admiration . . . we . . . prefer him to Charles, because he seems less dis-posed to tie himself down to conventional notions'.[17] Hallam liked the tone of this review, commenting on 'the odd style of his observations & the frank familiarity with which he calls them by their Christian names, just as if he had supped with them a hundred times.'[18] A few weeks later Tennyson sent Hallam a copy of his sonnet 'Check every outflash'. Hallam did not rest until he could get it into print.

Although Hallam's complaints are muted, the second half of the acad-emic year 1830–1 was a generally dispiriting one, given the enforced separation from the Tennysons, his now habitual lack of interest in acad-emic work and the fact that Henry had no plans to let him travel in the summer. In June, Hallam, along with Frederick Tennyson, visited Gladstone in Oxford. They went to concerts at the Sheldonian Theatre, and also spent time with Gaskell and Pickering. Hallam then returned to London in July, where he reported that he had been living 'like a hermit',[19] and devoting himself to reading and writing. Although he had previously claimed to find living in London more congenial to his intellectual life than living in Cambridge, not all the work that he did during July was entirely to his taste and Henry had clearly had a hand in some of it. Hallam found himself writing an 'interminable Essay' on Cicero on 'a table, crowded with Latin books, and a desk bursting with pompous paragraphs.'[20] He had also been (and this must have been at Henry's insistence) studying Justinian's *Institutes*, which were used as a student textbook on Roman law and which Henry would have seen as necessary reading for the next stage of Arthur's career. But there were diversions too. As usual when Hallam was in London, he took the opportunity to enjoy the cultural life of the capital, attending concerts by Paganini, of whom he was not greatly enamoured ('A fiddle to me is but a fiddle, turn it how you will'), seeing the soprano Guiditta Pasta in *Anna Bolena* (which enthused him rather more) as well as the ballerina Maria Taglioni ('the most graceful thing imaginable') and, of course, Fanny Kemble ('a person of genius').[21] It would be interesting to know to what extent these activities were viewed as acceptable by his parents: Julia Hallam in particular always retained a puritanical disapproval of the theatre, which she thought no fit place for a Christian. On 11 July the Hallam family decamped for the rest of the summer to a house at 6 Breed's Place, Hastings.

There were inevitable protestations about the dullness of Hastings, at least to begin with. 'Here there is nothing but wind and water; they talk to each other all day, and at such an illbred pitch of voice, that one cannot get in a word . . . [it] can never be considered the most odious place in England as long as St. Leonards [the neighbouring coastal town] is standing.'[22] Nevertheless, Hallam had to confess at the end of August, just before leaving Hastings, that his sojourn there had kept him 'much alone' as a result of which he had 'thought, read & written not a little'.[23]

The day after his arrival he wrote to Emily, who was not, over the summer months, in either good health or spirits. Her congenital tendency to melancholy and hypochondria could prove trying to Hallam, especially when it caused her to delay replying to his letters. Although he was always happy to offer her comfort as best he could, the correspondence of this period shows Hallam and Emily, not for the last time, in moods of mutual reproachfulness. Clearly Emily had recently told Hallam that she was only prepared to write to him when she was feeling cheerful, and wished to spare him the burden of offering sympathy when she was depressed. He took some exception to this and said 'I have no higher object on earth than to comfort you; do not depress me to an inferior aim; make not a holiday thing of me, fit to share your amusement, but unworthy of your grief!'. He offered his credentials as a support and a counsellor: 'Only remember how I love you at all times, in all moods, whatever pleases, whatever pains you; remember that I too the deep places of existence, and in those "valleys of the shadow of death" have learned some lessons that may do good to the soul of my beloved; remember that the bliss, for which we hope as Christians, takes its perennial complexion from sorrows upon earth'.[24] To counteract what might seem the rather preachy tone of these comments, Hallam also included a poem (subsequently printed in the *Remains* as *A Lover's Reproof*):

When two complaining spirits mingle,
  Saintly and calm their woes become.
Alas the Grief that bideth single,
  Whose heart is drear, whose lips are dumb!

My drooping lily, when the tears
  Of morning bow thy tender head,
Oh scatter them, and have no fears;
  They kill sometimes, if cherished.

Dear girl, the precious gift you gave
  Was of *yourself,* entire and free.
Why front *alone* Life's gloomy wave,
  And fling the brilliant foam to me?

Am I the lover of thy mirth –
  A trifling thing of sunny days –
A soul forbid, for want of worth,
  To tread with thee th' unpleasant ways?

No-trust me, love; if I delight
  To mark thy brightening hour of pleasure,
To deep-eyed Passion's watchful sight
  Thy sadness is a costlier treasure.[25]

In the absence of direct evidence it is often difficult to know exactly what Emily's feelings for Hallam were. His feelings for her were, in a sense, straightforward: not only did he find Emily attractive, but her attractiveness was increased by the knowledge that, unlike Anna Wintour, she could eventually be his, disapproving fathers notwithstanding. Doubtless her distance also added to her attractiveness. Like Anna she could be worshipped from afar, but much more confidently. In his emotional, just as much as in his literary life, Arthur Hallam was ardent and impulsive. Miss Tennyson, on the other hand, had more than enough time to consider the implications of the relationship she had entered into and to find Hallam's headlong nature at times overwhelming. If she did not actively resist him, she certainly knew when to withdraw into her own world, even though it was one often characterised by illness and low spirits which Hallam, with some reason, generally took to be psychosomatic.

There was a lapse of over three weeks before Hallam wrote to her again, and he once more did so feeling that he had offended her in some way: 'I forget what I did say in my last [letter]; but whatever it was, if it wounded you, I deserve to die a million deaths . . . Believe me, dearest . . . that I speak "nothing but in love of thee," and my reproachful words are but the fond exuberance of a tenderness, that reproaches not.' Although Hallam reiterated the fact that he had had 'long and severe experience of those melancholy sentiments you express', he felt strongly that Emily should not be allowed to indulge them, and offered some fairly common-place, not to say patronising, advice about keeping busy and saying her prayers: 'converse more, read more, think more upon subjects uncon-nected with yourself . . . But put your trust in God, Emily, and pray to him as He hath taught me to pray, that you and I may love each other dearly, dearly, but Him above all.' He encouraged her to keep up the study of Italian which she had recently started as 'nothing else in the world resem-bles the delight I take in Italian literature.'[26] Hallam often treated Emily as a pupil to be taught and admonished, particularly when she persisted in her low-spirited moods.

Emily spent rather a rootless summer, staying with her Lincolnshire aunts, first in Dalby and then in Louth. Her grandfather had at first refused to pay for her to spend the summer in Cheltenham, thus incurring Hallam's fury ('I never thought to be so glad of any one's death, as I feel I should be of his'),[27] though she did in the end go there in September with Alfred as chaperon. She remained uncommunicative for most of the month of August, causing Hallam rather icily to tell her that 'I really think I have earned by frequent writing on my own part a right to be preserved from anxiety by frequent hearing from Somersby'.[28]

Hallam turned the seclusion of his summer in Hastings to good literary use and became busier than ever on Tennyson's behalf. Although he reit-erated often enough his opinion that Tennyson's poems could never be generally popular, he worked very hard to bring them before the widest audience he could find and in so doing indulged in an unexpected but successful piece of literary opportunism. On 15 July he wrote to the publisher Edward Moxon who had just taken over the editorship of a new periodical, *The Englishman's Magazine*. After some initial flattery, Hallam went on to say that he understood from Milnes that Moxon would like to publish something by Tennyson for his next edition. He said that he would inform Tennyson of this, but in the meantime he enclosed the sonnet 'Check ev'ry outlash' and also a poem of his own ('I see her now, an elfin shape'). He also offered to write an article on Tennyson's poetry if Moxon would like to print it. This was the origin of what has become Hallam's best-known piece of critical writing.

Edward Moxon came from humble origins in Yorkshire. After having been apprenticed to a bookseller in Wakefield, he set off for London at the age of sixteen, working first for the publishers Longmans, and then for Hurst Chance and Co. He had written and published poetry himself from a young age and had got to know Charles Lamb and, through him, Samuel Rogers and Leigh Hunt. He had visited Wordsworth at Rydal Mount in 1826. Although the general demand for poetry was small at this time, Moxon decided to specialise in publishing it. He set up his shop at

64 New Bond Street in 1830 and brought out work by Lamb and Rogers. Five years later Wordsworth was to put his entire works in Moxon's hands and Moxon also in due course printed complete editions of Shelley and Keats as well as volumes by Tennyson, Browning and Patmore.

Encouraging Moxon to print Tennyson was an inspired *coup* on Hallam's part, though it was also an incongruous one. *The Englishman's Magazine* stood for everything which Hallam (once the Eton Whig, now the Cambridge Tory) and the Apostles most vehemently opposed. The magazine itself was short-lived, running only to seven monthly numbers between April and October 1831, but its credentials were explicitly radical. Its manifesto proclaimed that it saw itself operating in the spirit of Daniel Defoe 'the dauntless advocate of stubborn Truth . . . [who] went forth to do battle with error, intolerance and oppression . . . we are neither chained to a statesman's chariot, nor nailed to a trader's counter. It is a leading object of our ambition to be considered the representative of the intellectual dignity and moral worth of the unpretending majority of an enlightened nation.'[29] Reformist and democratic in purpose, each edition carried lengthy reports on the progress of the Parliamentary Reform Bill. It was also vocally opposed to slavery. Despite its editor's partiality for poetry, Tennyson, Hallam and Moxon were strange bedfellows, though it is worth remembering that W.J. Fox's enthusiastic review of Tennyson earlier in the year had also come from what could be called the radical press.

The first number of *The Englishman's Magazine* to appear openly under Moxon's editorship was that of August 1831 and Moxon was clear that he wanted it to be something special, a 'flash' number, as Hallam told Tennyson, when he was urging him to provide something for it. Hallam assured Tennyson that if he were to appear in it he would be in good company, as Moxon had already 'pressed Wordsworth, Southey and Charles Lamb into his service'.[30] Hallam, excited by the whole prospect, could well have been exaggerating: when the number was printed Wordsworth and Southey did not appear. Alongside Tennyson and Hallam, the other contributors were Thomas Hood, Leigh Hunt, John Clare, Thomas Pringle and Mrs Caroline Norton. Whilst this was not bad company for an emerging young poet of only undergraduate age, in practice it did not really amount to a flash number. There was no contribution from a major figure and Hallam and Tennyson themselves, of course, were virtually unknown. In the general way of reviews, Hallam's essay on Tennyson appeared anonymously.

Hallam appreciated well enough that if he wished to see a poem by Tennyson printed in the magazine, he would need to be cantankerous. Tennyson's co-operation could certainly not be depended upon. Moxon replied by return to Hallam's 15 July letter and Hallam, reporting this to Milnes three days later, wrote that 'His [Moxon's] reply is very civil . . . I had nothing of Alfred's by me, except that Sonnet I shewed you: this I sent, and Moxon seems charmed, and will print it instantly. I expect to be scolded for this . . . and in fact, it is a sad breach of trust, for I don't think he cares a straw for the Sonnet, and he is terribly fastidious about publication, as you know.'[31] He knew he would have to handle Tennyson carefully, so the following week he larded him with flattery, pointing out the inferiority of his own gifts: 'I, whose imagination is to yours as Pisgah to Canaan, the point of distant prospect to the place of actual possession . . . what with you is universal and all powerful . . . in me is checked and counteracted by many other impulses, tending to deaden the influence of the senses which were already less vivacious by nature.' It is in the very last lines of the letter that, strategically, Hallam reveals that he has sent the sonnet to Moxon, who has already printed it. 'You perhaps will be angry . . . I confess this is a breach of trust on my part, but I hope for your forgiveness.'[32] Tennyson's response is not recorded, though Hallam had told him about his own article.

Hallam's efforts behind Tennyson's back did not stop here. He wrote to Charles Merivale the following month, enlisting his help in the trail of literary deceptions that was being drawn around the poet. Merivale was enjoined to 'call upon Mr. Moxon, 64 New Bond Str., introducing yourself under shelter of my name and Alfred's, and to pop the question to him, "What do you pay your contributors? What will you pay Alfred Tennyson for monthly contributions?" Also, while your hand is in, to ask whether if Alfred was to get a new volume, ready to be published next season, Moxon would give him anything for the copyright, & if anything, *what*.'[33] Quite why Merivale had been deputed for this particular task is difficult to understand, and there is no evidence that he actually undertook it.

Hallam was characteristically deprecating about his article *On Some of The Characteristics of Modern Poetry, And On The Lyrical Poems of Alfred Tennyson*, writing to Edward Spedding that 'it was the hasty product of the evenings of one week.'[34] Subsequent critical opinion has been rather more favourable. The essay has been variously seen as foreshadowing the ideas of the symbolists and the imagists and perhaps its most distinguished adherent was W.B. Yeats, who said that 'When I began to write I avowed for my principles those of Arthur Hallam in his essay upon Tennyson . . . who had written but his early poems when Hallam wrote'.[35] More recent critics have taken favourable notice of it too. Peter Allen called it 'a brilliant critical essay, yet one that makes no concessions whatsoever to the prejudices of the ordinary reader', echoing James Spedding's comment that the essay was 'not written for the vulgar but it is dangerous to tell him [Hallam] so'.[36] Isobel Armstrong praises the essay's 'sophisticated carelessness'[37] and finds Hallam's analysis of individual poems more 'convincing than the cumbersome accounts of Fox.'[38]

The essay's title almost suggests two different essays being fused into one: as if a discussion of 'The Lyrical Poems of Alfred Tennyson' was an addendum to another topic, or that discussion of 'Some of The Characteristics of Modern Poetry' was an excuse for giving attention to Tennyson's recent poems. In fact the two parts of the essay, structurally distinct as they are, are closely bound up with each other.

As Armstrong points out it was a feature of nineteenth-century criticism 'to define subjects in terms of direct oppositions between two kinds of poetry',[39] an intellectual scheme which Hallam effectively pioneered. The first part of the essay sets up an opposition between 'the poetry of reflection' and 'the poetry of sensation'. Hallam's erstwhile 'favourite poet', Wordsworth, is now viewed, as the archetypal poet of 'reflection', as inferior to Shelley and Keats. Of Wordsworth he says: 'It is not true, as his exclusive admirers would have it, that the highest species of poetry is the reflective; it is a gross fallacy, that because certain opinions are acute or profound, the expression of them by the imagination must be eminently beautiful.' Thus an admirer of Wordsworth ' will be apt to mistake the pleasure he has in knowing a thing to be true, for the pleasure he would have in knowing it to be beautiful'. He sees Wordsworth's work as containing 'much . . . which is good as philosophy, powerful as rhetoric, but false as poetry'.

This dismissal enables Hallam to offer a critical defence of the so-called 'cockney school', by whom in practice he means Shelley and Keats, and it is here that Hallam's essay takes flight. He is, after all, entering into almost virgin critical territory in offering a sympathetic evaluation of these two poets, still largely unknown to the general reader and hitherto only the subjects of largely derisive reviews. Introducing the two poets into his argument, he says: 'the one [Shelley] was vast, impetuous, and sublime, the other seemed to be "fed with honey dew," and to have "drunk the milk of paradise". Unlike Wordsworth, these are 'poets of sensation . . . Susceptible of the slightest impulse from external nature, their fine organs trembled into emotion at colours, and sounds, and movements, unperceived or unregarded by duller temperaments. Rich and clear were their perceptions of visible forms, full and deep their feelings of music.' He emphasises their 'powerful tendency of imagination to a life of immediate sympathy with the external universe'.

In addressing himself to the question of the state of contemporary literature, he dissents from the utilitarian progressivism of Fox, believing that 'the age in which we live comes late in our national progress. That first raciness and juvenile vigour of literature . . . is gone never to return. Since that day we have undergone a period of degradation . . . [as a result of] the French contagion and the heresies of the Popian school.' One of the most interesting and original features of the essay is the way in which Hallam discusses recent literature in terms which begin to construct a definition of what would later be called 'the Romantic Revival', the sense that the period through which Keats and Shelley lived had brought about a return to something substantial and inspired in poetry after a period of aberration: 'With the close of the last century came an era of reaction, an era of painful struggle to bring our over-civilised condition of thought into union with the fresh productive spirit that brightened the morning of our literature.'

What connects Hallam's discussion of Keats and Shelley most closely with his discussion of Tennyson is the question of popularity. Hallam is adamant that, as 'Art is a lofty tree and may shoot up far beyond our grasp' the visions of what we would now call the Romantic Poets will be too rarefied for common reception: 'those writers will be always most popular who require the least degree of exertion . . . Hence, half the fashionable poems in the world are mere rhetoric, and half the remainder are, perhaps, not liked by the generality for their substantial merits'. This can, of course, be seen as special pleading on behalf of Tennyson whom Hallam conscientiously believed to be the likely property of only a small audience. In claiming that only a few choice spirits could appreciate him, Hallam was making a coterie poet of Tennyson, and whilst this might seem paradoxical in one who is trying to advance his friend's reputation, in view of the extremely hostile reviews that Tennyson's work was to receive over the coming years, Hallam was, in fact, being uncannily prescient.

In introducing Tennyson to his readers, Hallam makes serious claims for Tennyson's standing as a poet of sensation. There is obvious partiality here, but his assessment is not an injudicious one: 'a poet in the truest and highest sense . . . We think he has more definiteness and roundness of general conception than the late Mr. Keats [and unlike Shelley] he comes before the public unconnected with any political party or peculiar system of opinions . . . The features of original genius are clearly and strongly marked. The author imitates nobody.' Hallam's discussion of the features of individual poems show an insight which goes beyond mere rhapsody. The Hallam who had already said of 'Alfred's Mariana' that she 'grew up by assimilative force, out of the plaintive hint left two centuries ago by Shakespeare', had not only thought carefully about how his friend's poems actually worked but was also in command of an accomplished critical language. He laid down several of the terms in which Tennyson's poetry would continue to be discussed. He isolated 'five distinctive excellencies . . . First, his luxuriance of imagination, and at the same time his control over it. Secondly his power of embodying himself in ideal characters, or rather moods of character, with such extreme accuracy of adjustment, that the circumstances of the narration seem to have a natural correspondence with the predominant feeling, and, as it were, to be evolved from it by assimilative force. Thirdly his vivid, picturesque delineation of objects, and the peculiar skill with which he holds all of them *fused,* to borrow a metaphor from science, in a medium of strong emotion. Fourthly, the variety of his lyrical measures, and exquisite modulation of harmonious words and cadences to the swell and fall of the feelings expressed. Fifthly, the elevated habits of thought, implied in these compositions . . . imparting a mellow soberness of tone'.

It is perhaps inevitable, given the passage of time and the emergence of the Tennyson canon, that the individual poems which Hallam chooses for discussion can seem eccentric, and not representative of the essential Tennysonian voice. Hallam praises above all other poems *Recollections of the Arabian Nights* ('a perfect gallery of pictures') and makes great claims also for the naively gruesome *Ballad of Oriana,* which he not very convincingly links to the tradition of *Sir Patrick Spens* and the border ballads. He finds the *Supposed Confessions of a Second Rate Sensitive Mind* . . . full of deep insights into human nature.' He finds the poems about female characters to be 'like summaries of mighty dramas'. He concludes with a debating society squib that he is commending the volume 'to feeling hearts and imaginative tempers, not to the stupid readers, or the voracious readers, or the malignant readers, or the readers after dinner!'[40]

As will be seen, not all the readers of this article found either its content or its tone agreeable, though Hallam was by temperament much more able than Tennyson to weather the storms of controversy. In any discussion of Hallam's life, it is natural to speculate about how his career might have developed. This essay above all others indicates where his real intellectual strength lay. His own invocation of the 'Pisgah to Canaan' image sums up a great deal, as does his description of Tennyson and himself: 'you as poet, I in the humbler station as critic'.[41] Hallam was not likely to enjoy major distinction as a poet and this was abundantly clear, as he well knew, when comparisons with Tennyson were made, but his insight into the workings of literature was considerable and he would surely have become a leading literary-critical voice of the Victorian period if he had lived into it.

Hallam had taken Milnes into his confidence over the clandestine publication of Tennyson's poem in *The Englishman's Magazine* but the friendship between them experienced tensions over the summer from which it never fully recovered. Although Hallam could be fulsome enough to Milnes when the mood took him ('I . . . value highly an intercourse so refined and so agreeable, founded upon mutual regard, and ceme[nted] by some similarity of tastes, and common love of literature',[42] he never felt the warmth of regard for Milnes that Milnes felt for him. Milnes's affection for Hallam was genuine, as his elegies both for him, and later his sister, Ellen, show, but Hallam found the affection ultimately resistible. Peter Levi says, bluntly, that Milnes 'fell in love with Hallam but was severely rebuffed'.[43] Milnes did eventually marry, but it is more than possible that there was a sexual aspect to his admiration of Hallam, a point which has not passed unnoticed by those who wish to impute a homosexual dimension to the membership of the Apostles of Hallam's time, and which will be further discussed in CHAPTER SEVEN.

Milnes had left Cambridge in April 1830, so there was by now, inevitably, a greater distance between him and Hallam. Nevertheless, Hallam had taken Milnes into his confidence about his publishing plans. In writing to him about these on 18 July, Hallam added an initially rather mysterious comment that 'I was much pleased with your behaviour towards me in London, for you had some right to complain, and yet you had tact enough, and good temper enough to take the proper course. I am sorry I ever acted towards you with caprice; at the time I had reasons which seemed to justify my conduct.'[44] It is not at all clear to what Hallam is referring, though, knowing his occasional insensitivity and tactlessness towards his friends, it is not hard to imagine him offending Milnes, particularly when it is remembered that the poem he had written to him a couple of years earlier had contained an exhortation to behave with more seriousness. Milnes's reply has not survived but must have been sent, as Hallam took the matter up with him again two weeks later. On 31 July, after some introductory persiflage about their common friend, Tennant, Hallam's letter assumed the tone of rhetorical elaboration on which he often relied when sensitive or potentially embarrassing topics were to be raised. As was also often the case, Hallam showed himself a master of transition, moving almost imperceptibly from the frivolous to the serious:

> 'I thank you for what you say of my conversation, and I can return the compliment with very great sincerity. When you speak of "other more intimate relations being broken," you seem to labour under an illusion which I think it due to myself to endeavor to dispel, especially as your tone seems intended to convey reproach. I am not aware, my dear Milnes, that, in that lofty sense which you are accustomed to attach to the name of Friendship, we ever were, or ever could be friends. What is more to the purpose, I never fancied that we could, nor intended to make you fancy it. That exalted sentiment I do not ridicule – God forbid – nor consider as merely ideal: I have experienced it, and it thrills within me now – but not – pardon me, my dear Milnes, for speaking frankly – not for you . . . Whether it may not be better for you to take me on these terms, and to give up cheerfully the theory to which you have been visibly labouring to accommodate me . . . I leave you to consider.'[45]

What exactly the 'lofty sense ' or the 'exalted sentiment' are, the letter of course did not say, and it is possible to sense circumlocution as much as definition in the words that Hallam used. Clearly, Milnes's earlier letter had made some kind of protestation to Hallam, some suggestion that their friendship was, or should become, a specially intimate one. It is entirely characteristic of Hallam to respond with an air of dignified stand-offishness. His nature did not easily enter into close friendship, and, as has been already seen, his friendship with Gladstone had its repeated tensions and fractures. Even so, it is interesting that Hallam did not reject entirely the experience of 'exalted' friendship. The friendship which 'thrills' him was presumably that of Tennyson, who would inevitably, both as a superior poet to Milnes and as a potential brother-in-law, have had a higher claim on Hallam's time and affection than Milnes could have. His frank rejection of Milnes in this regard is unambiguous, though Milnes had a tougher skin than Gladstone and did not seem to bear Hallam any subsequent malice. Indeed, the force of Hallam's comments in this letter was to some extent blunted by the fact that the letter crossed with one from Milnes, and that Milnes, who had been travelling over the summer, had still not seen Hallam's letter a month later. Hallam was thus forced to reiterate his comments about Milnes's proffer of friendship. He accepted that they had a mutual esteem, and were bound by 'similarity of tastes', but 'With this Cordelialike proffer I recommend you to be content . . . I protested against that arriere pensee of yours, as ingenious as unfounded, which makes you assume that because I have not towards you the more elevated & vehement species of attachment I am therefore incapable of it altogether . . . I shall not willingly touch upon this subject again . . . but . . . I shall take the opportunity of thanking you from my heart for much in your conduct by which I have been pained at the time, but which I believe was meant well.'[46]

This was not the end of the correspondence between Hallam and Milnes, but there is no record of any more until well into the following year. The friendship between them thus inevitably weakened, though it is notable that, after Hallam's death, Milnes was one of the first of his friends to write to Henry Hallam, with a request that he be allowed to attend the funeral if it was going to be held in London.[47]

At the beginning of September the Hallam family left Hastings and Arthur and his father spent a fortnight in Devon and Cornwall, after which Arthur planned to visit Gaskell at his home in Yorkshire. Apart from bumping into his Cambridge friend Blakesley in Plymouth, the account of the trip to the west country which Hallam gave to his sister Ellen, sounds a rather dispiriting one: 'we were wet through on coach-tops, frozen on rivers in dark nights, famished at old houses, where there are inns, but no food.' There was, however, a visit to the Elton relations at Clevedon Court, interesting because it is the only visit of Arthur Hallam's to Clevedon of which there is an account in his own words, and it would seem to be the only visit which Hallam made there in his years of maturity. It was an unusual event in another way too. His Uncle Charles, having, as a result of his impulsive marriage to a dissenter, been estranged from his family, became reconciled with his father, Sir Abraham, in 1831, and was subsequently welcomed at Clevedon. In consequence Charles's children were complete strangers to Hallam, and he wrote to Ellen expressing helpless bemusement at being surrounded by members of his extended family whom he was scarcely able to recognise or name: 'I was left sitting in an endless circle of cousinly faces, just going through my ABC of family knowledge, repeating "You are not Kitty – you are Jane – " & so forth . . . Caroline & I behaved very cousinly to each other, and upon the whole I think I like her better than I expected – to be sure I did not expect much.' Reputedly, Hallam, used to the presence of younger siblings, got on well with children, but it is difficult not to imagine that he would really rather have preferred the company of the younger Tennysons at Somersby. He was also able to report that 'Harry & Julia were anxiously inquired after by all the old women & children in the lanes about Clevedon', showing that the Hallam connections, however infrequent their visits to the west country had been, were not forgotten.[48]

Slipping his father's leash in order to visit Gaskell in Yorkshire enabled Hallam to indulge in a little more deception. He had suggested that he might meet Tennyson, with Hull as a possible *rendez-vous*, but in the event a more pleasing possibility presented itself. As Emily and Alfred Tennyson were now in Cheltenham, Hallam joined them there, presumably telling his father that he was there to visit Alfred and keeping quiet about Emily. In the unlikely event that Hallam needed to square his conscience about this detour, he could doubtless have said that Henry had only forbidden visits to Somersby, so that he was not infringing the letter of the agreement which the two fathers had made earlier in the year, despite his having already been cavalier enough about its spirit. Certainly he was quite open about the visit in a subsequent letter to Frederick Tennyson: 'I spent a week . . . at Priory House Cheltenham, at the Board of Miss Corgan . . . & in the constant glory of seeing Emily, talking to her and sitting besides her.'[49]

Travelling on to Yorkshire and the Gaskell home at Thornes House, Wakefield, Hallam at first found Gaskell alone as his parents were away in Leamington. They spent their time riding and making various daily excursions, Hallam also claiming that he was about 'to take lessons in fishing'. They visited the nearby ruins of Bolton Abbey, which Hallam enjoyed, and also went to look at 'the Strid . . . a narrow hollow between sharp rocks, where somebody, about whom Wordsworth has written verses [*The Force of Prayer*], fell down, because his greyhound checked him as he took the leap.' This proved a less satisfactory visit as the Strid was 'unfortunately so swollen with rains that it looked for all the world like the other parts of the torrent.' In general Hallam liked the Yorkshire countryside, though found the towns smoky and monotonous. When the Gaskells returned from Leamington, Mrs Gaskell wiled away the evenings by playing the harp in the oval drawing room, while Hallam lay on the sofa and watched the reflections in the mirror as she played. As always, he reported well of Mrs. Gaskell: 'a clever woman, very amiable, and very full of conversation.'[50] Gaskell had been hoping to be nominated for the parliamentary seat of Wakefield at the next election, but, contrary to what had been expected, his uncle, who was the current incumbent, was persuaded not to stand down and consequently held onto the seat.

In reporting to Emily about his sojourn in Yorkshire, it was inevitable that Hallam would tell her something about Gaskell and about the history of their friendship. Although he accepted that by this time he and Gaskell had little in common apart from having been at Eton and subsequently in Italy together, he emphasised that '[Gaskell's] amiability, frankness and courtesy make his society always agreeable to me.' Talking about Gaskell also enabled Hallam to raise another, and potentially sensitive, subject: the 'English lady' that he and Gaskell had met in Italy, and about whom he needed to reassure Emily, who evidently already knew something about her:

> 'the fact is, it was not love I felt for that lady, although in other circum-
> stances it would have become love: but the nature of the case excluded all
> hope, and when the few weeks I passed in her society were over I became
> aware that the sentiments I had experienced had no basis to rest upon,
> although their effects on my mind, awakening and inspiriting all the latent
> powers of reflection and enthusiasm, were very extensive, and such as I
> shall feel in their consequences all my life.'

Although he goes on to add that Emily need not be jealous, as he could not 'see that face again . . . without one disloyal thought to you',[51] Hallam is clearly being disingenuous. His interest in Anna Wintour lasted longer than a 'few weeks' and, as has been seen, was still plaguing him throughout his first year at Cambridge. Indeed, the rapidity of his taking up with Emily herself was partly a reaction against what he saw as Anna's betrayal of him in becoming engaged to another. But the point needed to be made.

When Hallam returned to Cambridge in October it was in the knowledge that his undergraduate career was entering its final phase. There would be the BA examinations early in the new year, and, although he was not seeking honours, Henry would doubtless be hoping for a respectable showing at the very least, and Hallam's self-respect demanded much the same. Although pitched at an explicitly lower level than the Tripos examinations, the syllabus for the pass degree was closely prescribed and it included a substantial mathematical component. The syllabus fell into three parts. Part I comprised: 'Euclid's Elements, Principles of Algebra, Plane & Spherical Trigonometry, Conic Sections, Mechanics, Hydrostatics, Optics, Astronomy, Fluxions, Newton's Principia, Increments, &c., &c'. Part II required study of 'Beausobre's Introduction, Doddridge's and Paley's Evidences, the Greek Testament, Butler's Analogy, Paley's Moral Philosophy, Locke's Essay and Duncan's Logic.' Part III was more simply described: 'The Most celebrated Greek and Latin Classics'.[52]

Not much of this suggests that the preparation would be particularly enjoyable for someone of Hallam's interests, though his rather scanty correspondence during this period suggests that he was working hard for the examination, however unwillingly. He announced to Frederick Tennyson that the 'disdainful oriental beauty, whose name is Algebra' was going to dominate his thoughts as part of his 'studious habits next [i.e. this] term', though he also had to confess that he had made these kind of resolutions before without much success.[53] In mid-term he told Ellen that he was amusing himself in the evenings by reading Spanish, in compensation for the 'hard things' that he was forced to read in the mornings. Even Emily had to take second place for a while, as over the Christmas period Hallam feared that he would 'not have leisure to write to you at any length. You would not wish me to be plucked [i.e. fail], you know'.[54] He informed Brookfield at the same time that he had 'not a moment to spare from mathematics.'[55]

Hallam's scorning delights and living laborious days would have been made easier by the fact that most of his erstwhile closest friends were no longer in residence. The list of those who were present when Hallam read a paper to the Apostles on 29 October included new and unfamiliar names: Morrison, Farish and Heath. Garden and Tennant were also present and were certainly part of Hallam's circle, but very much second generation members of it. Even so, for all the work which Hallam was being forced to do for his degree examinations, there was leisure for a certain amount of independent intellectual activity. There were six meetings of the Apostles that term, at the first of which, on 29 October, Hallam read the paper already mentioned on the subject: 'Is there ground for believing that the existence of moral evil is absolutely necessary to the fulfilment of God's essential love for Christ?' This was the origin of Hallam's published essay *Theodicaea Novissima*.

The 'interminable essay' on Cicero on which Hallam had been working in July had also originated as an Apostolic paper the previous May on the Epicurean and Stoic philosophers. In its expanded form, it acquired the title *On the Philosophical Writings of Cicero* and was submitted for the Trinity College English Essay prize 'on some Literary, Moral, or Antiquarian subject', which it won. Although Hallam in his first year at Cambridge had been critical of the university's culture of emulation, his entries for the Chancellor's Gold Medal, as well as the college essay and declamation prizes showed him to possess well-developed competitive instincts when the circumstances suited him. One of the consequences of his gaining first prize in the previous December's declamation competition was that, in keeping with college tradition, he was required the following year to deliver an oration on a new subject. Hallam chose as his topic 'The influence of Italian upon English Literature', delivering the oration in the college chapel on 16 December in the presence of his father and of Alfred Tennyson, who had come specially to Cambridge to hear it, possibly surprising Hallam by doing so (a letter sent to Emily two days previously clearly assumes that Tennyson is in Lincolnshire). Both the essay and the declamation were early in 1832 printed as pamphlets, by W. Metcalfe of Cambridge who had also been responsible for printing the text of *Adonais*. Hallam dismissed the declamation as belonging to 'a vile mould of composition'[56] and although he believed that the Cicero essay was not the best he was capable of, he thought it was the better of the two pieces. Henry Hallam, though finding it 'perhaps too excursive from the prescribed subject',[57] took sufficient paternal pride in it to send copies to, among others, Samuel Rogers, with a covering note in which he excused himself for believing that Arthur's 'performances [were] a little out of the common.'[58] From Henry Hallam this was high praise. Arthur, too, despite his invariable detachment from what he had recently written, supervised the sending of a copy to his Uncle Henry Elton in Bristol, and also to his old tutor, Hawtrey, at Eton, informing Brookfield, who was acting as postman, in rather blasé fashion, that 'In the last [i.e. Hawtrey's copy] you may stick "from the Author" in my handwriting, if you chuse.'[59] As the tone of Hallam's words suggests, he did not (unlike his father) take Hawtrey unduly seriously, but he was certainly aping the life of a man of letters by printing and distributing signed copies of work and seeing that they found fit audience. His Uncle Henry was perhaps the closest of her three brothers to his mother, though he was an unlikely recipient of Arthur's essays, being by no means the most intellectual member of the Elton family. He showed his gratitude for the gift by writing his nephew a rather patronising letter, warning him of the dangers of intellectual arrogance, about which he clearly had firm views ('nothing is more likely to inflate a man more than a consciousness of intellectual superiority to his fellow Men', etc.). He enclosed some comments from 'a very Clever and Pious Cambridge friend' whom he clearly thought had understood Arthur's efforts better than he did.[60]

These three prose works, all of them substantial, not only show how active Hallam had been during the second half of 1831, but reflect both the depth and the range of his intellectual interests at the time. When the *Theodicaea* paper had been put to the vote, four Apostles (one of whom was Hallam himself) voted in favour of the question, and one (Tennant) opposed it. The fact that six members abstained is perhaps a comment on the subtlety (some might say opacity) of Hallam's argument. Indeed much the same reception had been given just over a year previously to Hallam's paper discussing Hartley's principles of Associationism, where five out of ten Apostles present 'found themselves unable to make up their minds.'[61] It was undoubtedly true that Hallam had raised the standard of Apostolic discussion. The questions put at the time of his joining the group two years earlier seem decidedly earthbound ('Whether England has passed her zenith'; 'Whether the . . . system of "The Division of Labour" . . . has been beneficial to the country'), especially in comparison with the sustained philosophical discourses which Hallam's later papers became, and which caused Donne to complain that, whilst accepting Hallam's promise as a philosopher, 'I cannot for the life understand why he uses so perverse a style. It has neither the pomp and circumstance of elegance, nor the clearness and force of argument.'[62]

The *Oxford English Dictionary,* states that the word 'Theodicea' is faulty etymology, being an 'erroneous Latinisation' of a word which had only existed since the philosopher Leibniz first used it, in French, in 1710. The dictionary's definition of the English derivative 'theodicy' is: 'a vindication of the divine attributes, esp[ecially] justice and holiness, in respect to the existence of evil; a writing, doctrine, or theory intended to "justify the ways of God to men"'. Broadly speaking, this describes the territory which Hallam's essay occupies. At root his work is a subjection of some fundamental tenets of Christian theology to a philosophical critique, though it is a critique which, the best part of two centuries later, inevitably strikes the reader as highly orthodox in its conclusions. Within the context of Hallam's life and writings it adds intellectual flesh to the comment which he had made a few months earlier to Tennyson about the tendency of Christianity to draw 'us all within its magic circle at last.' Perhaps this is why Tennyson always had such a high regard for it.

As the history of several of Hallam's contemporary Apostles shows, to serious and educated young men of this period, religious doubt was part of life. There was, at one extreme, Henry Alford and Francis Garden, each of whom was conventionally pious, and one of whom subsequently enjoyed a distinguished career in the church. At the other extreme there was Kemble, who, having announced an intention to take orders, felt ultimately unable to do so, and Donne, who left Cambridge without graduating, because he was unable, as required, to 'subscribe' that he was 'a *bona fide* member of the Church of England.'[63] Maurice, Sterling and, especially, Trench, though all subsequently ordained, suffered prolonged periods of spiritual struggle. Tennyson's doubts in *In Memoriam*, though not immediately perceived by the poem's first readers, and treated somewhat evasively by his son, were there to see, and were famously described by T.S. Eliot as being much more vividly apprehended than the poem's protestations of faith.[64]

It is worth remembering Hallam's own earlier spiritual struggles too, especially those which beset him in the dark spring of 1829, and which he later described to Milnes as 'grapples with Atheism' though adding that he had 'beat[en] the monster back, taking my stand on the strongholds of reason'.[65] In a protestant environment without the dogmatic certainties of Catholicism it was becoming more and more difficult for intelligent men to accept without question the tenets of Christianity in the light of developing philosophical and scientific thought. Nor had the institutional religion of Eton and Cambridge, combined with the prescribed and outdated apologetics of Doddridge and Paley, been any encouragement to a mature and considered faith. There had not been any suggestion (as there had been with Tennyson) of a career in the Church for Hallam, despite both his grandfathers having been clergymen. It is difficult not to see the *Theodicaea* as Hallam's acknowledgement of his arrival at a position of something like Church of England orthodoxy, as he asserts of his own personal beliefs at the end of the essay: 'the doctrine of a personal love for a personal God is assuredly no novelty, but has in all times been the vital principle of the church . . . and neither the Papal Hierarchy with its pomp of systematised errors, nor the worse apostacy of latitudinarian Protestantism have ever so far prevailed.'[66] It is also relevant that Hallam, seeing himself as shortly to be a married man (and the tone of his letters to Emily certainly bears this out), felt some responsibility as a spiritual, as well as an intellectual guide, to his future wife, despite his opinion that 'I do not think women ought to trouble themselves much with theology'.[67]

Hallam believed that it was incumbent upon Christians to 'give a reason for the faith that is in them', especially as Christianity was no longer to be considered as 'a topic apart from intellectual enquiry', and despite his conviction that the existence of God could not be proved by 'the unassisted efforts of man's reason'. Hallam starts from the premise that that the Bible is 'divinely authorised, and the scheme of human and divine things which it contains [are] essentially true.' God is love, and, despite the objections which can be made to this assertion (several of which Hallam considers), it was out of love that he created the world because love, just 'as it is the noblest quality of the human soul, must represent the noblest affection of the Divine Nature.' Christ thus becomes 'as the object of that Infinite Being's love, the necessary completion of his being.' Hallam raises the question of how Christ could reciprocate God's love given even his almost unimaginable inferiority to him. He could only do this through an encounter with evil. Since, Hallam says, 'the world as it exists, [is] full of sin and sorrow' only by 'a contest with evil', which exists largely 'because it was the necessary and only condition of Christ's being enabled to exert the highest acts of love, that any generated Being could perform.' This still fails to answer the question of why God permitted evil to exist in the world at all, a question which it is superficially, at least, blasphemous to ask, but which Hallam counters by asserting that God's greatness is more readily understood as a result of his having created 'a nature perfectly opposite' (and, by implication, inferior) to his own . . . the purpose of Christ's existence could not have been attained, and the essential nature of God could not have been fulfilled, without an actual contest between Christ and the powers of evil', though Hallam concedes that this 'contest' has involved the rest of humanity 'in its terrible proceedings'.

Hallam offers three reasons to explain why this is so. Firstly, that 'Divine Goodness [is] established rather than impeached by the fact of a ruined world . . . we are certainly not entitled to consider the perpetual misery of many individuals as incompatible with sovereign love.' Secondly, Christ, by 'chusing this mode . . . of warfare with evil . . .

displayed a perfect love for the lost souls of men.' Thirdly, the Holy Spirit was created as a means of ensuring that 'Christ might be loved, so to speak, from below as well as from above.' He then goes on to consider ('though [a] less important part of the subject') how Christ's sacrifice 'procured redemption for fallen man'. That is because love of Christ is the necessary preparation for love of God and because it is possible to know Christ through the gospels: 'we know him as an Elder Brother, a being of like thoughts, feelings, sensations, sufferings, with ourselves'. This gives the death of Christ its significance.

Hallam concludes by considering the arguments of potential opponents to his position, whom he does not expect will be atheists but deists, those who view God as an impersonal force and who would 'assert that a God animated by emotions resembling our own . . . is a figment of presumptuous imagination' though Hallam is emphatic that 'no system of Theism can subsist without the notion of some emotive principle in the Deity.' Ultimately, as already mentioned, his point is that 'the doctrine of a personal love for a personal God is assuredly no novelty, but has in all times been the vital principle of the church.'[68]

Motter sees this essay as 'the most interesting and important of Hallam's writings, being at once a kind of summation of [his] belief and practice',[69] but it seems likely that its original audience saw it rather differently. Their inability to marshal a strong sense either of agreement or disagreement with its arguments is a comment not only on its rhetorical dexterity, but on the fact that it was, indeed, a very personal 'summation of . . . belief and practice', the attempt of a sophisticated mind to construct a personal, yet consciously orthodox, theology. In point of influence, it is clearly inferior to the essay on Tennyson, which has remained a significant document in the history of nineteenth century aesthetics and has a much greater claim to true originality of thought. Hallam's attempts to 'justify the ways of God to men' ultimately present exactly the same problems as Milton's. As Henry Hallam, whose enthusiasm for the essay seems to have been markedly less than Tennyson's, noted: its 'hypothesis, like that of Leibnitz . . . resolves itself at last into an unproved assumption of its necessity', though he grants that is best viewed 'not as a solution of the greatest mystery of the universe, but as most characteristic of the author's mind, original and sublime . . . uniting . . . a fearless and unblenching spirit of inquiry into the highest objects of speculation with the most humble and reverential piety'.[70]

Whilst the *Theodicaea* was Hallam's most public statement on theological matters, it was by no means his last, and his letters increasingly contain Christian argument and exhortation. To Emily he tended to preach, writing to her in January 1832 about the 'reality of Evil' and redemption, and the necessity for a faith which is acknowledged 'by the heart not by the head', and a few months later, when she had clearly been depressed, he stressed his belief in the beauty and power of prayer.[71] A conspicuously sanctimonious tone also enters into his correspondence with the shortly-to-be-ordained Trench, with whom he clearly felt able to discuss spiritual matters, informing him in February that 'My hopes of earthly happiness . . . remain unscathed, but liable to many and terrible contingencies, which at times make me very wretched; but I thank God, Who has bestowed on me some measure of faith', returning to the question of eternal happiness again in his next letter. To Brookfield, who had apparently suffered some kind of disappointment or setback, he could also write that 'there is One, whose Spirit moves on the face of the waters, evermore, as on the first day, bringing light & peace out of chaotic darkness & confusion.'[72]

Henry Hallam's stricture on the Cicero essay (that it was 'perhaps too excursive from the prescribed subject') has been already noted and is fair comment, though Henry clearly had a higher opinion of this work than he did of the *Theodicaea*, and justified its apparent lack of focus by pointing out that Arthur was 'so deeply imbued with the higher philosophy, especially that of Plato . . . that he could not be expected to dwell much on the praises of Cicero in that respect.'[73] Perhaps Henry, like his son, is of the view that Cicero is rather small fry, philosophically speaking. Although Hallam finds things to praise and admire in Cicero's philosophical writings, the essay is another example of his enjoyment of arguing an extreme or at least an unfashionable case. This was something he particularly enjoyed doing in his debating speeches at Eton and another similarity which this essay shares with them is its young man's tendency to patronise the past, noticeably so when Hallam discusses the work of the Epicurean and Stoic philosophers.

Hallam's essay attempts neither to further nor to rehabilitate Cicero's standing as a philosopher. As with his discussions of Shelley or of Tennyson, Hallam takes pride in dealing with a figure who will necessarily be of interest to the few rather than the many. He claims that the current age, in its desire for instant gratification, is too debased in its tastes to appreciate Cicero: 'Cicero, the sedate, the patient, the practical, will [be unable to] retain his influence over the caprices of literary fashion. Already he is superseded in our public schools, and, I might add, were it not for the circumstances in which I am now writing, forgotten at our Universities . . . I do not think it probable that the generations to come . . . will restore either the philosophical works of Cicero, or that literature whose spirit they explore, to the immense popularity they once enjoyed.'[74]

Hallam's discussion of the Epicurean and Stoic Philosophers, from which the essay developed, clearly aimed to entertain its original Apostolic audience. Epicurus, they were told, having formulated the basic assumption of his philosophy: 'lost no time in communicating it to the world . . . but, unfortunately . . . he coupled it with another [idea], utterly unproved, and . . . not only incapable of truth, but productive of the most detrimental consequences to all who received it for truth. He asserted that as

Pleasure is a constituent part of every desire, so it must needs be the only object desired'. This, Hallam says, is 'a fallacy' which has ultimately proved attractive only to 'the profligate, or the feeble'. Nor are the Stoics spared. Their doctrine 'was wrong in the beginning, wrong in the middle, wrong in the end . . . [The Stoics] protested against the simple tenet, from which such fatal consequences were ostensibly derived . . . [they] subvert[ed] the fundamental distinctions of nature, in order to establish that adorable queen on what they considered a securer throne.'

In focusing on the philosophical writings of Cicero, Hallam acknowledges that he is dealing with a small, and by no means the best known part of Cicero's life and *oeuvre:* He cannot be separated from his position of Statesman and of '"Roman gentleman"'. He was also an orator: 'All of these influences (and some of them were not a little feverish and disturbing) he carried with him into the quiet fields and lucid atmosphere of philosophy.' Likewise, as a member of an essentially unphilosophical nation whose 'ordinary pursuits were practical, and their highest aims political', Cicero had no native tradition of philosophy to draw on, and was forced to adapt ideas from the great Greek thinkers in an intellectual environment in which philosophy had become 'an easy trade' and in which 'A minute fastidious casuistry supplied the place of . . . reasoning.' Cicero lacked 'the originality and freshness of the Grecian thinkers' and his own reading of Plato had been inadequate 'since he prefers the sanctions of morality provided by the latter Grecian schools to the sublime principle of love, as taught by the founder of the Academy.' In embracing Stoicism Cicero 'pledged himself to its errors, and became involved in its confusion'.

Nevertheless, Hallam does not dismiss Cicero as a thinker. He praises him as an ethical writer in 'That important division of Ethics, which enforces the moral necessity of self-restraint', and finds that Cicero's *De Amicitia* and *De Senectute* 'have a fine mellow tone of colouring, which sets them perhaps above all his other works in point of originality and beauty'. He is also very sympathetic to those things in Cicero which prefigure Christianity. In this respect Hallam's comments are entirely consistent with his conclusions in the *Theodicaea*. Hallam is clearly very keen to integrate Cicero's ideas with his own views on the philosophical basis of Christianity. In the pre-Christian era 'A school of philosophy stood in the place, and answered to the purpose, as far as it was able, of a national church . . . [and Christianity] brought the poor and unlearned into the possession of a pure code of moral opinion, that before had existed only for the wise.' One of the most important, and, to Hallam's mind, enduring, aspects of Cicero's philosophy was his apprehension of 'a Supreme Mind' and the consequent 'natural expectation of a future state' in which the immortal soul will exist after death and to whom Cicero 'promises the highest rewards to those who cultivated an active life, and busied themselves in political pursuits for the advantage of the state.'

Hallam concludes that, although Cicero was 'averse to original investigation', he is to be admired for 'the acute sagacity with which all varieties of opinion are subjected in turn to the elegance and freedom of liberal discussion'.[75] At root Hallam's views do not differ greatly from other writers on Cicero in the nineteenth century. The young John Henry Newman, in an essay published in 1824 (which it is unlikely that Hallam saw), also stressed the active rather than the contemplative nature of the Roman character, found Cicero an epitome of public virtue and integrity, but saw his philosophical writings as belated graftings onto the work of the Greeks, hampered by a language that was not attuned to philosophical discourse.[76] Later in the century Trollope was to present Cicero's as a 'humane, arguably proto-Christian moral and religious outlook', worthy of 'a fine senatorial parliamentarian and an anticipation of the English Christian gentleman'.[77]

Hallam's belief that the Cicero essay was a superior effort to his essay on the Italian influence on English Literature is demonstrably accurate, though in time he was to serve rather better the subject which fascinated him above all others. His reservations about the genre are well borne out in the resultant 'declamation'. The declamatory style is apparent throughout and, to a dispassionate reader, it is sometimes obtrusive and disabling, only just keeping on the right side of bombast. The tone is less balanced and judicious than it was in the essay on the Civil War of the previous year. Hallam's description of Chaucer, for example, as 'our beautiful morning star, whose beams earliest breaking through the dense darkness of our Northern Parnassus, did so pierce and dissipate its clouds', is decorative rather than scholarly, and although Hallam was dealing with a subject very close to his heart in this declamation, it is, just as much as the Cicero essay, open to the accusation of 'excursiveness', as only the last third of it deals specifically with subject of the Italian influence upon *English* Literature. Its exceptionally wide sweep of European cultural history is at times superficial, as when Hallam seeks to explain the influence of 'the Arabic imagination' on the presentation of 'amorous mysticism' and suggests that the seraglio, which might at first appear to be a prison in which women are kept as slaves, was also 'a temple . . . in which the Mussulman preserves the idol of his affections from vulgar gaze'. It is difficult not to believe that Hallam is trying, purposely, to embrace as wide a range of reference as he could in the aid of a consciously dazzling display.

One thing which the declamation does do, though, is to explain what it was about the Italian Renaissance which drew Hallam to it with such potency. It is at root a very subjective composition. Hallam associates Italian literature with an 'enthusiasm for the female character . . . [in which] the orient light of Poetry threw a full radiance on the natural heart of woman'. It is difficult not to be reminded of Hallam's period in Rome and the infatuation with Anna Wintour, an infatuation which, in turn, had involved her own fusion in Hallam's imagination with the lovers of Dante and Petrarch. Hallam does not separate the love poetry of Renaissance Italy from the language in which it is written, the language itself being also the subject of homage and eulogy. The Italian language, Hallam argues, was obviously the language of those who were the inheritors of the 'lost treasures of heathen civilization, the poets, historians, and philosophers of Greece and Rome.' At the time of 'the revival of literature' Italian authors 'felt their own thought expanded and miraculously strengthened . . . Italian [could take] into itself . . . the whole height, breadth, and depth of human knowledge, as it then stood'. This was also aided by the power and influence of the Catholic religion, an influence of which, in his own time, Hallam, as has been seen, was dismissive, but which in its medieval manifestations, takes on a much more attractive colouration: 'the splendours and pomps of the daily worship; the music and the incense, and the beautiful saints and the tombs of the martyrs – what strong hold must they have taken on the feelings of every Italian!'. Thus Hallam can sum up the predominating features of Italian literature: 'the first a full and joyous reception of former knowledge into their own very different habits of knowing; the second a deep and intimate expression of forms of Christianity'. Hallam's enthusiasm for the cultural monuments of the Italian renaissance was a genuine one, but it is difficult here not to think of a Cambridge undergraduate in winter yearning for the warm south.

Hallam's view of the contemporary state of Britain (and it is with this view that he concludes the declamation) is a gloomy one. He believes that revolution is at hand and sees evidence around him of a 'dispersion of those decencies and charities which custom produces and preserves'. In the face of this dissolution 'nothing possibly can be found to support men but a true spiritual Christianity.'[8]) In this conclusion, Hallam shows consistency with the *Theodicaea* and also with the Cicero essay. Hallam writes from a position of Christian orthodoxy, not as the result of any kind of evangelical conversion experience, but as the result of his having become convinced, philosophically, of the truths of Christian doctrine. This process of conviction had not been an easy one, as he subsequently wrote to Trench, with Apostolic earnestness:

'My hopes of earthly happiness, or if there be any word more appropriate to our pilgrim state . . . remain unscathed, but liable to many and terrible contingencies, which at times make me very wretched; but I thank God, Who has bestowed on me some measure of faith.'[79]

Hallam's writings at this time had another thematic connection. Hallam had much to say on the subject of love. Indeed it was in a discussion of the nature of human and divine love that the argument of the

Theodicaea began. Hallam postulated the creation of the world by God as indicative of his love for it, and argued that this love was not dissimilar from that 'exclusive and absorbing' experience, which 'whenever it exists in greatest perfection in our bosoms, we feel it sin and sacrilege to withdraw any considerable portion of our heart from the adored object.'[80] He went on to contemplate the idea that 'Philosophers who have fallen in love . . . tell us that the passion is grounded on a conviction, true or false, of similarity, and consequent irresistible desire of union or rather identification, as though we had suddenly found a bit of ourselves that had been dropt by mischance as we descended upon earth.' The philosophers in question, Hallam said, had generally been of the belief that 'this erotic feeling is of origin peculiarly divine.' Precisely who these philosophers were, Hallam did not reveal, and the reader senses some special pleading at this point, particularly in his interest in the 'erotic' which is not an area of human experience normally much referred to in theological discourse.

In the Cicero essay, Hallam again considered the nature of love, particularly as he believed that Cicero had wrongly rejected 'the sublime principle of love' as taught by Plato. What Hallam first said about love here was consistent with his comments in the *Theodiceae*: 'Love, in its simplest ethical sense . . . is the desire which one sentient being feels for another's gratification, and consequent aversion to another's pain. This is the broad and deep foundation of our moral nature'.[81] But Hallam went beyond the discussion of love in purely philosophical terms and looked at the question of Platonic love from a historical and cultural perspective, when he wrote that the 'frequent commendation of a more lively sentiment than has existed in other times between man and man, the misunderstanding of which has repelled several from the deep tenderness and splendid imaginations of the Phaedrus and the Symposium, but which was evidently resorted to by Plato, on account of the social prejudices which at that time depressed woman below her natural station'.[82] Although this passage has been read as a suggestion of, or possible apology for, latent homosexuality on Hallam's part,[83] in the absence of any other evidence of homosexual tendencies in Hallam, such an interpretation is an unlikely one, especially if taken out of the context of Hallam's other writings at the time. What it rather seems to show is Hallam's constructing a history of human sexuality in the light of his own emotional experiences and his reading.

Hallam's accounting for Greek homosexuality as a consequence of the 'depression' of women in that culture, links with the comments he makes in the essay on Italian literature about the position of women in the later era. He credits the medieval Italian poets with, in effect, discovering 'the female character . . . the orient light of Poetry threw a full radiance on the natural heart of woman', this, he believes was encouraged by Roman Catholicism which 'wrought in the heart of man a reverence for the weaker sex, both as teaching him to consider their equality with him in the sight of God . . . and as encouraging in himself those mild and tender qualities, which are the especial glory of womanhood'.[84] To Hallam, the eroticism of the Italian poets was perhaps the most important feature of their work.

The emergence of love as a significant subject in Hallam's writing clearly had an autobiographical explanation. Both the earlier, but lingering and not easily forgotten, involvement with Anna Wintour, and the more recent one with Emily Tennyson, kept the question of love very much alive in Hallam's mind, and the construction of his own history of European sexuality parallels his own sexual and literary development, from the male-centred sexual culture which his earliest classical reading reflected, to the emancipations of a more adult world in which the poetry he most admired reflected the intensities of his own emotional life. It is unlikely that Hallam was alone among his friends in thinking about love and about consequent notions of sexual morality An Apostles' meeting of the previous year had posed the question: 'Is the practice of Fornication justifiable on principles of expediency?'. The fact that only one Apostle thought that it was does not detract from the fact that the Apostles were clearly not afraid of discussing questions by which others would have been embarrassed.

The Christmas of 1831 proved something of an anti-climax after the triumphs of Trinity Chapel. Hallam's most notable Cambridge achievements were over. Only work for the Senate House Examination in January remained and Hallam stayed in Cambridge over Christmas in order to work: there is no record of his going home to London. He had already forewarned Emily that, with the expiry of his father's embargo on visiting her at the time of his twenty-first birthday in February, he would not be able to go to Somersby immediately, as his mother would like him home again for the first time in several months. Negotiating a visit to Somersby, even when it became technically 'legal', would in any case be a sensitive business. He wrote from Cambridge to John Frere on 27 December, claiming that he was 'expecting fully' to be 'plucked' in the examinations,[85] though he did spend some time in the company of Gladstone who visited Cambridge at the end of December. It is possible that Gladstone's visit was at Hallam's request as Gladstone's diary entry for 19 December records that Hallam had 'invited a renewal of our correspondence – to my *very* great joy. I ought to be very thankful for it.' Gladstone's sense of being condescended to by Hallam is yet again painfully present in these words, but his desire to see Hallam was so strong that he clearly wasted no time in making the journey to Cambridge.

The examinations for the BA degree, which Hallam sat in January 1832, were conducted according to well-defined rituals not obviously calculated to set anxious examinees' nerves at rest. On 13 January, the Friday morning before the start of the Lent Term, the 'Questionists' (as candidates were called) presented themselves, college by college, at the

Senate House, each group being led by a Master of Arts, specially appointed for the purpose and known as a 'father'. The Questionists were then, for administrative purposes, split into two groups which were examined separately. They each sat five examination papers, described in the official timetable as 'Homer, Virgil, Euclid, Paley and Arithmetic and Algebra'. The examinations were spaced over six days, and the results were announced (with what now seems unbelievable speed) on 21 January. In order to graduate, every Questionist had also to provide evidence that he subscribed to the doctrines of the Church of England, that he had passed the Previous Examination, and that he had 'kept' the necessary number of terms of residence (ten).

This latter requirement was to be a matter of minor irritation, as, technically, Hallam was in breach of it, having, as a result of illness, not resided for most of the summer term of 1829. It was thus incumbent upon him to provide the 'Caput' (a body comprising the Vice-Chancellor and the Professors of Divinity, Law and Physic, together with the Senior Regent and Non-Regent) with a medical certificate. Hallam was concerned that the certificate had not been drawn up by his physician 'in the proper forms' and that the Caput in its bureaucratic idiocy might well reject it. He urgently requested his father to arrange for another certificate to be sent, as otherwise he feared that he would be required to spend an extra term at Trinity before he could graduate. In the event, this was not to be the case, as Hallam was able to inform Emily on 22 January that he was now a Bachelor of Arts, and his time at Cambridge was over.

A few days later Hallam was apologising to Gladstone for not being well enough to write to him at length, though this was perhaps an excuse, as in all other respects he seemed healthy and active enough. He went off to join his family who were staying at Rose Hill, Tunbridge Wells, and he remained with them for the next month or so. Henry Hallam found the town 'excellent wintering' adding that 'We have a very small society of people we like, and play sixpenny whist when it might be dull else'.[86] Predictably, Arthur's views of the place were rather different, as the doggerel he included in a letter to J.W. Brookfield shows. Hallam, of course, is bored:

> Damned to a series of most awful dinners
> With coteries of ancient Tunbridge sinners,
> And cards, where all, save I, are always winners.[87]

As was generally the case when Hallam pronounced himself bored, he had plenty of time for reading and was beginning to plan a translation of Dante's *Vita Nuova* which he hoped would be ready towards the end of the year 'prefaced by some biographical chatter, & wound up by some philosophical balderdash about poetry & morality & metre & everything.' He was also decidedly apprehensive about the next stage of his education, as he wrote to Donne, who had left Cambridge and was now living a rustic life in Norfolk: 'I am about to become a nominal student of law . . . but . . . I have not much thought of practising. The life I have always desired is the very one you seem to be leading. A wife & a library – what more can man, being rational, require, unless it be a cigar?'[88] The mention of a wife perhaps explains why the news had somehow reached Oxford that Hallam's marriage was imminent: he received letters of congratulation from Doyle, Gaskell and Gladstone, though in fact he confessed himself to be 'getting very nervous about Somersby . . . Not a syllable have I spoken yet about my intentions to Pa or Ma.'[89]

Requests to visit Somersby would not be well-received by Henry, who had already taken the next stage of Arthur's career in hand. References to reading Justinian the previous summer show that Hallam had been given no option as to what was expected of him on graduation. Like his younger brother, and considerable numbers of other Old Etonians and Trinity men,[90] he was bound for the Inner Temple, to which he was admitted on 23 February 1832. He began to 'keep' his first term there in April. Henry writes of this period, somewhat smugly, that it was 'greatly [his] desire that [Arthur] should engage himself in the study of the law; not merely with professional views, but as a useful discipline for a mind too much occupied with habits of thought, which ennobling and important as they were, could not but separate him from the every-day business of life; and might, by their excess, in his susceptible temperament, be productive of considerable mischief'.[91] This was, of course, the old argument about the advantages of studying mathematics surfacing again in a different guise, and Arthur's reaction (already quoted in his letter to Donne) was a predictable one. 'Susceptible temperament' or not, Arthur was wedded to his 'ennobling' habits of mind, and Henry could not honestly claim much success so far in separating him from them.

PART TWO   *Mainly in London*

The legal training which young men of Hallam's generation underwent, like so much else in his education, might seem rather casual by more recent standards. Like Eton and Cambridge, the Inns of Court were institutions in need of reform. In the early nineteenth century their function was regulatory and social, rather than educational, and the Inner Temple manifested in both its buildings and its practices an air of 'genteel decline'.[1] At the time of Hallam's admission it was the smallest of the four Inns, though it expanded during the course of the century to replace Lincoln's Inn as the largest. The Inner Temple was alone amongst the Inns in requiring its entrants to pass an examination in 'classical attainments and the general subjects of a liberal education',[2] though the examination was seen less as a test of academic attainment than a sign that the candidate was of the right social type. The desire to be socially selective was deep-seated and was the result of the fact that potential barristers needed considerable private means in order to weather their first years at the bar when they would not receive any other income. Graduates of Oxford or Cambridge could be called to the bar after three years of 'reading' rather than five.

Whilst it would be wrong to dismiss the Inns of Court as merely finishing schools for young men of a certain class, it was undoubtedly true that many of those who were admitted had little intention of becoming professional lawyers (as Hallam's own remark about having 'not much thought of practising' hints). The Inns were attractive to potential students whose origins were in London[3] and also to those who wished to gain knowledge of the rudiments of the law in order to help them in running their estates. Once admitted to an Inn, there was no subsequent examination to be passed. Indeed, the idea of examining lawyers was considered in many quarters as ungenteel, as an incompetent practitioner would inevitably be found out and thus would not be able to develop a practice. The only formal qualification was to wait the necessary number of years and to eat a prescribed number of dinners in the Inn: three dinners per term, for twelve terms, hence the criticism that students were required merely to 'eat their way to the bar'.[4]

As the Inns did not provide any kind of tuition for their students, the students taught themselves by reading the standard law textbooks and apprenticing themselves to established practitioners. *Coke on Littleton* and Blackstone's *Commentaries on the Laws of England* formed the staple reading. Blackstone was an eighteenth-century judge who had been the first Professor of English Law at Oxford and whose star as a legal authority was very much in the ascendant at this time. Hallam did in fact claim some enthusiasm for 'the old fellow'[5] though his carelessness in leaving his copy on a boat during his summer trip to the Rhineland suggests that this enthusiasm might have been temporary.

For their practical training students undertook a pupilage with either a barrister, a special pleader, or an equity draftsman and conveyancer.[6] Those who wished to specialise in equity law were apprenticed to a conveyancer and usually worked in London, while those with an interest in common law were apprenticed to special pleaders and would work largely in the provincial assize courts.[7] Hallam's younger brother was to take the latter course, but Hallam himself was apprenticed to a Mr. Walters, who had a conveyancing practice in Lincoln's Inn Fields. Translating Dante, writing for journals, and the presence of Emily Tennyson in his life, meant that legal studies were far from uppermost in Hallam's mind for most of the time, and references to the Inner Temple in his letters are scanty and disparaging. He found the eating of dinners disagreeable 'for one is surrounded by hideous students in gowns & red whiskers, chattering about entails and mortgages'.[8] He found the dinners 'execrable' in quality and the company 'snobs'.[9]

Nevertheless Hallam was not thrown into the travails of the law immediately and indeed he followed his formal admission to the Inner Temple with what was the longest visit he had yet paid to Somersby, setting off two days later and remaining for five weeks until the end of March. He explained to Trench that he was visiting Somersby 'not only as the friend of Alfred Tennyson, but as the lover of his sister. An attachment on my part of near two years' standing, and a mutual engagement of one year, are, I fervently hope, only the commencement of an union which circumstances may not impair and the grave itself not conclude.'[10]

It was a period of great happiness. Hallam felt as though 'I had never known love till now . . . Never before have I known at one moment the luxury of actual delight, the reasonable assurance of its prolongation through a happy life.'[11] He was, like many lovers before and after him, convinced that his happiness in love was God-given. Whilst he complained that there were no horses available for riding and that the Tennyson sisters seemed less accomplished in their music-making than they used to be, it was clearly a busy period socially, with visits from Brookfield and Tennant, as well as Garden and Monteith, the latter of whom Frederick Tennyson feared were 'rather too magnificent for a little Parsonage in a remote corner of Lincolnshire'.[12] Brookfield in later years recorded his visit lyrically, transposing it in the memory from spring to summer, and recalling sitting up all night talking until daybreak, when, instead of going to bed, the young people walked out to watch the sun rising over the Wolds.

Unsurprsingly, the visit marked an intensification of the relationship between Hallam and Emily, so that Hallam's eventual parting from her at the end of March was acutely painful: 'bitter, even beyond what I had expected . . . I was quite faint, and the blood burned in my temples'.[13] From this time onwards both the tone and the frequency of the correspondence between Hallam and Emily changed, Hallam accepting that 'the last five weeks have fastened bonds of new, & invincible strength around our hearts . . . Let us pour out our moods to one another as freely, as tenderly . . . as when we sat side by side on the sofa.'[14] After Hallam's return to London a pattern was formed in which Emily generally wrote a letter each week which arrived on Saturday and to which Hallam replied by return, though, as will be seen, these letters charted misunderstandings as well as fond intimacies. Hallam's love for Emily was now the most important thing in his life, but it also brought anxieties with it. Hallam had asked to visit Emily's grandfather while he was in Lincolnshire, but had been refused on the grounds of old Mr. Tennyson's alleged ill-health. Entirely characteristically, the old man then complained that Hallam had ignored him. This lack of cooperation was to continue over the ensuing months. Setting out on his return journey, Hallam paid a private homage to the Tennyson family by visiting Dr. Tennyson's grave, where he prayed that he and Emily would enjoy a happy marriage. He returned to London, as he generally did, via Cambridge, and although he was able to meet friends, including Tennant and Brookfield there, he felt out of the swing of Cambridge life ('New customs, new topics, new slang phrases'),[15] even though he had left only weeks before. He had other things to occupy him now and was keen to move on. He did not look back on Cambridge with undue sentimentality, though he continued to visit it regularly.

This particular visit to Somersby was significant in another way too. Although it had been reported that Alfred was unwell, Hallam actually found him on good form and also discovered that he had been writing a great deal. He informed Trench delightedly that 'There is written the amount of a volume rather larger than the former, and certainly . . . more free from blemishes and more masterly in power'.[16] Recently completed poems included the first versions *The Palace of Art*, *Oenone*, *The Lotos Eaters* and *The Lady of Shalott* among others, and once more Hallam felt that he needed to take the business of publication in hand. He saw no reason for Tennyson to rush into print immediately, though he admitted that he would never feel 'easy or secure about your MSS until I see them fairly out of your control'.[17] To that end he employed Emily as a scribe as a means of ensuring he possessed as complete a set of the recent poems as possible, given Alfred's habitual carelessness with his manuscripts. Hallam continued to assemble manuscripts until the autumn, by which time he had arranged publication with Moxon, to whom he delivered the final versions of the poems in late September, though suggesting that Moxon waited a while before printing in case Tennyson continued to be indecisive about the poems' order.

Although Tennyson had been basking in the light of his friends' appreciation, and the reviews of Fox and of Hallam himself had ensured a favourable reception for the 1830 volume, this honeymoon period did not last. In May 1832, John Wilson, under his customary pseudonym of 'Christopher North', published a review in *Blackwood's Edinburgh Magazine* which took up the cudgels not only against Tennyson's poems, but against Hallam's essay. Wilson, who had reached a position of literary eminence in Edinburgh having sprung from humble origins in Paisley, took pride in the self-consciously pugnacious persona with which he had belaboured the reputations of a great many authors since the time of Byron. In an age when literary reviewing was generically ill-mannered (Francis Jeffrey's activities spring to mind also), Wilson was perhaps by this time its most celebrated exponent. William Hazlitt described him as 'a swaggering bully' and 'the bludgeon man'.[18] Wilson's review was one of exuberant malice, clearly enjoying lacerating the reputations of what he saw as two young 'cockney' upstarts. He began by blaming Hallam's essay for *The Englishman's Magazine*'s untimely demise: '[it]ought not to have died, for it threatened to be a very pleasant periodical. An essay "on the Genius of Alfred Tennyson," [sic] sent it to the grave. The superhuman-nay, supernatural-pomposity of that one paper, incapacitated the whole work for living one day longer in this unceremonious world . . . The Essay . . . awoke a general guffaw, and it expired in convulsions'.[19] Wilson also found Fox's praise of Tennyson in his *Westminster Review* article 'a perfect specimen of the super-hyperbolical ultra-extravagance of outrageous Cockney eulogistic foolishness'.[20] (No less).

As regards the general critical reception of Tennyson's work in the 1830s, this article was, sadly, cast in the shape of things to come, though neither Hallam nor Tennyson could have foreseen this. With hindsight, Hallam's decision to send Tennyson a copy of the review as soon as he had seen it seems miscalculated in the light of Tennyson's acute sensitivity to criticism. Although Hallam would doubtless have justified his action on the grounds that it was better that Tennyson should not come upon Wilson's comments unawares, his response illustrates a fundamental difference between the two men's characters. As Tennyson's self-appointed literary agent, Hallam inevitably believed that any publicity which his friend's work might receive would be advantageous and calculated to 'assist rather than hinder the march of your reputation',[21] and he confided to Brookfield that although he had 'a huge desire to kick' Wilson, 'all things considered the review will do good rather than harm'.[22] Hallam was amused rather than annoyed by the attack. More crucial in Hallam's reaction is the fact that he himself, nothing if not argumentative, thrived on controversy. Although he never himself took on Wilson directly, he was accustomed to giving every bit as much as he got when discussing literary matters. But Tennyson was stung and responded in time (and contrary to Hallam's advice) by publishing a rather maladroit poem attacking Wilson.

Although there are isolated references in his letters to feeling ill and depressed, Hallam's months in London following his return from Somersby were generally sociable and light-hearted ones. Henry Hallam referred to the period as one in which there was 'a gradual but very perceptible improvement in the cheerfulness of his spirits . . . in general he was animated and even gay; renewing or preserving his intercourse with some of those he had most valued at Eton and Cambridge'.[23] Someone of whom he saw much more at this time was Fanny Kemble, by whom, especially when she was performing, Hallam continued to be beguiled, although (like most of the critics) he was not particularly impressed with her when she played Lady Macbeth opposite her father. Macbeth was one of Charles Kemble's most celebrated roles, but Hallam found Fanny's performance disappointing in comparison with that of her aunt, Mrs. Siddons. He dined with the Kembles shortly afterwards, when John Kemble brought dire reports of post-revolutionary Paris from which he had just returned. On his visits to the Kembles, Hallam was able to discover that Fanny Kemble was more than just a stage star. She was widely read and would have preferred a career as a writer had she not been prevented by a severe streak of self-criticism from being satisfied with what she wrote. Hallam witnessed two further appearances by Fanny, both in plays by James Sheridan Knowles, the first one in a play called *Julia*. Although the play itself was undistinguished, Hallam enjoyed Fanny's performance, and shortly afterwards dined with her again, when he 'sat next to her, & had much conversation with her, Certainly she is a very striking person.'[24] In early May he saw her in another play by Knowles, *The Hunchback*, in which 'Miss Kemble acted still more magnificently than the 1st. time'.[25]

Hallam's flirtations with Fanny may have been innocent in intention, but they were the mark of a natural ladies' man. Although Fanny was not the best friend to Hallam's reputation after his death, she was clearly much taken by him at the time, confiding in her journal that: 'I am not sure that I do not like him the best of all John's friends. Besides being so clever, he is so gentle, charming and winning.'[26] It is not difficult to imagine what the always susceptible Hallam's reactions to Fanny's attentions would have been, nor their effect upon his vanity, but that he communicated his feelings about Fanny with abandon in letters to Emily shows thoughtlessness and insensitivity. The fact that Emily, in response to Hallam's letters, often complained of feeling unwell at this time, does not, therefore, seem entirely coincidental. Emily may have appeared the weaker vessel, and Hallam often took a rather imperious attitude towards her, but she was, and continued to be, more than capable of playing psychological games with him when she chose.

A frequent cause of frustration to Hallam at this time was Emily's (clearly calculated) refusal to do anything other than hint about the state of her health. Emily possessed her share of the Tennyson hypochondria, and she was clearly not above using it in order to taunt Hallam. Hence on 28 April, he expresses disappointment that she has described herself merely as 'As well as *usual*'. Hallam takes this to imply 'difficult' behaviour on Emily's part: 'I fear it means frequent pain & sadness; it means not coming down to breakfast, & not going in to dinner; it means now in the end of April all it would have meant in the middle of March' [i.e. when Hallam was staying with her]. Hallam duly exhorted her to a greater resolution 'that we may both have strength to resist a self-idolatrous tendency to the indulgence of despondent or of sanguine moods, or any that are not consecrated by the desire of pleasing God.'[27] He counselled her 'not to esteem all painful emotions deeper and truer than the joyful ones',[28] whilst providing enthusiastic reports of Miss Kemble's acting and his various social encounters with her. He asks Emily to put her trust in prayer. At one point she claimed to be too ill to write at all (though describing her illness as 'only a cold'),[29] and her brother Charles wrote in her place.

By the beginning of June Hallam was again taking a severe tone and he lectured Emily: 'For God's sake do not leave me in ignorance of any change that occurs in your health: I cannot make out from what you now say what kind of illness you have had, whether an aggravation of your constant annoyances, or something quite new & distinct. Charles spoke of "epidemic cold", but a word of that sort means anything. Tell me truly, have you only suffered what others in the family have suffered, or is your former complaint made worse? . . . Have you been under Dr. Bousfield's care? What does he tell you? I am determined, when I next come to Somersby, to see him, & learn from him his real opinion.'[30] Had he lived to marry Emily, Arthur Hallam could well have proved every bit as authoritarian a husband as Henry, from whose intransigence he was himself now again suffering.

Hallam was receiving no encouragement in his relationship with Emily from either of their families. As well as the difficulty posed by old Mr. Tennyson ('that wrongheaded grandfather of yours')[31], Hallam had to report to Emily that

> 'my prospect of attaining the only earthly happiness possible for me, my union with yourself, depends entirely on my father's will. It would not depend at all on his will had I any money, not drawn from his purse; but I have not; nor is it probable that I should succeed in gaining any for several years. I have represented to my father so strongly how important it is to my happiness, my health, perhaps my life, that I should not be left so long in a condition of miserable suspense, uncertainty, & divided existence . . . He cannot endure the idea of my withdrawing myself from the society in which he has been accustomed to move, or abandoning the profession which he chose for me, at least until I have practised it.'[32]

In short Henry was concealing social snobbery behind a mask of economic pragmatism.

Despite these tribulations, Hallam continued to keep in touch with his Cambridge friends. On 12 May he reported to Emily that he had just returned from an Apostolic dinner, in which Alfred Tennyson's health had been drunk, and, according to Merivale, the 'best part . . . was the mutual recriminations of Spedding and Hallam for killing *The Englishman,* and their joint indignation at Blackwood for cutting him up after death'.[33] Despite (or perhaps because of) the controversy arising from Wilson's review of the 1830 volume, Tennyson was undoubtedly viewed as the Apostles' greatest celebrity and the following month Hallam was able to herald Tennyson's imminent arrival in London by informing John Kemble 'I have news for you, great news – Alfred the great will be in town . . . He lingers now at Cambridge with Tennant. He talks of going abroad instantly, from which I shall endeavor to dissuade him.'[34] Tennyson's London visit was viewed with keen anticipation by the other Apostles too and James Spedding also wrote in similar terms: 'The great Alfred is here . . . smoking all the day, and we went . . . on a pilgrimage to see him; to wit, Two Heaths, my brother and myself, and meeting Allen on the way, we took him along with us, and when we arrived at the place appointed we found A.T. and A.H.H. and J.M.K. So we made a goodly company, and did as we do at Cambridge'.[35] Apart from conversation and smoking, Hallam also complained on one occasion of being exhausted after dancing all night, and recorded Tennyson's first visit to dinner with his family in Wimpole Street. Tennyson was at first very nervous, though he eventually became more animated 'on mention of some water-insects of his acquaintance.'

Hallam introduced Tennyson to John Kemble's family. Fanny Kemble had become a great enthusiast for Tennyson's poems, and her sister had made a transcription of *The Lady Of Shalott* (presumably, as it was not yet in print, it had been read to her by Hallam). Hallam, in Tennyson's company made a second visit to see Fanny in *The Hunchback* in which he believed she had acted 'better than ever . . . I think, *because she knew Alfred was there.*'[36] Certainly Fanny took a great liking to Tennyson, one which to some extent supplanted her earlier interest in Hallam. She freely and publicly proclaimed him the greatest of living poets, and although she found his 'sarcastic expression' and lengthy silences disconcerting, she admitted to admiration and love of him in the light of his poetic achievements.[37] Tennyson read Fanny's own unpublished play, *The Star of Seville*, of which he had a high opinion (inevitably higher than Fanny's own) though her earlier play *Francis the First*, had had proved a success when it had been produced at The Covent Garden Theatre in March.[38]

Clearly much fun was had amidst this talented and extrovert family. James Spedding's brother, Edward, reported a Sunday evening spent at the Kembles' house in which he heard 'French and German oaths and curses set to music', songs from Fanny, a recitation by Tennyson of *The Legend of Fair Women*, and some mimicry from John Kemble after which Tennyson, not to be outdone, performed his own party pieces, including his imitation of the sun coming out from behind a cloud.[39]

Hallam failed in his attempt to discourage Tennyson from travelling abroad. Tennyson remained vague about his plans for a time, but then, on what seems like the spur of the moment, decided to go to Germany and persuaded Hallam to go with him. Hallam took Emily by surprise when he wrote to her in a letter of 30 June that he and Alfred were setting off the very next day 'up the Rhine for three weeks! He [Alfred] complained so of his hard lot in being forced to travel alone, that I took compassion on him, & in spite of law and relatives &c. I am going'.[40] He consoled Emily by promising to go straight to Somersby on his return. Whatever guilt he felt about leaving Emily at such short notice was presumably compensated for by his sense of freedom at being able at last to come and go without having to ask his father's permission. Nor, evidently, was his commitment to his legal studies strong enough to detain him in London.

The speed with which travelling arrangements could be made in 1832 is unimaginable today, though the rather impromptu way in which this voyage was undertaken might go some way to explaining why it turned out to be a not entirely satisfactory one. It is also interesting to speculate about why Germany was chosen as the destination. John Kemble's enthusiastic reports of his period of residence in Germany might have influenced Tennyson, and Hallam had at one stage briefly contemplated going off to a German university for a time. Even so Hallam was relatively unusual for one of his generation in being more interested in Italian than in German culture, and, as he had already twice visited the Rhine Valley with his parents, it seems unlikely that he would have gone to Germany at this time if Tennyson had not persuaded him to. In his choice of destination, Tennyson was doing no more than reflecting popular taste, as Rhine journeys were particularly fashionable among English tourists at the time.

They set off for Holland on the steamboat *Batavier* ('as illbuilt & unpleasant a vessel as I ever saw'[41]), where, on arrival, after 24 hours at sea, they found themselves in quarantine. There had been a cholera epidemic in Holland (London had recently seen cases too), as a result of which incoming travellers were offered the alternative of either being moved to a quarantine island under Dutch guard or remaining on their boat in the Maas river. Hallam and Tennyson took the latter option and were quartered on the boat for a further six days. The conditions were appalling: cabins were dirty and infested with insects, the ship's attendants were surly, and Hallam said that the dinners provided were the worst that he had ever eaten. They were allowed off the boat only to walk for a few paces under armed guard and in fear of being shot or having their quarantine period doubled if they strayed. On one occasion another boat from London drew alongside them which actually had cases of cholera on board. The poor people were taken ashore where they could be seen dying one by one. At night Hallam had the melancholy experience of watching boats coming to land at the island where the corpses of victims were subsequently dissected and buried. This did little for the travellers' morale and Hallam even threatened to swim back to England. They also feared that the damp conditions on board and their closeness to an infected boat might lead to the spread of cholera among their fellow passengers. In a final gesture of frustration, Hallam and Tennyson went out on deck and pulled down the Dutch colours. Eventually they were allowed to stay in Rotterdam. Frances Brookfield reported an old story that Hallam, to please his father, had taken six volumes of Herodotus with him, along with some philosophy books, for his own enjoyment. Be that as it may, Hallam certainly took a copy of Blackstone with him, but contrived to leave it behind on the boat. Arrangements were subsequently made to have the book returned for collection at John Kemble's house. Both Hallam and Tennyson were short of money, and not therefore best pleased by the extortionate prices they were charged for their food. Hallam described the conditions in a letter to Kemble, rising rhetorically to the occasion and speaking of 'lying in a mud-yellow river, between two of the flattest, ugliest banks in Christendom . . . My wit is exhausted, & I fear smacks of the stagnant ditches which regale our sight & smell, & I believe furnish the water we drink'.[42]

Although Tennyson had been the moving spirit behind this trip, as they passed through Holland he was resolutely unwilling to enjoy the scenery, which he thought was too like Lincolnshire. Hallam was fairly jaundiced too, though he liked the quaintness of Rotterdam with its 'Ships, houses, trees all mingled pell-mell; & looking glasses hung out of every window.'[43] They subsequently visited Delft, the Hague and Nimwegen, before continuing up the Rhine into Germany. Tennyson remained irritable and hard-to-please (Hallam said he was suffering 'paralysis of the brain') firmly sticking to his view that 'the Rhine was no more south than England', and asserting obstinately that he could have designed a better river himself. Similar sentiments had actually been expressed by Henry Hallam fourteen years before, when he made his remark about the Rhine at Cologne reminding him of the Thames at Battersea. Eventually reaching Cologne themselves, Hallam and Tennyson were much cheered by the great, though still not completed, cathedral. Hallam found Cologne 'the paradise of painted glass . . . The Cathedral is unfinished & if completed on the original plan will be the most stupendous & magnificent in the world.' He also mentioned seeing the cathedral's greatest treasure, the Tomb of The Three Kings 'nearly all of pure massy gold, studded with rich precious stones'.[44] After Cologne, they visited the neighbouring and smaller but elegant city of Bonn, birthplace of Beethoven, and which Hallam thought bore 'a sort of family likeness' to Cambridge.

From Bonn, Hallam and Tennyson took a 'luxurious climb' up the Drachenfels mountain, the luxury taking the form a horse-drawn carriage. Upon reaching the summit, they ate cherries beneath the wall of the castle. They then went on to the island of Nonnewerth, where they spent the night in what had been an old Benedictine convent with fine views of the mountains and river. On their way there, being rowed across stream by an old woman, they narrowly avoided being run down by a passing steamer, Hallam adding to the danger of the situation by trying to take charge of the navigation. Further stops were made at Boppart and Andernach, and they reached their journey's end at Bingen, just short of Mainz. Hallam reported that they had 'drunk infinite Rhenish, smoked illimitable Porto Rico, & eaten of German dinners enough to kill twenty men of robust constitution.'[45] They returned in mid-July: rather a brief trip by the standards of the day, but presumably limited by shortage of money. They returned by way of Aix La Chappelle to Belgium, and then via Brussels to the Channel coast. Tennyson had been diverted at Aix by the spectacle of a statue of the virgin on the cathedral roof whose dress blew about in the wind to reveal that she was wearing 'foul linen' underneath. A further reminder of the hazards that attended foreign travel was provided when their coach overturned in a ditch. Hallam claimed that he had commandeered a posse of fifty Belgians to right it, by pushing it backwards through a hedge into an orchard. His subsequent accounts of this trip differed from Tennyson's. Hallam was, according to Spedding, 'brimful of adventures and anecdotes' whereas Tennyson's version was more prosaic.[46] Hallam generally found that travel provided him with a lot to say, and he was clearly not above spicing up his accounts when he had the right audience. Tennyson, although keen to embark on it, had clearly not found the trip much fun.

Returning to England and wishing to go to Somersby, Hallam again had to be devious. He had informed his father, by letter from Germany, of his intended visit to Lincolnshire and managed to avoid him on his return to London (the Hallam family were out of town at the time). He clearly did not want to run the risk of Henry's trying to prohibit the visit and went so far as to swear Kemble to secrecy about his movements should Kemble encounter Henry in the meantime. Hallam and Tennyson travelled northwards together in the first week of August, staying in Cambridge en route, where they met James Spedding who invited them to breakfast, and was regaled with their travellers' tales, in the company of Tennant and Edward Lushington.

If Hallam's visit to Somersby in April of 1832 had been a happy and romantic affair, his August visit was much more fraught. He told Brookfield that he had been 'very unwell, & very wretched . . . suffering the pressure of a severe anxiety, which, although past, has left me much worn in spirit . . . I have been very miserable since I saw you: my hopes grow fainter & fewer . . . Somersby looks glorious in full pride of leafy summer. I would I could fully enjoy it: but ghosts of the Past & wraiths of the Future are perpetually troubling me.' The continued intransigence on the part of both families over the question of his marriage to Emily was preying on his mind and casting dark clouds over what he must have hoped would be a much happier stay. In particular he was driven to despair by the obduracy of his own family, declaring to Brookfield that if he was successful in gaining Emily's hand, it would be at the cost of 'the affection of my own family, the faces of my home, the faces of my infancy'.[47] Soon after arrival at Somersby, Hallam had paid a visit to Rev. T.H. Rawnsley, Rector of Halton Holgate, who had been appointed Emily's guardian after Dr. Tennyson's death, but of whose existence Hallam had previously been unaware. Rawnsley, too, had been unaware that 'young Hallam' (as he referred to him) considered himself engaged to Emily. Rawnsley was not himself an obviously vindictive man and he tried his best to be fair and reasonable, but he was clearly caught in a situation in which it was impossible to be an intermediary in negotiating a wedding settlement about which the two relevant parties had no desire to negotiate at all.

After Arthur's visit to him, Rawnsley wrote to Henry Hallam, from whom he received a reply dated 22 August, just over a week after Arthur's letter to Brookfield. In order to appreciate both its tone and its detail, the text of Henry's letter needs to be quoted in full:

Sir,

The subject of your letter is by no means new to me, but has been the cause of great perplexity & solicitude for a considerable time. In the early part of 1831, a correspondence took place between the late Dr. Tennyson & myself, which is doubtless in the possession of Mrs. T. & to which I should desire you to have recourse. It will there appear that I stated very explicitly the difficulties that stood in the way of my consent to my son's wishes, partly on account of his age, but still more from my inability to make him such allowance as could suffice by any means to maintain a family as respectably as the situation of the parties required. Dr. Tennyson's answer to my letter was an excellent one; & he appeared to coincide altogether in the views I had taken of the subject.

It was certainly my hope, & was intimated by me as delicately as I could, that the young lady would have released a promise made by a boy of 19, who had neither his father's consent, nor any reasonable prospect of fulfilling the engagement. I stipulated with my son that he should not go to Somersby *during his minority*; & Dr. Tennyson felt that, on his own & his daughter's account, he could not think of inviting him.

The lamented death of Dr.T. took place not long after this; & nothing passed between my son & myself on the subject till last spring, when, having come of age, he expressed his wish to go to Somersby. I could not object to this, having limited my prohibition to his minority; & it came out about this time, that a correspondence had been kept up all along with the young lady. If this was done with Mrs. Tennyson's approbation, I must say that, making every allowance for a mother's feelings, under distressing circumstances, she had done all in her power to frustrate not only my intentions, but those of her husband as signified to me. My son considered himself too far engaged in honour by this correspondence, & by the sort of renewal of their mutual promises which had taken place, to marry any other woman – in which it was impossible for me not to concur. But this of course left the objections to their union grounded on *want* of adequate income just as before. Of my son's *present* visit to Somersby I had no knowledge or suspicion, till he informed me of it by a letter from the continent, to which he had gone for a short time with Mr. Alfred Tennyson.

My uniform language to my son has been, that it would give me the utmost pleasure to see him happy; but that I am bound to consider the claims of my other children, by which I mean not only their claims to an adequate provision after my death, but to partake in the advantages of my fortune during my life. He has entered on the study of the law, a profession which I know to be expensive, & which, for several years, cannot afford him the slightest return. His abilities however are excellent, &, if rightly directed, may, it is to be hoped, in some mode or other become serviceable hereafter to his worldly interests.

My circumstances do not permit me to make a larger allowance to my son, in the event of marriage, than £600 per annum; & as to do this may possibly subject me to some degree of inconvenience, I cannot think of going farther. It is in fact a liberal offer, considering all the circumstances, & one which I have never yet named to him. I do not immediately see any other resource which he can have at present towards augmenting his income, except what the bounty of Mr. Tennyson may supply. I wish this part of my letter to be confidential, & only communicated to the two Mr. Tennysons. I may here observe, that till your letter arrived I was wholly ignorant of the existence of guardians, & did not even know that Miss E.T. was a minor.

I shall be perfectly willing to make an adequate settlement on any lady whom my son may marry with my consent.[48]

Henry Hallam was not at root an ungenerous man and Rawnsley considered this letter 'kind and liberal'. In terms of the financial provisions it set out, this is fair comment. Henry Hallam's proposed allowance to Arthur, though not amounting to a fortune, was not a niggardly one. He was doubling the allowance of £300 per year which Arthur had had at Cambridge, and the sum he offered was well in excess of the annual stipend of a clergyman, schoolmaster or university fellow (though they would, of course, generally be provided with free accommodation). What is particularly striking about this letter, however, is the tone in which Henry Hallam's proposals are expressed. The letter sounds irritable and suggests that Henry feels that he has been both inconvenienced and undermined. He is openly censorious of what he sees as Mrs. Tennyson's unwarranted interference in a matter about which he and her husband had made an agreement; he is stung at hearing for the first time that Emily has a guardian and that she is a minor (clearly Arthur had been very selective in what he had told his father about her); and he takes few pains to disguise his disapproval of Arthur's being encouraged to visit Somersby without his own permission. It is also clear that he had not himself so far taken the relationship particularly seriously, apparently believing that Emily would have thought better of it before too long. Henry's final paragraph, suggesting that he would happily make a generous allowance were Arthur to marry someone he approved of, is less than tactful. Henry Hallam was not a poor man, and his playing the part of one in this letter is disingenuous. His elaborate pleas of poverty are not convincing, and his reference to the financial 'inconvenience' to which Arthur's marriage would put him sounds pusillanimous. There is no sense in any part of the letter that Henry's cooperation with the Tennysons (if it can even be called that) is other than grudging.

Rawnsley wasted little time in writing to Emily's Uncle Charles (now rejoicing under the name of Tennyson d'Eyncourt), and asked that he and Mr Tennyson should confer on what Rawnsley's reply to Mr. Hallam should be. Rawnsley was thus authorised to communicate the terms of old Mr. Tennyson's settlement. Mr Tennyson was prepared to make Emily an allowance of £70 per year during his lifetime, and, on his death she was to receive a seventh part of the proceeds from the sale of one of his estates. This would probably amount to a sum of about £3000. Mr Tennyson was perfectly happy to accept whatever sum Mr. Hallam chose to settle.

The apparent reasonableness of old Mr. Tennyson's terms should not be allowed to detract from the fact that he was in practice offering very little, and that negotiations between two self-assured and substantial men, both of them used to having their own way, were about to turn difficult. Both Henry Hallam and Mr Tennyson were negotiating over a marriage which they wished to discourage but were not able to prevent, and which was, in consequence, likely to bring out the worst in both of them. Jack Kolb believes that Henry thought the Tennysons were being opportunistic and in consequence he was testing the genuineness of their faith,[49] but the fact that the next stage in the negotiations on the Hallam side was conducted by Arthur himself seems to point to the fact that Henry had considerable distaste for the whole business and had chosen not to spend any more time on it. Arthur, after all, could be as ruthless as anybody when pursuing his own ends, even though, as it turned out, he was too hot-headed on this occasion.

To begin with, Arthur claimed to be proceeding with his father's full authorisation. He reported bluntly to Charles Tennyson d'Eyncourt that his father had found Mr. Tennyson's terms 'certainly less satisfactory than he had hoped' and trusted therefore that he might reconsider them. By means of compromise, in addition to the £600 per annum already offered, Henry Hallam was prepared to offer a jointure of £500 on Emily, but felt that the £3000 legacy promised on Mr. Tennyson's death was insufficient. He therefore suggested that Mr. Tennyson should settle £4000 to himself in his lifetime to be held in trust for Emily until his death, raised either from a mortgage on his estates or from any other source he might think appropriate. In the event of Mr. Tennyson's agreeing to these terms, Mr Hallam would be happy for the marriage to take place, though he wished to 'reserve to his own discretion the appointment of the time.'

Arthur then went onto make a plea for Charles to use his influence with his father, as 'This engagement is irrevocable; much unhappiness or at least much anxiety will result from such a delay of its completion, as must probably occur before my own exertions can have added anything to my income. I am aware that Mr. Tennyson has numerous claims upon his liberality; but I had hoped that upon an occasion such as his granddaughter's marriage, & that by no means a marriage which he can consider disadvantageous, he might be induced to [make] her a larger allowance than he would otherwise have thought expedient.' Hallam ended by assuring Charles that he was happy to meet him to discuss the matter further next time Charles was in London, and that his father would be happy to do likewise.[50]

If the final lines of the letter seem emollient, the rest of it obviously isn't. Although Hallam believed that 'The expressions he [Henry] authorised me to use were of a very conciliatory & courteous character',[51] Henry's demands of Mr. Tennyson are presumptuous, and the fact that they are communicated through Arthur adds insult to injury. Arthur's assertion that the engagement is 'irrevocable' would, in its context, also be provocative. Hallam's true feelings on the matter were revealed in a letter to Gaskell on 8 September. Gaskell himself had recently married, so Hallam presumably felt it was acceptable to make a clean breast of his current dilemma:

'A negotiation has been going on between my father and the old man whose only good quality is his relationship to the person I love best in the world. The wretch makes most shabby, beggarly offers, which my father considers inadequate; and unless I can by hook or crook induce him to bid higher, I am not likely to be married before the Millennium.'[52]

Hallam by now saw the negotiations as being entirely his responsibility rather than his father's, and, pursuing his ends 'by hook or crook', he decided to enlist the support of Frederick Tennyson, as the eldest son of the family, though he was unaware of the fact that old Mr. Tennyson had instructed Charles that 'Frederick may be made no party in this business.'[53] Although making no secret of his belief that Mr. Tennyson's offer was one of 'execrable shabbiness',[54] he asked for Frederick's help in the case of Mr. Tennyson's remaining obdurate, and indeed had a plan to offer: perhaps one of the Tennyson aunts (Aunt Bourne or Aunt Russell) could be prevailed upon 'to settle 40 or 50£' per year on Emily. More than this, as Frederick's expectations, as a future head of the family, were bound to be considerable, Hallam even went so far as to suggest that the £4000 requested by Henry could come in the form as a charge on Frederick's future estate.

'Am I an impudent fellow to make so cool a proposal?' Hallam asked Frederick, doubtless rhetorically, but accurately predicting the reaction of any reader of this particular letter. Then follows the emotional appeal: 'it is for you to consider whether what is given for Emily's interest is not given for the welfare of the whole family . . . The hearthstone which you would thus contribute to raise would be a sure and lasting asylum . . . of comfort to you all, when the foot of an alien shall be on the soil of Somersby. The projects of union, & mutual alleviation of life's sorrows, which we have so often formed half jokingly, might be realised beyond our wildest wishes.'[55]

If Frederick made any reply it has not survived, but in any case Hallam's letter was quickly overtaken by events. The very next day, Charles Tennyson d'Eyncourt wrote to Hallam from Lincolnshire, informing him that Mr. Tennyson 'desires me to say that he cannot . . . break into the arrangements . . . made for a large family of which the portion he designs for Miss Emily Tennyson is a part. I am also to add that having fully made up his own mind he requests that all future communications may be made through Mr. Rawnsley.'[56] In short, from the Tennyson side, negotiations were over. It was as well that Mr. Tennyson never saw the contents of Hallam's letter to Frederick.

Hallam had been rebuffed by Mr. Tennyson, and, by implication, by Charles Tennyson d'Eyncourt also; he had made a self-confessedly 'impudent' proposal to Frederick when chances of success were slim. So now, in some desperation, he decided to approach the only other suitable male Tennyson left, Alfred's cousin George, son of Charles, and a Trinity contemporary. Hallam requested 'half an hour's conversation' with him on 19 September, though then perhaps thought better of it, claiming subsequently that he was 'prevented' from seeing him on the appointed day, and asking George to let him know 'if you hear anything about my affairs that may be of any importance to me.' He was forced to confess the 'complete failure' of his recent negotiations, which had 'made matters worse instead of better. The old man seems angry at an attempt to influence him through his son, & your father seems angry at being troubled with the subject.'[57] To anyone other than a young man in love, this state of affairs would hardly be surprising. After a month's effort and tribulation, the prospects for Hallam's marriage to Emily were bleaker than ever and there seemed little hope of any immediate improvement. Mr. Tennyson continued to merit the complaints which Hallam (none too tactfully) enjoyed making about him and Henry Hallam was spared the pain of having to see his son marry someone he had not himself actually met.

Hallam's final strategy was to try to enlist the help of the Tennysons' Aunt Bourne, who had been generous in offering Alfred financial assistance while he was at Cambridge. Hallam was alarmed to discover that at the time he wrote she was actually staying with Charles Tennyson d'Eyncourt, 'the very individual, whom of all others I least wished to know I had written to her!'[58] The delay in her reply he attributed to the letter not having been delivered, though he did eventually hear from her about a month later. Her letter was sympathetic in general terms, though she did not make any specific commitment.

It is not certain exactly how much Emily knew about the difficulties of which she was the blameless cause. Hallam's letters to her at this time are less frequent and he clearly does not feel under any obligation to keep her up to date with the chapter and verse of the family negotiations. Hallam had told her of his father's letter to Rawnsley and put a bold face on it by suggesting that both his parents thought that this would constitute 'a decided advance' to their affair: 'I have been more hopeful & cheerful the last two or three days . . . I feel a courage within me to brave ill fortune . . . nothing can happen to do us real injury, so long as we are true to ourselves'.[59] Hallam seems to be keeping most of his doubts and perplexities from her. Most certainly the things he said to his friends at the time suggest much more emotional pain than is shown in his letters to Emily.

In other respects the summer was a happier and more productive one. Henry Hallam had moved the family to Croydon Lodge, and Hallam accommodated himself to country life, as he had done before, with some, but not too much complaint. Croydon he found 'not positively ugly, but its neighbourhood to a dusty London road, daily & almost hourly travelled by innumerable coaches, is a very unpleasant, though sometimes a convenient circumstance.' He found the house itself comfortable, and enjoyed the rustic surroundings, 'fields . . . with cows & horses in them'. There was an assortment of dogs (one of whom attacked his younger brother Harry), pigs, a bull and some beehives.[60] He gave Tennyson a *resume* of his daily routine: 'about ½ past 8 in the morning, I find myself dressed. I sometimes take a turn in the garden until the great bell summons to prayers & breakfast. A microscope is then produced if the day be sunny and my Father examines various subjects of the animal & vegetable kingdom, then ½ an hour music by my sister. Inundated with Mozart and Beethoven I go up to my room to read about "Real Property" till 2, then walk; then talk or German reading or more music with the sister. Dinner at 6, As soon as my father makes the stir of his chair as a prelude to rising after desert, [sic] I tap my sister on the shoulder, take a candle and up we go to my room. Where I smoke & read German till ½ past 8 when we are called down to tea, then I read or write till 11.'[61] He also told Emily that during the evenings he smoked his pipe and talked about her to Ellen, though his pleasant existence was disturbed when he heard of the sudden death of Edward Spedding, brother of James, which Tennyson was to commemorate in a sonnet. Edward, Hallam thought, 'was more sensitive than his brother.'[62]

Throughout the summer Hallam continued to busy himself with the manuscripts of Tennyson's new poems. He was now the intermediary between the poet and his publisher, urging Tennyson to send as much material as possible and expressing occasional frustration at his indecisiveness. Hallam told Tennyson in mid-September that Moxon was 'impatient to begin the volume',[63] though Hallam's threat to decide on the order of the poems himself suggests that the impatience was as much his as anybody else's. Tennyson continued to supply new material until the end of the month (including the sonnet 'My life is full of weary days' which is addressed to Hallam), by which time Hallam delivered the poems to

Moxon, but instructed him to wait before printing them in case Tennyson changed his mind again. By mid-October he was staying with Douglas Heath and reading the first proofs along with Heath and W.H. Thompson, in 'an arbor in the garden' during a spell of particularly wet weather. Clearly the business of proof-reading went beyond merely checking typography, as Hallam had suggestions to make about verbal details too. He particularly liked *The Lady of Shalott*, telling Tennyson 'You were indeed happily inspired when the idea of that poem first rose in your imagination.'[64] Tennyson did the final proof-reading himself, dealing with Moxon directly for the first time, but remaining even at that stage, uncertain about which of the poems 'lying by me'[65] merited publication. Despite being urged by Hallam and other friends to include *The Lover's Tale*, Tennyson's stubbornness prevailed and the poem did not appear. Hallam saw the last set of proofs as well, finding the type 'very pretty, but the volume will, I fear, be small. My admiration of it increases, if possible.'[66]

Hallam also had literary work of his own at this time. He sent a sonnet about a picture of the adoration in Cologne Cathedral to William Maginn of *Fraser's Magazine*, urging his credentials not only as an already published poet, but as 'as good a Tory as your heart can wish'.[67] This could well have been the last poem which Hallam composed, as he had by this stage virtually ceased to write poetry at all, though as a response to a picture, it is reminiscent of his very earliest poems about the paintings he had seen in Florence at the Pitti Palace in the autumn of 1827. The picture in Cologne was by Stefan Lochner and presented the scene of the adoration in an idealised setting, rather than in the more conventional stable.[68] Although *Fraser's Magazine* published the poem in February 1833, it subsequently remained unprinted and was included neither in the *Remains*, nor in Motter's collected *Writings*:

There were no crowns, no gold, no jewels bright
  Of strange tiaras, on the saintly brows
  Of Mary Nazarene, what time she rose
Beside the manger, trembling at the sight
Of the three wanderers, and their new starlight.
  They were no kings; nor were their garments those
  I see before me, rich in deepen'd glows
Of Eastern crimson, zoned with chrysolite.
Yet would I not from yonder frame remove
  One colour or one form; nor for the show
  Of real things those higher truths let go,
Fresh on this canvass from the painter's soul –
  Pure elements of faith, and joy, and love,
Wrought into one by Art's divine control.[69]

However, Hallam's chief work that summer was of a very different kind. Earlier in 1832, a substantial volume by Gabriele Rossetti, *Disquisizioni Sullo Spirito Antipapale*, had been published (in Italian) in London, running to all of 460 pages. Rossetti, an Italian *émigré* (and father of Dante Gabriel, Christina and William Michael) had recently been appointed Professor of Italian at King's College, London. Rossetti had had an eventful and precarious early life, though he was a man of genuine culture and sophistication. Born in Naples of humble origins, he had, as a result of a generous patron, been able to attend the University, where his studies had included philosophy and classics. He was a freemason and also belonged to the revolutionary Italian political movement, the *Carbonari*. Indeed his political activities during the time of the uprising of 1820 forced him into hiding from which he was saved by the sympathetic intervention of Admiral Sir Graham Moore and his wife, who smuggled him away, first to Malta, and then to London. He had been helped also by John Hookham Frere senior, the father of Hallam's friend John Frere, and had been effective in cultivating influential friends, including Coleridge and the Dante scholar, H.F. Cary.

Rossetti's own studies in Dante had begun about the time of his arrival in London. He embarked on a projected three-volume *Comento* on Dante in 1825, although only two volumes were completed. It was published on a subscription basis, two of its earliest subscribers being Samuel Rogers and Henry Hallam, though overall its sales were poor. Rossetti, partly as a result of his own experience of secret societies and of freemasonry in Italy, had become convinced that Dante had belonged to a covert Ghibelline and anti-Roman society in Florence, which had a secret vocabulary, known as *gergo* by which private messages of an anti-Papal nature were encoded in his poetry. Although these ideas provoked ridicule in some quarters, the *Comento* was not, in general, badly received, and Rossetti developed his ideas further in what was to become the *Disquizioni*. By this time an unorthodox but interesting reading of Dante had developed into a mighty conspiracy theory which embraced Petrarch and Boccaccio as well. Rossetti's biographer, E.R. Vincent, sums up Rossetti's theory as follows: 'Stated in the briefest possible way, Rossetti's belief was that from early times there had existed a secret society with humanitarian and secular aims which had united its members in opposition to political and ecclesiastical tyranny . . . In it many of the chief heretical movements of history found their inspiration, particularly those that were directed against the papacy and its secular claims. It exists in the modern world as the force behind Freemasonry'. Thus having begun by believing that Dante had belonged to such a secret society and communicated to his fellow members by a code and a system of private symbols, Rossetti in due course expanded his theory until it became, preposterously, 'the universal key to the understanding of all literature'.[70] The theory seemed at its most reasonable when applied to the allegory of the

Divina Comedia but much less so when applied to non-allegorical literature and to biography. Following his own personal logic, Rossetti turned
Dante not only into a freemason and anti-Papist, but into an anti-
Christian. His argumentative method, if so it could be called, rested on
'nonsensical anagrams and acrostics', decontextualised quotations and a
'complacency and childish pride'.[71]

Hallam had taken Rossetti's book with him when he set out for the
Rhine with Tennyson and had finished reading it whilst quarantined in
Holland. He had written to Kemble at the time that he was 'puzzled what
to do about him. Not convinced, I am yet staggered . . . I cannot bring
myself to concede the full extent of so wide & unsettling a theory: yet I
cannot help thinking there must be something in it . . . I should hardly feel
satisfied to review the book, without further examination of its materials'.[72] This is a measured and moderate first response to the book, indeed
it is considerably more restrained than Hallam's review was to be. Clearly
the subject matter was fascinating to him, focussing as it did on the poet
in whom he had the greatest interest. By the end of August he told Kemble
that he had already written 'ten or twelve pages' of a review[73] and was
trying to persuade one of the literary journals to print it. He approached
The Foreign Quarterly Review, *The Quarterly Review* and *The
Edinburgh Review* but with no success. The fact of Rossetti's book being
published in Italian restricted its range of potential readers (a two-volume
English translation was to appear in 1834) and *The Edinburgh* had
already found someone else to review it. Hallam therefore arranged to
have his *Remarks on Professor Rossetti's "Disquizioni Sullo Spirito
Antipapale"* published as a pamphlet by Moxon in October. The *Remarks*
appeared anonymously, or rather pseudonymously, being initialled
'T.H.E.A.' This was specifically at Hallam's request, as he 'took fright at
some things I had said about Christianity & matters appertaining to it
. . . having no wish to earn the reputation of an Atheist or a Mystic.' He
also jokingly enquired of Kemble if Rossetti was a big man because 'I
flatter myself, if he calls at my house to lick me, I have English stuff enow
in my fists to floor a beggarly Italian.'[74]

It is easy with hindsight to see Hallam's *Remarks* as a sledgehammer
being used to crack a nut. The essay is Hallam's longest sustained prose
work. The pamphlet runs to sixty pages of text with a further sixteen
pages of notes. Whilst much of it is taken up with an animated and witty
demolition of Rossetti's theories, in the final section Hallam offers his
own views about the medieval Italian poets and their religious and
cultural context. Although Rossetti expounded his theory at length in his
book, it is not at root at all difficult to demolish, particularly when Hallam
resorts to the traditional reviewer's strategy of *reductio ad absurdum*.

Hallam's fundamental and repeated objection to Rossetti's theories is
that they are not grounded in any ascertainable historical fact, being 'alike
contrary to sound philosophy, and to the records of history.'[75] He subse-

quently complains that 'we require positive proof of [the secret society's] existence in the first place, and afterwards of every additional inch of ground assigned to its progress . . . But the gentleman, with whom we have to do, never stops, never deliberates, never doubts. On he drives, in full conviction that all his past reading is in his favour, and full faith that all his further reading will confirm it.'[76] Hallam is not convinced by Rossetti's promise to reveal his documentary evidence in a subsequent volume.

The tone of Hallam's *Remarks* is, for the most part, one of spirited enjoyment. He has fun in exposing the absurdities of Rossetti's theories and brings all his debating society panache to the task. This is best illustrated when, for the first time, and, of course, highly tendentiously, he presents a summary of Rossetti's position: 'It must be acknowledged . . . the theory we are about to consider has its brilliant side. A secret society we are told . . . has continued, from the earliest historical point at which its workings can be traced, to exercise an almost universal influence on the condition of the civilised world . . . the destinies of Europe have been in their hands; and the great revolutions which have agitated us are almost entirely due to their indefatigable operation. No track of literature has been untrodden by these masked assailants . . . The genius of Luther was no more than a puppet, infallibly directed by their invisible agency.'[77]

Even when Hallam appears to be treating Rossetti more indulgently, his comments are subverted by irony, words of apparent praise quickly turning themselves by degrees into trenchant criticism. Hallam writes of Rossetti's style, for example, that it is 'lively and often rises to eloquence, while the nature of his hypothesis lends to historical details all the wildness and novelty of romance. He has amassed considerable information on the limited range of subjects which regard his immediate pursuit, but he appears to want extensive reading and that philosophical discrimination which might be expected to arise from it . . . The most heterogeneous elements are pressed into the service of his hypotheses with almost tyrannical eagerness . . . A man must be careful indeed, in whose words Signor Rossetti would not discover something to help out his argument.'[78]

What irritates Hallam is not simply Rossetti's sublime wrong-headedness, but the way in which his theories ultimately reduce the stature of the poets with whom they deal, particularly Dante. Representing Dante as an anti-Papist, anti-Christian, freemason is aesthetically as well as historically monstrous and it is for this reason that Hallam feels obliged to defend the reputation of the poet whom he venerated above all others. In terms reminiscent of his college declamation of the previous December, Hallam evokes what he sees as the spirit of medieval Christianity: 'The Beautiful was everywhere around men, waiting, and, as it were, calling for their love . . . Is it wonderful that the feeling of reverence for that august name, the Church . . . should, in that day, have been often irresistible in the minds of imaginative men[?]' Rossetti's treatment of Dante in whom 'The spirit of Catholic Christianity breathes in every line, lessens the 'dignity and magnificence' of his poetry which are 'materially lowered by such a hypothesis.'[79]

Like many people who hold extreme or absurd opinions, Rossetti was highly sensitive to criticism and Hallam's jokes about the possibility of physical violence were made in genuine anticipation of an angry response. Hallam's *Remarks* had not been afraid to patronise a man who was more than old enough to be his father, and it must have taken some hardness of skin on Rossetti's part to accept Hallam's expectation of 'much amusement' from his 'further researches'.[80] In fact Rossetti received Hallam's *Remarks* in good part, one of his biographers noting that it was the only review which he valued.[81] More significantly, the pamphlet received the plaudits of Leigh Hunt, who sent Hallam, via Moxon, a present of a copy of Shelley's *Masque of Anarchy*, though Hallam, in his reply to Hunt, distanced himself from the extremes of enthusiasm which he and his friends had felt for Shelley at Cambridge. In the same letter he drew his attention to Tennyson's forthcoming volume ('much superior, in my judgement, to the first') but, with that detachment that always characterised his attitude to his own work after publication, he apologised for the *Remarks* and claimed that the pamphlet had been written 'too hastily, & with few books at hand.'[82]

Hallam had written in the *Remarks* of Dante's *La Vita Nuova*: 'No one can have read that singular work without having found his progress perpetually checked, and his pleasure impaired, by the occurrence of passages apparently unintelligible, or presenting only an unimportant meaning, in phrases the most laborious and involved'.[83] It was a desire to make this 'singular work' more accessible which caused Hallam to embark on his most substantial (though uncompleted and little known) work on Dante. He had written to Tennyson in January, whilst still at Cambridge, saying that he wanted to pick his brains about 'metres which may be serviceable, as well as for my philosophy in the notes as for my actual handiwork in the text'.[84] Although it is unlikely that Hallam had begun translating *La Vita Nuova* at this point, his comments to Tennyson indicate the scope of what he had planned: a fully edited text in English, with explanatory notes. He had already, as has been mentioned, outlined this project in a letter to Donne.

It is not difficult to see why Hallam would be drawn to *La Vita Nuova*. The work's presentation of Dante's tragically unrequited love for Beatrice would, over and above his general enthusiasm for the Italian poetry of the period, strike especial chords. Hallam's love for Emily Tennyson was, technically, not unrequited, but the problems posed by geographical separation and unhelpful families inevitably meant that Hallam was forced to love from a distance and suffer the agonies of longing for what must have often seemed the unattainable. His earlier interest in Anna Wintour had been experienced in almost conscious imitation of Dante and Beatrice.

La Vita Nuova itself is something of a hybrid (a fact which must have contributed to Hallam's frustration at its difficulties). At root it tells one of the best-known love stories in western literature, but it does so in two parallel ways: through a sequence of sonnets and *canzoni,* and through a linking prose narrative, which comments on the structure of the poems, as well as providing an autobiographical account of the circumstances which prompted them. It is in the prose account that most of the text's obscurities lie, and Hallam's explication of it, had he completed it, would have been very useful, as, at the time he was working on it, there was no other English translation of *La Vita Nuova* at all. Charles Lyell's versions of the sonnets and *canzoni* appeared in 1835; the first translation of the entire work appeared in 1846, and Dante Gabriel Rossetti's translations (also of the entire work) which became the best-known version in English, appeared in 1861. Hallam translated 23 of Dante's 25 sonnets, plus one sonnet by Cavalcanti, and one *canzone.* No work by him on the prose sections survives, if indeed it was ever begun.

Henry Hallam, who knew his Dante well, was critical of Arthur's translations, finding them 'rather too literal and consequently harsh',[85] as a result of which he not only excluded them from the *Remains,* but destroyed his copy of the manuscript. It was only through their survival in a manuscript possessed by Hallam's Cambridge friend, John Heath, that caused them to be rediscovered in 1935. If Dante Gabriel Rossetti's translations are to be taken as the obvious comparison, Henry Hallam's strictures on his son's work seem severe. Hallam's translations, by the side of Rossetti's can, it is true, feel rather bloodless, but in their rather penny-plain poetic language they gain in directness and economy and avoid the occasionally self-conscious archaisms that are characteristic of Rossetti. It is, of course, a minor literary irony that Dante Gabriel Rossetti's translations were made by the son of the very man who had so irritated Hallam by suggesting that Beatrice existed only as a figment of the poet's imagination.

An interesting parallel to Hallam's English translation of Dante was his review of an Italian translation of *Paradise Lost* by Guido Sorelli, ('very trifling, an article of three pages only' as he wrote to Tennyson[86]), on which he worked during September 1832, and which appeared in *The Foreign Quarterly* in October. Sorelli, though a Florentine by birth, was resident in England and had even dedicated his translation to Queen Adelaide. Whilst Hallam was in general terms approving of Sorelli's efforts, he did not find him among those 'few who constitute [Milton's] first class of translators' and he inevitably found himself considering the question of translation generally, applying the same kind of criteria to Sorelli's Milton as his father would do to Arthur's own work on Dante. Hallam raises the fundamental question as to whether poetry can be satisfactorily translated at all: 'How poor and meagre a part of any master-work can be transplanted unto a foreign mould?' In particular, he feels that Sorelli has damaged parts of the poem 'by the substitution of a flaccid paraphrase for an energetic expression, or the insertion of a paren- thesis that weakens instead of explaining.' The fact that Hallam concludes 'that we feel the utter hopelessness of seeing a real translation of Milton',[87] is the end of a not significantly different response to Sorelli than was Henry Hallam's in his suppression of his son's version of *La Vita Nuova*.

Hallam's literary activities were not curtailed by his beginning work in Walters' conveyancing office, though he felt annoyed at being interrupted from them. He started at the office at the end of October and wrote to Emily after what was probably his first week that 'All my mornings I now spend in a Conveyancer's office, copying precedents of Deeds & so forth – not very hard work, to be sure, but irksome, especially as it destroys the prime of the day, & leaves the mind fatigued & irritable for the rest of it . . . There are three more besides myself, two of whom are Cambridge men, whom I know; we have a snug fire, & a newspaper; we yawn in concert, & sometimes chat. About three o'clock I get loose, so, you see, the imprisonment is but short.'[88] As Hallam's description shows, his atti- tude to the law was ambivalent: he inevitably found that it robbed him of that part of the day which he would have devoted to literary work, but in the end the activity and company were tolerable, especially if he did not take them too seriously. A couple of weeks later, he was able to report that he had drawn up his first conveyance 'by which Miss Joan Hogeson alias Hoggeson has "bargained, sold, granted, released & confirmed" certain Butcher's shops in Barley Market in Tavistock in the Co. of Devon to Mr. Christopher Vickry Bridgeman. It covered eighteen folio pages – I wish him joy of his beef & mutton.'[89] Henry Hallam maintained the view that Arthur enjoyed his legal work, and on at least one occasion made efforts to advance his son's prospects by introducing him to Sir John Bosanquet, Judge of Common Pleas, an old Eton and Christ Church contemporary of Henry's. Although Hallam complained at Christmas that he was restricted by only being allowed eight weeks holiday a year, which had to be taken piecemeal, it did not keep him from Somersby or prevent him from travelling in Europe with his father the following summer. Though references to his legal work in his letters are few, Hallam remained, technically at least, a trainee lawyer until his death.

Being permanently resident in London again, Hallam resumed his full social life. Although he occasionally declared that London depressed him, he was clearly finding plenty of congenial diversions. He informed Emily that he had been enchanted by the company of John Heath's sister, Julia, 'under whose fascinating influence I remained for two rainy days. She is not handsome, but her eyes are lively & pleasant, and her countenance wears an expression of intelligent archness.'[90] As always there were visits to the theatre. On 22 October he went to Covent Garden to see *The Vision of the Bard*, a play by James Sheridan Knowles, composed in tribute to Sir Walter Scott, who had died only the previous month. The play presented a series of scenes illustrating Scott's novels and poems. Five days later, Hallam saw Knowles's *The Hunchback* again, this time with Ellen Tree rather than Fanny Kemble as the female lead, though Hallam, predictably, still preferred Fanny in the part. Hallam also did some acting himself when he attended an evening of charades, organised by Charlotte Sotheby at her guardian uncle's house in Essex. On arrival Hallam was received most warmly as he was the only male present, and, without undue false modesty, he enthused to Emily that his 'most decided success was in the character of Pygmalion. Charlotte Sotheby was my Statue: she looked it to perfection.' Hallam ended up wearing as costume Charlotte's dressing gown, which was 'declared very Grecian'.[91] Hallam crowned his performance with a blank-verse speech, which he had specially composed for the occasion, and which survived to be published in the *Remains*.

Although he anticipated that Emily would think him disloyal for saying so, Hallam finished his account of his performance by singing the praises of his hostess and her sister: 'They are both agreeable girls, & full of lively, somewhat satirical conversation, yet not without tokens of deep & strong feeling, ready to come when called for.'[92] They were in fact part of quite a lengthy catalogue of attractive young women who came into Hallam's acquaintance at this time. Apart from Julia Heath, Fanny Kemble and the Sotheby sisters, there were also two more sisters, an otherwise unidentified Emily and Marianne at Blackheath. Hallam's repeated references to his flirting with his female friends were ill-judged. Robert Bernard Martin finds his behaviour 'pathetically immature and unintentionally cruel . . . deriving from Arthur's deep frustration at their inability to marry.' He thinks that this shows that 'the auguries were not good for their happiness'.[93]

In Hallam's letters to Emily, there is plenty of evidence to contradict this latter point. The relationship was to suffer a crisis at the end of the year but in the autumn of 1832, from Hallam's side, it seemed as close as ever: in September he had sent Emily, in celebration of her twenty-first birthday, a parcel consisting of a transcription by his sister Ellen of a Beethoven piano duet, a French translation of de La Motte Fouqué's *Undine,* and a pair of gold earrings, going on to declare that

'You are so dear & good a creature; you have had so much to suffer; your tender frame is so susceptible of agitating impressions from memory & imagination – I ought to deal with you delicately, as with a trembling flower . . . It is now near three years since you arose upon my life, like a star. At first the beams were clear, but distant; their brightness & their warmth have been increasing ever; but they have not yet reached their meridian and I yearn for the hour of their fullness with impetuous, believing hope.'[94]

A month later he tells her: 'I am enthroned in the love of Emily, &

regard all other things as below the concern of my royalty. You too are enthroned; you sit, a queen beside me, on a triumphal car, behind which follows a long train of fair captives conquered by my valour.'[95] These are ardent and moving words, though they do proceed from the pen of an extremely fluent and well-read writer with the aim of persuading Emily that his feelings about her are entirely sincere. Hallam's references to the intelligence and the charms of his female acquaintances in London might be seen as a means of injecting a flirtatious tone into his correspondence with Emily, especially as he takes pains on more than one occasion to assure her that none of the young ladies concerned can rival her. Nevertheless, they do not sound like the words of an innately monogamous man. Nor was Hallam above putting his Lincolnshire fiancée in what he thought was her place, exhorting her to do good works and visit the sick: '"Pure religion & undefiled" says the Apostle "is to *visit* the widow & the fatherless in their affliction."'[96] It is difficult not to find this condescending, coming, as it did, from one who was in the midst of theatres, dinners and charades, and, although Hallam insisted to her that his heart was not in these things, Emily had plenty of time to consider the implications of his letters and to come to her own conclusions about them.

Much excitement was generated by the appearance of Tennyson's *Poems* at the beginning of December. It was favourably reviewed in *The Athenaeum* on 1st December, though *The Literary Gazette* a week later was much less enthusiastic, and, sadly, much more in keeping with the general tone of reviews of Tennyson's work at this time. Although William Jerdan, the *Gazette*'s editor, granted Tennyson some felicity in the description of nature, he placed him firmly in 'The Baa-Lamb School' of poets and added a cruel parody of *The Lady of Shalott* to his review. As usual, Hallam was unfazed by the criticism, but begged Emily not to mention it to Alfred. Hallam instead took pride in the physical appearance of the book, writing on 5 December that 'It shines in Moxon's window, resplendent with lilac covers, & tempting passengers, I hope irresistibly. Near a hundred copies are sold, which is pretty well for the first two days.'[97] Although Hallam was delighted with the poems in general terms, he was irritated by Tennyson's obstinacy in refusing to make the corrections which he had suggested, and reported a similar reaction from Alfred's friends in Cambridge, though the book was also selling well there.

There had again been some fear that the Tennysons might have to leave Somersby but this came to nothing, and Hallam spent the Christmas of 1832 with the family there. Although he had been much looking forward to his visit, and he subsequently claimed it had been the most enjoyable period he had spent in Lincolnshire, his stay did in one very important way prove a disappointment. Although Emily had been well enough to join in the dancing and to venture outside, for much of the time that Hallam was there she was confined to her room. Given her behaviour on Hallam's previous visit, this state of affairs was not entirely unprecedented, but it was obviously worrying. Hallam had scolded Emily before about her not coming down to breakfast and staying in bed till mid-day, and shortly before he left London, he had urged her to 'Be visible – that's a good girl – when I arrive.'[98] He clearly had some premonition of what her behaviour might be like. Although there had been no particular suggestion of physical illness on Emily's part in the months leading up to Christmas, Hallam did write of 'a hunger of imagination preying upon your mind which I want to see blunted'.[99] Hallam's tendency, as on previous occasions, was to see Emily's condition as hypochondria, and it is hard not to agree with him. Such surviving accounts of this Christmas period as there are seem to suggest that the general atmosphere in the Rectory was festive enough,[100] and the Tennysons, as a family, always knew how to enjoy themselves. Hallam and Emily, however, were, for part of the time at least, reduced to writing each other little notes in Italian. Perhaps this was an attempt on Hallam's part to create a private language between them that would be impenetrable to other eyes. Hallam begs Emily to 'think of me. Have pity on my unhappiness if not on your own'.[101] Emily's replies are mundane and non-committal, asking him about the weather and what he has been doing.

It is difficult not to see Emily's withdrawal from Hallam's company as being a tactical one. Whether this was the result of a specific cooling of her feelings as a result of Hallam's wide-ranging flirtations in London, or whether she was simply overwhelmed by the presence of his extremely forceful personality, is hard to tell. Henry Hallam had never concealed the fact that he thought Arthur's behaviour towards Emily was rash and there is good reason to think that, given plenty of time for reflection, and mindful of her own family's attitude to the relationship, Emily had come to a similar conclusion. Her desire to be in Hallam's company was clearly less strong than his to be in hers, and his own ardour appeared undimmed, writing once more, when the time came of his 'horror of sudden loneliness' upon leaving her.[102]

After a two weeks' stay, Hallam left Somersby on Monday, 7 January 1833. He took the coach from Spilsby, in the company of a garrulous elderly spinster. Breaking his journey at Cambridge, he arrived at Trinity College at midnight where he was regaled with mulled claret before spending the rest of the night on Brookfield's sofa. As on the previous occasion, his arrival at Cambridge found him urging Emily to write to him immediately, despite his only just having left her: 'I long, I burn to know whether you are better or worse or just the same: write to me dearest, one line.' Nevertheless, Cambridge provided him with social comforts of its own traditional kind, and he spent tobacco-filled hours with Brookfield, Garden and Monteith, before taking 'the very slowest coach that ever travelled' back to London.[103]

Emily continued to have doubts about the sincerity of Hallam's feelings towards her, and matters came to a head in mid-February. She accused him of having grown less fond of her, to which he quickly responded that he loved her 'better than anything in the world . . . when I say that I love *you*, I mean that I love your true & enduring self, with all your noble capacities of good, all that fits you for life on earth & in heaven'.[104] This is a noble and eloquent statement but one which did not prevent him from once more expressing the view that her 'overwrought sensibility, too much concentred by circumstances on itself' and exacerbated by illness, had caused her not only to underestimate the strength of his feelings for her, but also to recoil from talking frankly to him about hers *'for fear I should like you less afterwards'*. The self-'depreciation' of which he also accuses her was no doubt the result of Emily's feeling isolated in Lincolnshire whilst Hallam carried on philandering in London. Emily suffered more than anyone, even more than Gladstone, from Hallam's culpable lack of tact, which this very letter bears out when he goes on to talk about yet another female acquaintance, a Miss Morris 'a very amiable young lady', who has read his review of the Milton translation in *The Foreign Quarterly,* and being much impressed with it, has 'made a dead set at me'.[105] This boasting (for such it is) skews considerably the protestations of love to Emily which Hallam made in the first part of the letter, though yet again he fails to see this.

Nevertheless, in the short term Emily was mollified, and Hallam chose to describe the matter as a 'little broullerie' which was 'settled a l'aimable', suggesting that her recent feelings had been influenced by 'headache or discomfort'.[106] He told her that he was well occupied with legal studies in the morning and metaphysical ones at night, though he clearly had plenty of time to enjoy social and cultural diversions. He breakfasted with Gladstone, had meetings with old Apostolic friends and saw Charles Tennyson, in whose company he visited Heath and Tennant. There were visits to the ballet and opera (*Don Giovanni,* about which he was particularly enthusiastic), as well as an aristocratic party at Lady Lansdowne's to celebrate the Queen's birthday. He was also reading Jane Austen, whom he much liked, preferring *Emma* to *Mansfield Park.*

Hallam's literary activity took yet another new turn in March when he informed Emily that he had just completed a 'Memoir of Voltaire'. This was the first of three short biographical studies (the other two were of Petrarch and Burke) which Hallam was commissioned to write for a series called *Gallery of Portraits, with Memoirs* published under the aegis of The Society for the Diffusion of Useful Knowledge. This society had come into being in 1826 and Henry Hallam was a member of its committee, which presumably explains why Arthur was invited to contribute. The series had begun in the previous summer and ran, in monthly instalments, for three years, earning in the process a sneering description as a 'Penny Magazine' from *Tait's Edinburgh Magazine,*[107] though the Society's aim to spread literary and scientific knowledge among the humbler classes was an entirely worthy one. The Voltaire essay was published first, the other two appearing (they were all anonymous) posthumously. Hallam's dismissiveness of his own literary work is familiar enough by now, though it seems likely that he genuinely viewed these portraits as hack work, telling Emily that at £5 for 'eight or nine pages', the writing was not very demanding, and that he was happy at the thought of writing more of them.

Voltaire, Petrarch and Burke are a diverse, even incongruous trio, but Hallam's comments on all three authors are vigorous, astute and detailed. The portraits are all eloquent and show familiarity with not only the lives but the historical backgrounds of the figures concerned. Perhaps unsurprisingly, the portrait of Petrarch is the most extensive and appreciative. Burke, (whose complete works Gladstone had presented him with on leaving Eton) Hallam had always admired, though his study of Voltaire reveals some impatience with its subject, whose life Hallam cannot write about without irony occasionally breaking in, about whose limitations as a philosopher he is emphatic, and of whose atheism he disapproves.

The year 1833 was a cold spring with some late snow, to which Hallam attributed Emily's continued illness. Although the nature and symptoms of this illness were never precisely divulged (vague references were made to Emily's liver) she claimed to have been feeling 'Very *unwell*'.[108] A gap of three weeks in their correspondence followed, during which time Alfred Tennyson appeared in London for an extended stay, accompanied by his elder sister, Mary. Once more it is difficult not to find calculation in Emily's behaviour. By claiming to be unwell, she was clearly excusing herself from visiting London and exposing herself to the scrutiny of Arthur's family. The surrogate appearance of Mary was, to say the least, strange. Mary was attractive and more outgoing than her younger sister, and immediately became a great favourite with the Hallams who did not, of course, have the problem of having to accommodate her as a future daughter-in-law. She formed a sisterly friendship with Ellen Hallam as well as impressing Mrs Hallam with her charm. Alfred, despite his tendency to taciturnity and gruffness, managed to get on well with Henry Hallam, though he maintained in his later years that he had always found Henry's disputatiousness difficult to cope with. The Hallams generously gave dinner parties which included not only the Tennysons, but also Cambridge friends of Arthur and Alfred.

Alfred and Mary took the opportunity to do as much sightseeing as possible. Although Tennyson's professed purpose in visiting London had been to see the Elgin Marbles, their activities took a rather more scientific direction. As well as a visit to the Zoological Gardens, they went twice 'to that fairy palace, the Gallery of Practical Science.' On the first occasion they examined drops of rainwater in a giant microscope, and on the second 'saw the wonderful Magnets' and also Perkins's cannonball-firing steam gun. They took in Kensington Gardens, Hyde Park and the Pantechnicon (a newly-opened bazaar, or department store, in Belgrave Square). There were boating trips in the company of the Heath brothers and their younger sister, and, on Easter Sunday, a rather more solemn visit to Westminster Abbey, where they heard 'a magnificent Handel anthem' and a sermon from an (unidentified) bishop. Apart from the Hallams' dinners, there was also one with the Heaths, but most significantly a supper party at Moxon's where Tennyson stayed till 3 a.m., meeting his publisher, and also Leigh Hunt, in the flesh for the first time.

Hallam was exhilarated by the Tennysons' visit and felt that it had been a great success. Not surprisingly he experienced a sense of anti-climax when they left, claiming to feel 'glumpy', though at the same time convinced that 'a great barrier was broken down between my own family & that of my adoption. I have tasted a rich foretaste of future union. I have shewn Ellen a sister'.[109] Whoever had been responsible for the surrogacy, it had clearly worked, and at least Hallam was convinced that the prospects for his marriage had become easier. If his parents accepted Mary, the logic went, they would therefore accept Emily: this was indeed to be the case, but in circumstances that Hallam could not have foreseen. The fact that Hallam also believed (erroneously as it transpired) that old Mr Tennyson was 'dangerously ill' was cheering in its own way too, though the old man did, in the event, outlive him by the best part of two years.

London was in the grip of an influenza epidemic in March to which Hallam succumbed. He was seriously ill for two weeks with a heavy intermittent fever, attacks of which would last for about five hours, leaving him weak and prostrated for the rest of the day, and often sleepless at night. He was permitted only a liquid diet, which lowered his spirits, and was also plied with quinine on alternate days as a means of trying to prevent further feverish onsets. He was still unfit for work at the beginning of May, when, although the most debilitating symptoms had gone, he was experiencing 'great languor' which prevented him from doing much and kept him from Somersby which he was very keen to visit again soon. Although Blakesley had reported previously that Hallam was looking healthier and had put on weight, he had been experiencing recurrences of his severe headaches and it was certainly Henry Hallam's view that his son never properly recovered from this bout of influenza.

Concern for his health is perhaps the reason why Hallam was much under parental control over the summer months. In late May his mother on 'a whim' took Hallam, his brother, sisters and governess, for a week's stay at the Green Man Hotel at Blackheath, then still essentially a country village, despite being within commuting distance of Hallam's office (six miles each way 'on the broiling top of a coach').[110] The weather was warm and the fresh air was invigorating, though Hallam suspected that Tennyson would not have viewed the area as being 'real' countryside, especially as there was much noise from the horses crossing the heath and coming to rest in the inn yard.

On their return to Wimpole Street, the Hallams played host to Arthur's cousin Caroline Elton, who was due 'to take a month of town'. Arthur had, originally, expressed dismay at the thought of squiring her through 'balls, theatres, sights &c.' In the event her arrival had been delayed for a month as a result of the influenza. She was shortly to marry and had been esteemed as 'a great beauty, a leading belle at Clifton',[111] though Mrs Hallam found her less attractive than Mary Tennyson.

By this time Henry Hallam had planned another foreign tour for himself and Arthur alone. It was to last for six weeks and start at the beginning of August. As might be expected, Hallam was none too enthusiastic at the prospect, which, according to Stephen Spring Rice, was undertaken 'much to his disgust as he says that "too much contact between the governor and the governed is the worst possible thing"'.[112] Hallam, after all, was now a seasoned foreign traveller in his own right, and his lack of enthusiasm for a tour which would obviously be undertaken on terms acceptable to his father was understandable. Despite this impending prospect, however, Hallam did manage to spend most of July at Somersby, whilst the rest of his family was staying with their Elton relatives at Clevedon Court. What was unusual about Hallam's stay this time was that Alfred Tennyson was not there. He was enjoying one of his nomadic periods. He had been in Cambridge at the beginning of the month, and had then spent some time 'in a regular Camb[ridge] debauchery style' in London, with his brother Frederick and other friends,[113] before going off to Scotland to stay with Robert Monteith. It seems highly probable that Hallam and Tennyson, as a result of their respective journeyings did not see each other before Hallam left for the continent. Kemble had hoped that Hallam would join the company in Cambridge whilst Tennyson was there, but there is no evidence that he did. The letter that Hallam wrote to Tennyson from London on 31 July, only three days before his departure, was a particularly affectionate one, but it seemed to indicate that it had been some considerable time since the friends had met. Its words have become some of Hallam's best-known ones: 'I feel tonight what I own has been too uncommon with me of late, a strong desire to write to you. I do own I feel the want of you at some times more than at others; a sort of yearning for dear old Alfred comes upon me and that without any particular apparent reason. I missed you much at Somersby.'

But the main reason for Hallam's writing this letter was to ask Tennyson to address subsequent correspondence to him in Vienna 'whither I am going on Saturday'.[114] Tennyson had clearly not been privy to Hallam's travelling plans which had, in any case, been hatched rather impulsively by Henry. Hallam Tennyson, in his *Memoir*, originated the story, subsequently retold by Charles Tennyson (and unquestioned by both Robert Bernard Martin and Peter Levi in their biographies), that Tennyson rushed down from Scotland in order to say goodbye to Hallam before he left for the continent, thus providing a *mise en scène* for a last meeting between them. There are a number of reasons why this was unlikely, indeed impossible. Firstly, Hallam's departure was not in itself unduly significant. Six-week continental tours were not unusual in the Tennyson/Hallam circle, and the two friends had often been apart for periods of several weeks at a time. Secondly, Tennyson, in Scotland, was far too distant to make a sudden trip to London just to say goodbye. More crucially, as Hallam's letter is dated 31 July and his departure was on 3 August, not even the most efficient postal and transport services would have provided enough time for a meeting in London to be arranged and to take place. Charles Tennyson's description of a dinner with Moxon and Leigh Hunt which went on until 4.30 a.m. on the night preceding Hallam's departure sounds remarkably like the dinner that had already taken place in May. It is the unsentimental, but in the end, unsurprising, truth, that Hallam went on his last journey with no formal leave-taking from his most celebrated friend.

Precisely what Henry Hallam's motives were in undertaking this trip are not clear, though it was certainly the case that the arrangements had been made at the last minute. The most likely explanation is that Henry believed that Arthur needed to travel in order to recover his health, and Arthur subsequently reported from Vienna on the benefits of mountain air and scenery to his mental and physical well-being. It has also been suggested that Henry once again wished to assert his control over Arthur, by preventing him from undertaking yet another foreign trip on his own initiative, and thereby hoping to take his mind off Emily. Arthur believed that his father was now reconciled to his union with her, but this was not necessarily the case. Mary Tennyson was not Emily after all. Either way, the proposed itinerary was a characteristically gruelling one, not obviously calculated to answer the needs of a convalescent. Its ultimate destination was Budapest, then a remote and exotic city, beyond the usual European tourist routes. The plan was that Hallam and his father would travel through Flanders into the Ardennes, then (presumably through Switzerland) to Lake Constance, the Tyrol, Innsbruck, Salzburg and Vienna, where they would take time sightseeing before going onto the Hungarian capital. However unenthusiastic Hallam might have felt at the journey's prospect, it did once more afford him the opportunity to excel as a travel writer. Where, five years earlier, Gladstone had been the chief recipient of his recorded impressions, it was now Emily who was to hear detailed accounts of his experiences.

Crossing the channel by steamboat did not prove a particularly comfortable experience: the crossing took twelve hours and the boat was small and cramped and had no private cabins. It also pitched rather heavily and made many of the passengers (including Hallam) sea-sick. Nor was Hallam's stomach much relieved by the sight of two French women feeding their dog the juice from the currant pie which they were eating, before finishing off the rest of it themselves from the same plate.

It was also very cold. They stayed overnight in Calais, and then made for Lille. Hallam liked the Flanders landscape and enjoyed watching the peasants harvesting. They stayed at Cassel (where Hallam and Tennyson had stayed on their way to the Pyrenees) and visited the cathedrals at Mons and Tournay, before crossing the border into Belgium and descending to Namur (from where Hallam wrote to Emily). Hallam was amused by a postillion at Ath, who had driven him and Tennyson three years previously and remembered them, recalling that they had been carrying a copy of Virgil with them. He thought that Hallam was looking much better than when he had seen him last.

Hallam wrote to Emily from Salzburg on 24 August, bringing her up to date on what had been happening during the two weeks since leaving Namur. He took up the travelogue from the time of his arrival at the Austrian border. From Lake Constance, they had travelled to Bregenz, capital of the Vorarlberg region and stayed at a small village called Bludenz, before crossing the Arlberg pass in rain and cloud. Hallam was very much a child of his time in being moved by wild and mountainous scenery of the sort that had thrilled him in the Alps, the Scottish Highlands and the Pyrenees. As he told Emily, enthusiastically: 'I felt my spirits rise at feeling myself once more among my old favourite objects – the torrent rushing impetuously beneath me, its turbid grey waters flashing into white foam along the rocky channel – the ragged green of the declivities beside it, strewed with numerous & irregular fragments of rock – the pines above these stretching up the mountain, into the cloud – the waterfall, swollen with recent storms, gushing down in all directions.' They went on to Innsbruck, capital of the Tyrol, which Hallam was very happy to visit again (he had last been there on his way back from Italy five years ago, with his head full of Anna Wintour). Hallam thought that the chief sight worth seeing there was the Chapel of the Emperor Maximilian, which contained not only the Emperor's tomb, but 28 bronze statues of Austrian princes 'semi colossal in size'. Hallam's enthusiasm for the works of art which he encountered, however, was not matched by that for the natives of the Tyrol, whom he dismissed as 'an uncivilised race, possessing apparently the virtues & vices of the savage state.' He also sent Emily a pen and ink sketch of the scene at Konigsee, which they had visited the previous day.

The city of Salzburg drove Hallam to superlatives: 'I am not sure that of all the delightful situations in the world, the most delightful is not that of *Salzburg.*' He was not the first or the last visitor to respond to the Italianate feel of this least Germanic of cities: 'spacious squares, with handsome fountains – large, wellbuilt streets – the architecture elegant, & somewhat effeminate – the environs laid out in the most pleasant lanes & avenues you can imagine.' He wished that Emily were with him and indeed even entertained the momentary hope that they might live together there some day, though when he passed through the city again on his return journey he revised his opinion.[115]

From Salzburg Hallam and his father set out for a three-day excursion into the mountains. Hallam was not thrilled by the chateau at Heilbronn ('laid out in the worst possible taste'), but had a great deal more to say about the salt mines at Hallein. In order to see these, all visitors, irrespective of sex, had to change into miner's white overalls, which inevitably made them look grotesque. They descended, by slow degrees, to the bowels of the earth, first of all walking along a narrow corridor, wide enough only for one abreast, then, by means of a sequence of slides, they arrived at 'an immense subterraneous lake' which they were ferried across by boat. Hallam thought of Acheron. Then they all had to sit astride a cart improvised from planks and pulled by a running man, until: 'we perceived a glimmer of light ahead; gradually it widened & brightened; & at length we had the satisfaction of rushing out into broad day, with blinded eyes and oppressed limbs.' Making their way back to Salzburg, they stayed overnight at the village of Werfen, where preparations were being made for a wedding. Although Hallam thought the bride, a minor aristocrat, was far too heavily built to be attractive, he was keen to see the wedding take place and he got up early to watch it, though had to leave before the service was over as the horses were ready to return. After excursions to neighbouring lakes and the waterfall at the Traun See, the Hallams then made their way from Salzburg to Vienna.[116]

Arrival at Vienna found Hallam in high spirits, which he attributed to the effects of mountain scenery: 'I do not think mountains ever seemed so sublime to me as this time in Tyrol & Salzburg.' His first letter from Vienna was addressed jointly to Emily and Alfred Tennyson. He liked the city though he had less to say directly about it than about Salzburg. Again he wrote approvingly of the design of the wide squares and streets, 'everything wears an appearance of gaiety and liveliness.' He compared Vienna with Paris, finding Vienna 'more uniformly handsome'. He found the Prater insipid, but was ecstatic about the Imperial Gallery. Recalling previous journeys to museums and galleries with Alfred, he could not resist sharing his impressions of his favourite Venetian painters with him: 'the gallery is grand and I longed for you . . . such Giorgiones, Palmas, Bordones, Paul Veroneses! and oh Alfred such Titians! by heaven that man could paint.' There were other cultural delights apart from the purely visual: four visits to the theatre, and two to the opera, for Herold's swashbuckling *Zampa* ('full of devilry & flames & speaking statues') and Meyebeer's *Robert le Diable* ('a most effective opera').[117]

Needless to say, Hallam's initial misgivings about this European journey had now been completely swept away, and his characteristic enthusiasm for travel (and travellers' tales) was rekindled, even to the point of announcing to Emily, as they left Vienna en route to Budapest, 'I always had a decided inclination for Hungary', despite the fact that they had now left mountainous scenery well and truly behind them and had to contemplate Hungary's vast central plain, 'very ill cultivated, & in most parts [it] presents the appearance of an extensive, irregular common, with trees growing over it in a scattered manner.' Hallam thought the peasantry looked wild and 'Asiatic', and he felt as if he was now travelling beyond the bounds of Europe. On the one night in which he slept in a Hungarian village, he believed that he had 'never been so near the extreme limits of civilisation: the people brought no towels or basin till they were sent for, & declared it was their custom to put only one sheet, & that a short one, on their beds.' Accomplished linguist that he was, he inevitably tried to learn some Hungarian, which he found rather exotic. He managed to acquire some basic vocabulary and was amused to discover that 'Nem' (Emily's family nickname) was Hungarian for 'no' ('I hope you like your new dignity as a Magyar negative'). Linguistically, matters were helped by the fact that German was spoken in certain parts of the country though the report that some of the aristocracy still spoke Latin proved by this time to be largely unfounded.

Hallam visited the four principal Hungarian towns: Preßburg, Raab, Gran and Pesth. Preßburg he found rather German in atmosphere, though he enjoyed watching a firework display and the views of the Danube. Raab and Gran seemed more authentically Hungarian, but Pesth impressed him most: 'I had no notion that after three days' travel through barbarism I shd. emerge into a splendid capital.' Pesth was at that time joined to Buda by a bridge of boats. Its river frontage reminded Hallam of the Lungarno at Florence, though he thought the Danube was the more impressive river. Although Pesth was of less historical interest than Buda, Hallam thought it 'far the better in appearance'.[118]

In writing to Emily with this news on 11 September, Hallam took the opportunity to wish a happy birthday to Mary Tennyson, in whose honour he claimed he would raise a glass of Tokay, and he told Emily a little more about his proposed itinerary: he and his father were about to return to Vienna where they would stay for a day or two before striking northwards to Prague. This was turning into an extended tour, and Hallam's original estimate that it would last for six weeks was obviously a conservative one. The precise date for the return was not known, though it looked increasingly as if Hallam and his father would not be back until the very end of the month at the earliest; indeed they might even be travelling until the beginning of October. By that time Hallam's friends were expecting him to see him again in London.

But these expectations were not to be fulfilled. On 1 October, Alfred's friend John Heath was staying with the Tennysons at Somersby and was sitting with the family at dinner. Alfred's sister Matilda had been at a dancing class in Spilsby and had taken the opportunity to visit the post office there and bring back any letters that were waiting. One of the letters was in an unknown hand, with an unfamiliar postmark, and was addressed to Alfred, but with the instruction that, in his absence, the letter should be opened by Mrs. Tennyson. Matilda gave Alfred the letter which he read before immediately leaving the dining room. He asked Emily to follow him.

Four days after he had written his last letter to Emily, Arthur Hallam had been found dead in his hotel room in Vienna. Alfred broke this appalling news to his sister and caught her in his arms as she fainted.

CHAPTER SEVEN

A *Creature of Glorious Promise*
Death and Transfiguration

The letter had come from Henry Elton, Hallam's uncle, in Clifton, Bristol and was dated 1st October 1833:

My dear Sir,
At the desire of a most afflicted family, I write to you, because they are unequal, from the Abyss of grief into which they have fallen, to do it themselves.

Your friend Sir, and my much loved Nephew, Arthur Hallam, is no more – it has pleased God, to remove him from this his first scene of Existence, to that better World, for which he was Created.

He died at Vienna on his return from Bud, by Apoplexy, and I believe his remains come by sea from Trieste.

Mr Hallam arrived this Morning in 3 Princes Buildings. [Henry Elton's home in Bristol]

May that Great Being, in whose hands are the Destinies of Man – and who has promised to comfort all that Mourn pour the Balm of Consolation on all the Families who are bowed down by this unexpected dispensation!

I have just seen Mr Hallam, who begs I will tell you, that he will write himself as soon as his Heart will let him. Poor Arthur had a slight attack of Ague – which he had often had – Order'd his fire to be lighted – and talked with as much cheerfulness as usual – He suddenly became insensible and his Spirit departed without Pain – The Physician endeavour'd to get any Blood from him – and on Examination it was the General Opinion, that he could not have lived long – This was also Dr. Holland's opinion – The account I have endeavour'd to give you, is merely what I have been able to gather, but the family of course are in too great distress, to enter into details –

I am, dear Sir –
Your very Obt. Sevt.
HENRY ELTON.[1]

* "A Creature of Glorious Promise" was a phrase used by Francis Doyle to Henry Hallam, October 1833.

217

There is no easy way to break bad news, and how the news of Hallam's death could have been broken more sensitively is beyond imagination. Clearly Henry Elton tried very hard to provide the Tennysons with the unthinkable tidings as best he could (and, outside of Hallam's family, they were the first to be informed), but the impact of his letter must have been all the more impossible to bear because of its own artlessness and embarrassment. Henry Elton was not at all a literary man and he found it understandably difficult to articulate his own feelings of loss, and to balance these with the need to communicate factual detail. The letter's incoherence is part of its distressing power. It evokes (and would have evoked) an uncomprehending numbness in its reader. Even in ages more attuned to premature and unexpected death than our own, the sudden ending of a close friend's life was still a shock, particularly when he himself had shown in his recent communications every sign of health and strength. That Alfred Tennyson remembered this moment for the rest of his life is not surprising, nor is the fact that Emily was prostrated for the whole year which followed Arthur's death. As Frederick Tennyson subsequently put it: 'His loss . . . is a blow from which you will may well suppose, we shall not easily recover.'[2]

Inevitably, with time, more details emerged and by 11 October Francis Doyle could write to Gladstone with what has become perhaps the most generally accepted account of the circumstances of Hallam's death:

> 'Hallam was taken ill on arriving in Vienna as he believed with a return of his ague [i.e. the influenza from which he had been suffering in the spring]. He felt uncomfortable and chilly the whole of the next day and in consequence asked a fire to be lighted. In this condition he remained until the Evening; then he said that he felt himself rather better, that he thought the Ague fit was passing off, and that he should send the courier out to get some sack in order to prevent a return of the complaint. Mr. Hallam then said that as Arthur felt himself less unwell, he should go out and take a walk, which he did, leaving him upon the Sofa. On his return Arthur was still lying down, but his head was in a different position. Mr. Hallam, struck with this (though apparently after some time), spoke to him and received no answer – a Surgeon was immediately sent off, who opened a vein in his arm and another in his hand, but no blood followed and he expired almost immediately. It seems to have been some sort of apoplectic seizure, I presume in some respects similar to those rushes of blood under which he laboured at Cambridge – the fact of his having been subject to such an ailment terminating at his early age in that fatal manner would seem to indicate that something must have been organically wrong in the conformation of his head.'[3]

It was in its own way a source of consolation to Hallam's family and friends (and especially to his father) to believe that 'he could not have lived long', though their reasons for thinking so were not really based on strong medical evidence. It seems certainly to have been the case that Hallam never enjoyed a robust constitution, a state of affairs which was not helped by his compulsive energy and occasional hyperactivity. He had been excused physical exercise as a schoolboy and people who met him socially had described him as delicate and occasionally sickly-looking. Gladstone had spoken of Hallam's occasional high colouration after he had been studying hard and his friends knew of his frequent headaches. Yet none of these symptoms are, or were, life-threatening in themselves. Contrary to popular opinion, there is no necessary correlation between a ruddy complexion and high blood-pressure, for example, nor is there one between severe headaches and cerebral malfunctioning. Hallam's tendency to headaches was probably the condition subsequently to become known as migraine (and it was one which he shared with his mother).

On 10 October, Henry Hallam did, as promised, write to Tennyson from Bristol:

> We cannot express in letters what we would say to each other – therefore I must request you to meet me in Wimpole Street on Thursday next at one. It may be some faint mitigation of sorrow, meantime, that your poor friend was not lost by any improvidence or neglect, and that he must, in all probability, have been snatched away at no distant period, possibly when the bereavement might have been further aggravated, if indeed that could be.
>
> I beg you to give my kindest regards to your mother; but especially to assure your poor sister Emily of my heart-felt and lasting affection. All that remains to me now is to cherish his memory, and to love those whom he loved. She above all is ever a sacred object of my thoughts. God knows how much we have felt for her and for you.
>
> Yours most faithfully,
H. Hallam[4]

This is more a note than a letter, significant for what it leaves out as much as for what it includes, though its tone of self-justification is unmistakable, exonerating its author (presumably) from any accusation of responsibility for the death, and, indeed, emphasising once more its virtual inevitability. Henry Elton's letter did not say very much about the immediate circumstances of Arthur's death, and this one, which might have been expected to say more, says even less. The same is true of the account which Henry Hallam subsequently gave in the *Remains*, where he talks of Arthur's 'deranged circulation' and 'a sudden rush of blood to the head [which] put an instantaneous end to his life. The mysteriousness of such a dreadful termination to a disorder, generally of so little importance, and this instance of the slightest kind, has been diminished by an examination which shewed a weakness of the cerebral vessels, and a want of sufficient energy in the heart'.[5] The death certificate bluntly gave the cause of death as 'schlagfluss' or 'stroke'.

Henry Hallam's memoir in the *Remains* was an essay meant for general, though restricted, circulation, and he consequently chronicled Arthur's death using layman's language. He was keen to treat the matter with due tact, concealing the point that 'the examination' to which he referred was in fact a full post-mortem, as legally required, of which the pathologist's report (written in Latin) survives. Vienna was probably Europe's leading medical centre at this time, and the examination was carried out on 17 September, two days after Arthur's death, by Karl Von Rokitanski, who subsequently enjoyed a reputation as 'the most eminent pathologist in Europe'.[6] Rokitansky reported in detail on what he found but did not offer any hypothesis of his own about the cause of death. His most significant findings were: that the death was quick (probably with some convulsions); that the heart was of normal size (hence there was no hypertension); the lungs were distended, discoloured and partly obstructed, and contained a large amount of blood; the liver and gall-bladder were enlarged and blood-filled, and the spleen was on the point of rupture. Most significantly of all, the skull also contained large amounts of blood.

This last fact establishes the principal cause of Hallam's death as some kind of brain haemorrhage. Brain haemorrhages can be caused by high blood pressure, but only in people much older than Hallam was. It is more likely that Hallam suffered a haemorrhage resulting from the bursting of a congenital 'berry' aneurism (the clinical term for a swollen blood vessel). Although milder forms of this condition need not prove fatal, where there is severe bleeding patients lose consciousness almost instantly and death generally results within a few hours. This seems accurately to fit the circumstances of Hallam's death, and is consistent with the deposits of blood found in the skull.[7] However, it is clear that there were other serious symptoms too. The condition of Hallam's lungs suggests that what Henry Hallam thought was a recurrence of the influenza which Arthur had suffered in the spring could well have been the onset of pneumonia. The condition of his other organs is more difficult to explain, but could be consistent with some kind of bacterial infection, or even incipient leukaemia. Henry Hallam's insistence that Arthur's death would have occurred anyway was not fanciful, and the presence of an undiagnosed aneurysm could have exactly the same effect on the sufferer today as it did then.

Arranging for the post-mortem and for the return of Arthur's body kept Henry in Vienna for some time after Arthur's death. He had written to his highly distinguished family doctor and personal friend, Dr. (later Sir Henry) Holland on the day after Arthur's death to inform him of the event. Indeed, until Henry's return to the family on 28 September, Holland was the only person apart from himself who knew about it. Henry chose not to inform the family until he could do so in person.[8] They were staying, during his absence, with Henry Elton in Bristol, and they were to remain there until early December. The difficulties which Henry Hallam experienced in Vienna must have taxed his emotional resources to their extreme. There were insurmountable problems about the burial of Arthur's body: Henry had had to involve the British Ambassador in the face of bureaucratic complications, attempts at extortion, and intransigence about the interment of a protestant in a catholic cemetery.[9] Henry may have been forced to make the complicated arrangements for the shipping of Arthur's remains from Trieste because there was simply no alternative. It was unusual for the body of someone who had died abroad not to be buried there, and it was to be more than three months before Arthur's remains finally arrived in England. Before Arthur's body was taken from the hotel, *Goldene Birne* in the Landstrasse, Henry cut off a lock of his hair. It still exists.

Inevitably reports of Hallam's death spread quickly. On 3 October, Francis Doyle, Hallam's Eton friend who lived across the road from him in Wimpole Street, called at Hallam's house to enquire when he would be returning from Europe, only to be told by a housemaid that 'Mr. Arthur' had been dead for a fortnight. So shocked was Doyle that he did not stay to ask for details but immediately went off to write to Gladstone and Gaskell. Gladstone received the news three days later. His diary entry for that day is thus significant, not only for being the earliest recorded reaction to Hallam's death by one of his friends, but also for being the first of a series of tributes which Gladstone was to pay to Hallam's memory over the next sixty years. Indeed, after Tennyson, Gladstone was the principal perpetuator of the Hallam legend, despite the repeated misunderstandings that had characterised their friendship. Indeed, as has already been noted, to Gladstone, Hallam became much easier to cope with as a memory than as a presence. His diary entry for 6 October 1833 reads:

'Post hour today brought me a melancholy announcement – the death of Arthur Hallam. This intelligence was deeply oppressive, even to my selfish disposition. I mourn in him, for myself, my earliest near friend: for my fellow creatures, one who would have adorned his age and country, a mind full of beauty and of power, attaining almost to that ideal standard, of which it is presumption to expect an example in natural life. When shall I see his like? . . . I walked upon the hills to muse upon this very mournful event, which cuts me to the heart. Alas for his family and his intended bride!'[10]

Gladstone duly wrote in condolence to Henry Hallam, as did Arthur's other Eton friends, Gaskell and Doyle. To Gaskell: 'The place which he had in my heart can never be refilled. The happiest associations in my life were inseparably connected with him . . . dear Arthur has exchanged what must have been a career of brilliant usefulness in this world for pure and lasting happiness in the next.' To Doyle, there was never 'so admirable and excellent a being as my dear friend Arthur . . . a beloved friend abounding in all those amiable qualities which excite and retain attachment, but also as a creature of glorious promise who could not have failed to . . . benefit mankind'.[11]

Authors of letters of condolence are not upon oath, and an element of exaggeration is perhaps to be expected. Nevertheless there are common features in these early reactions to Hallam's death. All three of the Eton friends, Gaskell and Doyle in particular, wish to claim an almost exclusive possession of their 'dear friend Arthur' and they protest a much closer friendship with him than he would have acknowledged himself. During the last few years of his life, Doyle and Gaskell had been at best at the periphery of Hallam's social circle, and the intensity of their sense of loss caused them instead to describe a friendship which they *would like* to have had. Arthur Hallam in death became a great many people's property. The other significant common feature of these tributes, of course, is their apprehension of great, though ultimately ill-defined, gifts, of a kind that 'would have adorned [their] age and country'. This belief was not unjustified, and it was the basis above all others on which the construction of the Arthur Hallam legend depended.

Amongst the Apostles too the floodgates opened. They had lost the man whom they saw as their intellectual leader. They had also basked in the radiance of his personality and his friendship. As a self-consciously fraternal grouping, the Apostles felt not only a collective sense of loss, but a need for mutual support. W.C. Lubenow sums this up neatly when he writes: 'Hallam's death confirmed Apostolic solidarity . . . Grief consolidated the meaning of friendship for the Apostles. Yet death also froze their dead friends in the ice of legend, making them something more, and less, than they actually were.'[12] When John Kemble broke the news to his sister, Fanny, he said: 'This is a loss which will most assuredly be felt by this age, for if ever man was born for great things he was. Never was a more powerful intellect joined to a purer and holier heart; and the whole illuminated with the richest imagination, with the most sparkling yet the kindest wit'.[13] Robert Monteith went further, and wrote of Hallam in language suggestive of Tennyson's bereaved Bedevere in *Morte d'Arthur*: 'He was so much a centre round which we moved, that now there seems a possibility of many connections being all but dissolved. Since Hallam's death I almost feel like an old man looking back on many friendships as something bygone.'[14] Henry Alford, who had always been one of the most devoted of Hallam's worshippers, summed up the matter to Charles Merivale with an unexpected eloquence: 'I do not remember any thing for many years which has distressed me so much as his death; I sometimes sit and think of it until I feel quite unhappy. It seems, indeed, a loud and terrible stroke from the reality of things upon the fairy building of our youth'. He wrote to his cousin (and fiancée), Fanny: 'I have lately lost a very dear and intimate college friend, Hallam, who died suddenly at Vienna. He was a man of wonderful mind and knowledge on all subjects, hardly credible at his age-younger than myself. He was well acquainted with our own, French, German, Italian, and Spanish literature, besides being a good classical scholar, and of the most tender, affectionate disposition; and there was something admirably simple and earnest in all he said or did. I long ago set him down for the most wonderful person altogether I knew.'[15]

Alford also celebrated Hallam's passing in verse ('Gentle soul/ That ever moved among us in a veil/ Of heavenly lustre') as did Francis Doyle, Charles Elton (Arthur's uncle) and Charles Tennyson. Most poignant of all, though, are Emily Tennyson's words:

Renew my heart in heavenly love,
Take all my sin away,
That I may be his bride above
For an eternal day
Oh fatal journey to the South
Which cost my Arthur's life,
A little time would but have passed
Ere I'd been made his wife.[16]

Additionally, if no other proof was needed that Tennyson's *In Memoriam* did not spring fully formed upon the world, there was the tribute from Richard Monckton Milnes. Milnes had been the first of Arthur's friends to write in condolence to Henry Hallam, requesting, with some presumption, permission to attend the funeral, should it be held in London, and claiming (not very convincingly) to have cut short his travels on the continent in order specifically to renew his intimacy with Hallam. Milnes offered his own verse tribute in *On the Death of _____:*

I thought, how should I see him first,
How should our hands first meet,
Within his room,- upon the stair,-
At the corner of the street?
I thought, where should I hear him first,
How catch his greeting tone,-
And thus I went up to his door,
And they told me he was gone![17]

There is a clear prefigurement here of what is perhaps the best-known lyric of *In Memoriam,* Section VII, ('Dark house by which once more I stand'). Milnes's poem was published in 1838 and the section of *In Memoriam* in question was not composed until ten years later, so it is more than likely that Tennyson had read it. But Milnes's desire to commemorate Hallam did not stop with this poem. He was preparing to publish, as a result of his recent travels, *Memorials of a Tour in Greece*, and he dedicated the book, which appeared the following year, to Hallam's memory, informing Henry Hallam when he did so that it was 'an open testimony to the affectionate admiration with which I regarded one, whom I loved with the truth of early friendship, and you with a parent's passion . . . I hold his kind words and earnest admonitions in the best part of my heart, I have his noble and tender letters by my side, and I feel secure from any charge of presumption in thus addressing you, under the shield of his sacred memory.'[18] Other friends were less headlong in their reactions, but Francis Doyle was in due course to call his son Arthur, in Hallam's memory, just as Tennyson's first son was Hallam and in the Elton family there have been descendants bearing the name of Hallam in every generation to the present day.

But it is of course Tennyson's reaction to Hallam's death which has been most frequently chronicled. In 1949, for example, Charles Tennyson, drawing on what will be seen as the received and essentially nineteenth-century representation of Hallam's death, would write:

'For Alfred a sudden and brutal stroke had annihilated in a moment a love "passing the love of women". The prop, round which his own growth had twined itself for four fruitful years, was suddenly removed . . . During the first months of his sorrow waves of depression swept over him, so dark that he often longed for death. The sudden extinction of his friend, with all his infinite capacity for affection and his brilliant promise, struck at the very roots of his will to live.'[19]

In fact Alfred Tennyson was more resilient than these remarks suggest. On the very day that Gladstone heard the news of Hallam's death, Tennyson wrote the first of the lyrics ('Fair ship that from the Italian shore') which would subsequently grow into *In Memoriam*. He did not hesitate to take up Henry Hallam's invitation to meet him a week thence in London on 17 October (it could well have been his memory this visit to the 'dark house' in Wimpole Street which was the origin of Section VII). He stayed in London for at least a week, sociably visiting friends, including Edward Fitzgerald, who wrote to Donne with some exhilaration that Tennyson was in town and had been writing 'fresh poems . . . finer . . . than any he has done'.[20] Fitzgerald's verdict was accurate. The poems in question, although they included several short pieces and fragments which did not appear until after Tennyson's death, also included the final version of *The Two Voices*, along with the new poems *St. Simeon Stylites, Hark! The dogs howl, On a Mourner, Ulysses* and its companion

Tithon (later to appear as *Tithonus*) and *Tiresias*. The ensuing months would also see Tennyson working on *Morte d'Arthur* (there is a reference to this poem in a letter from Stephen Spring Rice, dated 27 November),[21] and *Oh that 'Twere Possible* ('the "germ" of "Maud"')

Tennyson's sufferings after Hallam's death were considerable and well-documented. He later spoke of having to endure an experience which 'seemed to me to shatter all my life so that I desired to die rather than to live'.[22] Tennant observed a 'bitterness of spirit' in him[23] and Tennyson declined a party invitation from Sophia Rawnsley, his attractive young Lincolnshire neighbour, on the grounds that 'It would be of no use to come among you with an uncheerful mind – and old remembrances sometimes come most powerfully upon me in the midst of society.'[24] But he was not completely overwhelmed. The fact that he did not publish another volume of verse until 1842 caused the later Victorians to speak of Tennyson's 'ten years' silence'. In reality the 1830s were in many ways Tennyson's most productive decade and the reason he chose not to publish was the result of hostile reviewers rather than of creative paralysis. In addition to 'Christopher North', there had been another savage attack, this time from J.W. Croker in *The Quarterly Review* in April 1833. Croker was a most influential reviewer and the *Quarterly* had been described as 'the next book to God's Bible'.[25] Not to be outdone by North, Croker announced his intention to 'undertake Tennyson and hope to make another Keats of him.'[26] His was the most crushing review of all, and the one which probably had the deepest effect on Tennyson.

To Tennyson, Hallam's death was not merely a stimulus to new work: it was also an intervention into existing projects. A good example of this is *The Two Voices*. For well over half a century, Tennyson's biographers, following Hallam Tennyson's *Memoir*, believed that this poem (originally entitled *Thoughts of a Suicide*) was Tennyson's first grief-stricken response to Hallam's death. In fact three-quarters of the poem, including its most apparently despairing sections, were already in existence and, if any biographical reading of the poem is sought, it is a distinct possibility that the 'Suicide' whose feelings are being represented in the poem is Hallam rather than Tennyson. Hallam himself, it should be remembered, had approached the same subject in *Lines Written in Great Depression of Mind*, in March 1829. The evidence that Tennyson was in a suicidal state after the death of Hallam is much less powerful than was once, rather blindly, assumed.

Tennyson worked in a completely different way in *Ulysses*, of which he subsequently said that: 'There is more about myself in Ulysses which was written under the sense of loss and that all had gone by, but that still life must be fought out to the end. It was more written with the feeling of his [Hallam's] loss upon me than many poems in 'In Memoriam'.[27] The interweaving of autobiography with dramatic monologue in the poems of this period is intricate, so that where *The Two Voices* might seem to be a directly biographical poem but turns out not to be, so *Ulysses*, which seems securely placed in the world of literary epic, is one of the most directly autobiographical poems which Tennyson wrote, and it is unusual to find a poet inviting us to read a poem against what might seem to be its own grain. A poem which ends with the exhortation 'To strive, to seek, to find and not to yield' does not sound as if it springs from feelings of bereavement and loss. Nevertheless, when it is remembered that the Ulysses of Tennyson's poem is not the Homeric hero of the *Odyssey*, but the ageing figure whom Dante presents in the *Inferno*, the sense of enervation in the poem's voice becomes easier to understand. Tennyson's Ulysses is irritated with the common lot of life and favours a sentimental engagement with past achievements, which coexists with a supreme vagueness as to what the direction of his proposed final voyage will be. As Robert Bernard Martin says: 'the poem is full of the *need* of going forward not progress itself; there is much exhortation, little action'.[28] Ulysses' very desire 'To sail beyond the sunset, and the baths/ of all the western stars until I die' is, in its asymptotic imprecision, a sign of confusion rather than of clarity about the future.

Of equal relevance is the slightly later *Morte d'Arthur*. Tennyson had for some time been contemplating the composition of a long Arthurian poem, which he believed it would take him twenty years to write, but which, after Croker's review, he lacked the confidence to undertake. Tennyson's Arthurian poems became, in time, perhaps the major works of his early laureate years, but their origins lie in the autumn of 1833, when Tennyson, so to speak, began his Arthurian project at the end. Although Tennyson's account of King Arthur's death derives from Malory, it is a Malory from whom a great deal has been air-brushed. On the human level, the poem only contains two men: Arthur and Bedevere, and its psychological centre is the mourning Bedevere rather than the dying Arthur. Arthur is distant and uncompromising, offering no satisfactory answer to Bedevere's anguished plea 'Ah my Lord Arthur, whither shall I go?' and leaving the tragic, surviving, Bedevere 'revolving many memories' as he watches Arthur's body being taken to its resting place by boat, just as the body of Tennyson's own Arthur was.[29]

Although Tennyson was still receiving letters of condolence in December, such as the one from the sanctimonious Francis Garden ('they that sow in tears, shall reap in joy' etc), so there was a new presence in his social circle in Lincolnshire who has his own perspective on Hallam's death. John Rashdall, whom Tennyson had known (probably more as acquaintance than friend) at Cambridge, was now The Rev. John Rashdall and had, in September 1833, just settled into a curacy in Lincolnshire at Orby, near Spilsby, which put him well within riding distance of the Tennyson family. He had not been at Trinity, nor had he been part of the Apostolic circle, facts which might go some way to explain his diary entry for 10 October, where he writes, with an apparent absence of concern:

'Hallam is dead! – such is life: the accomplished – vain, philosophic Hallam, dead, on a sudden – at 23 [sic] – Indeed true philosophy ought always to be saying – the thing is needful'.[31] He had been told of Hallam's death by Mary Tennyson. Rashdall was a pious young man of an evangelical temper and (at least in the pages of his diary) a degree of self-importance. This serves to make his unexpectedly heartless remark about Hallam all the more noteworthy, but it is a salutary reminder of how Hallam could appear to those who were not in his charmed circle, and it is reminiscent of the opinion expressed by Gladstone's elder brothers who had also found Hallam vain when they met him in Rome.

Although Rashdall was closer to Frederick Tennyson (of whose immortal soul he despaired), he was also in touch with the rest of the family at this time and his diary has interesting light to shed on Alfred Tennyson's activities. Rashdall's own sympathy was directed particularly towards Emily, who, he wrote, was 'in deepest misery as well as poor Hallam's Father, who says he has now nothing left but to "love those whom he loved", and that Emily as one to whom his son was attached will always be to him an object of the most sacred regard. He will perhaps do something for her, or Alfred: Money for a Tour would be desirable to occupy her mind: – I can hardly conceive a greater calamity. Mr. H was to have settled 800£ *a year* [sic] on his marriage'. Likewise, Tennyson's cousin, Julia, though pointing out that 'all the Somersby family seem to feel it severely', singles out 'Poor Emily' rather than Alfred for her particular sympathy on account of her 'great affliction'.[32]

Despite his declining the invitation from Sophia Rawnsley, Tennyson appears to have had a sociable time over the Christmas period of 1833, one which, as R.W. Rader was the first to point out, did not bear overmuch resemblance to the first of the Christmases described in *In Memoriam*.[33] On Boxing Day, the 'Tennysons' (presumably Frederick and Alfred) joined Rashdall over a barrel of oysters which 'they nearly emptied'; on 30 December Alfred and Mary dined with Rashdall at the Rawnsleys and danced until past midnight. The following day, Rashdall (priestly conscience or no) slept in until noon, before being visited by Henry Rawnsley and Alfred Tennyson, who smoked all afternoon before going out for a 'windy walk'. On Thursday 2nd January, Alfred sent a message to Rashdall inviting him to Somersby to meet Robert Tennant (who was visiting) the following day. Rashdall spent the afternoon and evening there, sitting up with Tennyson and Tennant till 3 a.m.

That fact that Tennyson's activities on 3rd January 1834 are recorded has an especial interest, as this was the day on which Arthur Hallam's remains were finally laid to rest in Clevedon Church. The shipping of the body back to England had proved even more difficult than Henry could have anticipated and was perhaps the source of the complaint he made in a letter to Tennyson in December that his own grief over Arthur's loss was increasing rather than diminishing with time. Arthur's body did not leave

Trieste until the beginning of December, and Henry did not at first expect its arrival until mid-January. In fact it arrived at the end of December, though even so there were causes for anxiety, as that month had seen a series of freak storms, severely affecting shipping in the English Channel and elsewhere. There had even been a hurricane at Dover, the port where the body was finally landed, though Henry had originally expected it to put in at Bristol, which was much the nearer port to Clevedon. Tennyson's *In Memoriam* was written in the belief that this had actually been the case, Tennyson being rather taken aback when he learned of his error several decades later.

From Dover Arthur's mortal remains were borne in a solemn cortège of three carriages, pulled by sixteen black Hanoverian horses. The lead coffin was taken in overnight at each place at which the cortège stopped, and was, on the day of the funeral, carried from Clevedon Court to St. Andrew's church (a distance of about two miles) by six Elton estate workers. The funeral service was simple and there were no flowers. The Vicar of Clevedon, Rev. William Newland Pedder, officiated. Along with the coffin, a small square box, thought to contain Hallam's heart, was interred in the Elton family vault in the church's south transept, where, in time, the large memorial tablet was inscribed:

TO THE MEMORY OF
ARTHUR HENRY HALLAM,
OF TRINITY COLLEGE, CAMBRIDGE, BA,
ELDEST SON OF HENRY HALLAM, ESQUIRE,
AND OF JULIA MARIA, HIS WIFE,
DAUGHTER OF SIR ABRAHAM ELTON, BART.,
OF CLEVEDON COURT,
WHO WAS SNATCHED AWAY BY SUDDEN DEATH,
AT VIENNA, ON SEPTEMBER 15TH, 1833,
IN THE 23RD YEAR OF HIS AGE,
AND NOW IN THIS OBSCURE AND SOLITARY
CHURCH,
REPOSE THE MORTAL REMAINS OF
ONE TOO EARLY LOST FOR PUBLIC FAME,
BUT ALREADY CONSPICUOUS AMONG HIS
CONTEMPORARIES
FOR THE BRIGHTNESS OF HIS GENIUS,
THE DEPTH OF HIS UNDERSTANDING
THE NOBLENESS OF HIS DISPOSITION,
THE FERVOUR OF HIS PIETY,
AND THE PURITY OF HIS LIFE

Vale decisive,
Vale dilectissime, desideratissime,
requiescas in pace
Pater ac mater hic posthac requiescamus tecum,
usque ad tubam

Although the author of the current guidebook to Clevedon Parish Church describes these words as 'rather verbose',[34] there is in fact nothing exaggerated in them, and the Latin ones are particularly moving: they commemorate Arthur Hallam in terms that his friends would have recognised and which are entirely in keeping with his posthumous reputation. It seems likely that the 'obscure and solitary church' had been chosen with care as Arthur's last resting place. It was the church in which Henry and Julia Elton had been married, and, apart from its association with his mother's family, it was also, as Henry said, appropriate 'on account of its still and sequestered situation, on a lone hill that overhangs the Bristol channel.'[35] The tablet, of course, can still be seen there.

Tennyson was not among the mourners present. A letter to him from Henry Hallam, dated 9 December, went so far as to offer him a seat in his own carriage, thus treating Tennyson with the respect normally only extended to close family members. Indeed, given that neither Hallam's mother nor sisters attended the funeral, Tennyson and Henry Hallam would effectively have been the chief mourners. Although Henry had written 'I have been informed that you have expressed a wish to attend our dear Arthur's funeral', Tennyson must have quickly changed his mind, for, when Henry wrote to him to inform him of the funeral's date, he did so as a matter of information only, adding that 'My first thought was not to write to you till all was over. But you may have been apprehensive for the safety of the vessel . . . Use your own discretion about telling your sister'.[36]

Tennyson's reasons for not attending Hallam's funeral are unclear and can only be surmised. Rashdall reported later in January that Tennyson had stayed with him for three days and that he 'improves greatly: has evidently a mind yearning for fellowship; for the joys of friendship and love. Hallam seems to have left his heart a widowed one'. The last phrase inevitably suggests that Tennyson had read to Rashdall the 'Fair ship' lyric from *In Memoriam* in which the poet speaks of his being 'widowed'; if not, Rashdall's description becomes an uncannily acute one. It accepts that Tennyson has taken time to come to terms with Hallam's death, though, again, it does not suggest someone who has been totally overtaken by it. If Tennyson did not feel emotionally strong enough to attend Hallam's funeral, he clearly had no difficulty in dancing until the small hours when the mood took him, and felt no need to 'keep' the day on which the funeral took place. His refusal to attend is most likely explained by his characteristic shyness, which would have made him hesitant about taking his place in Henry Hallam's carriage, and appearing prominently amongst Arthur's rather grand Elton relations.

The three months which followed the death of Arthur, had, of course, been all but unbearable to the Hallam family. Henry's confession that his grief grew rather than diminished with time was no doubt correct, but it was nothing besides the grief which Ellen Hallam articulated in her Journal. She had begun to keep a journal on 1 November 1833, little more than a month after the news of Arthur's death had reached her. Ellen claimed that her purpose in writing was 'the humble hope that through the Divine Blessing, I may derive great spiritual advantages from the regular practice of writing down every day something that I have done, read, heard or thought in the course of it'.[37] Ellen's quickness of mind and wide intellectual sympathies meant that her journal recorded much about a life which was seriously and thoughtfully led. It cannot, however, conceal the fact that the prompting of the journal was the shock of Arthur's absence, and it is to this that it repeatedly, indeed compulsively, returns. Apart from the frequent references to a general heaviness of heart and spirits, Ellen clings to her cherished memories of the brother to whom she had always been especially close: 'He who was "a star my way to bless" is gone & with him all my happiness.' The arrival of the ship bringing back Arthur's body on 28 December 'opened every wound afresh' and she recalled that 'About this time three years ago we had a conversation in this same room, which I can *never never* forget. He opened his whole heart to me & disclosed to me his attachment. I thought myself then very unhappy . . . But . . . in looking back so far . . . that hour, I have felt . . . to be one of the sweetest of my existence.' On the day of the funeral she wrote: 'how little did I dream of this coming storm, this awful change, this utter annihilation of everything akin to happiness.' On 4 January, the following day, she was able to report that 'Dearest Papa is just arrived. Oh! How much he has gone through since last he was here.'

The almost wilful detachment which Tennyson had shown in declining to attend the funeral subsequently manifested itself in another way. The previous November Robert Tennant had written to him, suggesting that 'whatever writings Arthur has left should be collected and published, that there may be some memorial of him amongst us'. Tennant goes on to suggest that Tennyson might like to 'intimate to Mr. Hallam' that this was 'the general wish of his friends.'[38] Tennyson never liked being told what to do, and there is no evidence that he acceded to Tennant's request. Nevertheless, Tennant was voicing the general view of the other members of the Hallam circle: Gladstone, Gaskell and Doyle had already made the same suggestion to Henry Hallam the previous month, and Tennant himself then took up the matter with Henry, offering to provide help in supplying copies of the papers which Arthur had given to the Apostles, and assuring Henry that 'It would . . . give me great pleasure to be able to assist in preserving the memory of one who was the dearest friend I am ever likely to know.' Tennant also suggested that the *Vita Nuova* sonnets were in general worthy of inclusion even though he thought that some might require 'considerable alteration'.[39] Henry himself eventually wrote to Tennyson in February to tell him that it was now his intention 'to print, for private friends only, a few of those pieces which have already appeared, with some poems and perhaps prose papers that I have in my possession.' He then asked Tennyson a favour: 'Perhaps you would do something. I should desire to have the character of [Arthur's] mind, his favourite studies and pursuits, his habits and views, delineated. I shall not apply to too many persons; but it has been suggested to me that Spedding will be better able to assist'.[40] He asked Tennyson for Spedding's address so that he could contact him.

Tennyson was the most obvious person from whom to request this favour. Apart from the closeness of the Hallam and Tennyson families, Alfred was the best-known and most widely published writer within Arthur's circle. What Henry completely failed to recognise, however, was that Tennyson never had any taste or aptitude for writing prose (this famously extended even to the writing of letters). Although Tennyson subsequently told his grandfather that 'my heart seemed too crushed and all my energies too paralysed',[41] to comply with Mr. Hallam's request, he expressed the matter differently to Henry himself, replying to him only a very few days later: 'I attempted to draw up a memoir of [Arthur's] life and character, but I failed to do him justice. I failed even to please myself. I could scarcely have pleased you.' In the event Henry wrote the bulk of the memoir himself and supplemented it with material provided by Spedding and Gladstone. Perhaps Tennyson was being more than merely tactful when he added the hope that he would 'be able at a future period to concentrate whatever powers I may possess on the construction of some tribute'.[42] Tennyson was always his own man, and his effective refusal to help Henry Hallam in the way he required was characteristic. Neither Henry Hallam nor the literary world in general was to be disappointed by the tribute to Arthur which Tennyson would eventually produce, and it is not an exaggeration to say that nobody (not even its author) could at this time have predicted the form which it would take.

Spedding wrote to Henry Hallam on 3 March 1834, agreeing to provide material for the preface, and, with becoming modesty, added that 'I fear I can add little to what you will learn from others . . . I know that the step you have resolved on, will be acceptable [to Arthur's Cambridge friends] than any other . . . shortly as my friendship with your son has been permitted to last, his memory stands side by side with my Brother's'.[43] Despite his doubts about his fitness for the task, Spedding completed his portrait in less than a week and sent it to Henry on 11 March. It was included in the *Remains* exactly as written.

The *Remains in Prose and Verse of Arthur Henry Hallam* appeared in July 1834, though there were to be seven subsequent reprintings. The first edition was issued by W. Nicol, of 51 Pall Mall, and ran to 100 copies which were distributed privately by Henry Hallam. Subsequent editions appeared under the imprint of John Murray, and, later, Elkin Mathews and John Lane. There were also two American editions, published in 1863 and 1893 respectively.[44] Henry's *Preface* consisted of a memoir of Arthur, interspersed with letters provided by Spedding and Gladstone, which contained reminiscences relating broadly to university and schooldays respectively. Henry writes as one 'whose eyes must long be dim with tears, and whose hopes on this side of the tomb are broken down for ever'. His words, after all, had been penned only a few months after Arthur's death, with the full shock of the event still very clear in his mind. It is unsurprising that he should cherish with a father's warmth the memory 'of this extraordinary young man.' There is no reason whatsoever to suspect exaggeration in Henry's words when he writes of his late son's 'premature abilities [being] not more conspicuous than an almost faultless disposition, sustained by a more calm self-command than has often been witnessed in that season of life. The sweetness of temper which distinguished his childhood, became with the advance of manhood an habitual benevolence, and ultimately ripened into that exalted principle of love towards God and man which animated and almost absorbed his soul during the latter part of his life . . . He seemed to tread the earth as a spirit from some better world . . . we must feel not only the bereavement of those to whom he was dear, but the loss which mankind have sustained by the withdrawing of such a light.'[45]

But Henry Hallam's view of Arthur is not merely pious, and despite the almost beatific terms which he sometimes uses, there is another, and very different dimension to Henry's portrait. When he asked Tennyson for his contribution, Henry requested first of all that he should deal with the 'character of [Arthur's] mind', and it is Arthur as an intellectual being with whom Henry largely concerns himself, writing with particular elegance and precision about his son's mental characteristics. He stresses Arthur's precociousness as a child, his wide reading, his facility in languages, his prolific efforts in prose and verse. He speaks of Arthur's Eton poetry as bearing 'very striking marks of superior powers' (though he doesn't include any of it in the collection). He goes on to say that 'Poetry with him was not an amusement but the natural and almost necessary language of genuine emotion . . . That he was a poet by nature, these remains will sufficiently prove'. We hear too of Arthur's rapid progress in the Italian language and the authoritative praise of his Italian poems. Henry also asserts that Arthur was 'conversant with the great features of ancient and modern history', and, in the exalted company of his closest Cambridge friends, 'sought above all things, the knowledge of truth, and the perception of beauty.[46]

However, there is another and contrasting vein which runs through Henry's *Preface* to the extent of almost subverting the claims he makes for Arthur's intellectual gifts. Henry is forthright and unforgiving about Arthur's lack of formal academic success. Indeed it is difficult not to feel that Henry is registering a sense of disappointment which the historian's desire to represent the truth cannot in the end suppress. Arthur's lack of aptitude for classical studies is repeatedly emphasised. Both the foreign tours which the young Arthur undertook with his parents are seen in retrospect as having been impediments to his progress in the classical languages, as is also the innately wide-ranging nature of his intellect which found concentration on repetitive tasks distasteful. At Eton, Henry says, Arthur was 'a good, though not perhaps a first-rate, scholar in the Latin and Greek languages. The loss of time, relatively to this object, in travelling, but, far more, his increasing avidity for a different kind of knowledge, and the strong bent of his mind to subjects which exercise other faculties . . . will sufficiently account for what might seem a comparative deficiency in classical learning.' Nor does Henry pass over the fact of Arthur's lack of interest in the composition of Latin verse. He takes the traditional Etonian view that this area of study was 'the chief test of . . . literary talent.' In his membership of the Eton Society, Henry says, 'he declined still more from the usual paths of study, and abated perhaps somewhat of his regard for the writers of antiquity'.[47] At Cambridge 'he was not formed to obtain great academical reputation . . . In truth he was very indifferent to success of this kind; and conscious as he must have been of a high reputation among his contemporaries, he could not think that he stood in need of any University distinctions . . . It was, however, to be regretted, that he never paid the least attention to mathematical studies . . . A little more practice in the strict logic of geometry, a little more familiarity with the physical laws of the universe, and the phenomena to which they relate, would probably have repressed the tendency to vague and mystical speculation which he was fond of indulging'. Henry specifically draws attention to Arthur's poor memory which he also believed contributed to his lack of academic achievement: 'He could remember anything . . . that was associated with an idea. But he seemed, at least after he reached manhood, to want almost wholly the power . . . of retaining with regularity and exactness, a number of unimportant uninteresting particulars.'[48]

Henry's response to Arthur's death was naturally and necessarily a complex one, compounded of a sense of loss, of guilt, and of talent unfulfilled. It was unanimously agreed among all who knew him that Arthur Hallam's life had promised much: the fact of his not having achieved measurable academic success added to, rather than detracted from, this perception.

Of the two interpolated letters by Gladstone and Spedding, Gladstone's is the shorter. Its tone, as might be expected, is measured and reverential, though Gladstone apologises for its 'slovenliness and insufficiency'. It was by no means the last of the public tributes which Gladstone was to pay to the man of whose superior gifts he remained in awe for the rest of his life: 'it was of him above all his contemporaries, that great and lofty expectations were to be formed . . . if he is judged by the works which he has left behind him, the estimate formed of his powers, however high, will yet be completely inadequate.' Gladstone speaks of Hallam the Eton schoolboy as being something of an oracle amongst his friends: 'As a critic there was no one upon whose taste and judgement I had so great a reliance. I never was sure that I thoroughly understood or appreciated any poem till I had discussed it with him.'[49] The rest of Gladstone's 'sketch' (his word) is largely given over to discussing Hallam's tastes in literature.

It has already been noted that Henry Hallam from the beginning had intended to elicit James Spedding's help with the *Remains*, though why he did this is not entirely clear. There is no evidence that he knew Spedding particularly well (certainly in the way that he knew Tennyson or Gladstone) and this was borne out by the fact of his having to ask Tennyson for Spedding's address. Nevertheless, Henry's choice was an inspired one. Spedding's portrait of Hallam is brilliant and, although, as was noted in CHAPTER FOUR (where this passage has already been quoted), it freezes Hallam in its reader's mind as a perpetual undergraduate, there is no other writing about Hallam which makes his personality and presence so immediate. When Spedding begins by saying that he could 'scarcely hope to describe to you the feelings with which I regarded him, much less the daily beauty of his life out of which they grew' he has, of course, already begun to bring Hallam alive.

Spedding praises Hallam, but without sentimentality. Spedding's Hallam is brilliant and gifted, but fallible and idiosyncratic: 'He was commonly to be found in some friend's room, reading or conversing: a habit which he himself felt to be a fault and a loss-and he had occasional fits of reformation, when he adhered to hours and plans of reading with a perseverance which left no doubt of his power to become a strict economiser of time . . . I never saw him idle. He might seem to be lounging or only amusing himself; but his mind, as far as I could judge, was always active and active for good . . . He could read or discuss metaphysics as he lay on the sofa after dinner, surrounded by a noisy party . . . He was fond of society – the society (at least) which he could command at Cambridge . . . And he was looked up to by all as the life and grace of the party.' Like Henry Hallam, Spedding accepted that, in the formal sense, Hallam's Cambridge studies were 'desultory', but balanced this by pointing out that he would never refuse an argument.

On the question of how Hallam's great gifts would have been employed if he had lived, Spedding makes much the same point that Francis Doyle made about Hallam at Eton, suggesting that the very diversity of his gifts prevented him from developing any single one of them to its fullest extent: 'the compositions which he has left (marvellous as they are) are inadequate evidences of his actual power . . . His powers had not yet arranged themselves into the harmony for which they were designed. He sometimes allowed one to interfere with the due exercise of another . . . he was not . . . a very *patient* thinker. He read, thought, and composed with great rapidity . . . so that he did not do full justice either to his author, or himself, or his reader . . . His own theories he was constantly changing and modifying'.

Spedding finally pays tribute to Hallam as 'friend and companion': 'While we were together it left me nothing to desire . . . when I first knew him he was subject to occasional fits of mental depression . . . [but] With me he was all summer-always cheerful, always kind-pleasant in all his moods . . . No man tempered wit and wisdom so gracefully . . . I little dreamed how soon his name might become a sacred one.'[50]

That Arthur Hallam was uniquely promising is the feature that all who knew him were agreed upon, but the nature of the promise is inevitably ill-defined. The natural consequence of Hallam's mixture of personal and intellectual qualities made him hard to categorise and the shape of his possible achievements was in consequence the harder to predict. Tennyson's belief, expressed in *In Memoriam*, that he was formed for 'civic virtue' seems bloodless, and turns Hallam into the kind of public figure from whose shade he himself would probably all too speedily have fled. By the time of his death, Hallam had already shed his political and poetical skins: the former did not survive Eton, and the latter did not survive his association with Tennyson. But he was a prose writer of great incisiveness and style, in possession of a vast hinterland of reading and information. He was particularly celebrated amongst his friends as a 'metaphysician', and whilst this does not automatically mean that he had the necessary originality of thought to become a major philosopher, he undoubtedly had the dialectical skill to join the ranks of what we now think of as the Victorian sages: those writers, predominantly of non-fiction, who were potent and respected interpreters of their age. Although Hallam was not formed to be an historian on his father's model, he would almost certainly have at least equalled his father's stature as a man of letters, and, specifically, as a writer on philosophy and aesthetics.

If his comments in the preface are anything to go by, Henry Hallam was more partial to Arthur as a poet than as prose writer, and the *Remains* is essentially an anthology of poems to which some prose works have been added (though they form a not inconsiderable proportion of the volume). Henry's strictures on the *Theodicaea Novissima* and on Arthur's Cicero essay have already been noted and he included the former only at the prompting of Tennyson. Even so, Henry is selective in the poems which he included. The *Remains* makes no effort at being a Complete Poetical Works (which it quite easily could have been). Just as Henry's biographical notes had made no reference to Anna Wintour, or to Arthur's involvement with the Spanish revolutionaries, so the principles by which Henry selected the poems for the *Remains* were calculated to promote and preserve a particular image of Arthur. He sought advice from Francis Doyle and also, possibly, James Milnes Gaskell,[51] but reserved the final decision to himself. Of the poems already published in 1830 Henry excluded *Lines Written in Great Depression of Mind* and *Lines Addressed to Alfred Tennyson* (the rather interesting poem, previously quoted, about Hallam's encounter with the mad girl in the asylum). As an editorial principle he thus suppressed two of the most personal, and indeed most powerful, of Arthur's earlier poems. Those of the 1830 collection which are reprinted are generally more anodyne, including several of the occasional pieces written on the Scottish tour in the summer of 1829, along with a number of other poems presumably selected to show Arthur's versatility. Thus there are six of his Italian sonnets, a translation from Schiller, an Eton verse exercise and *Timbuctoo*. Although Henry had no great opinion of the latter work, its status as a competition piece presumably ensured its presence. Of the 42 poems contained in the *Remains*, approximately half are new, and nine are directly concerned with Hallam's love for Emily Tennyson. Clearly Henry felt much happier about printing these, than he did about printing the poems relating to Anna Wintour.

Despite the *Remains* enjoying a number of subsequent reprintings, it is unlikely that it ever reached a very large audience, and was indeed never meant to. After 1850, Hallam came to be known, above all else, through Tennyson's *In Memoriam* rather than through his own work. Writing on the centenary of his death in 1933, T.H. Vail Motter could say: 'To most people Arthur Hallam's name is familiar, but his work and all else that his name stood for a hundred years ago are but vague shadows'.[52]

Alhough Hallam's death inevitably sundered the friendship between himself and Tennyson, it did actually serve to bring the Hallam and Tennyson families closer together. The death of Arthur seems to have softened Henry Hallam's heart in several ways, one of which was his taking upon himself a quasi-paternal role towards Emily. Emily's health had suffered as a result of the heavy and unexpected loss which she had been forced to bear in the autumn of 1833, and which, however complex her feelings for Arthur were, removed at one stroke the most important being in her life. Tennyson family tradition provides a touching portrait of her at this time, originally included by Hallam Tennyson in the *Memoir*: 'In consequence of her sudden and terrible grief', he wrote, 'my aunt Emily was ill for many months, and very slowly recovered. "We were waiting for her," writes one of her friends, "in the drawing-room the first day since her loss that she had been able to meet anyone, and she came at last, dressed in deep mourning, a shadow of her former self, but with one white rose in her black hair as her Arthur loved to see her.'[53] Although its author openly accepts that this portrait of Emily is based on hearsay, it is the only one of her at this time which has survived.

Henry Hallam's interventions in Arthur's life often seemed severe and unsympathetic and were capable of causing resentment, if not anger, on the part of his son. Nor was he a man easily to give way to outward shows of feeling. Nevertheless, a part of his grief at Arthur's death was bound up in his sense that he himself bore some responsibility for it. The letter which he had written to Alfred Tennyson in October 1833, as has been noted, had a self-justifying tone, which his assurance that Arthur's death would have been inevitable merely underlined. Henry could not but have been aware that Arthur had died without having married the woman to whom he was betrothed, and that this situation was in no small way the result of his own discouragement. It has even been suggested that Arthur's ill-health in the spring and summer of 1833 had been exacerbated by his anxieties about when, and whether, his marriage to Emily would ever be allowed to take place.[54]

Despite the fact that he had still not yet met her, Henry invited Emily to visit his family in London in the autumn of 1834. She stayed for four months, becoming an even more cherished member of the family circle than Mary Tennyson had been, and happily taking on the role of additional sister (and confidante) of Ellen, to whom she became very close. Further extended visits were paid in 1837 and 1838. Alfred joined her for part at least of both these visits, and, in September 1838, showed Julia Hallam some sections of *In Memoriam*, the fair copies of which have been preserved in the Elton family papers, thus constituting the earliest extant manuscript versions of these lyrics.[55] Henry Hallam settled £300 per year on Emily for the rest of his life. This sum constituted half the annual allowance he had originally proposed to give to Arthur. He was also to leave Emily £1000 in his will. In brief, he came to view her as a dependant, as did his wife, who went so far as to describe Emily as her 'widowed daughter'.[56] It was clearly intended that Emily was to become a perpetual widow despite the fact that she had never actually been married.

It seems that the Tennyson family took much the same view. As Philip L. Elliott has pointed out in his study of the manuscript history of the *Memoir*,[57] Hallam Tennyson went to some trouble to excise any reference in the work to Emily's later life. No readers of the *Memoir* would know that Emily confounded everybody's expectations of her by subsequently marrying, an action which did not go down at all well (even Alfred was said to have disapproved,[58] especially as her husband was, of all things, a naval officer, believed to be no better than 'a midshipman'). Richard Jesse was, in fact, a Lieutenant, and he came from a perfectly respectable family, but he was still, in naval terms, only a middle-ranker. Jane Elton, Arthur's cousin, was shocked to the root of her being when she heard of Emily's engagement (Emily was married in January 1842) and she wrote to her sister making abundantly clear why this was. It was an insult to Hallam and Elton family dignity, and the social snobbery which had always been present in the background of previous negotiations between the Hallams and the Tennysons, rose, Kraken-like, to the surface in Jane's letter. Clearly Arthur's reputation was now unassailable and Emily was seen not only as insulting his memory but as besmirching the role which both families had bestowed on her (Jane had even on one occasion referred to Emily as 'a kind of Nun.') Jane's unconsciously entertaining letter merits lengthy quotation:

> 'What do you think? . . . Emily Tennyson is actually going to be married – and to whom after such a man as Arthur Hallam. To a boy in the Navy, *supposed* to be a Midshipman. It is *a state secret* that Uncle H. allows Emily anything per annum, so don't mention it to anyone. Is it not extra-ordinary–painful–unbelievable? . . . can you conceive anyone whom he had loved, putting up with another? I feel so distressed about this, really it quite *hurts* me, I had such a romantic admiration for her, looked at her with such pity, and now all my feeling about her is bouleversed . . . Julia Hallam always considered her quite as her own sister, and of course Uncle H. could never have contemplated her marrying again (it is just the same thing as marrying again) . . . If the Gentleman were a man of astounding talents one would try and get over it, but all one hears is that he is R.N.'[59]

The subject figured in Jane's correspondence for some time, though at no point could she ever bring herself to refer to Jesse by name ('one nobody had ever heard of'). She stuck firmly to the opinion that Henry Hallam's allowance to Emily had been made in order 'to obviate' the necessity of marriage.[60] The fact that Emily had on one occasion mentioned to Mrs. Hallam, that, in the event of her mother's death (which would be bound to occur before long), she would need to look to her future financial state, also told against her, as it seemed to suggest not only that she was marrying for money, but that she was less grateful than she should have been for Henry's munificence. Henry himself, however, remained equable, and sent Emily a wedding gift, accompanied by a note wishing her well. He also became godfather to Emily's son, who was to become yet another to swell the ranks of those bearing the forenames Arthur Hallam.[61]

In the years after Arthur's death, for all the complexities of their history and circumstances, the Tennyson family prospered more than the Hallams did. Both Emily and Alfred married, produced children, and lived for longer than their biblical span. The subsequent history of the Hallam family, however, was permeated by tragedy and Henry Hallam had, within a very few years, the melancholy duty of adding a further three memorial tablets to the one which had already been raised in Clevedon church in commemoration of Arthur.

Ellen Hallam's journal covering the period which followed Arthur's death has already been quoted. Ellen shared Arthur's tendency to melan-choly, and, although she was described by her cousin Frances as being 'beautiful and of a thoughtful and discerning mind', another cousin, Mary, insisted that 'Ellen was not happy in this life. She took no interest in the pleasures & enjoyments of this world, but God led her through a mysterious path-through conflict and melancholy of mind- to seek that peace which passeth all understanding.'[62] On 15 June 1837, having just recovered from a bout of measles, she joined her mother and younger sister for their reading of the psalms after Sunday breakfast, and, uttering no more than a gentle sigh, 'put her head on her mother's shoulder and died'.[63] She was just short of her twenty-first birthday. Although Henry's stoicism encouraged him to report subsequently that his wife, Julia, was 'wonderfully resigned. Her mature faith in Heaven yields to no storm',[64] Julia seems never to have fully recovered her spirits after Ellen's death. The family observed a lengthy period of mourning, leaving London for Sevenoaks, where they 'lived in strict retirement' for some months. The Reverend Alfred Gatty, later to write a study of *In Memoriam*, reported seeing 'the sorrowing couple at church in garments of the deepest mourning; and the fine brow of Mr. Hallam resting on his hand, as he stood during the service in pensive devotion'.[65]

Following the death of Ellen, Julia Hallam kept her own journal for nearly three years. It does not make for comfortable reading, as Julia's mental state at this time was evidently very precarious. Her unhappy history of miscarriages and stillbirths made her prone to a range of illnesses, both real and imagined; she found her husband at times frustratingly remote and preoccupied; above all else, after the death of three of her children, her concern for the safety and well-being her youngest, Harry, became pathologically obsessive.

The family led a rather peripatetic existence during these years, suggesting an unwillingness to remain for long amidst the melancholy associations of Wimpole Street. They returned from Sevenoaks to 'our desolate home' in London on 2nd January 1838, but there was a nine-month sojourn at Pinner later that year, and a slightly shorter one near Southampton for the second half of 1839. Henry was just as affected as his wife was by the death of his two elder children in such quick succession, but the intensity of their bereavement proved a barrier rather than an encouragement to communication between Henry and Julia. Although Julia records an occasion on which Henry 'wept at my side' while they were out on a country walk, more characteristic of the journal is the complaint that Henry 'seemed indisposed to talk – perhaps our thoughts were full of the same subject. O how I wish that this reserve on serious matters would cease – I think I would be more comfort to him, if he would sometimes talk of those dear ones who are gone.' For all Julia's deference to him as 'my dear husband', Henry was clearly far from easy to live with. Julia records disagreements, which even if they were only of 'trifling importance', still convinced her that she 'ought quietly to have sacrificed my own will in compliance with his wishes.' Although Henry withdrew from society for a while, by the time they had returned to London he resumed his rounds of dinner parties, at which Julia was a far from willing presence, whether as guest or (especially) as hostess. Julia noted that Henry needed 'excitement' in order to sustain his spirits. During the periods in Sevenoaks and Pinner he made frequent excursions 'to town', and was also buoyed up by the writing of his *Literary History of Europe*, whose completion left him depressed. It is difficult not to think that this work provided a kind of therapy, even though it inevitably served to distance him even further from his wife. Another difficulty lay in the husband and wife's different attitude to religion. Julia complained of the infrequency of Henry's attendance at communion and Henry objected to Julia's efforts to indoctrinate Harry with prayers and bible readings, believing that he should be allowed to develop his own faith in his own way.

On the 23 March, 1840 (her fifty-seventh birthday) Julia was taken ill with influenza, which she had almost certainly caught from her sister-in-law, Elisabeth. Worn down as she was, both physically and mentally, she did not recover from it, and died on 28 April. The last written words of her journal are a prayer for the protection of Harry.[66]

Henry now had two children left to him: his daughter Julia, and Harry. Harry was born in 1824 and was consequently 13 years younger than Arthur in whose life he did not figure greatly. But it was inevitable that, after Arthur's death, Harry would come to fill the very large gap in Henry's life that Arthur had left, and become the focus of his expectations.

Henry was fortunate that Harry, like his elder brother, was gifted, and his career followed the same trajectory as Arthur's had done: Eton, Trinity and the Inner Temple. The traditional difference between the elder and the younger son is noticeable when contrasting Arthur's and Harry's temperaments. Harry was more easy-going and biddable than Arthur, less prone to sudden enthusiasms and to fluctuations between periods of despair and hyperactivity. Those who had known Harry at Eton, however, spoke of him in terms very similar to those which had been applied to Arthur, noting 'a singular sweetness of temper . . . [a] great facility in learning . . . both his masters, and those of his schoolfellows who saw much of him, were struck with the general forwardness of his intellect, as well as the breadth and solidity with which the foundations of his education had been laid. His literary taste and information were uniformly recognised by his contemporaries as greatly in advance of their own. At an age when most boys are reading Scott or Byron, he studied Bacon and delighted in Wordsworth and Dante'. As was the case with Arthur, the wide-ranging nature of Harry's literary enthusiasms prevented him from developing any great interest in the classical curriculum, though he did, at the age of fifteen, enter for the recently introduced Newcastle Scholarship and gained the medal for second place. He was less of a public figure at Eton than his elder brother had been, though he did speak at the Society 'where his speeches were . . . noted for ease and clearness.' However, it seems that his innate sensitivity to other people's feelings made him a less combative speaker than Arthur, who enjoyed being provocative and delighted in showing off his rhetorical gifts. Harry was described by one of his school friends as 'gentle, retiring, thoughtful . . . affectionate, without envy or jealousy.'[67]

At Cambridge, he acquitted himself with reasonable distinction. Although, like Arthur, he had only limited interest in Classics and Mathematics, he was, by official university criteria, more successful than his elder brother, gaining second class honours (known as Optimes) in the Mathematics Tripos and a Chancellor's Medal in Classics. He went so far as to sit the examination for a fellowship at Trinity, though was unsuccessful at a first attempt. It was believed that he could well have been successful had he tried again the following year. He was also a member of the Apostles where he was said to have spoken 'quietly, earnestly, logically, and convincingly . . . he was . . . possessed with a spirit of candour and tenderness.' Harry never came to dominate this society in the way that Arthur had done, though he spread his wings into a new direction and founded the 'Historical Debating Club' which existed to 'encourage a more philosophical habit in style, argument, and choice of subjects' than was pursued in the Union, which he generally eschewed. He became especially celebrated for his impromptu remarks and speeches.[68]

On leaving Cambridge, Harry began his legal training, though, unlike Arthur, he had a career at the bar in mind. He joined the Midland Circuit, though his first impressions of the provincial life of a junior barrister were not favourable. Like Arthur, he found that it caused an interruption to the studies that he was really interested in (in his case, English history and political economy). Also, at the beginning of his career, he was on circuit largely in order to look for work. He complained to his sister Julia from Lincoln that he had not yet had a brief, that mess dinners were overpriced and not very good, that his lodgings were poor, and that he objected to having to pay for champagne every night. He looked forward, as soon as he could, to joining her and her father, who were travelling in Germany.[69]

Henry Hallam had undertaken another extensive foreign tour that summer, initially in the company of his daughter Julia, but on the understanding that Harry would also be with them for at least part of the time. Harry joined his father in the Rhine Valley. From there they travelled through Bavaria and Austria to Venice, Florence and Rome on an itinerary which, at least in its later stages, very much paralleled the one undertaken with Arthur more than twenty years before.

But another, and scarcely credible, parallel occurred. After leaving Rome, Harry was taken ill with a fever, probably typhus. The family continued their journey to Siena but Harry's condition remained unstable. Henry wrote home one day to say that he thought Harry was sinking; the next day Harry rallied and Henry felt more optimistic. But eventually tragedy overtook the family once more and on 25 October, Henry had to report that Harry had died, 'talking of his friends at home, sending his dear love to them, – apologising for giving such an amount of trouble to everybody.'[70] He had just turned twenty-six. Once more, Henry was faced with the melancholy responsibility of supervising the return of his son's remains to Clevedon. The funeral service took place on 23 December 1850 and was conducted by Arthur's old Cambridge friend, now the Reverend W.H. Brookfield, who was married to Arthur's cousin Frances. After the service, Brookfield wrote to his wife that 'Poor dear Mr. Hallam bore up with all the fortitude that might be expected from so manly a character consistently with the tenderness of one so affectionate . . . at the close of the solemnity he went down into the vault, and seemed for a few moments difficult to be got back again, but after perhaps less than a minute his self command returned and Captain Elton led him back.' Thackeray, who also attended the service, added that Henry had gone into the vault in order to kiss his son's coffin.[71]

This time Henry's grief knew fewer bounds and the stoicism which had enabled him to survive Arthur's death was less obvious. When Macaulay called to see him on his return to London, Henry wept openly before him, and to Samuel Rogers he wrote that 'there is now nothing to fill the gap, nothing to take off from the solitude of my last days . . . nothing to preserve my name and memory when I go home and am no more seen.'[72] Two years later, Julia married Sir John Lennard of Pickhurst, near Bromley, in Kent and Henry, after suffering a paralytic stroke in 1854, went to live with them there. He was a semi-invalid for the rest of his life, though visitors reported well of him. Sir Henry Holland felt that this final illness had brought about 'a placid gentleness over the sterner qualities of the mind.'[73] Another visitor thought that his mind was not 'dimmed, and there is nothing senile in his aspect . . . His mind seems bright and his spirits seem light'.[74] He died on 21 January 1859 in his eighty-second year, and was buried at Clevedon, the last of his branch of the Hallam line to bear the family name. The words inscribed on his tomb were suggested by Alfred Tennyson.

Despite the tragedies which had befallen Henry Hallam and his family, Henry had remained active and had for long been a respected national figure. He had declined both a Baronetcy and the Regius Professorship of Modern History at Oxford. After his death a committee of the great and the good was formed, chaired by Lord Lansdowne, and including Richard Monckton Milnes and Alfred Tennyson, with the purpose of erecting, by public subscription, a statue of him. The collected subscriptions totalled £1300 and the committee first of all hoped that the statue would be placed in Westminster Abbey, but the Dean (Arthur's Apostolic friend R.C. Trench, and a member of the committee) said that he was not able to authorise this construction, so the statue was eventually unveiled in the crypt of St. Paul's Cathedral. The sculptor was William Theed. Henry Holland, who had also been a member of the organising committee, believed that that the statue 'strikingly pourtrays his massive intellectual features, and the general aspect of the man'.[75] He was also pleased that the inscription was written in English rather than Latin. In addition to this, E.C. Hawtrey, Henry Hallam's friend and the former tutor of his sons, arranged for a bust of Henry to be placed in the Upper School at Eton, where those Old Etonians 'distinguished in Science, Theology, Literature or Politics, & in military or naval duties' were commemorated.[76] It can still be seen there.

That Arthur Hallam's name would become better known than that of his father would have seemed improbable to Henry Hallam's contemporaries, even though Tennyson's *In Memoriam* had appeared nine years before Henry's death. Despite Tennyson's stated intention in 1834 of providing in due course his own tribute to Hallam, it is unlikely that he was clear about what direction he was moving in when he began work on the disparate group of poems which he at first referred to simply as his *Elegies*. What had particularly characterised the reaction of Hallam's friends to his death was not only their acute sense of a great personal loss, but an equally powerful sense that Hallam's death was the world's loss too.

Hallam's posthumous reputation effectively passed through two phases. At first, what might be described as the essentially Apostolic response solidified, over a period of seventeen years, into *In Memoriam*. After the publication of this work, Hallam became not just Apostolic but public property, and the figure of Hallam as Tennyson represented him became the one that was generally accepted as definitive. Indeed, Hallam has almost invariably been 'read' largely as an extension of Tennyson, and as an integral part of Tennyson's biography, to the point of virtually ceasing to be an autonomous character with his own identity. He was subsumed not only by the most capacious poetic imagination of nineteenth-century England, but into what has often been seen as that century's most iconic English poem. In Valentine Cunningham's words: 'Hallam's death [was] . . . perhaps, the most significant event of all for Victorian poetry.'[77] Even so, it is a poem which has proved, ever since its first appearance, particularly susceptible to misreading.

The circumstances surrounding the publication of *In Memoriam, A.H.H.* in 1850 are well known. Despite its attempts at anonymity, the identity of both author and subject were leaked to the press shortly before its first edition appeared. The clamour of critical approval which the poem then met with all but beggars belief. Not only was it a complete contrast to the hostile reception which most of Tennyson's previous work had received, but the widespread enthusiasm which accompanied *In Memoriam* showed the degree of public interest which a lengthy and philosophical poem could provoke in mid-nineteenth-century Britain. Equally well known is the fact of the poem's later appropriation by the recently widowed Queen Victoria, who found it instantly and immediately answerable to her own state. Tennyson had struck an important contemporary emotional nerve. His friends had been right: they had been urging him for decades to seek a large and 'significant' subject as a suitable use of his talents. Tennyson had taken his time, but the urgings had not been misplaced.

The early reviews were strikingly unanimous in both tone and content, even if that unanimity often led to partial and reductive readings of the poem. The first reviewers, after all, had not had much time to reflect on the poem at the length it requires and can perhaps be excused for finding only those things in it which they wished to find. Charles Kingsley, possibly the poem's most authoritative reviewer, provided a particularly succinct accolade when he wrote in *Fraser's Magazine* that he thought *In Memoriam* 'the noblest English Christian poem which several centuries have seen.' Coventry Patmore's words were even more emphatic: 'the best religious poetry that has ever been written in our language.' In general the poem was seen as almost bracingly optimistic. G.H. Lewes wrote that he would 'be surprised if it does not become the solace and delight of every house where poetry is loved. A true and hopeful spirit breathes from its pages . . . All who have sorrowed will listen with delight to the chastened strains here poured forth in *In Memoriam.*' The *Examiner,* whose reviewer was probably John Forster, judged it to be 'the record of a healthy and vigorous mind working its way, through suffering, up to settled equipoise and hopeful resignation.' A great deal more was written in a similar vein.[78]

What is noticeable about these reviews is what they leave out: there is mention of the poem's faith, but not of its doubt, or of its representation of the problems of bereavement and the unappeasable sense of separation that goes with them. There is no apprehension of a described natural world which is hostile as well as beautiful. Most significantly, in these reviews there is virtually no mention of Hallam, who has, for the moment, largely disappeared, though he was to find his way back before long.

In the year following the publication of *In Memoriam*, a short article about Arthur Hallam appeared in an unlikely quarter. Dr. John Brown, an Edinburgh physician, wrote regular literary articles for *The North British Review* (some of which he subsequently collected and published in book form), and, presumably in the light of *In Memoriam*'s popularity, he felt moved to offer some kind of tribute to the poem's subject (if Hallam can be so called). Brown must have seen a copy of the *Remains*, as he shows familiarity not only with its contents, but with Henry Hallam's preface which he quotes almost in its entirety. In the development of the Hallam mythology Brown's article is significant in two respects: firstly, he seems to have been the first person outside of the Hallam circle to write about Hallam at length and in an apparently authoritative way. Although Brown knew Hallam only through the *Remains* and *In Memoriam*, he spoke of him as of a personal acquaintance, and a saintly one at that: 'to each one of us the death of Arthur Hallam-his thoughts and affections-his views of God, of our relations to Him, of duty, of the meaning and worth of this world and the next – where he now is – have an individual significance. He is bound up with our bundle of life; we must be the better or the worse of having known what manner of man he was'.[79]

Brown also feels free to reconstruct Hallam's character in his own image. If Hallam had occasionally in his schooldays been seen as prone to solemnity, in Brown's hands he is almost an anchorite, characterised by a 'power of giving himself up to the search after absolute truth, and the contemplation of supreme goodness'. Brown rates the *Theodicaea* particularly highly: 'it is an endeavour to get nearer God-to assert His eternal Providence . . . We know no performance more wonderful for such a boy. Pascal might have written it.'[80] At least Tennyson thought that Hallam was only 'half-divine'.

The second way in which Brown's article is significant is that its reading of *In Memoriam* is couched in terms which would become increasingly familiar as the nineteenth century wore on. Brown writes: 'There is no excessive or misplaced affection here; it is all founded in fact: while everywhere and throughout it all, affection – a love that is wonderful – meets us first and leaves us last, giving form and substance and grace, and the breath of life and love, to everything that the poet's thick-coming fancies so exquisitely frame.'[81] Although Hallam Tennyson was happy to give this essay currency (he included it in a volume called *Tennyson and his Friends* in 1911), Brown's reading of *In Memoriam* was, as will be seen, in certain ways the opposite of Hallam Tennyson's own: only someone substantially in ignorance of the poem's origins and structure could state that 'it is all founded on fact', though Tennyson's other early biographers (and there was a surprising number of them) without exception believed this to be the case.

The earliest biography of Tennyson to have anything like definitive status was Hallam Tennyson's *Memoir* of 1897 in which certain apparently canonical features of the story of Hallam's death were incorporated. Phillip L. Elliott sums these up as follows: 'The Arthur Hallam–Alfred Tennyson legend which Hallam seemed to be trying to promote is this: Tennyson and his family were prostrated after Arthur Hallam's death, not stirring from Somersby, that Alfred Tennyson did not visit Clevedon Church until he consecrated his marriage by doing so, that no one (until Emily [his wife] in 1850) took the place of Arthur Hallam as Tennyson's literary advisor, [and] that Hallam's memory burned brightly, ultimately inspiring "Crossing the Bar".'[82]

Hallam Tennyson's version of events is not entirely reliable, and (particularly in respect of Tennyson's being 'prostrated' and 'not stirring from Somersby'), easily repudiated, but it is, even so, considerably more authoritative than the versions offered by other hands. In the crop of shorter biographical studies which appeared after Tennyson's death, it is easy to see what his loss of Arthur Hallam had become in the literary imagination of late-Victorian England. To Arthur Waugh (father of Evelyn) in

1892: 'Alfred Tennyson was too much overwhelmed to work. Even poetry failed to charm him from his sorrow. It was not until many years afterwards that his grief was to find voice'.[83] R.F. Horton, whose 1900 biography of the poet rejoiced under the title: *Alfred Tennyson, A Saintly Life*, laid a spurious claim to a much greater insight into Tennyson's psychological state, when he wrote of Hallam's death, that 'the effect was not physical but spiritual. His soul rocked to and fro, like a building shaken by an earthquake . . . Out of his unutterable grief he set to work slowly to build up . . . the noblest memorial that was ever raised to a dead friend.'[84] In Andrew Lang's *Tennyson* (1901) 'the news [of Hallam's death] fell like a thunderbolt from a serene sky. Tennyson's and Hallam's love had been [quoting Kingsley] "passing the love of women"'.[85]

These accounts (if so they can be called) of Hallam's death contain a number of common elements. Their language is dramatic, almost apocalyptic in tone, and metaphor (earthquakes, thunderbolts, etc.) is brought in as a substitute for knowledge. These writers had no access to any reliable information about the actual events of 1833, nor did they know enough about the textual history of *In Memoriam* to offer a reading of it which could define the relationship between Tennyson and Hallam with the subtlety which it requires. In the absence of greater knowledge, all these critics were forced to read *In Memoriam* in a distortingly literal way, a way which Hallam Tennyson, for all his desire to mythologise his father, vigorously attempted to discourage. He did so by quoting his father's own words on the subject:

'It must be remembered . . . that this is a poem, not an actual biography. It is founded on our friendship, on the engagement of Arthur Hallam to my sister, on his sudden death at Vienna, just before the time fixed for their marriage, and on his burial at Clevedon Church. The poem concludes with the marriage of my youngest sister Cecilia. It was meant to be a kind of *Divina Commedia*, ending with happiness. The sections were written at many different places, and as the phases of our intercourse came to my memory and suggested them. I did not write them with any view of weaving them into a whole, or for publication, until I found that I had written so many. The different moods of sorrow as in a drama are dramatically given . . . . .'I' is not always the author speaking of himself, but the voice of the human race speaking thro' him. After the death of A.H.H., the divisions of the poem are made by first Xmas Eve (Section XXVIII), Second Xmas (LXXVIII), Third Xmas Eve (CIV and CV, etc).'[86]

Tennyson additionally made a number of comments on the poem to James (later Sir James) Knowles, the architect of his house at Aldworth, but also a man with serious literary interests who went on to become editor of *The Nineteenth Century*, which is where Tennyson's comments, originally dictated in 1870–1, eventually appeared. Apart from offering glosses on particular lines and stanzas, Tennyson offers some general remarks on the poem which are broadly consistent with those he made to his son. Tennyson says that the 'poem begins with death and ends in promise of a new life-a sort of divine comedy-cheerful at the close. It's a very impersonal poem as well as personal . . . It is rather the cry of the whole human race than mine . . . It's too hopeful this poem . . . .more than I am myself . . . .The general way of its being written was so queer that if there were a blank space, I would put in a poem.'[87]

Literary critics are not in general given to co-operating with authors who try to tell them how their works should be read, but Tennyson's comments on *In Memoriam* have both a coherence and a plausibility which means they need to be taken seriously and need not necessarily involve too much clipping of literary-critical wings. Tennyson is emphatic on four fundamental points. (i) *The poem is a poem, not an autobiography. It is 'impersonal' as much as it is personal.* (ii) *The emotions represented in it, are represented 'as in a drama'* (i.e. a dramatic monologue, such as *Ulysses* or *Tithonus*), *and so the voice is not to be thought of simply as the individual voice of the poet.* (iii) *That the poem's movement towards a hopeful conclusion is to some extent imposed (the poet doesn't finally share that hope) and that* (iv) *this was a structure which needed to be imposed as a means of bringing some kind of order to a diffuse collection of lyrics, composed almost randomly over a long period of time.*

One or two further points may be added. It is quite well known, for example, that the poem's prologue was the last section to be written; the marriage of Tennyson's sister, Cecilia, which is described in the poem's final lyric, had actually taken place eight years previously, before much of the rest of the poem had been written, hence it is not, in terms of strict chronology, a conclusion; the poem appears to present a sequence of events and feelings which occurred over a period of approximately three years (marked by the three Christmases), whereas the individual lyrics themselves were composed over a much longer period. T.S. Eliot's often quoted comment that *In Memoriam* reads like 'a diary, the concentrated diary of a man confessing himself',[88] thus needs some adjustment: a diary, by definition, records events in a chronological order, but the chronology of *In Memoriam* was manufactured primarily with aesthetic principles in mind.

Whilst it can be said that these rather pedantic considerations have no bearing on the emotional impact of the poem, they do have a bearing upon the poem's representation of Arthur Hallam, which Aidan Day has described by saying: 'There are two levels of reference to Hallam throughout . . . The first is the autobiographical and the real. The other, running concurrently and sometimes overlapping with the first, is the mythological.'[89] It has also been said that, in comparison with other poems in the English elegiac tradition, *In Memoriam* is notably personal and intimate in tone and in its evocations of a previously shared life. By the side of *Lycidas, Adonais* or *Thyrsis* (the generally cited examples) this is indeed the case, yet any honest and detailed reading of *In Memoriam* must inevitably lead also to the conclusion, best summed up by Timothy Peltason, that 'Arthur Hallam himself is not a vivid presence, but a vivid absence' in the poem',[90] a fact which is underlined by the image of reaching hands ('Reach out dead hands to comfort me', Tennyson at a crucial moment beseeches (LXXX)). There is a yearning for assurance that Hallam still exists in the (or an) afterlife: that parallel universe which contains him.

Hallam's elusiveness as a flesh-and-blood figure is also increased by Tennyson's descriptions of him in relative terms (that is relative to himself. Like Gladstone, Tennyson repeatedly expresses a conscious feeling of inferiority). Hallam is presented as consistently superior to the poet, indeed as a paragon: 'The man I held as half-divine' (XIV); 'one whose rank exceeds [my own] (LX);'he was rich where I was poor' (LXXIX); 'the master-bowman' (LXXXVII); 'thrice as large as man' (CIII); 'manhood fused with female grace' (CIX); 'A soul on highest mission sent' (CXIII); 'A life that all the Muses decked' (LXXXV). This resourceful hyperbole on Tennyson's part has inevitably become the basis on which generations of readers have formed their impressions of Arthur Hallam, but knowledge of his biography, and of the history of his relationship with Tennyson, reveals that there was much greater equality between the two men than the poem allows. If Tennyson had the highest regard for Hallam's abilities, it was even more significantly the case that Hallam had the highest regard for Tennyson's. It was Hallam, after all, who, in admiration of his friend's genius, had given up writing poetry, as being only Pisgah to Tennyson's Canaan, and who had instead put his energies into the important but much humbler roles of being Tennyson's agent, editor and sponsor.

The places in *In Memoriam* where Tennyson offers direct description of Hallam are those in which his superhuman status is most insisted upon. This is seen particularly in the sequence of lyrics from CIX to CXXX. In the first of these Tennyson writes of Hallam's:

> Heart-affluence in discursive talk
>   From household fountains never dry;
>   The critic clearness of an eye
> That saw through all the Muses' walk;
>
> Seraphic intellect and force
>   To seize and throw the doubts of man;
>   Impassioned logic, which outran
> The hearer in its fiery course;

High nature amorous of the good,
　But touched with no ascetic gloom;
　And passion pure in snowy bloom
Through all the years of April blood;

A love of freedom rarely felt,
　Of freedom in her regal seat
　Of England; not the schoolboy heat,
The blind hysterics of the Celt;

And manhood fused with female grace,
　In such a sort, the child would twine
　A trustful hand, unasked, in thine,
And find his comfort in thy face

Tennyson's affectionate recollection of his friend in this lyric leads by degrees to the construction of a mythic Hallam. Tennyson speaks of the 'fusion' of male and female qualities in Hallam, but the lyric fuses a number of other things too. First there is the unquestioned, and unchallenged, superiority of Hallam's intellect, an intellect which is not only of a seemingly unearthly origin, but which also possesses an energetic, almost violent, 'fiery' power which does not merely handle concepts, but can 'seize and throw' them. Yet this transcendent intelligence is also 'amorous of the good': it is not merely ornamental, and its very desire for 'the good' itself in its turn becomes fused with a commitment to political freedom, ultimately sanctioned as wholesomely patriotic. The practical outcome of this multifarious giftedness would have led, lyric CXIII predicts, to Hallam's life becoming, if he had lived:

A life in civic action warm,
　A soul on highest mission sent,
　A potent voice of Parliament,
A pillar steadfast in the storm.

If *In Memoriam* is a monument to Hallam, it also makes Hallam into a monument. The poem insists on a golden chain of connections from intellectual brilliance, through moral distinction, to civic eminence. Any contemporary reader who knew only the outline of Hallam's life and background would presumably have accepted this formulation without argument, though a knowledge of the details of his life inevitably draws attention to the essentially fictional nature of figure who has been constructed. Timothy Peltason is deeply critical of this aspect of *In Memoriam*, drawing attention to its 'unreal and conventional fancies' which 'distract the poet and . . . weaken the poem.'[91]
But these details defined the later nineteenth century's perceptions of

Arthur Hallam and it is worth examining the ways in which what might be called the heroic depiction of Hallam subsequently developed. As has been noted, in parallel to Tennyson's writing about Hallam, there was also Gladstone's. Gladstone did not take leave of Hallam after he had made his contribution to the *Remains* and he was still writing about him in the 1890s, by which time, after Tennyson's death, he had become the chief curator of the Hallam reputation. In a letter to the bookseller, Bernard Quaritch, which was reproduced in *The Times*, in December 1896, Gladstone drew attention to his having been given by Arthur a copy of Henry Hallam's *Constitutional History* as a leaving present at Eton, and made use of the opportunity to mention that Hallam was 'at that time my dearest friend.'[92] In January 1898 (the year of his death), Gladstone wrote an article for *The Daily Telegraph*, entitled *Personal Recollections of Arthur H. Hallam*, in which various of what had by that time become recognisably canonical features of Hallam were evoked. The terms in which Gladstone's judgements were couched were the familiar ones. Hallam was a paragon in every conceivable way:

'It is the simple truth that Arthur Henry Hallam was a spirit so exceptional, that everything with which he was brought into relation during his shortened passage through the world came to be, through this contact, glorified by a touch of the ideal . . . at Eton . . . he stood supreme among all his fellows . . . any competent witness would at once have declared him the best scholar . . . of the whole school.'

Gladstone, like Tennyson, also fuses the intellectual superiority with the moral and in consequence sees Hallam (inaccurately) as embodying a supreme contentment with life. To Hallam success never automatically led to happiness, but, even so, Gladstone wrote: 'Arthur Hallam's life at Eton was certainly a very happy life. He enjoyed work, he enjoyed society . . . His temper was as sweet as his manners were winning. His conduct was without a spot or even a speck. He was that rare and blessed creature *anima naturaliter Christiana*.' Most characteristic of all, is Gladstone's reiteration of his own sense of inferiority to Hallam 'not only . . . in knowledge and dialectical ability, but my mind was "cabined, cribbed, confined" by an intolerance which I ascribe to my having been brought up in what were then termed evangelical ideas.'[93]

If Gladstone contributes to the beatification of Hallam, full canonisation was to come eight years later. In 1906, Frances Mary Brookfield published her book *The Cambridge Apostles*. Frances Brookfield, daughter of Hallam's cousin Jane Elton and her husband, his Cambridge friend, The Rev. J.W. Brookfield, produced what was, until the work of Peter Allen (1978) and W.C. Lubenow (1998) the standard study of the Cambridge Apostles of Hallam's time. Although the book is essentially anecdotal, highly unreliable, and almost totally lacking in any sense of chronology, Brookfield is a natural writer and talks with exuberance about the Hallam circle in a way which, despite the necessary caveats, is still highly readable. Her history of the Apostles takes the form of a series of character-sketches of its principal members which obviously owe not a little to family tradition and gossip (though her husband had not in fact been an Apostle himself). Frances Brookfield is not so much in awe of these young demi-gods as in love with them. 'It is a remarkable fact', she wrote, 'that all these intellectual giants were endowed, not only with prodigious faculties, but with extraordinary good looks.'[94] Her fulsomeness about Tennyson, for example, caused her to insist that his 'greatness as a man was quite independent of his genius as a poet. He would have been a great man though he had never written a verse . . . he was strikingly handsome . . . splendid of face and strong of limb.'[95] As might be expected, Brookfield, with equal licence and a comparable assumption of personal acquaintanceship, was particularly effusive about Hallam, who floats through her narrative (as he had done through Gladstone's) on a cloud of superlatives: 'His childhood was not like that of others. The scope and capacity of his mind was so prodigious and so early evident that his parents . . . were startled by it and when they realised how prodigally he was endowed became almost afraid to contemplate or speak of his gifts . . . [his Apostolic friends] were all at once captivated by him. They saw his charm and felt his strength and "bowed before him in conscious inferiority in everything." There was a personal as well as a mental attraction about this extraordinary youth which contributed to his singular power of fascination . . . few people born into this world ever in so short an existence made such an impression upon his fellows of distinct individuality and uncommon power as did this gifted youth. Knowledge, success, friendship, love, all were his, and each in its most perfect form.' Even allowing for family partiality, the hagiographic thrust of this portrait, not to mention its palpable inaccuracies, all but turns Hallam's brief life into the subject of a fairy-tale. Indeed Brookfield represents Hallam's life as attaining its own kind of aesthetic perfection and completeness: 'Favoured in his birth, in his gifts, *in his death* [my italics] and in the great memorial written thereon'. Of his relationship with Emily Tennyson, Brookfield writes: 'His affection for his friend's sister was the great and real emotion of his young life and rounds off and completes a career of singular beauty.'[96] This is Hallam without tears: the divinely gifted genius, whose death, by this time, is seen as almost fortunate: at least in so far as it granted him an eternal life on earth, it 'rounded off his career' in the most aesthetically satisfying of ways. To a reader familiar with *In Memoriam*, and especially to one familiar with the *Remains*, Brookfield's account of Hallam's life (and it was a widely read one) is a lyrical travesty.

But it is worth returning to Aidan Day's comment that in *In Memoriam,* the mythic Arthur Hallam coexists with the personal one.

Whilst the poem undeniably mythologises Hallam, this is by no means all it does. It has things to say about Tennyson's relationship with Hallam, a relationship which is often represented in the most intimate of terms. Whilst Tennyson insisted that the poem's narrating voice was not his, but often 'the voice of the human race', it is worth examining what characteristics that ostensibly impersonal voice possessed.

However impersonal Tennyson wished the voice of *In Memoriam* to seem, it was certainly a voice which was not afraid to speak of love. If Tennyson's relationship with the dead Arthur Hallam is imaged in terms of reaching hands, it is also imaged in terms of sundered marriage. The very first section of the poem to be written, only days after Tennyson had heard of Hallam's death, famously presents the writer as a grieving widow ('My Arthur, whom I shall not see/ Till all my widowed race be run' (IX)).The fact of Arthur Hallam's intended marriage to Emily is obviously relevant to his relationship with Tennyson, but it is noteworthy that when Tennyson refers to this marriage, he sees himself as much as Emily as Hallam's 'partner in the flowery walk' (LXXXIV) and later, when he imagines 'Two partners of a married life', he adds that 'I looked on these and thought of thee' (XCVII). Tennyson's relationship with Hallam is often figured in male/female terms. Tennyson himself is sometimes the man, sometimes the woman. In lyric XIII, the sympathy is with the grieving widower, disconsolate at finding himself alone in what had been the intimacy of the marriage bed. In lyric LX, the poet compares himself with 'some poor girl whose heart is set/ On one whose rank exceeds her own'. The love which these examples illustrate is also of an intensely possessive kind: 'The shape of him I loved, and love/ For ever' (CIII); 'Dear heavenly friend that canst not die,/ Mine, mine, for ever, ever mine' (CXXIX). Tennyson also places this love in a clinching literary context by invoking the shade of Shakespeare's sonnets: 'I loved thee, Spirit, and love, nor can/ The soul of Shakespeare love thee more' (LXI).

Tennyson had more than once in his earlier literary career been accused by reviewers of effeminacy, and in poems from *Mariana* onwards there had been examples of Tennyson's identification with female characters and sensibilities. Not very long after its publication, the intimate and feminised voice which is audible in parts of *In Memoriam* attracted attention, and it was attention of a frankly unsympathetic kind.

In November 1851 (in other words about eighteen months after *In Memoriam*'s appearance and its almost unanimously enthusiastic reception) there was an article about it in *The Times*. Its author has been generally believed to be Manley Hopkins (father of Gerard) and the article was printed in a column headed *The Thunderer*. It was thus an opportunity for Manley Hopkins to sound off, and he clearly felt that *In Memoriam* had had too much adulation and that Tennyson and his poem needed cutting down to size. The almost satirical tone of parts of the article is reminiscent of those early reviews by which Tennyson had been so stung. After objecting to 'the enormous exaggeration of the grief,' the writer goes on:

> 'A second defect, which has painfully come out as often as we take up the volume, is the tone of – may we say so! – amatory tenderness . . . Very sweet and plaintive these verses are; but who would not give them a feminine application? Shakespeare may be considered the founder of this style in English. In classical and Oriental poetry it is unpleasantly familiar. His mysterious sonnets present the startling peculiarity of transferring every epithet of womanly endearment to a masculine friend.'[97]

Although expressing distaste for the task, *The Times* review opened up what has subsequently become a major and persistent question about *In Memoriam*. Exactly what is the reader to make of this 'tone . . . of amatory tenderness' which is much more powerful, at least in its immediate and local effects, than the poem's more generalised representation of matters of faith and doubt?

For Tennyson's late Victorian and Edwardian biographers, the question of homosexuality, in literature as in life, could easily be side-stepped with urbane decorum (Kingsley's 'love passing the love of women' was an invaluable and often invoked expression when talking of Tennyson and Hallam). These writers avoided the sense of embarrassment and irritation that seemed to inform *The Times* article. Indeed, as late as 1949 Sir Charles Tennyson, notwithstanding the insights offered by developments in the study of psychology, could breezily attempt to deflect the question of his subject's sexuality:

> 'There is . . . no evidence that during these years, [he was referring specifically to 1830–1] Tennyson had any serious love affair, and one is tempted to infer that his affections were still so wholly absorbed in his friendship with Arthur that there was no room for any deep attachment to a woman.'[98]

Yet the parallel with Shakespeare's sonnets, drawn by *The Times*, as well as by Tennyson himself, inevitably moved the poem on to contentious ground. As Louis Crompton remarks, *In Memoriam* 'had . . . taken its place beside Shakespeare's sonnets as a problematic expression of male affection.'[99] Shakespeare's sonnets tended to make nineteenth-century readers uneasy. Henry Hallam was particularly dismissive of them, believing that it was 'impossible not to wish that Shakespeare had never written them. There is a weakness and folly in all excessive and mis-placed affection, which is not redeemed by the touches of nobler sentiments.'[100] He deplored their effects on 'young men of poetical tempers'. Benjamin Jowett, recalling Tennyson's own love for the sonnets, felt a need to apologise for him: 'It would not have been manly or natural to have lived in it always. But in that peculiar phase of mind he found the sonnets a deeper expression of the never to be forgotten love which he felt' [i.e. for Hallam].[101]

It seems likely that Tennyson himself was aware that a homosexual interpretation could easily be put upon parts of *In Memoriam*. As well as his distancing of himself from the poem and the repeated assertions that it was not autobiographical, textual scholarship has been able to reveal the extent to which Tennyson continued to revise and excise in both his manuscript and printed versions. Susan Shatto and Marian Shaw have noted in their edition of *In Memoriam* several examples of 'Tennyson's deliberate attempt to obscure and make less personal the references to himself and Arthur Hallam'.[102] They cite fifteen instances altogether, some of which are perhaps of more significance than others. For present purposes, three examples will serve as illustrations.

Firstly, in Section XCIII, stanza 4, the printed version reads:

Descend, and touch, and enter; hear
  The wish too strong for words to name;
  That in the blindness of the frame
My ghost may feel that thine is near.[103]

The first line of the stanza in manuscript, which Tennyson subsequently repudiated, reads much more intimately: 'Stoop soul & touch me: wed me: hear'

In Section XLIII, the fourth and final stanza reads:

And love will last as pure and whole
  As when he loved me here in Time,
  And at the spiritual prime
Rewaken with the dawning soul.

Tennyson also clearly felt some concern about the first line of this stanza. The relatively anodyne line which he eventually decided upon, replaces two previous attempts, both of which discuss love in much more personal and possessive terms, the original 'And therefore that our love was true', being followed by 'And thus our love, for ever new.'[104] The attempt to direct attention away from the intimate and confessional, is again apparent in the second stanza of Section LI:

Shall he for whose applause I strove,
  I had such reverence for his blame,
  See with clear eye some hidden shame
And I be lessen'd in his love?

In a previous version, the 'some hidden shame' of the third line of this stanza, was the ostensibly more revealing 'my secret shame.'[105]

In these examples we see particularly clearly the suppression of detail which might otherwise be read as quasi-erotic in favour of something more restrained and neutral, and there is also anecdotal evidence of Tennyson's sensitivity to what he saw as misinterpretation of the poem. Among the comments which he made to James Knowles, was the one about the opening of lyric CXXII. This lyric begins with the line: 'Oh, wast thou with me, dearest then'. About this Tennyson said with defensive vehemence: 'If anybody thinks I called him "dearest" in his life they are much mistaken, for I never even called him "dear".'[106] Hallam Tennyson was also complicit in editorial suppression, excising in the *Memoir* the second half of the Jowett passage about Shakespeare's sonnets which has been quoted, and destroying his father's correspondence with Hallam, though as both Tennyson and Hallam families were withholding with correspondence when it suited them, the significance of this can be exaggerated. Tennyson was a notoriously unwilling letter writer, so it is unlikely that there would have been much extant correspondence anyway (during the time of Hallam's courtship, communication with Alfred was sometimes done by means of Hallam's letters to Emily). The very protective position taken by Hallam's descendants to the correspondence relating to his affair with Anna Wintour was not dissimilar. Nevertheless it is hard not to think that Hallam Tennyson, compiling the *Memoir* of his father in the 1890s, had been influenced by the emergence of the first public British literary homosexual.

Critical attitudes to the question of *In Memoriam*'s perceived sexual overtones have tended to parallel public attitudes to homosexuality in general. One tradition of writing about the poem has been uncomfortable about its possible homosexuality, as if therewith the poem contains some kind of dark secret which undermines its status, and for which some kind of apology needs to made. Just as the Victorian critics were, in the manner of Kingsley, able to by-pass the subject, even as recently as 1969 Gerhard Joseph worked hard to turn Hallam into an ultimately untroubling religious symbol, writing that 'Hallam is . . . occasionally, if obliquely, or by analogy, addressed as a woman (mother, sister, or beloved) who can serve as man's best approach to an erotic union with God'.[107] R.W. Rader finds it necessary, however he might himself read the autobiographical information, to enrol the poem on what he sees as the right moral side:

'Tennyson's feeling for Hallam almost certainly had homosexual components, but that quite certainly he could have had no conscious awareness, or conception, of the possibility that his feeling could have been given physical expression; the very impossibility – the fact that the relationship was absolutely *untinged by sensuality* [my italics] was . . . the very fact that made it possible for him to feel so deeply.'[108]

The rather Jesuitical tone of this passage is only enhanced by the fact that it appears as a footnote.

Christopher Ricks's treatment of the subject in 1972 is not entirely uninfluenced by this tradition when he says: 'It is not only a post-Freudian world which finds some cause for *anxiety* here [my italics]' and he says of the parallels between *In Memoriam* and Shakespeare's sonnets. 'Anybody who believes that Tennyson's feelings for Hallam were not homosexual should try to say why.' Yet Ricks's finding this possible sexual dimension of the poem a cause for 'anxiety' causes him to slip the leash of critical authority by saying that 'crucial acts of definition will have to be left to the psychologists and psychiatrists.'[109]

But there is also a tradition of writing about *In Memoriam* – particularly from explicitly gay critics – which sees the apparent homosexuality of the poem as its most significant feature, and a feature which does not need to be apologised for or explained away. Whilst this approach to the poem brings an apparently refreshing openness to the matter, it parallels the position of *In Memoriam*'s earliest reviewers in having taken an *a priori* decision about what it wishes to find in it. By Tennyson's time poets had had a tendency to acquire their personal myths: Coleridge took opium; Byron died in Greece; Shelley drowned; Keats died of consumption in Rome. These myths inevitably tended to make their subjects more exotic, as did, in time, Browning's eloping to Florence with Elizabeth Barrett. The Tennyson myth was less dramatic, but had its own attractiveness: his best friend died when Tennyson was 24 and Tennyson never fully recovered from the trauma. Readers approaching *In Memoriam* via this route will readily assume, therefore, that it is the fruit of a homosexual relationship and (as anyone who has tried to teach the poem to students will know) this is a view which can be particularly resistant to reason.

There is in fact a long history of homosexual appropriations of *In Memoriam*. Graham Robb, in his study of nineteenth-century attitudes to homosexuality, has pointed out that a canon of texts was coming into existence 'in which gay men and women discovered themselves, regardless of the author's intentions or sexuality'. He illustrates this point by quoting from the German sexual reformer Magnus Hirschfeld whose journal for 1900 contained a bibliography of works likely to appeal to a homosexual readership. It included writings by Rimbaud, Swinburne and Michaelangelo, but also *In Memoriam*. Robb also cites a novel by Edward Prime-Stevenson in which a homosexual character has on his bookshelves works by 'Tibullus, Hafiz, Shakespeare, Whitman, Tennyson, Rachilde amd Sturgis.'[110]

In Memoriam is a moving tribute to a friendship between two young men which was tragically cut short. As such it is easy to see how the poem could (and can) be appropriated by a homosexual readership, just as it could be, for entirely different reasons, by Queen Victoria. To suggest that either its author or it subject was a homosexual is a different matter. The fact that he did not marry until he was turned forty (and until he had completed *In Memoriam*) can be cited as evidence that Tennyson was not unduly interested in women, though the history of his very long-drawn out relationship with the woman who eventually became his wife, not to mention other love affairs in the 1830s, also need to be considered. It is likewise misleading to cite *In Memoriam* alone as a key to Tennyson's sexual nature. *Maud* is arguably a much more personal poem (Tennyson called it 'my pet bantling'), and its sometimes quite flagrant eroticism is strongly heterosexual. It is also very easy for a reader who learns about Tennyson's friendship with Hallam only through the medium of *In Memoriam* to see that friendship as existing in a vacuum. Hallam was not Tennyson's only friend, nor Tennyson Hallam's. Their own friendship had its context. Hallam was by no means the only one of Tennyson's Cambridge friends to be invited to Somersby, and he was certainly not the only one to fall in love with a Tennyson sister. John Heath was engaged to Mary for a time, and another Trinity contemporary, Edward Lushington married Cecilia. Alfred and his elder brother Charles' wives were sisters. Although Tennyson was shy and often awkward in company, he could be sociable enough when he chose, and had his own circle of friends both at Cambridge and later in London: Spedding, Trench and (later) Edward Fitzgerald all figured significantly in his life. To assume that Hallam was Tennyson's only friend is mistaken. Even the assumption that Tennyson, in life as opposed to art, viewed him as his 'best' friend lacks clinching proof.

None of the commentators on *In Memoriam* who have been cited were writing with the full degree of knowledge about Arthur Hallam which became available on the publication of his collected letters in 1981. If it is a temptation for critics to suggest that there *might have been* a homosexual element in Tennyson's feelings for Hallam (and it can be no more than 'might have') there seems little likelihood that there was anything homosexual in Hallam's feelings for Tennyson. There is no doubt from the vast amount of Hallam's correspondence which does survive (let alone a considerable body of his poetry) that he was extremely susceptible to the attractions of women and in modern parlance could best be described as highly-sexed. Not only was there the lengthy and often painful experience of his first love for Anna Wintour, there was also the interest (on the rebound from Anna) in Anne Robertson, the moth-like attraction to the flame of Fanny Kemble, and the flirting with Charlotte Sotheby, quite apart from the more sustained and eventually more adult love for Emily, a love which those who have read only *In Memoriam* inevitably undervalue.

It is not surprising either that the sexual mores of the Cambridge Apostles in the early nineteenth century have been a source of interest to critics and biographers. In the later era of Forster and Keynes and Bloomsbury, the society had a distinctly homosexual flavour, just as it was to have in the age of Blunt and Burgess. In Hallam's time the atmosphere was rather different. Although the Apostles existed in an environment in which male friendship could often be intense and was taken very seriously (as Thackeray noted: 'What *passions* our friendships were'[111]). it was also an environment in which there was no generally defined pattern of homosexual behaviour or identity.[112] It is possible that, having attended public schools as the Apostles generally had, some experience of homoeroticism might have been acquired, though there is little direct evidence that there was much sexual behaviour among the boys in the Eton of Hallam's time. The prevalence of homosexuality in public schools (Byron's Harrow notwithstanding) is in general an historically later phenomenon. In the early nineteenth century, whilst homoeroticism certainly existed, it did so with few explicit terms of reference. Richard Monckton Milnes has already been portrayed as someone whose behaviour conformed in many respects to that of a more modern homosexual (though he eventually married), and there seems little doubt that he found Hallam immediately attractive when he met him. The comparable, and more complex, feelings which Gladstone had for Hallam could well have had a sexual element in them (Gladstone's quickness to take offence and feel rejected, are clearly significant) but Hallam resisted being possessed, either by Gladstone or by Milnes, manifesting what Jack Kolb has described as his '*noli me tangere*'[113] attitude to those who offered him their friendship. His occasional lack of sensitivity in his dealings with both of them (and especially with Gladstone) seems to indicate that he was unaware of the effect which he could have on his male friends.

Attempts to find evidence of homosexuality in Hallam's own writings have generally proved nugatory. Peter Allen, in his 1978 study of the Apostles, quotes from Hallam's letter to Milnes of 1st September 1829 (already discussed in CHAPTER THREE) in which Hallam refers to 'the basest passions [which have] roused themselves in the dark caverns of my nature',[114] but he quotes them out of context: they actually refer to Hallam's struggles with atheism. Richard Dellamora, accepting this reading, even goes so far as to assert that the passage 'may be taken as a veiled confession of genital attraction to other men'.[115] Allen also cites the section of Hallam's essay on Cicero in which he discusses Plato's 'commendation' of love between men.[116] But writing about Plato's 'commendation' of male love is not of itself a sign that the author feels guilt about his own sexual leanings, or that he is recommending homosexuality to others. Sometimes an essay on Cicero is just an essay on Cicero.

Dellamora goes further than Allen in seeking evidence for personal intimacies amongst the Apostles, though his assertions, whilst bold in their claims, are generally coy about their sources. Hallam's unmarried Apostolic friends, in particular Spedding, Lushington and Venables are scrutinised. Dellamora quotes comments from Sir Henry Taylor about the 'depths of tenderness' that Spedding concealed from all but a few intimates, concluding that this shows that Spedding was 'strongly, perhaps sexually, attracted to other men.' With Henry Lushington and George Venables he is on ostensibly stronger ground, as they openly lived together and had been close friends since their schooldays at Charterhouse, though the evidence that Venables was in love with Lushington is contained in Venables' Journals which Dellamora tells us are not publicly available for inspection, and cannot therefore be quoted.[117]

Whilst it is certainly fair to note that some of the Apostles remained unmarried, there are other aspects of the group's sexual behaviour which are equally worthy of examination. Hallam's Apostolic friends resembled neither Bloomsbury on the one hand nor the Oxford Movement on the other, their behaviour being characterised neither by open promiscuity nor by self-conscious abstinence. There was a tendency towards early marriages, clearly undertaken as a means of perpetuating caste identity. It is interesting that of Hallam's Trinity College contemporaries, Alford, Donne and Trench all married their cousins. William Brookfield married Hallam's cousin. Hallam's father had married the sister of an Oxford contemporary. Only Hallam's death prevented another early (and essentially dynastic) marriage.

Arthur Hallam's nineteenth-century descendants do not seem to have been exercised by the nature of his sexual proclivities: they preferred to present him as having no sexual proclivities at all, and Anna Wintour's presence as the skeleton in the cupboard was to provoke some ill-feeling amongst the Hallam relicts in the 1880s. What was left of Hallam's family inevitably remained vigilant in its guardianship of his memory and reputation. The widespread popularity of *In Memoriam* made this, for the most part, a straightforward task, though, as their not particularly justified objections to Emily Tennyson's marriage had shown, family pride could be roused when it was felt that any violence was being done to the image of Arthur which they cherished.

In 1883, ten years after the death of Hallam's school friend James Milnes Gaskell, Gaskell's journalist son, Charles, decided to print a collection of the letters which his father had written from Eton, Italy and Oxford. These were first circulated privately as *Records of an Eton Schoolboy*, and some of them have already been quoted in CHAPTER TWO, presenting, as they were intended to do, an invaluable glimpse into Eton life in the 1820s. Charles Milnes Gaskell was also quite explicit that his book had another purpose: to celebrate the memory of Arthur Hallam, whose death had occurred exactly fifty years previously and to whom some of his father's correspondence had been addressed. Charles Milnes Gaskell was concerned that few members of his own generation knew anything about Hallam other than that he was the inspiration for Tennyson's *In Memoriam*.[118] Additionally Gladstone had always been keen that more of Hallam's correspondence should be available and, after he had seen Gaskell's *Records*, suggested that, if the volume were to be published, he would be happy to see his own correspondence with Hallam included. Gaskell thought that this was a good idea, especially as the correspondence in question related to the events and personalities of a half a century ago and thus would be unlikely to cause offence. Consequently he proposed that, as 'No . . . objection can now be urged . . . we shall give the letters *in extenso*'.[119]

Gaskell's belief that there would be 'no . . . objection' to the publication of the letters was premature. Both Gaskell, and his intermediary, Joanna Richardson, wrote to Julia Lennard, Hallam's remaining sister, asking for her agreement to publish them. Joanna Richardson even went so far as to suggest that 'I think the publication of [Hallam's] letters in their high tone shd. do good with other young men.'[120]

Julia Lennard at first consented in principle but she was not happy about the inclusion of those letters which related to Hallam's time in Italy and particularly to Anna Wintour. Francis Doyle, who wrote a fulsome introduction to the *Records*, clearly saw no problem in their references to 'The boyish fancy for Miss Wintour . . . [which] was quite natural, [and] might have happened to any boy'.[121] Julia, however, remained adamant, writing to Gaskell that: 'Should the book be published, I sd. Like some of the letters from Italy omitted as well as the two I have mentioned before . . . I must ask that nothing may be published without first being submitted to me for my approval.'[122] This was as far as Julia could get in attempting to place an embargo on the letters, but Gaskell's book appeared all the same and the world heard for the first time something about Arthur's amorous exploits in Rome, tame though they would inevitably have seemed by then, though Charles Gaskell managed to add insult to injury by asserting that Anna Wintour had 'inspired Arthur Hallam's best verses'.[123]

This was not a comment calculated to go down well with the family of the Poet Laureate (who with some reason believed that Hallam's best verses were those inspired by Emily), and when a copy of the first, privately printed, edition of the *Records* arrived at Farringford, it was kept from Tennyson's eyes. Hallam Tennyson wrote to Julia that his father had 'set your brother on such a pinnacle before all the world, that anything now published concerning your brother can only detract from his fame . . . my father has such a deep love for him that he would fain keep all critics at a distance from him'. Tennyson's wife concurred, expressing relief that the volume had only at that stage been printed privately, 'lest the public ideal of your brother should in any way be disturbed', adding, with a touching sweetness that in consequence 'we have withheld the book from my Ally.'[124]

This incident indicates just how well-protected Arthur Hallam's memory had become, but there would always be those of a more iconoclastic bent who wished to be critical of it and Hallam's apparently impregnable reputation was not complete proof against attack. As has already been seen, the tendency of late-Victorian biographers of Tennyson had been to turn both him and Hallam into more or less fictional characters, but other points of view were occasionally expressed. Thomas R. Lounsbury published the first part of a projected two-volume biography of Tennyson in America in 1915. *The Life and Times of Tennyson* deals with the poet's life up to 1850. Perhaps the fact that the second volume was never completed has contributed to this biography's relative neglect (there is no reference to it in the British Library catalogue, for example), but at the time of its appearance it was undoubtedly the most scholarly biography of Tennyson which had been written, being much more detailed than the *Memoir*. Lounsbury devoted a whole chapter to Hallam, which was careful, well-informed and refreshingly lacking in sentimentality. Lounsbury discussed the tributes which were paid to Hallam after his death, but acknowledged their inevitable partiality, pointing out that, after all, their authors were 'at the time of their utterance, in some cases little more than boys.' He accepted that he was being controversial in daring to question the by then almost canonical words of Hallam's friends and contemporaries, but he did not flinch from facing the issue which they pose, when he wrote that 'the pages of history are strewn with the lives of men of unfulfilled promise, of men whose apparently high prospects of success have never ripened into fruition.' He cast a cold eye on Hallam's actual achievements, emphasising his lack of academic success at Cambridge and his limitations as a poet ('The verse he wrote was good of its kind; but it is no better than what scores and even hundreds of accomplished men have written'). He was also harsh (though with less justification) on the prose writings, in which he found 'little charm of manner . . . There is nowhere exhibited any of that lightness of touch, that grace, that peculiar happiness of expression, which indicates the existence of the consummate master of prose'.[125] It is not clear how much of Hallam's prose Lounsbury had actually read. If he had read more than the few pieces contained in the *Remains*, (presumably the only examples available), he might possibly have been more generous.

Although Lounsbury was the first person to present a cogently sceptical view of Hallam in a serious academic context, ever since Hallam's death there had been individual dissenting voices, and Lounsbury ended his own chapter by quoting at length from one of them: Fanny Kemble. It is ironic that Fanny, whom Hallam, for a time at least, idolised, should so resolutely have refused to subscribe totally to the generally accepted view of Hallam. Most certainly she is prepared to agree that there 'was a gentleness and purity almost virginal in his voice, manner and countenance . . . On Arthur Hallam's brow and eyes this heavenly light, so fugitive on other human faces, rested habitually, as if he was thinking and seeing in heaven.' But this was not before she had confessed, rather more tartly, that his 'early death . . . and the imperishable monument of love raised by Tennyson's genius to his memory, have tended to give him a pre-eminence among the companions of his youth which I do not think his abilities would have won for him had he lived; though they were undoubtedly of a high order.'[126]

Much the same view was taken by W.H. Thompson, an Apostle, later to have a distinguished academic career as Cambridge's Regius Professor of Greek, and as Master of Trinity. He reported at the time of Hallam's death that Tennyson seemed 'less overcome than one would have expected',[127] and subsequently opined, when asked, that 'Tennyson, beyond doubt' was the greater man.[128]

There had also been those, who, existing outside the aura of Hallam's personal 'sweetness', had found him vain and posturing. He could seem overbearing, argumentative and self-centred, and Rashdall's comment about the 'vain, philosophical Arthur Hallam', is too pithy to forget, especially as it came from the pen of an otherwise rather serious young man, not much given to flights of satirical humour. Above all, though, there are the opinions of A.C. Benson, who greatly relished taking the axe to Hallam's reputation in what still remains the most comprehensively hostile treatment of it. His *Fasti Etonenses*, 'A biographical history of Eton selected from the lives of celebrated Etonians', published in 1899, might be expected to be cosily reverential in its accounts of 'celebrated Etonians', written, as it was, from within the walls (Benson was an Eton Housemaster at the time), but the case is quite the opposite.

Benson's initial proposition that Hallam 'has perhaps been more gloriously monumentalised than any other living man of the century', represents an artful exaggeration, which gives Benson just the rhetorical cue which he needs to attack Hallam on several fronts. First of all, there are his letters, which 'it is difficult to read . . . without forming an impression unfavourable to Hallam. The letters appear, even with all due allowances, to be tinged with unhealthy precocity, and by what we should call priggishness, developed to a painful degree' and, to prove his point, Benson quotes two short extracts from his letters to Gaskell, both confessedly, of a self-absorbed and almost narcissistic kind ('I am a moping, peevish, creature', etc.). He then goes on to assert that 'Hallam . . . was not always so amiable as his biographers would have us think', and quotes an anecdote: 'Lord Dudley told Francis Hare that he had dined with Henry Hallam and his son Arthur in Italy when "it did my heart good to sit by, and hear how the son snubbed the father, remembering how often the father had unmercifully snubbed me."' Finally there is his poetry: 'Hallam's poems do not show great promise. Those belonging to the year 1829 are written in a strain of despondency and dejection, chiefly due to the state of his health'.[129]

Given that the air of veneration which surrounded Hallam can easily enough turn fetid, Benson's hostility to him is quite bracing, even if, in the end, he does not always seem to have chosen the best grounds on which to attack him. Benson's judgement on the poetry is fair, but his strictures on the letters would be more reasonable if the letters quoted were the only ones which there were. That Hallam was 'not always so amiable as his biographers would have us think', depends upon which biographers Benson has in mind, but to the present one, the thought of Arthur Hallam (aged seventeen at the time) publicly snubbing his notoriously disputatious father verges on the sublime.

Nor does Benson spare Hallam's physical appearance, criticising not only the 'inferior artist' who executed the portrait of Hallam which still hangs at Eton, but also the picture's subject: 'a rubicund, good-humoured, almost beery-looking young man, with a sly and sensual cast of the eye.'[130] Most certainly the portrait in question is bold in its coloration, but it is noteworthy that Benson's inveteracy fixes Hallam in his reader's imagination in terms exactly the opposite from those in which he was generally recalled by those who knew him (as for example, Fanny Kemble, in the comments just quoted.) Reports of Hallam's appearance tended to emphasise delicacy and frailty.

Relatively few pictorial representations of Hallam survive, and, apart from the portrait already mentioned, none of them were the work of professional artists. There is an anonymous painting which may possibly be of Hallam as a child, otherwise there are extant drawings by Anne Sellwood and James Spedding (both of which are reproduced). As already mentioned, the painting by Mr Harden of the party aboard the ship from Bordeaux to Dublin in 1830 shows Hallam only from behind. The bust of Hallam by Sir Francis Chantrey, now at Trinity College, Cambridge, was executed only after Hallam's death and consequently seems rather formal and expressionless. It is thus not easy to gain any clear appreciation of what Hallam actually looked like. Perhaps this is one reason why there has been a tendency in the construction of his myth to insist on his physical attractiveness. Fanny Kemble's description of Hallam's appearance at least came from someone who actually knew him, but when Roy Jenkins, in an otherwise unflattering series of references to Hallam in his biography of Gladstone, claims that Hallam was 'thought dazzlingly beautiful',[131] it can only be concluded that even an author as hostile to Hallam as Jenkins is unthinkingly buying into the Hallam mythology created by Frances Brookfield and others.

Although he was not speaking specifically of his physical appearance, Jack Kolb has referred to Arthur Hallam's 'elusive attractiveness',[132] yet it is Kolb's own edition of Hallam's letters, published in 1981, which more than anything else challenges this apparent elusiveness and comes closest to showing us Hallam in his habit as he lived. Although Kolb also makes the point that Hallam's life has an 'incomplete, unformed quality . . . curiously appropriate to his permanent embodiment in *In Memoriam*',[133] it was also, as the present study has attempted to show, a surprisingly full and varied life. If the 'unformed' nature of Hallam's life is the inevitable result of its premature end, it was nevertheless a life lived fervently, in which a great deal was done in a great many areas, with considerable energy and over a very short period. So much of Hallam's life reads as if it is the life of someone considerably older than he actually was. His work as poet, critic, translator, editor, not to mention his associations with publishers, poets and actors, was, so to speak, thoroughly *adult*, yet carried out for the most part whilst he was still only of undergraduate age. The generally agreed view that Hallam's life was one of great promise should never be allowed to overshadow the fact that it was also a life of unusual achievement.

In the veneration which came to surround Hallam's memory, it is precisely this personal dynamism which has been forgotten and the tragedy of his life lies not only in its brevity, but in the way in which later generations have been led, particularly by *In Memoriam*, to associate Hallam so indissolubly with Tennyson that he has been granted too little by way of immortality on his own terms. It has been the fate of Arthur Hallam's short life to be taken as read, rather than to be read.

A story persisted in the Tennyson family which has a particularly symbolic resonance. In late September 1833, Alfred's sisters, Mary and Matilda, were walking near their home in Somersby and, although the news of Hallam's death had not yet reached them, they were convinced that they had seen his ghost. The figure of a tall young man, dressed in white, was observed walking ahead of them until suddenly it left the lane and disappeared into the hedge. Matilda was so frightened that she went home in floods of tears.[134]

It is as a phenomenon just beyond the reach of physical reality that Hallam has largely been perceived since his death. It has served so many to grant him his own special status: superhuman, almost supernatural, iconic, but bearing only a glancing reference to the man of flesh and blood.

In Clevedon, visitors still invoke the ghost of his memory as they make their way up and down Poets' Walk.

Notes

CHAPTER ONE *Naturally Disputatious*: Father and Son, 1811–1822

1   Tennyson, *In Memoriam*, XVIII.
2   Tennyson, *In Memoriam*, XIV.
3   *Remains*, pp. iii–v.
4   Britton, *History and Antiquities* (1830), p. 68.
5   Dictionary of National Biography (1890), vol. 24, p. 96.
6   Ch Ch., vol. 14.
7   Victoria County History (Staffordshire), vol. 17, p. 21.
8   Card, *Eton Established* (2001), p. 99.
9   Maxwell Lyte, *History of Eton College* (1899), p. 358.
10 Card, p. 100.
11 Ch Ch., vol. 12.
12 Clark, *Henry Hallam* (1982), p. 1.
13 Ticknor, *Life, Letters and Journals* (1876), vol. 2, p. 148.
14 Letters, p. 239.
15 Trin. Add. Ms. d27.
16 Sanders, *The Holland House Circle* (1908), p. 225.
17 Trin. Add. Ms. d28.
18 Ramsden, *Correspondence of Two Brothers* (1906), pp. 58–60.
19 Clark, p. 4.
20 Clark, p. 5.
21 Dagnall, *Creating a Good Impression* (1994), pp. 83–5.
22 M. Elton, *Annals of the Elton Family* (1994), p. 108.
23 C. and F. Brookfield, *Mrs Brookfield and her Circle* (1906), p. 115.
24 Elton, *ibid.*
25 BL. Add. Ms. 81295B.
26 *Ibid.*
27 *Writings*, p. 92.
28 Ch Ch., vol. 9.
29 Elton, p. 141.
30 BL. Add. Ms. 81295B.
31 Clive, *Scotch Reviewers* (1957), p. 35.
32 Clive, p. 42.
33 McGann (ed.), *Byron, Complete Poetical Works*, vol. 1, pp. 245–6.
34 *Ibid.*, p. 408.
35 Virgin, *Sydney Smith* (1994), p. 119.
36 Hudson, *Holland House in Kensington* (1967), p. 61.
37 Hayward, *Lord Lansdowne* (1872), p. 6.

38 Holland, *Recollections of a Past Life* (1872), p. 227.
39 Fox, *Journal* (1923), pp. 152–3.
40 Martineau, *Autobiography* (1967), p. 249.
41 Sanders, p. 224.
42 Martineau, *ibid.*
43 Ticknor, vol. 2, p. 145.
44 Ch Ch., vol. 12.
45 Hayward, p. 23.
46 Sanders, p. 226.
47 Ramsden, pp. 119, 125.
48 *In Memoriam,* VII.
49 Ramsden, p. 248.
50 Ramsden, p. 250.
51 *Remains*, p. iv.
52 Ramsden, *ibid.*
53 BL. Add. Ms. 81295A.
54 Ch Ch., vol. 10.
55 *Remains*, p. v.
56 Victoria History of Putney (1912, repr. 1996), p. 5.
57 E. Hammond, *Bygone Putney* (1898), p. 58.
58 Festing Jones, *Samuel Butler* (1919), vol. 1, pp. 228–9.
59 Holland, p. 226n.
60 BL. Add. Ms. 81296.

CHAPTER TWO An Unreformed Education: Eton College, 1822–1827

 1 Jenkins, *Gladstone* (1995), p. 10.
 2 Letters, p. 118.
 3 Chandos, *Boys Together* (1984), p. 25.
 4 Card, p. 119.
 5 Tucker, *Eton of Old* (1892), pp. 73–4; 76–7.
 6 Letters, p. 100.
 7 Wilkinson, *Reminiscences of Eton* (1888), p. 48.
 8 Maxwell Lyte, p. 391.
 9 *Remains*, p. vii.
10 Ch Ch., vol. 11.
11 *Remains*, pp. v, viii.
12 Wilkinson, p. 48.
13 Chandos, p. 32.
14 Doyle, *Reminiscences and Opinions* (1886), p. 30.
15 Sterry, *Annals of Eton College* (1898), p. 229.
16 Benson, *Fasti Etonenses* (1899), p. 279.
17 *Ibid.*, p. 331.
18 Hollis, *Eton: A History* (1960), p. 207.
19 Tucker, p. 84.
20 Benson, p. 303.
21 *Ibid.*, p. 281.
22 Chandos, p. 218.
23 *Etoniana*, no. 71, p. 328.

24 Letters, p. 96.
25 Sterry, p. 257.
26 Tucker, p. 40.
27 Lawrence (ed.), *The Encouragement of Learning* (1980), p. 23.
28 Benson, p. 299.
29 Ch Ch., vol, 9.
30 Gaskell (ed.), *An Eton Boy* (1939), p. 39.
31 *Ibid.*, p. 29.
32 *Ibid.*, p. 74.
33 Letters, p. 43.
34 Ch Ch., vol. 9.
35 Brooke and Sorensen (eds.), *The Prime Minister's Papers: Gladstone, vol.* *1* (1971), p. 24.
36 Card, p. 145.
37 Wilkinson, p. 30.
38 Ch Ch., vol. 13.
39 F.St.J. Thackeray, *Memoir of Dr. Hawtrey* (1896), p. 58.
40 *Ibid.*, p. 54.
41 *Ibid.*, p. 86.
42 BL. Add. Ms.81296.
43 Gaskell (1939), p. 80.
44 Brooke and Sorensen, p. 30.
45 Doyle, pp. 41, 43.
46 Brooke and Sorensen, *ibid.*
47 *Remains*, pp. xxxvi, xxxvii.
48 H. Hallam, *The Constitutional History of England* (1827), vol. 1, p. 8.
49 Burrow, *A Liberal Descent* (1981), p. 15.
50 Maxwell Lyte, p. 409.
51 Sterry, p. 248.
52 Gaskell (1939), p. 77.
53 Doyle, p. 32.
54 Letters, p. 95.
55 Lawrence, p. 27.
56 Doyle, pp. 35–6.
57 Gladstone, *Diaries* (1968), vol. 1, 26/6/26.
58 *Ibid.*, 25/2/26.
59 Letters, p. 48.
60 *Ibid.*, p. 51.
61 Gladstone, *Diaries*, 29/4/26.
62 Letters, p. 54.
63 *Remains*, p. vii.
64 Gladstone, *Diaries*, 14/5/26.
65 Letters, p. 54.
66 *Ibid.*, p. 58.
67 *Etoniana*, no. 71, p. 328.
68 Gladstone, *Diaries*, 27/7/26.
69 Letters, p. 63.
70 *Ibid.*, p. 65.
71 *Ibid.*, p. 68.

72 *Ibid.*, p. 69.
73 *Ibid.*, p. 72.
74 *Ibid.*, p. 81.
75 *Ibid.*, pp. 72–5.
76 *Ibid.*, pp. 86–7.
77 *Ibid.*, p. 91.
78 Gaskell (1939), pp. 109, 103.
79 Gladstone, *Diaries*, 24/9/26.
80 *Ibid.*, 12/3/27, Letters, p. 121.
81 Gladstone, *Diaries*, 5/11/26.
82 Brooke and Sorensen, p. 31.
83 Doyle, p. 40.
84 Dr. Edward Littleton, private correspondence with the author.
85 Brooke and Sorensen, pp. 29–30.
86 Sterry, pp. 250–51.
87 Letters, p. 123.
88 *Ibid.*, p. 155.
89 *Ibid.*, p. 49.
90 *Ibid.*, p. 118.
91 Gaskell (1939), p. 83.
92 BL. Add. Ms. 81296.
93 Gaskell (1939), p. 84.
94 Letters, p. 123.
95 Gladstone, *Diaries*, 28/3/27.
96 Letters, p. 122.
97 *Ibid.*, p. 143.
98 Gaskell (1939), pp. 103–4.
99 Letters, p. 99.
100 *Ibid.*, p. 154.
101 Kolb (1999), pp. 38–41.
102 Brock and Curthoys, *History of the University of Oxford* (1997), p. 40.
103 Letters, p. 217.
104 Gaskell (1939), p. 57.
105 Letters, p. 129.
106 *Ibid.*, pp. 139, 141.
107 *Ibid.*, p. 131.
108 Brooke and Sorensen, p. 190.
109 Letters, pp.146, 150.
110 Gladstone, *Diaries*, 22/5/27.
111 Brooke and Sorensen, p. 192.
112 Gladstone, *Diaries*, 4/6/27.
113 BL. Add. Ms. 1296
114 Brooke and Sorensen, p. 193.
115 Letters, pp. 145–6.
116 *Ibid.*, p. 146.
117 *The Eton Miscellany*, vol. 1, p. 215.
118 *Remains*, p. ix.
119 *The Eton Miscellany*, vol. 1, pp. 61, 125, 161.
120 Ch Ch., vol. 11.

121 Brooke and Sorensen, p. 196.
122 Letters, p. 171.
123 *Etoniana*, No. 58, p. 115.
124 Gaskell (1939), p. 107.
125 Gladstone, *Diaries*, 23/7/27.
126 BL. Add. Ms. 81296.
127 Letters, p. 157n.
128 *The Times*, 24 December 1896.
129 Letters, p. 162.
130 *Ibid.*, p. 172.
131 *Ibid.*, p. 154.
132 *Ibid.*, pp. 162, 171, 164.
133 Gaskell (1939), p. 100.
134 Morley, *Life of William Ewart Gladstone* (1903), vol. 1, p. 38.
135 Letters, p. 158.
136 *Ibid.* p. 161
137 *Ibid.* pp. 179, 177, 185, 180

CHAPTER THREE *A Farewell to the South*: Italy, 1827–1828

1 Letters, p. 219n.
2 *Remains*, p. xiv.
3 Letters, p. 216.
4 Starke, *Information and Directions for Travellers on The Continent* (5th ed. 1824), p. vi.
5 Hale (ed.), *The Italian Journey of Samuel Rogers* (1956), pp. 75–7.
6 *Ibid.*, p. 81.
7 Starke, p. 125.
8 Hale, p. 71.
9 Starke, p. 23–4.
10 Letters, p. 174.
11 BL. Add. Ms. 81298A.
12 Letters, p. 174.
13 Hale, p. 96.
14 Letters, p. 175.
15 Starke, p. 42.
16 Letters, p. 176.
17 *Ibid.*, p. 181.
18 *Ibid.*, p. 180.
19 *Remains*, pp. xii–xiii.
20 Writings, p. 3.
21 Letters, p. 182.
22 Hale, p. 88.
23 Letters, pp. 177, 179.
24 *Ibid.*, p. 184.
25 *Ibid.*, p. 190.
26 *Ibid.*, p. 192n.
27 *Ibid.*, p. 186.
28 *Remains*, pp. x–xi.

29 Letters, p. 189.
30 Eaton, *Rome In The Nineteenth Century* (1820), vol. 3, pp. 231–2, 238.
31 *Ibid.*, vol. 3, p. 64.
32 Letters, p. 190.
33 *Ibid.*, p. 191.
34 Writings, p. 212,
35 Letters, p. 186.
36 See Eaton, vol. 2, pp. 173–4, also Martin, *Narrative of a Three Year's Residence in Italy* (1828), p. 122.
37 Writings, pp. 5–6.
38 Ch Ch., vol. 8.
39 Letters, p. 197n.
40 Gaskell (1939), pp. 128–9.
41 Ch Ch., vol.8.
42 Writings, p. 4.
43 Letters, p. 195.
44 Hale, p. 67.
45 Letters, p. 199.
46 *Ibid.*, p. 200.
47 *Ibid.*, p. 202.
48 Starke, p. 230.
49 Letters, p. 206.
50 *Ibid.*, pp. 204–5.
51 Gaskell (1939), p. 142.
52 Letters, p. 206.
53 *Ibid.*, p. 209.
54 *Ibid.*, p. 530.
55 Writings, p. 8.
56 *Ibid.*, pp. 20–23.
57 *Ibid.*, p. 20.
58 Trin. Add. Ms. D28.
59 Letters, p. 216.
60 Letters, pp. 210–14.
61 Ricks, vol. 2, p. 18.
62 *Remains*, p.10.
63 Letters, p. 217.
64 *Ibid.*, p. 236.
65 *Ibid.*, pp. 217–18.
66 *Ibid.*, pp. 229, 233.
67 *Ibid.*, p. 187n.
68 *Ibid.*, pp. 223–33.
69 *Ibid.*, p. 217.

CHAPTER FOUR '*Cambridge I hate intensely*': Trinity College, 1828–1829

1 *Remains*, pp. xxi–xxii.
2 Wemyss Reid, *Life, Letters and Friendships of Richard Monckton Milnes* (1890), p. 59.

3   *In Memoriam*, LXXXVII; CIX.
4   F.M. Brookfield, *The Cambridge Apostles* (1906), p. 126.
5   H. Tennyson, *Tennysion A Memoir* (1897), vol. 1, p. 66n.
6   Allen, *The Cambridge Apostles: The Early Years* (1978), p. 11.
7   Searby, *A History of the University of Cambridge*, vol. 3, p. 166.
8   *Ibid.*, p. 191.
9   *Ibid.*, p. 235.
10 Wemyss Reid, p. 57.
11 *Ibid.*, p. 71.
12 Letters, p. 243.
13 Searby, p. 67.
14 Allen, p. 12.
15 Smith and Stray (eds.), *Teaching and Learning in Nineteenth Century Cambridge* (2001), p. 126.
16 F.O. Alford, *The Life, Journals and Letters of Henry Alford, DD* (1874), p. 44.
17 Wemyss Reid, p. 64.
18 Brock and Curthoys, p. 26.
19 Smith and Stray, p. 34.
20 Pope-Hennessy, *Monckton Milnes The Years of Promise* (1949), p. 1.
21 Rouse Bell, *Trinity College, Cambridge* (1906), pp. 29–30.
22 Pope-Hennessy, p. 11.
23 Moorman, *William Wordsworth The Later Years* (1965), p. 424.
24 Winstanley, *Early Victorian Cambridge* (1940), p. 58.
25 *Ibid.*, p. 60.
26 *Ibid.*, p. 71.
27 Rouse Bell, p. 89.
28 Letters, p. 244.
29 DNB, vol. LX (1899), p. 460.
30 Gill, *Wordsworth and the Victorians* (1998), p. 56.
31 Ticknor, vol. 2, p. 152.
32 Rouse Bell, p. 92.
33 DNB, *ibid.*
34 Williams, *Passing the Torch* (1991), p. 121.
35 *Ibid.*, p. 122.
36 Letters, p. 244.
37 Martin, p. 56.
38 *Ibid.*, p. 55.
39 Allen, p. 16.
40 Alford, p. 49.
41 Letters, p. 243.
42 *Ibid.*, p. 249.
43 *Ibid.*, pp. 255–7.
44 Allen, p. 75.
45 Letters, p. 244.
46 *Ibid.*, p. 256.
47 *Ibid.*, p. 245.
48 E. Leedham-Green, *A Concise History of the University of Cambridge* (1996), p. 139.

49 Pope-Hennessy, p. 15.
50 Allen, p. 43.
51 Letters, p. 244.
52 *Ibid.*, p. 255.
53 *Ibid.*, p. 249.
54 *Ibid.*, pp. 241, 245.
55 *Ibid.*, p. 249.
56 *Ibid.*, p. 257.
57 *Ibid.*, p. 253n.
58 *Ibid.*, p. 288.
59 *Ibid.*, p. 257.
60 *Ibid.*, p. 259.
61 *Ibid.*, p. 260.
62 BL. Add. Ms. 81296.
63 Letters, p. 263.
64 *Ibid.*, p. 276.
65 *Ibid.*, pp. 273–4.
66 Wemyss Reid, p. 62.
67 Letters, pp. 279–80.
68 *Ibid.*, pp. 276–7.
69 Wemyss Reid, p. 67.
70 *Ibid.*, p. 49.
71 Pope-Hennessy, p. 19.
72 F.M. Brookfield, p. 234.
73 *Ibid.*, p. 250.
74 Wemyss Reid, pp. 59, 62.
75 Letters, p. 277.
76 *Ibid.*, p. 276.
77 *Ibid.*, p. 268.
78 *Ibid.*, p. 288.
79 *Ibid.*, p. 291.
80 *Ibid.*, pp. 282–4.
81 Writings, p. 34.
82 Letters, p. 287.
83 Writings, p. 33.
84 Culler, *The Poetry of Tennyson* (1977), p. 22.
85 Bryant, *The African Genesis of Tennyson's 'Timbuctoo'*, TRB, vol. 3 (1981), pp. 196–201.
86 Lang and Shannon, p. 41.
87 Letters, p. 318.
88 Ricks, vol. 1, p. 190.
89 Letters, p. 275n.
90 Day, *The Spirit of Fable*, TRB, vol. 4 (1983), p. 60.
91 Writings, p. 42.
92 BL. Add. Ms. 81296.
93 *Remains*, p. xxxviii.
94 BL. Add. Ms. 81296.
95 Letters, p. 298n.
96 *A Meeting and A Farewell*, Writings, p. 36.

97 *Remains*, p. xvii.
98 Letters, p. 297.
99 *Ibid.*, p. 294.
100 Wemyss Reid, pp. 65–6.
101 Letters, p. 292.
102 *Ibid.*, p. 294.
103 *Ibid.*, pp, 296, 316.
104 Writings, p. 48.
105 *Ibid.*, pp. 51–2.
106 Letters, p. 297.
107 *Ibid.*, p. 299.
108 Clive, p. 48.
109 Letters, p. 297.
110 *Ibid.*, pp. 257–8.
111 Writings, pp. 70–74.
112 Lockhart, *Life of Sir Walter Scott* (one volume edition, 1848), p. 314.
113 Writings, p. 62.
114 Letters, p. 318.
115 *Ibid.*, p. 304.
116 Writings, pp. 66–7.
117 Letters, p. 309.
118 *Ibid.*, p. 334.
119 *Ibid.*, p. 326.
120 *Ibid.*, p. 329.
121 *Ibid.*, p. 312.
122 *Ibid.*, p. 333–4.
123 *Ibid.*, p. 312.
124 *Ibid.*, p. 334.
125 *Ibid.*, pp. 308–9.
126 *Ibid.*, p. 329.
127 *Ibid.*, p. 317.
128 Gladstone, *Diaries,* vol. 1, 16/9/29.
129 Martin, p. 98.
130 Wemyss Reid, p. 72.

CHAPTER FIVE *Living Awfully Fast*: The Apostles and Somersby, 1829–1831

1 Martin, p. 60.
2 Nicolson, *Tennyson: Aspects of His Life Character and Poetry* (1923), p. 15.
3 Ricks, vol. 1, p. 186.
4 Writings, p. 45.
5 Martin, *Ibid.*
6 Letters, p. 372.
7 Carlyle, *The Life of John Sterling* (1851), pp. 46, 66.
8 Allen, p. 15.
9 *Ibid.*, p. 8.
10 Armstrong, *Victorian Poetry* (1994), pp. 39, 52.

11 Allen, p. 78.
12 *Ibid.*, p. 6.
13 *Ibid.*, p. 8.
14 Merivale, *Autobiography* (1888), p. 98.
15 Allen, p. 7.
16 Lubenow, *The Cambridge Apostles 1820–1914* (1998), pp. 30–31.
17 Letter, Tennyson Research Centre, Lincoln.
18 *Ibid.*
19 Letters, pp. 343–4.
20 *Ibid.*, p. 336.
21 Pope-Hennessy, p. 23.
22 Wemyss Reid, p. 72.
23 Allen, p. 51.
24 Pope-Hennessy, p. 24.
25 Letters, p. 341n.
26 Wemyss Reid, p. 78.
27 Writings, p. 75.
28 Wemyss Reid, p. 91.
29 Ricks, vol. 1, p. 240.
30 Wemyss Reid, p. 76.
31 Forman (ed.), *The Poetical Works of Percy Bysshe Shelley* (1877), vol. 4, p. 5.
32 Granniss, *A Descriptive Catalogue of . . . First Editions . . . of . . . Shelley* (1923), p. 73.
33 Kolb (1977) (1), p. 37.
34 *Ibid.*
35 Letters, p. 348.
36 Hayward, p. 15.
37 *Ibid.*, p. 21.
38 Martin, p. 101.
39 David, *Fanny Kemble A Performed Life,* p. xi.
40 Kolb (1977) (1), *ibid.*
41 Writings, p. 83.
42 C. Tennyson, *Alfred Tennyson* (1949, revised 1968), p. 84.
43 Letters, p. 353.
44 *Ibid.*, p. 354.
45 F.M. Brookfield, p. 164.
46 Weymss Reid, p. 84.
47 C. Tennyson, p. 87.
48 Letters, p. 365.
49 *Remains*, pp. xxxviii–xxxix.
50 Nowell-Smith, *A.H. Hallam's 'Poems 1830'*, The Book Collector (1959), vol. 8, pp. 430–31.
51 Letters, p. 363.
52 *Ibid.*, p. 365 .
53 Hagen, *Tennyson and his Publishers* (1979), p. 15.
54 Letters, pp. 360–61.
55 Large, *The Tennyson Family and their Villages* (1999), pp. 10, 60.
56 VP., p. 6.

57 Letters, p. 675.
58 Martin, p. 104.
59 BL. Add. Ms. 74090A.
60 Evans, *'A Flute of Arcady' Autograph Poems of . . . Arthur Henry Hallam,* British Library Journal, vol. 25 (1999), pp. 212–233.
61 VP., p. 3.
62 Writings, p. 88.
63 *Ibid.*
64 *In Memoriam*, LXXXIX.
65 Writings, p. 97.
66 R. Adicks, *'The Garden Trees': A Collaboration Between Tennyson and Hallam*, TRB, vol. 5 (1971), p. 147.
67 Writings, p. 99.
68 Gladstone, *Diaries*, vol. 1, 22/6/30.
69 Letters, pp. 368–9.
70 *Ibid.*, pp. 371–2.
71 *Ibid.*, p. 356.
72 F.M. Brookfield, p. 162.
73 Martin, p. 116.
74 Merivale, p. 72.
75 F.M. Brookfield, p. 338.
76 *Ibid.*, p. 282.
77 *Ibid.*, p. 259.
78 Pope-Hennessy, p. 13.
79 Alford, p. 39.
80 *Ibid.*, p. 65.
81 Carlyle, p. 84.
82 Trench, *Letters and Memorials of Richard Chenevix Trench* (1888), vol. 1, p. 32.
83 *Ibid.*, p. 37.
84 *Ibid.*, p. 72.
85 Allen, p. 106.
86 Martin, p. 118.
87 Letters, p. 374.
88 *Ibid.*, p. 379.
89 *Ibid.*, p. 387.
90 Sambrook, *Cambridge Apostles at a Spanish Tragedy*, English Miscellany, vol. 16 (1965), pp. 183–194.
91 Carlyle, p. 116.
92 Trench, p. 70.
93 F.M. Brookfield, p. 337.
94 H. Tennyson, vol. 1, p. 52.
95 Letters, p. 375.
96 *Ibid.*
97 *Ibid.*, p. 377n.
98 Martin, p. 121.
99 See Garfield, The *Last Journey of William Huskisson* (2002).
100 Letters, p. 379.
101 Letters, p. 387.

102 Victoria County History of Cambridgeshire, vol. 2, p. 117 (1948).
103 Merivale, p. 149.
104 Hobsbaum and Rude, *Captain Swing* (2nd ed., 1973), p. 134.
105 Alford, pp. 61–2.
106 Merivale, p. 149.
107 Martin, p. 125.
108 Lushington and Venables, *Joint Compositions* (Undated).
109 Letters, p. 390.
110 *Ibid.*, p. 391n.
111 Martin, p. 126.
112 Alford, pp. 62–5.
113 Clayden, *Rogers and his Contemporaries* (1899), pp. 350, 367.

CHAPTER SIX A Young Man of Letters, 1831–1833

PART ONE *The Last of Cambridge*

1 Letters, p. 445n.
2 Writings, pp. 93–5.
3 Martin, p. 130.
4 *Ibid.*
5 Letters, p. 407.
6 *Ibid.*, p. 413.
7 *Ibid.*, pp. 415–16.
8 *Ibid.*, p. 418.
9 *Ibid.*, pp. 420–21.
10 *Ibid.*, p. 423.
11 Merivale, p. 151.
12 Letters, p. 472.
13 *Ibid.*, p. 446.
14 Reprinted in Armstrong, *Victorian Scrutinies* (1972), p. 74.
15 *Ibid.*, pp. 76–7.
16 Letters, p. 396.
17 *Ibid.*, p. 410n.
18 *Ibid.*, p. 418.
19 *Ibid.*, p. 472.
20 *Ibid.*, p. 430.
21 *Ibid.*, p. 472.
22 *Ibid.*, pp. 448–9.
23 *Ibid.*, p. 465.
24 *Ibid.*, pp. 433–4.
25 Writings, p. 102.
26 Letters, pp. 455–6.
27 *Ibid.*, p. 455.
28 *Ibid.*, p. 475.
29 *The Englishman's Magazine*, vol. 1 (1831), pp. 1–2.
30 Letters, p. 441.
31 *Ibid.*, p. 443.
32 *Ibid.*, p. 446.
33 *Ibid.*, p. 460.

34 *Ibid.*, p. 467.
35 Yeats, *Essays* (1924), p. 431.
36 Allen, pp. 144–5.
37 Armstrong (1993), p. 66.
38 Armstrong (1972), p. 19.
39 *Ibid.*, p. 13.
40 Writings, pp. 183–198.
41 Letters, p. 463.
42 *Ibid.*, p. 453.
43 Levi, *Tennyson* (1993), p. 58.
44 Letters, p. 444.
45 *Ibid.*, pp. 453–4.
46 *Ibid.*, pp. 464–5.
47 Ch Ch., vol. 15.
48 Letters, pp. 479–80.
49 *Ibid.*, p. 487.
50 *Ibid.*, pp. 480–85.
51 *Ibid.*, p. 483.
52 Cambridge University Calendar (1832), p. 167.
53 Letters, p. 487.
54 *Ibid.*, p. 496.
55 *Ibid.*, p. 500.
56 *Ibid.*, p. 504.
57 *Remains*, p. xviii.
58 Clayden, vol. 2, p. 72.
59 Letters, p. 516.
60 *Ibid.*, p. 528.
61 Allen, p. 155.
62 Letters, p. 513n.
63 Cambridge University Calendar (1832), p. 100.
64 Kermode (ed.), *Selected Prose of T.S. Eliot* (1975), p. 245.
65 Letters, p. 312.
66 Writings, p. 212.
67 Letters, p. 509.
68 Writings, pp. 200–12.
69 *Ibid.*, p. 199.
70 *Remains*, p. xxxix.
71 Letters, pp. 508, 568.
72 *Ibid.*, pp. 523, 525.
73 *Remains*, p. xviii.
74 Writings, p. 181.
75 *Ibid.*, pp. 145–179.
76 Newman, *Historical Sketches* (1872, reprinted 1901), pp. 245–300.
77 Vance, *The Victorians and Ancient Rome* (1997), p. 78.
78 Writings, pp. 213–234.
79 Letters, p. 523.
80 Writings, p. 203.
81 *Ibid.*, p. 157.
82 *Ibid.*, p. 159.

83 Allen, p. 157.
84 Writings, p. 218.
85 Letters, p. 498.
86 Clayden, vol. 2, p. 72.
87 Letters, p. 515.
88 *Ibid.*, p. 512.
89 *Ibid.*, p. 516.
90 Duman, *The English and Colonial Bars in the Nineteenth Century* (1983), pp. 22, 24.
91 *Remains*, p. xxx.

PART TWO   *Mainly in London*

1 Noel, *A Portrait of the Inner Temple* (2002), p. 37.
2 Duman, p. 20.
3 *Ibid.*, p. 10.
4 Noel, *ibid.*
5 Letters, p. 522.
6 Duman, p. 26.
7 *Ibid.*, p. 84.
8 Letters, p. 554.
9 *Ibid.*, p. 566.
10 *Ibid.*, p. 534.
11 *Ibid.*, p. 536.
12 Lang and Shannon, p. 72.
13 Letters, p. 542.
14 *Ibid.*, p. 546.
15 *Ibid.*, p. 549.
16 *Ibid.*, p. 539.
17 *Ibid.*, p. 549.
18 Wu, *William Hazlitt* (2008), p. 253.
19 Armstrong (1972), p. 108.
20 *Ibid.*, p. 112.
21 Letters, p. 562.
22 *Ibid.*, p. 566.
23 *Remains*, pp. xxxiii–xxxiv.
24 Letters, p. 563.
25 *Ibid.*, p. 569.
26 Kemble, *Record of a Girlhood* (1878), vol. 3, p. 193.
27 Letters, pp. 559–60.
28 *Ibid.*, p. 568.
29 *Ibid.*, p. 587.
30 *Ibid.*, p. 593.
31 *Ibid.*, p. 575.
32 *Ibid.*, pp. 593–4.
33 Merivale, p. 171.
34 Letters, p. 597.
35 Lang and Shannon, p. 74.
36 Letters, pp. 601–2.

37 Kemble, vol. 3, p. 209.
38 David, p. 32.
39 Allen, p. 148.
40 Letters, p. 604.
41 *Ibid.*, p. 610.
42 *Ibid.*, pp. 606–7.
43 *Ibid.*, p. 611.
44 *Ibid.*, p. 613.
45 *Ibid.*, p. 616.
46 Martin, p. 155.
47 Letters, p. 618.
48 *Ibid.*, pp. 622–3.
49 Kolb (1977) (1), p. 45.
50 Letters, pp. 636–7.
51 *Ibid.*, p. 642.
52 *Ibid.*, p. 639.
53 *Ibid.*, p. 644n.
54 *Ibid.*, p. 642.
55 *Ibid.*, p. 644.
56 *Ibid.*, p. 645.
57 *Ibid.*, p. 649.
58 *Ibid.*, p. 654.
59 *Ibid.*, p. 625.
60 *Ibid.*, p. 626.
61 *Ibid.*, p. 646.
62 *Ibid.*, p. 638.
63 *Ibid.*, p. 646.
64 *Ibid.*, p. 661.
65 Lang and Shannon, p. 81.
66 Letters, p. 667.
67 *Ibid.*, p. 650.
68 Kolb (1977) (2), pp. 373–6.
69 Letters, p. 650n.
70 Vincent, *Gabriele Rossetti in England* (1936), p. 73.
71 Waller, *The Rossetti Family 1824–1854* (1932), p. 94.
72 Letters, p. 607.
73 *Ibid.*, p. 628.
74 *Ibid.*, p. 667.
75 'T.H.E.A.' *Remarks on Professor Rossetti's "Disquisizioni Sullo Spirito Antipapale"* (1832), Preface (unpaginated).
76 *Ibid.*, pp. 14–15.
77 *Ibid.*, pp. 9–11.
78 *Ibid.*, p. 8.
79 *Ibid.*, pp. 56–7.
80 *Ibid.*, p. 48.
81 Waller, p. 97.
82 Letters, p. 683.
83 T.H.E.A., p. 20.
84 Letters, p. 502.

85 *Remains*, p. xxxii.
86 Letters, p. 678.
87 Writings, p. 236.
88 Letters, p. 674.
89 *Ibid.*, p. 681.
90 *Ibid.*, p. 663.
91 *Ibid.*, pp. 687, 695.
92 *Ibid.*, p. 688.
93 Martin, p. 158.
94 Letters, p. 670.
95 *Ibid.*, p. 694.
96 *Ibid.*, p. 698.
97 *Ibid.*, p. 697.
98 *Ibid.*, p. 706.
99 *Ibid.*, p. 700.
100 Martin, p. 166.
101 Letters, p. 711.
102 *Ibid.*, p. 715.
103 *Ibid.*, p. 714.
104 *Ibid.*, p. 724.
105 *Ibid.*, pp. 725–6.
106 *Ibid.*, p. 728.
107 Writings, p. 280.
108 Letters, p. 736.
109 *Ibid.*, pp. 747–8.
110 *Ibid.*, p. 763.
111 *Ibid.*, p. 749.
112 Allen, p. 153.
113 Letters, p. 768n.
114 *Ibid.*, p. 767.
115 *Ibid.*, pp. 773–5.
116 *Ibid.*, pp. 778–80.
117 *Ibid.*, pp. 784–5, 790.
118 *Ibid.*, pp. 787–9.

CHAPTER SEVEN *A Creature of Great Promise*: Death and
   Transfiguration
1 Letters, p. 792.
2 Martin, p. 184.
3 Letters, p. 793n.
4 Lang and Shannon, p. 94.
5 *Remains*, pp. xxxiv–xxxv.
6 Kolb (1986), p. 44.
7 Dr Edward Littleton, private correspondence with author.
8 Holland, p. 227.
9 Kolb (1986), p. 40.
10 Gladstone *Diaries*, vol. 2 (1968), 6/10/33.
11 Ch Ch., vol. 15.

12 Lubenow, pp. 80. 83.
13 H. Tennyson, vol. 1, p. 106.
14 Lang and Shannon, p. 103.
15 Alford, pp. 92–4.
16 BL. Add. Ms. 81296.
17 Milnes, *Poems of Many Years* (1838), p. 190.
18 Pope-Hennessy, p. 72.
19 C. Tennyson, p. 145.
20 Lang and Shannon, p. 95.
21 *Ibid.*, p. 99.
22 Martin, p. 189.
23 Lang and Shannon, p. 97.
24 *Ibid.*, p. 105.
25 H. Tennyson, vol. 1, p. 94.
26 Martin, p. 169.
27 Ray, *Tennyson reads 'Maud'* (1968), p. 37.
28 Martin, p. 186.
29 See also Blocksidge, *Tennyson and the Two Last Men On Earth*, English Review, vol. 4 (1992), pp. 8–13.
30 Lang and Shannon, p. 103.
31 Rashdall, Diary, Bodleian Library, Oxford, Eng. Misc. e351 (unpaginated).
32 Rader, *Tennyson in the Year of Hallam's Death*, PMLA, vol. 77, p. 419 (1962).
33 *Ibid.*, p. 421.
34 Sandford, *Clevedon Parish Church* (1987, revised 2000), p. 31.
35 *Remains*, p. xxxv.
36 Lang and Shannon, p. 105.
37 BL. Add. Ms. 81298B.
38 Lang and Shannon, p. 97.
39 Ch Ch., vol. 15.
40 Lang and Shannon, p. 107.
41 *Ibid.*, p. 112.
42 *Ibid.*, p. 108.
43 Ch Ch., vol. 15.
44 Motter, *Arthur Hallam's Centenary: A Bibliographical Note*, The Yale University Library Gazette (1934), pp. 107–8.
45 *Remains*, pp. xxxv–xxxvi.
46 *Ibid.*, pp. ix, xviii, xv.
47 *Ibid.*, pp. v, vi, viii.
48 *Ibid.*, pp. xiv–xvi.
49 *Ibid.*, pp. xxvi–xxix.
50 *Ibid.*, pp. xxi–xxvi.
51 Evans, pp. 220–21.
52 Motter, p. 105.
53 H. Tennyson, vol. 1, pp. 108–9.
54 Kolb (1977) (1), p. 41.
55 BL. Add. Ms. 81295B, 81296.
56 BL. Add. Ms. 81295B.
57 P. Elliott, *The Making of 'The Memoir'* (1978), p. 27.

58 Letters, p. 801.
59 C. and F. Brookfield, pp. 102–3.
60 *Ibid.*, pp. 105, 110.
61 Letters, p. 799.
62 A.H. Elton, *A Few Years in the Life of Mary Elizabeth Elton* (1878), pp. 78–9.
63 M. Elton, p. 162.
64 C. and F. Brookfield, p. 36.
65 Gatty, *A Key to Lord Tennyson's 'In Memoriam'* (3rd ed., 1885), p. 72n.
66 BL. Add. Ms. 81295.
67 *Remains* (2nd ed. 1853), pp. xlviii–xlvix.
68 *Ibid.*, pp. lii–liii.
69 Ch Ch., vol. 15.
70 C. and F. Brookfield, p. 332.
71 *Ibid.*, pp. 339–41.
72 Clayden, vol. 2, p. 379.
73 Holland, p. 227.
74 Clark, p. 29.
75 Holland, *ibid.*
76 Ch Ch., vol. 13.
77 Cunningham, *The Victorians* (2000), p. 311.
78 Shannon, *Tennyson and the Reviewers* (1952), pp. 142–6.
79 H. Tennyson, *Tennyson and His Friends* (1911), p. 471.
80 *Ibid.*, p. 460.
81 *Ibid.*, p. 445.
82 Elliott, p. 27.
83 Waugh, *Alfred, Lord Tennyson* (1892), p. 67.
84 Horton, *Alfred Tennyson* (1900), p. 64.
85 A. Lang, *Alfred Tennyson* (1901), p. 31.
86 H. Tennyson, vol. 1, pp. 304–5.
87 Ray, pp. 37–8, 41.
88 Kermode (ed.), p. 243.
89 Day, *Tennyson's Scepticism* (2005), p. 127.
90 Peltason, *Reading 'In Memoriam'* (1985), p. 15.
91 *Ibid.*, p. 132.
92 *The Times*, 24 December 1896.
93 *The Daily Telegraph*, 5 January, 1898.
94 F.M. Brookfield, p. 188.
95 *Ibid.*, pp. 308–9.
96 *Ibid.*, pp. 123, 126, 153, 156.
97 Reproduced in Hunt (ed.), *Tennyson 'In Memoriam' A Casebook* (1970) p. 104.
98 C. Tennyson, p. 103.
99 Crompton, *Byron and Greek Love* (1985, repr. 1998), p. 364.
100 H. Hallam, *An Introduction to the Literature of Europe* (1839), vol. 3, pp. 504, 501.
101 Quoted in P. Hammond, *Love Between Men in English Literature* (1996), p. 149.
102 Shatto and Shaw (eds.), *Tennyson: In Memoriam* (1982), p. 25.

103 *Ibid.*, p. 110.
104 *Ibid.*, p. 71.
105 *Ibid.*, p. 76.
106 Ray, p. 41.
107 Joseph, *Tennysonian Love* (1969), p. 68.
108 Rader, *Tennyson's 'Maud': The Biographical Genesis* (1963), p. 145n.
109 Ricks, *Tennyson* (1972), pp. 215–16.
110 Robb, *Strangers* (2003), pp. 225–6.
111 H. Tennyson (1911) p. 115.
112 Weeks, *Sex, Politics and Society* (2nd ed., 1989), p. 109.
113 Letters, p. 32.
114 *Ibid.*, p. 312.
115 Dellamora, *Masculine Desire* (1990), p. 22.
116 Allen, p. 157.
117 Dellamora, p. 21.
118 Gaskell (ed.), *Records of an Eton Schoolboy* (1883), p. 23.
119 *Ibid.*, p. 221.
120 Ch Ch., vol. 13.
121 *Ibid.*
122 *Ibid.*
123 Gaskell (1883), p. 105.
124 Ch Ch., vol. 13.
125 Lounsbury, *The Life and Times of Tennyson 1809–1850* (1915), pp. 609–613.
126 Kemble, vol. 2, pp. 2–3.
127 Thorn, *Tennyson* (1992), p. 123.
128 Martin, p. 183.
129 Benson, pp. 343–6.
130 *Ibid.*, p. 345.
131 Jenkins, p. 16.
132 Kolb (1973), p. 172.
133 *Ibid.*
134 Martin, pp. 182–3.

Bibliography

Abbreviations

BL. Add. Ms.   Elton family papers in British Library.

Ch Ch.   Hallam family papers in Christ Church Library, Oxford (17 volumes).

DNB   1890 *Dictionary of National Biography* London: Smith Elder.

Lang and Shannon   Lang, C.Y. and Shannon, E.F. (eds) 1982: *The Letters of Alfred, Lord Tennyson*, vol. i, 1821–50. Oxford: Oxford University Press.

Letters   Kolb, J 1981: *The Letters of Arthur Henry Hallam*, Columbus: Ohio State University Press.

Martin   Martin, R.B. 1980: *Tennyson: The Unquiet Heart*, Oxford: Clarendon Press 1980.

Remains   Hallam, H. (ed.) 1834: *Remains, in Verse and Prose, of Arthur Henry Hallam*, Privately Printed.

Ricks   Ricks, C. (ed.) 1987 *The Poems of Tennyson in Three Volumes*, Harlow: Longman.

TRB   The Tennyson Research Bulletin.

Trin. Add. Ms.   Hallam papers in Trinity College Library, Cambridge.

VP   Tennyson, C. and F.T. Baker, F.T. (eds.) 1963: *Some Unpublished Poems by Arthur Henry Hallam*, (Victorian Poetry, vol. 3, supplement, Summer 1965, reprinted as *Publications of the Tennyson Society*, No. 3).

Writings   Motter, T.H.V. (ed.) 1943: *The Writings of Arthur Hallam*, New York and London: Oxford University Press.

Adicks, R. 1971: *The Garden Trees: A Collaboration Between Tennyson and Hallam* (TRB, 5, 1971, p. 147).

Alford, F.O. 1874: *The Life, Journals and Letters of Henry Alford, DD*, London: Rivington.

Alford, H. 3rd edition 1859: *The Poetical Works of Henry Alford*, London: Rivington.

Allen, P. 1978: *The Cambridge Apostles: The Early Years*, Cambridge: Cambridge University Press.

Armstrong, I. 1972: *Victorian Scrutinies, Reviews of Poetry 1830–1870*, London: Athlone Press.

Armstrong, I. 1993: *Victorian Poetry, Poetry, Poetics and Politics*, London and New York: Routledge.

Austen Leigh, R.A. 1921: *Eton College Register 1698–1752* Eton: Spottiswoode Ballantyne.

Austen Leigh, R.A. 1927: *Eton College Register 1753–1790* Eton: Spottiswoode Ballantyne.

Bellot, H.H.L. 1902: *The Inner and Middle Temple*, London: Methuen.

Benson, A.C. 1899: *Fasti Etonenses* Eton: Drake.

Blocksidge, M. 1992: *Tennyson and the Two Last Men On Earth*, The English Review, vol. 2, no. 4, pp. 8–13.

Britton, J. 1830: *The History and Antiquities of the Abbey and Cathedral Church of Bristol*, London: Longman.

Brock, M.G. and Curthoys, M.C. (eds.) 1997: *The History of the University of Oxford* vol. 6 Part I, Oxford: Clarendon Press.

Brooke, J. and Sorensen, M. (eds.) 1971: *The Prime Minister's Papers: Gladstone, vol. 1, Autobiographica*, London: HMSO.

Brookfield, C. and F. 1906: *Mrs Brookfield and her Circle*, London: Pitman.

Brookfield, F.M. 1906: *The Cambridge Apostles*, London: Pitman.

Bryant, H.B. 1981: *The African Genesis of Tennyson's 'Timbuctoo'* (TRB, vol.3, pp. 196–201).

Burrow, J. 1981: *A Liberal Descent: Victorian Historians and the English Past*, Cambridge: Cambridge University Press.

'W.L.C.' 1865: *Etoniana, Ancient and Modern*, Edinburgh: Blackwood.

Cambridge University Calendar, 1832.

Card, T. 2001: *Eton Established*, London: Murray.

Carlyle, T. 1851: *The Life of John Sterling*, London: Chapman and Hall.

Chandos, J. 1984: *Boys Together*, London: Hutchinson.

Clark, P. 1982: *Henry Hallam*, Boston: Twayne.

Clayden, P.W. 1889: *Rogers and His Contemporaries*, London: Smith Elder.

Clive, J. 1957: *Scotch Reviewers The Edinburgh Review 1802–15*, London: Faber.

Crompton, L. 1985, repr. 1998: *Byron and Greek Love*, Swaffham: Gay Men's Press.

Culler, A.D. 1977: *The Poetry of Tennyson*, Newhaven: Yale University Press.

Cunningham, V. 2000 *The Victorians: An Anthology of Poetry and Poetics*, Oxford: Blackwell.

Dagnall, H. 1994: *Creating a Good Impression: Three Hundred Years of the Stamp Office and Stamp Duties*, London: HMSO.

David, D. 2007: *Fanny Kemble A Performed Life*, Philadelphia: Pennsylvania University Press.

Day, A. 1983: *The Spirit of Fable: Arthur Hallam and Romantic Values in Tennyson's 'Timbuctoo'* (TRB, vol. 4, no. 2, 1983).

Day, A. 2005: *Tennyson's Scepticism*, Basingstoke: Palgrave Macmillan.

Dellamora, R. 1990: *Masculine Desire. The Sexual Politics of Victorian Aestheticism*, Chapel Hill: North Carolina University Press.

Doyle, F.H. 1886: *Reminiscences and Opinions*, London: Longmans Green.

Duman, D. 1983: *The English and Colonial Bars in the Nineteenth Century*, London: Croom Helm.

Eaton, C. 1820: *Rome in the Nineteenth Century: Referring to a period of residence in Rome, 1817–1818*, Edinburgh: Hurst, Robinson, Constable.

Elliott, P.L. 1978: *The Making of the 'Memoir'*, Greenville: Furman University Press.

Elton, A.H. (ed.) 1877: *A Few Years Of The Life Of Mary Elizabeth Elton*, Clevedon: privately published.

Elton, M. 1994: *Annals of the Elton Family, Bristol Merchants & Somerset Landowners*, Far Thrupp: Sutton.

The Englishman's Magazine, Vols. 1 and 2 (April–October 1831).

Etoniana, Nos. 58, 71, Eton College: privately published.

The Eton Miscellany (1827).

Evans, R. 1999: *A Flute of Arcady: Autograph poems of Tennyson's Friend, Arthur Henry Hallam*, The British Library Journal, Vol. 25, 1999 pp. 212–233.

Festing Jones, H. 1919: *Samuel Butler: A Memoir*, London: Macmillan.

Forman, H.B. (ed.) 1877: *The Poetical Works of Percy Bysshe Shelley*, London: Reeves and Turner.

Fox, H.E. (ed. Earl of Ilchester) 1923: *The Journal of the Hon. Henry Edward Fox*, London: Thornton Butterworth.

Garfield, S. 2002: *The Last Journey of William Huskisson*, London: Faber.

Gaskell, C.M. (ed.) 1883: *Records of an Eton Schoolboy*, London: privately published.

Gaskell, C.M. (ed.) 1939: *An Eton Boy*, London: privately published.

Gatty, A.J. (3rd edition) 1885: *A Key to Lord Tennyson's 'In Memoriam'*, London: Bell.

Gill, S.1998: *Wordsworth and the Victorians*, Oxford: Oxford University Press.

Gladstone, W.E. (ed. M.R.D. Foot) 1968: *Diaries,* vols. i and ii, Oxford: Clarendon Press.

Granniss, R.S. 1923: *A Descriptive Catalogue of the First Editions in Book Form of the Writings of Percy Bysshe Shelley*, New York: Grollier Club.

Hagen, J.S. 1979: *Tennyson and his Publishers*, London: Macmillan.

Hale, J.R. (ed.) 1956: *The Italian Journal of Samuel Rogers*, London: Faber.

Hallam, H. 1827: *The Constitutional History of England*, London: John Murray.

Hallam, H. 1837–9: *Introduction To The Literature of Europe, In Fifteenth, Sixteenth, and Seventeenth Centuries*, London: John Murray.

Hammond, E. 1898: *Bygone Putney*, Kingston: Surrey Comet.

Hammond, P. 1996: *Love Between Men in English Literature*, Basingstoke and London: Macmillan.

Hayward, A. 1872: *Lord Lansdowne: A Biographical Sketch*, London: reprinted from *The Saturday Review*.

Hobsbaum, E. and Rude, G. 2nd edition, 1973: *Captain Swing*, Harmondsworth: Penguin Books.

Holland, H. 1870: *Recollections of a Past Life*, London: Spottiswoode.

Hollis, C. 1960: *Eton: A History*, London: Hollis and Carter.

Horton, R.F. 1900: *Alfred Tennyson, A Saintly Life*, London: Dent.

Hudson, D.1967: *Holland House in Kensington*, London: Peter Davies.

Hunt, J.D. (ed.) 1970: *Tennyson 'In Memoriam'* A Casebook, London: Macmillan.

Ilchester, Earl of 1937: *Chronicles of Holland House*, London: Murray.

Jenkins, R. 1995: *Gladstone*, London: Macmillan.

Johnson, C.B. (ed.) 1905: *William Bodham Donne and his Friends*, London: Methuen.

Joseph, G. 1969: *Tennysonian Love*, Minneapolis: Minnesota University Press.

Kemble, F. 1878: *Record of a Girlhood*, London: Bentley.

Kermode, F. (ed.) 1975: *Selected Prose of T.S. Eliot*, London: Faber.

Kolb, J. 1973: *The Hero and his Worshippers: The History of Arthur Hallam's Letters* (Bulletin of the John Rylands Library of Manchester, vol. 56, pp. 150–173).

Kolb, J. 1977(a): *Arthur Hallam and Emily Tennyson* (Review of English Studies, vol. 28, 1977, pp. 32–48).

Kolb, J. 1977(b): *They Were No Kings: An unrecorded sonnet by Hallam*, (Victorian Poetry, vol. 15, 1977, pp. 373–6).

Kolb, J. 1986: *Morte d'Arthur: The Death of Arthur Henry Hallam*, (Biography, vol. 9, 1986, pp. 37–58).

Kolb, J. 1999: *Christ Church or Trinity? Arthur Hallam's Matriculation*, (American Notes and Queries, vol. 12, no. 3, 1999, pp. 38–41).

Kolb, J. 2000: *Hallam, Tennyson, Homosexuality and the Critics* (Philological Quarterly, vol. 79, 2000, pp. 365–96).

Lang, A. 1901: *Alfred Tennyson*, Edinburgh: Blackwood.

Large, J. 1999: *The Tennyson Family & Their Villages*, privately published.

Lawrence P.S.H. (ed.) 1980: *The Encouragement of Learning*, Salisbury: Michael Russell.

Leedham-Green, E. 1996: *A Concise History of the University of Cambridge*, Cambridge: Cambridge University Press.

Levi, P. 1993: *Tennyson*, London: Macmillan.

Lockhart, J.G. (One volume edition) 1848: *Life of Sir Walter Scott*, London: Hutchinson.

Lounsbury, T.R. 1915: *The Life and Times of Tennyson 1809–1850*, Newhaven and London: Yale University Press.

Lubenow, W.C. 1998: *The Cambridge Apostles 1820–1914*, Cambridge: Cambridge University Press.

Lushington, H. and Venables, G.S. (Undated): *Joint Compositions*, London: McGowan.

McGann, J. (ed.) 1980: *Byron The Complete Poetical Works*, vol. I, Oxford: Clarendon Press.

Martin, S. 1828: *Narrative of a Three Year's Residence in Italy, 1819–1822*, London: publisher unknown.

Martineau, H. (ed. L.H. Peterson). 2007: *Autobiography*, Plymouth, Ontario: Broadview Press.

Maxwell Lyte, H.C. (3rd edition) 1899: *A History of Eton College*, London: Macmillan.

Merivale, C. 1898: *Autobiography*, Oxford: privately published.

Merriam, H.G. 1939: *Edward Moxon Publisher of Poets*, New York: Columbia University Press.

Milnes, R.M. 1838: *Poems of Many Years*, London: Moxon.

Moorman. M. 1965: *William Wordsworth, The Later Years 1803–1850*, Oxford and London: Oxford University Press.

Morley, J. 1903: *The Life of William Ewart Gladstone*, London and New York: Macmillan.

Motter, T.H.V. 1934: *Arthur Hallam's Centenary: A Bibliographical Note*, (The Yale University Library Gazette, vol. 8, 1934).

Newman, J.H. 1872, reprinted 1901: *Historical Sketches*, London: Pickering.

Nicolson, Harold 1923, *Tennyson: Aspects of His Life Character and Poetry*, London: Constable.

Noel, G. 2002: *A Portrait of The Inner Temple*, Norwich: Russell.

Nowell-Smith, S. 1959: *A.H. Hallam's 'Poems, 1830'* (The Book Collector, vol. 8, 1959 pp. 430–1).

Ollard, R. 1982: *An English Education*, London: Collins.

Peltason, T. 1985: *Reading 'In Memoriam'*, Princeton: Princeton University Press.

Pinion, F.B. 1990: *A Tennyson Chronology*, London: Macmillan.

Pope-Hennessy, J. 1949: *Monckton Milnes: The Years of Promise, 1809–1851*, London: Constable.

Rader, R.W. 1962: *Tennyson in the year of Hallam's death* (PMLA, vol. 77, pp. 419–24).

Rader, R.W. 1963: *Tennyson's 'Maud' The Biographical Genesis*, Berkeley: California University Press.

Ramsden, G. (ed.) 1906: *Correspondence of Two Brothers*, London: Longmans.

Ray, G.N. 1968: *Tennyson reads 'Maud'*, Vancouver: University of British Columbia.

Rashdall, J: Diary (Bodleian ms.: Eng. misc. e351).

Ricks, C. 1972: *Tennyson*, London and New York: Macmillan.

Robb, G. 2003: *Strangers*, London: Picador.

Rosenberg, J.D. 1992: *'Stopping for Death': Tennyson's 'In Memoriam'*, (Victorian Poetry, vol. 30, nos. 3 and 4, 1992).

Rouse Bell, W.W. 1906: *Trinity College, Cambridge*, London: Dent.

Rouse Bell, W.W. and Venn, J.A. (eds.) 1911: *Admissions to Trinity College, Cambridge*, vol. 4, London: Macmillan.

Sambrook, A.J. 1965: *Cambridge Apostles at a Spanish Tragedy* (English Miscellany, vol. 16, 1965, pp. 183–194).

Sanders, L. 1908: *The Holland House Circle*, London: Methuen.

Sandford, E.N.T. 1987, revised 2000: *Clevedon Parish Church*, Clevedon: privately published.

Searby, P. 1997: *A History of the University of Cambridge*, vol. 3, 1750–1870, Cambridge: Cambridge University Press.

Sinfield, A. 1986: *Alfred Tennyson*, Oxford: Blackwell.

Shannon, E.F. 1952: *Tennyson and the Reviewers*, Cambridge, Mass.: Harvard University Press.

Shatto, S. and Shaw, M. (eds.) 1982: *Tennyson 'In Memoriam'*, Oxford: Clarendon Press.

Smith, J. and Stray, C. (eds.) 2001: *Teaching and Learning in Nineteenth Century Cambridge*, Woodbridge: Boydell.

Stair Douglas, Mrs (2nd edition) 1882: *The Life and Selections from the Correspondence of William Whewell, DD.*, London: Kegan Paul.

Stapylton, H.E.C. 1864: *Eton School Lists 1791–1850*, Eton: Williams.

Starke, M. (5th edition) 1824: *Information and Directions For Travellers On The Continent*, London: publisher unknown.

Sterry, W. 1898: *Annals of Eton College*, London: Methuen.

Tennyson, C. 1949 (revised 1968): *Alfred Tennyson*, London: Macmillan.

Tennyson, H. 1897: *Tennyson: A Memoir*, London: Macmillan.

Tennyson, H. 1911: *Tennyson and his Friends*, London: Macmillan.

Thackeray, F.St.J. 1896: *Memoir of Edmund Craven Hawtrey*, London: Bell.

Thorn, M. 1992: *Tennyson*, London: Little Brown.

Thwaite, A. 1996: *Emily Tennyson*, London: Faber.

Ticknor, G. (ed. G.S. Hillard) 1876: *Life, Letters and Journals of George S. Ticknor*, London: Sampson Lowe.

Todhunter, I. 1876 (repr. 1970): *William Whewell*, Farnborough: Gregg International.

Trench, M. (ed.) 1888: *Letters and Memorials of Richard Chenevix Trench*, London: Kegan Paul.

Tucker, W.D. 1892: *Eton of Old*, Griffith Farran.

Vance, N. 1997: *The Victorians and Ancient Rome*, Oxford: Blackwell.

Venn. J.A. (ed.) 1940: *Alumni Cantabrigiensis*, Part 2, vol. I, Cambridge Cambridge University Press.

Victoria County History of Cambridgeshire, vol. 2, 1948, vol. 3, 1959, Oxford: Oxford University Press.

Victoria County History of Staffordshire, 1976, vol. 17 Oxford: Oxford University Press.

Victoria History of Putney 1912 (reprinted 1996) London: London Local History Reprints.

Vincent, E.R. 1936: *Gabriele Rossetti in England*, Oxford: Clarendon Press.

Virgin, P. 1994: *Sydney Smith*, London: HarperCollins.

Waller, R.D. 1932: *The Rossetti Family 1824–1854*, Manchester: Manchester University Press.

Waugh, A. 1892: *Alfred Lord Tennyson A Study of His Life and Work*, London: Heinemann.

Weeks, J. (2nd edition) 1989: *Sex, Politics and Society*, London and New York: Longmans.

Wemyss Reid, T. 1890: *Life, Letters and Friendships of Richard Monckton Milnes*, London: Cassell.

Wilkinson, C.A. 1888: *Reminiscences of Eton*, London: Hurst and Blackett.

Williams, P. 1991: *Passing the Torch: Whewell's Philosophy and the Principles of English University Education* (in M. Fisch and S. Schaffer (eds.), *William Whewell: A Composite Portrait*), Oxford: Oxford University Press.

Windscheffel, R.C. 2008: *Reading Gladstone*, Basingstoke: Palgrave Macmillan.

Winstanley, D.A. 1940: *Early Victorian Cambridge*, Cambridge: Cambridge University Press.

Wu, Duncan 2008: *William Hazlitt: The First Modern Man*, Oxford and New York: Oxford University Press.

Yeats, W.B. 1924: *Essays*, London: Macmillan.

Index

marriage negotiations, 194–6
memorial tablet, 1, 228–9
memory, 88, 93, 233
mental breakdown (1829), 11, 87,
   98–100, 103–4, 109, 110–11, 155
pictorial representations, 263
posthumous reputation, 243–64
return of his body, 2, 220–1, 227–8
state of health, 18, 41, 62–3, 97–8,
   103–5, 210, 237
views on University of London, 6
views Wimpole Street as home, 17
relationships
AT holds as half-divine, 2, 245, 248
AT's visit to London (1832), 187–8
AT's visit to London (1833), 209–10
attraction to Anna Wintour, 8,
   66–74, 75, 80, 97, 105, 107, 111,
   127, 129, 133, 158, 168, 176–7,
   179, 202, 236, 255, 257, 259, 260
attraction to Anne Robertson, 70,
   107, 257
attraction to Emily, 131, 132–5, 149,
   152, 158, 179, 183–4, 202, 251,
   257
criticism of Gladstone's abilities, 51
Doyle's views on, 31, 234
with Ellen, 17, 35, 110
Emily's feelings for, 158
engagement to Emily, 16
first meeting with Emily, 126
friendship with Alford, 87, 141
friendship with AT, 55, 101–2, 112,
   113, 116, 132, 139, 166, 252–7
friendship with Fanny Kemble,
   126–7, 139, 157, 185–6, 188, 205,
   257
friendship with Farr, 42
friendship with Frere, 90, 95
friendship with Gaskell, 22, 31, 37,
   64, 66–7, 70–1, 73, 77, 168
friendship with Gladstone, 22, 31,
   32, 37, 38, 40–2, 53–5, 77, 112,
   137–9, 165, 208, 258
friendship with Kemble, 90, 118, 127
friendship with Milnes, 95–6, 111,
   122, 124, 139, 164–6, 258
friendship with Spedding, 140–1
friendship with Tennant, 122, 165
gift to Gladstone, 51–2, 250
Gladstone's gift of works of Burke,
   51–2, 209
Gladstone's visit (1831), 179

influence on AT, 135
influence of his mother, 11
meets Scott (1829), 106, 107, 108
regard for Maurice, 118
views on Farr, 89
visit to Gladstone (1831), 156
Wintour's engagement to Healey,
   111
travels
European tour (1818), 17–18
European tour (1822), 18
European tour (1827–28), 52, 53–4,
   56–75
European tour (1833), 211–16
European tour journal (1827–8), 58,
   59–61
Florence (1827), 61–2
French Alps (1827), 59–60
Genoa (1827), 60
Germany (1832), 74, 188–91, 200
Innsbruck (1828), 73–4
Italy (1827–28), 57–8, 60–73, 74–5
meets Gaskell in Italy (1827), 62, 63,
   64, 65, 66–7, 73
Naples (1828), 69–73
Normandy (1829), 105
Paris (1827), 59
Rome (1827), 57, 58, 62–9
Scotland (1829), 106–8
Venice (1828), 73
visit to Ireland (1825), 20–1
visits
Bowood, 14, 126
Cheltenham (1831), 167
Clevedon Court (1831), 166–7
Croydon Lodge (1832), 197
dislike of Brighton (1828–29), 91
Forest House (1830), 146
Hastings (1831), 157–66
Holland House, 14
Malvern (1829), 110–11
Somersby, 16, 131–6, 149, 152,
   183–4, 191, 206–7, 211
Sutton Court residence (summer
   1826), 38–9
trip to the west country (1831),
   166–7
Tunbridge Wells (1832), 180
Yorkshire (1831), 166, 167–8
works
'A Farewell to Glenarbach', 108
'The Battle of the Boyne', 49
biographical studies, 208–9